DO
WE
DREAM
UNDER
THE
SAME
SKY

僕らは同じ空のもと
夢をみているのだろうか

DO WE DREAM UNDER THE SAME SKY

Though written out, without a question mark at the end of the sentence, it's only an opening to an idea.

In the past years, with the Global pandemic and the exertion of White Supremacy tendencies in the US as well as Nationalists Populist in many parts of the global world, I'd like for the exhibition to refocus our mindset and perspectives.

With many of these thoughts in mind, I'd like the potential of Okayama Art Summit 2022 to be focused on peripheral practices by artists who may share in common their itinerant backgrounds. By "itinerant," I mean that most of the artists in this selection are coming from cultural and social backgrounds that are diverse. Though they may have their practices and their locations in the center of western artistic hegemony, we could understand that their positioning in that (western) hegemony, is based on their identification with positions other than western. That their lives and histories are constructed indifferent to the west.

The dream here, is to dream in a sky of difference, in a sky of multiplicity, of narratives of representation that are peripheral to the western canon. That the dream is for us (the participants and the viewer) to experience representations, which are outside of our normative position. That the dream can open us to stories and lives and ways of thinking, looking, hearing, being, existing beyond the hopes, the aspirations, and dreams that we ourselves are touched by in our daily structures.

Okayama Art Summit 2022
Artistic Director
Rirkrit Tiravanija

Rirkrit Tiravanija

Born in 1961 in Buenos Aires, Argentina, Thai artist Rirkrit Tiravanija is known for a practice that overturns traditional exhibition formats in favor of social interactions through the sharing of everyday activities such as cooking, eating and reading. Creating environments that reject the primacy of the art object, and instead focus on use value and the bringing of people together through simple acts and environments of communal care, Tiravanija's work challenges expectations around labour and virtuosity. Tiravanija is on the faculty of the School of the Arts at Columbia University, and is a founding member and curator of *Utopia Station*, a collective project of artists, art historians and curators. He also helped establish an educational-ecological project known as *The Land Foundation*, located near Chiang Mai, Thailand.

僕らは同じ空のもと夢をみているのだろうか

疑問文としてすべての要素を備えていながらも文末に疑問符のないこのセンテンスは、アイディアの入り口にしかすぎません。

この数年間、世界的パンデミックに加え、アメリカ国内の白人至上主義や世界各地のナショナリスト的ポピュリストの趨勢が強まってきたという背景を踏まえて、私はこの展覧会を私たちの意識や視点を変革するものにしたいと考えています。

こうした様々な思いを巡らし、岡山芸術交流2022については、できれば「旅人」という共通の背景をもつアーティストの周辺的な活動に特に集中したいと考えています。「旅人」というのは、選定されたアーティストのほとんどが異質な文化的あるいは社会的背景をもっているという意味です。彼らの多くが、活動や制作拠点を西洋の芸術的ヘゲモニーの中心に置きながらも、その（西洋的）ヘゲモニーのなかでの自らの位置づけにおいては、西洋以外の立場からのアイデンティティが根底にあります。彼らの人生と歴史は、西洋との違いによって形づくられているのです。

ここで言う夢とは、違いのある空や、多元性のある空で見る夢、つまり、西洋的規範の周縁にある物語表現のなかで見る夢を意味しています。私たち（参加者と鑑賞者）からすると自らが規範的とみなす世界の外にある表現を経験するということです。その夢は物語や人生に対して私たちを開き、希望や熱望、日々の社会構造のなかで触れる夢を超えたところにある、考え方、ものの見方、聞き方、そして存在の仕方に対して私たちを晒してくれるものなのです。

岡山芸術交流 2022
アーティスティックディレクター
リクリット・ティラヴァーニャ

リクリット・ティラヴァーニャ

1961年、アルゼンチン、ブエノスアイレス生まれ。タイ人アーティストであるティラヴァーニャは、料理や食、読書といった日常的な行為の共有を通じて観客と交流する場を設け、従来の展示形式をくつがえす表現で知られる。芸術作品の優位性を否定し、作品の使用価値および単純な行為と助け合いによって人と人を結びつける空間を構築することで、労働やアート鑑賞のあり方に挑む。現在、米・コロンビア大学芸術大学院教授を務める。アーティスト・美術史家・キュレーターによる共同プロジェクト「Utopia Station」創設メンバーであり、キュレーター。また、タイのチェンマイ近郊にある教育および環境保全プロジェクト「The Land Foundation」の設立にも携わる。

CONTENTS

目次

僕らは
同じ
空のもと
夢を
みて
いる
のだろうか

むかし
むかし
のこと

鏡の
荒野に

たくさんの
人々

太陽が
消えても
僕らには
光が
ある

影は
まだすべてを
覆ってはいない

部屋
全体が
みえる
けれど
そこには
誰も
いない

みんな
集まれ

美しい
海を
つくるのも
一粒
一粒の
水滴だ

バカげた
現実に
闘いを
挑もう

希望の
角度は
人
それぞれ

ダイナマイト
こそは
すべて

火が
なければ
灰も
出ない

幸福
とは
あたたかな
ガム

魂の
ほんとうの
目は
水だ

この
社会に
残された
時間は
もう

長くは
ない

黒き
堆肥に
跪け

未來は
自然の
なかに
ある

文＝リクリット・ティラヴァーニャ
訳＝秋元孝文

DO
WE
DREAM
UNDER
THE
SAME
SKY

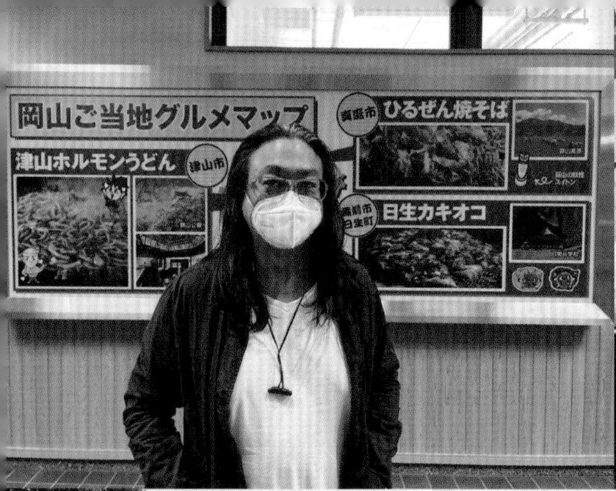
岡山ご当地グルメマップ
ひるぜん焼そば
津山ホルモンうどん
津山市
日生カキオコ
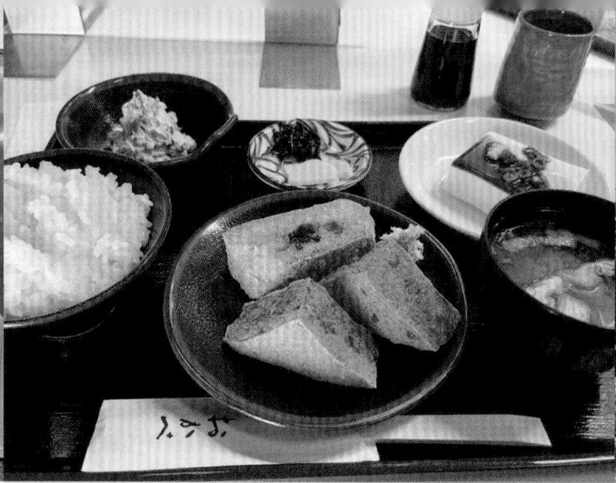
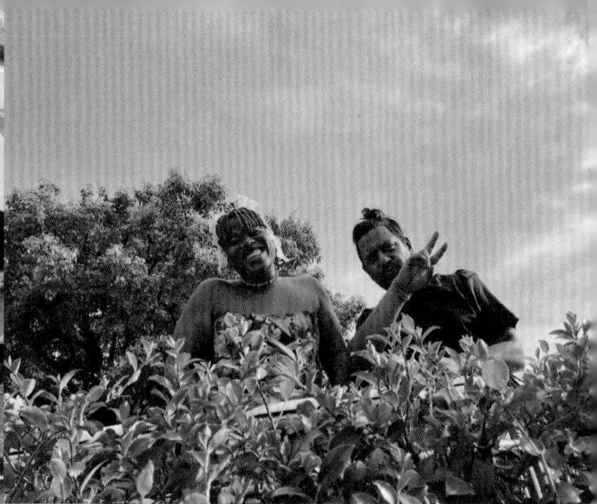
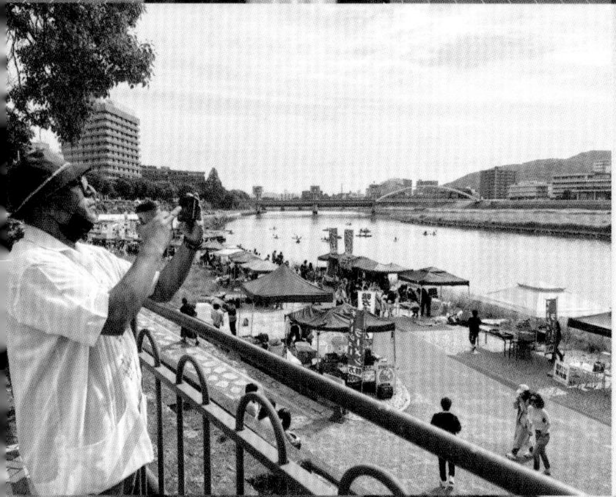
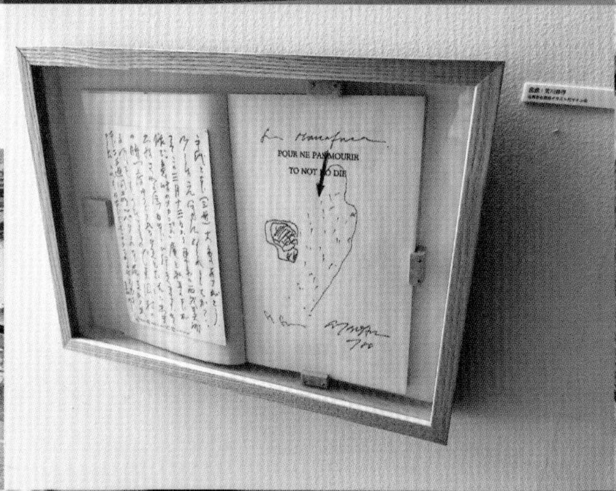
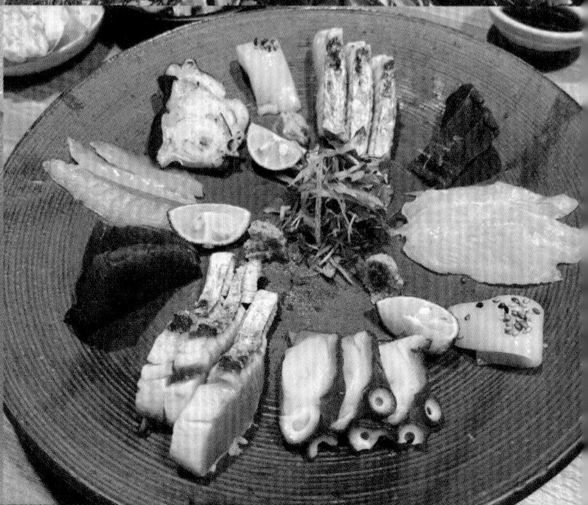
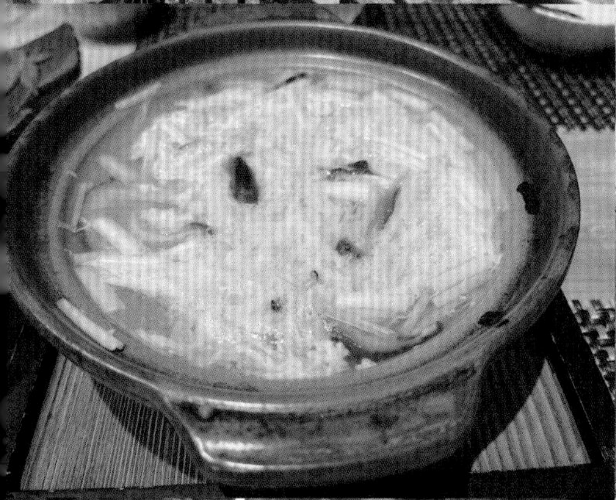
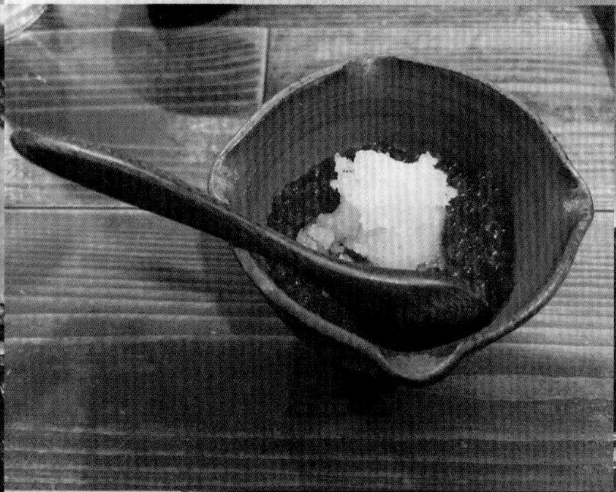
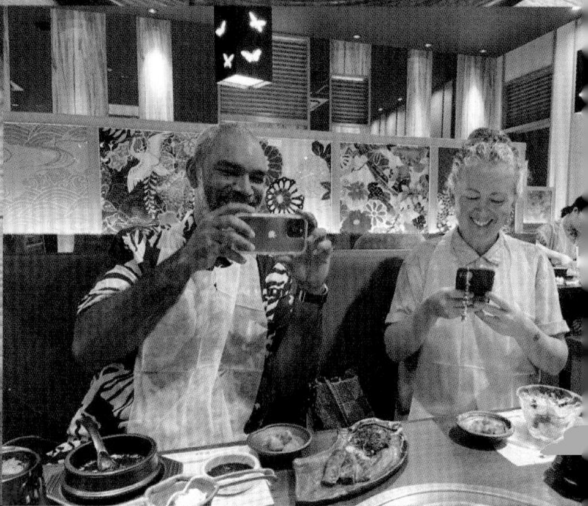
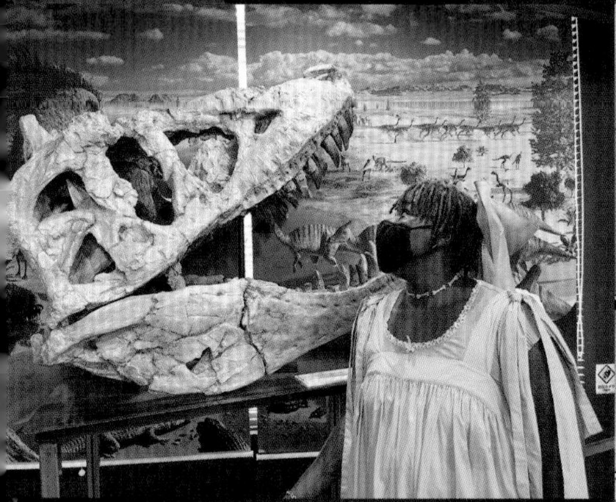
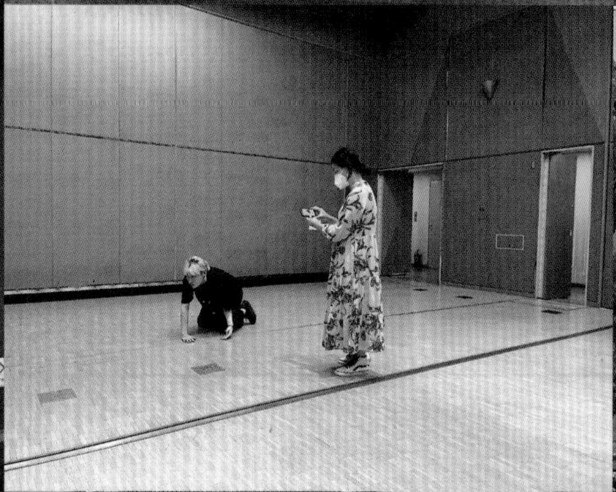
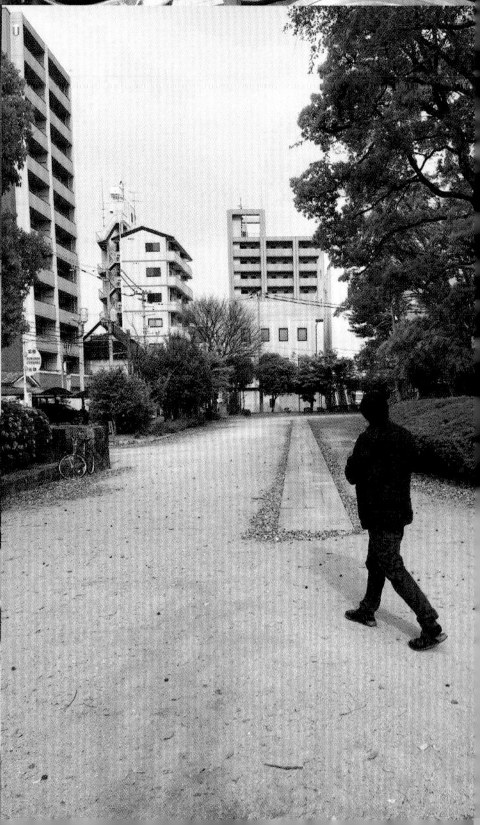
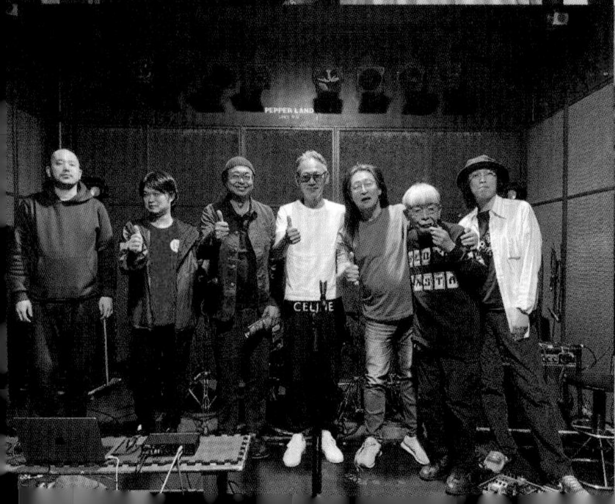
PEPPER LAND
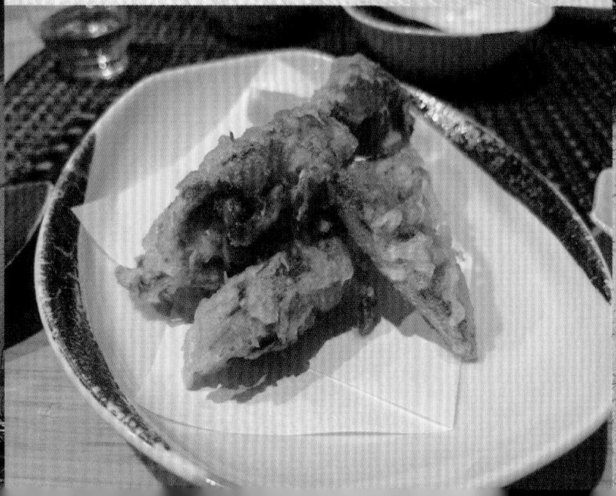

ONCE
UPON
A
TIME

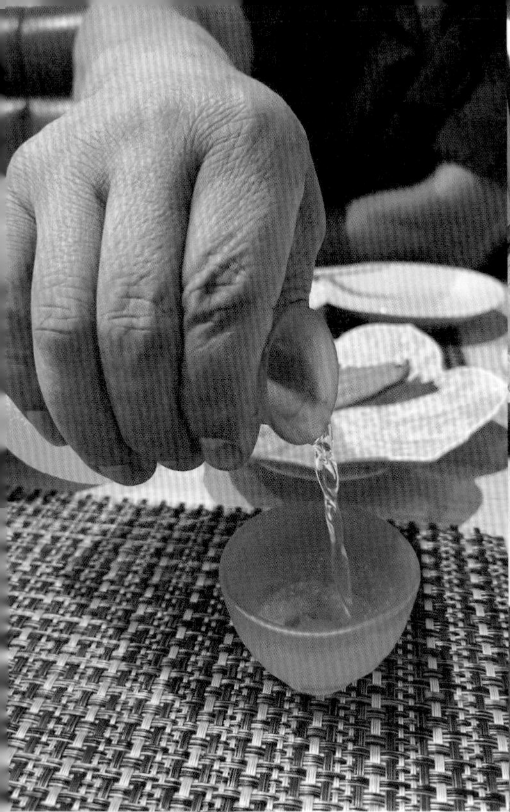
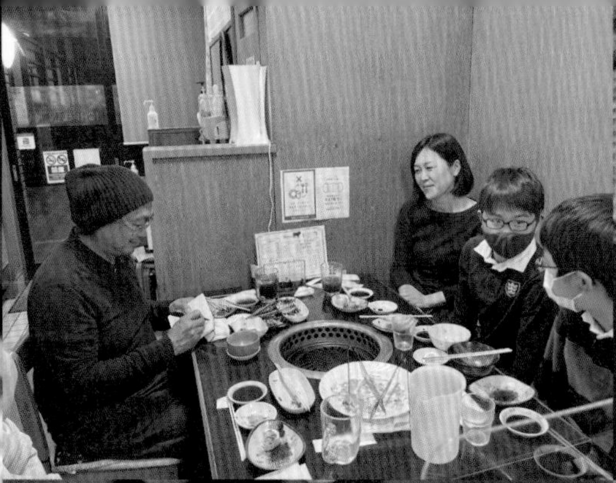
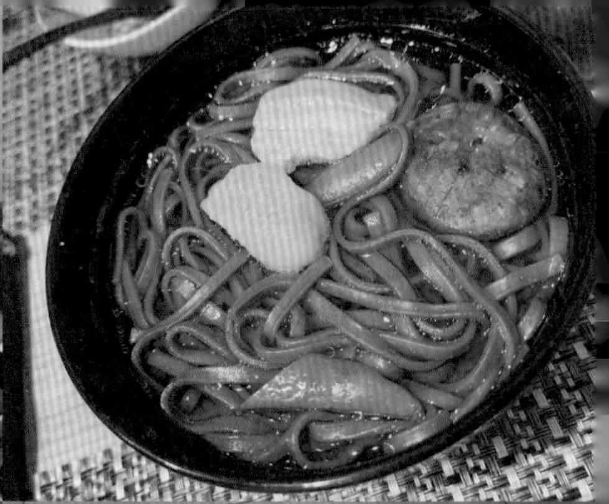
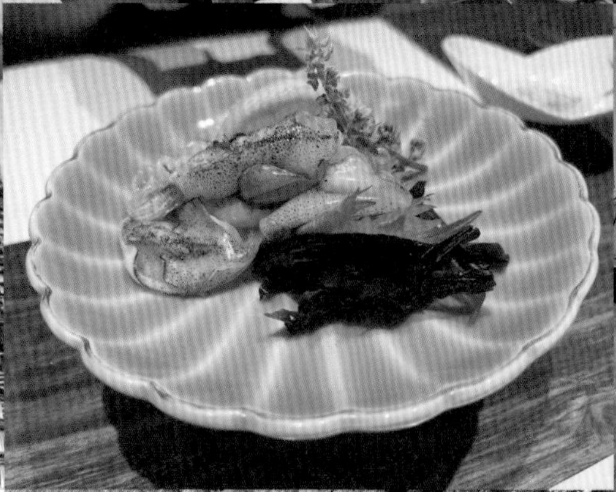
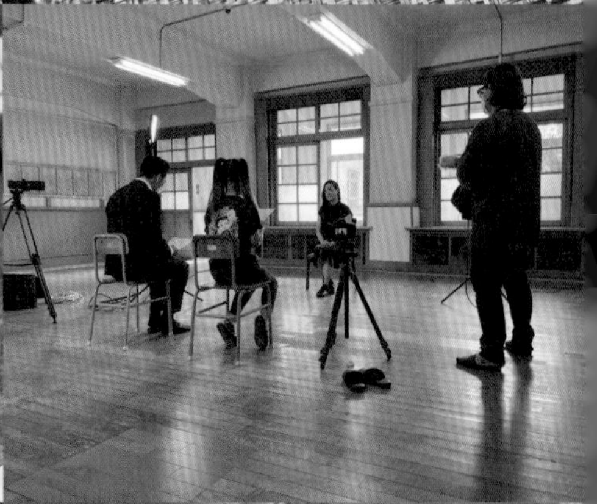
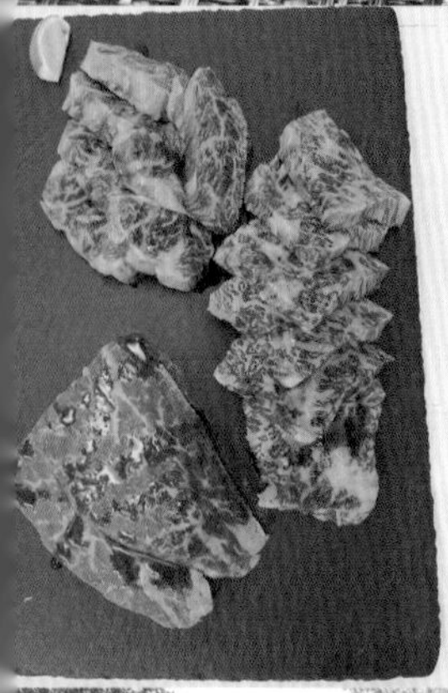
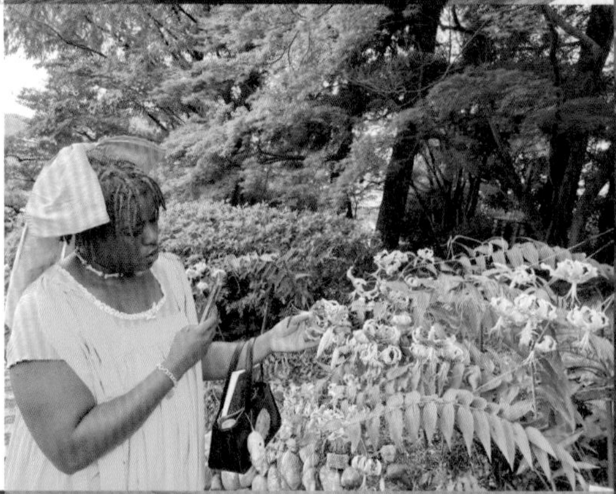
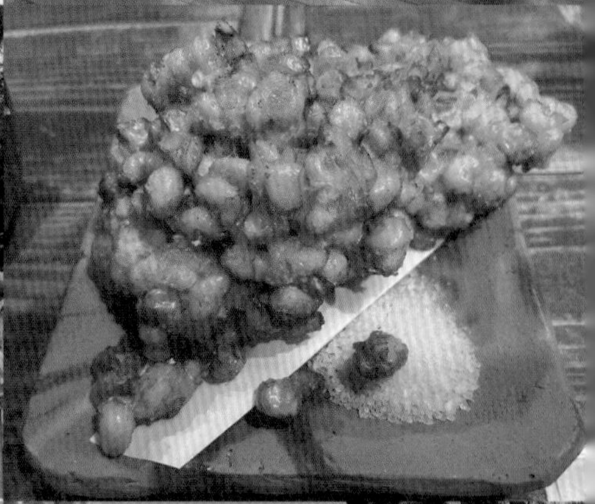
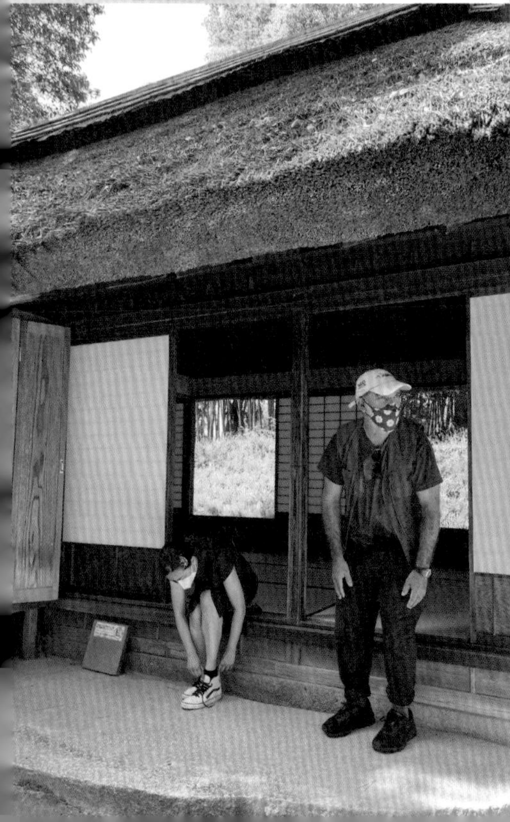
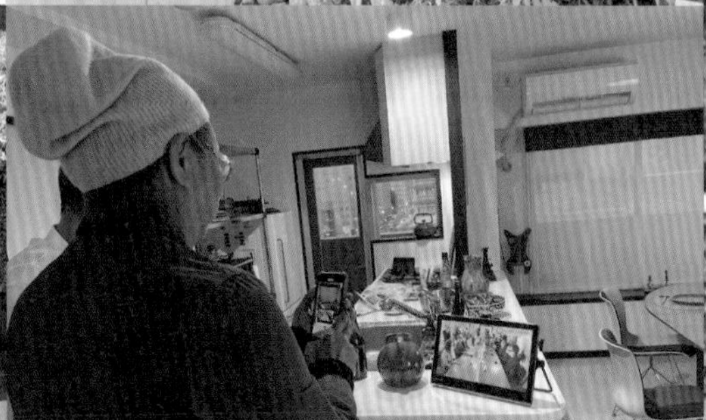
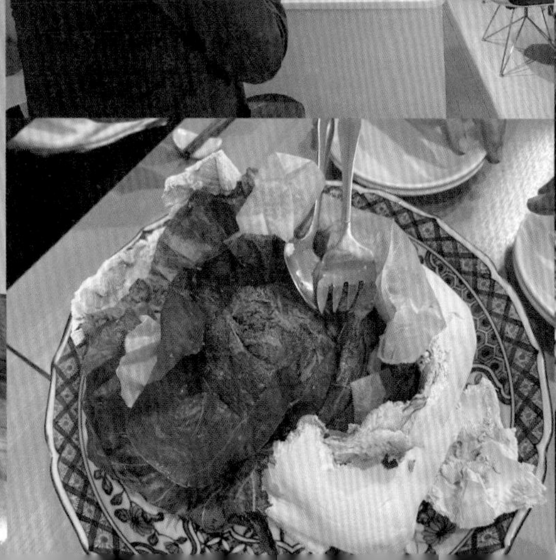
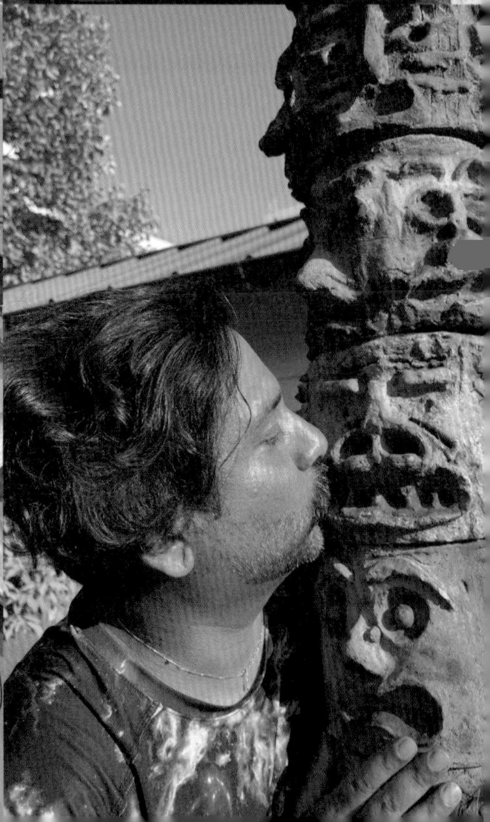

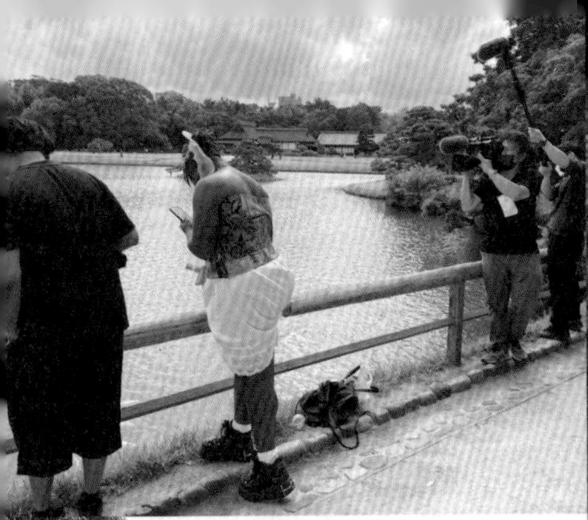
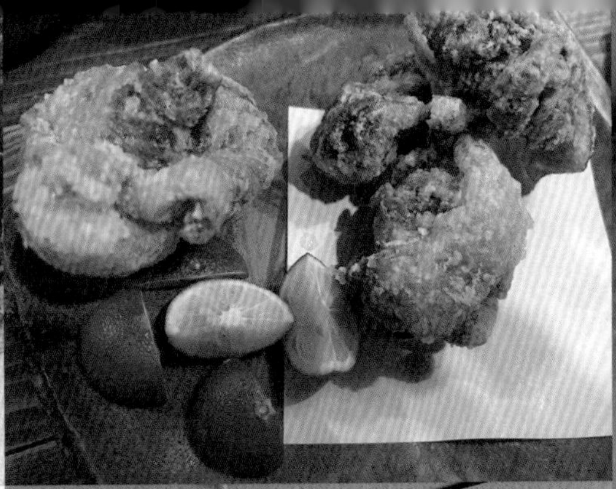
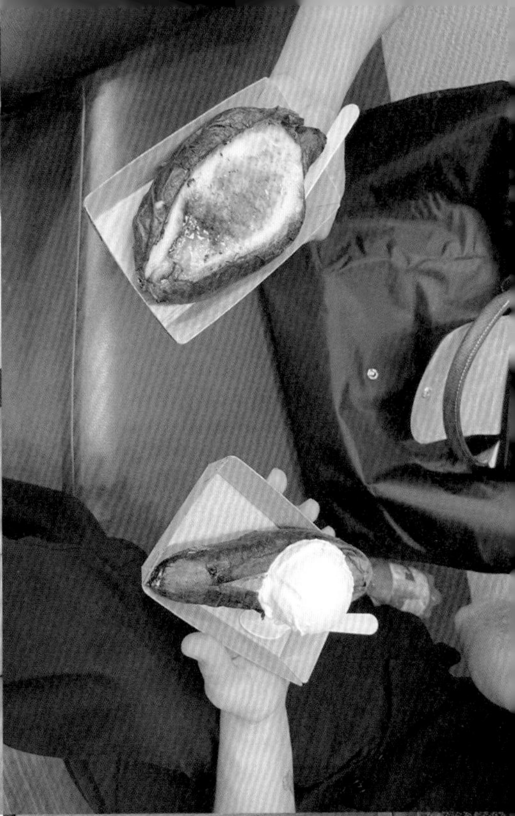
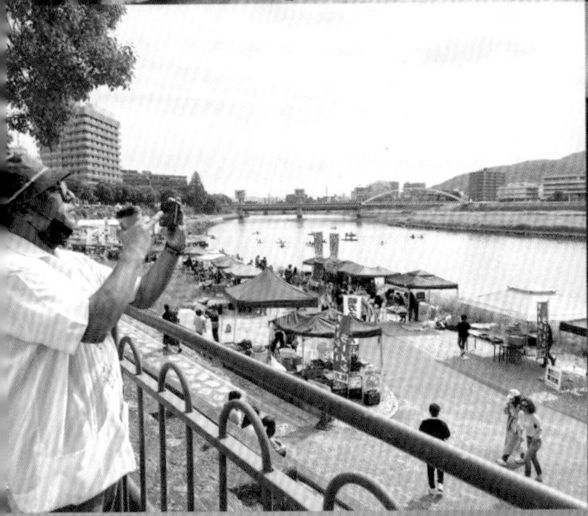
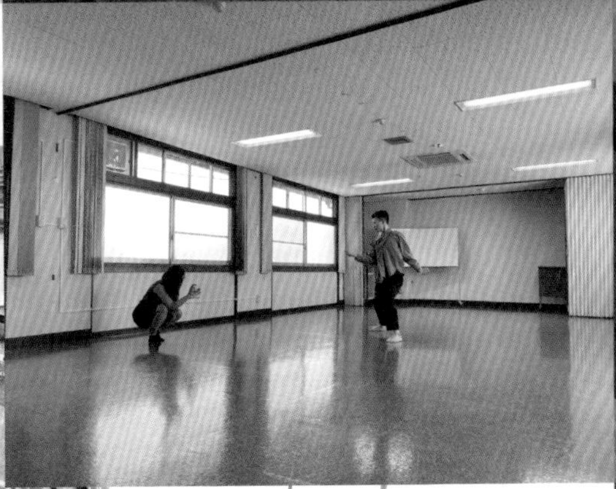
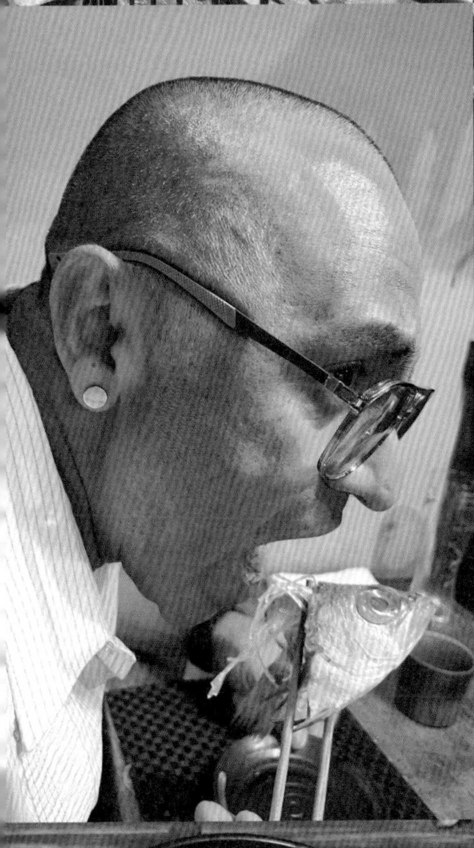
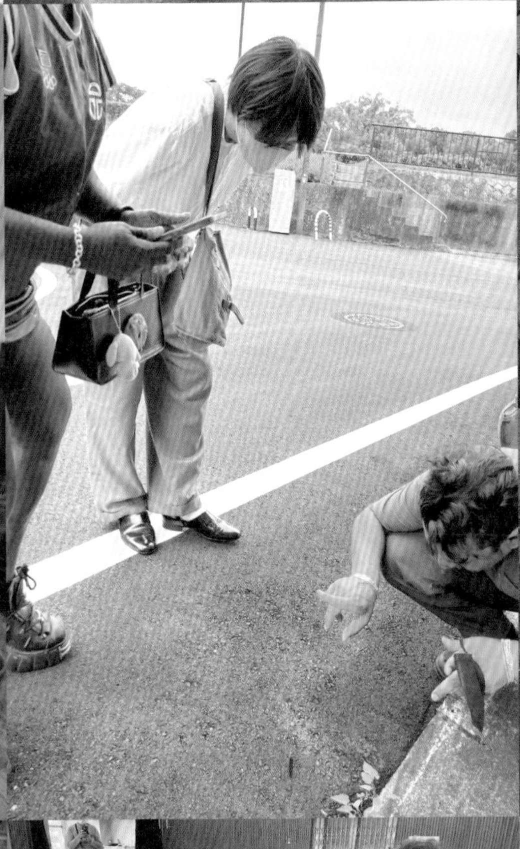
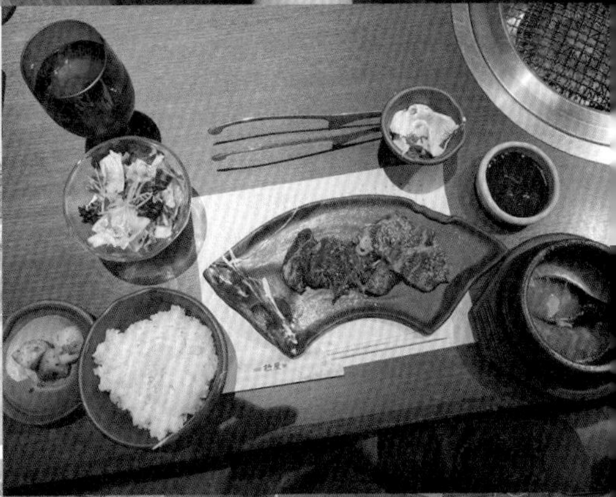
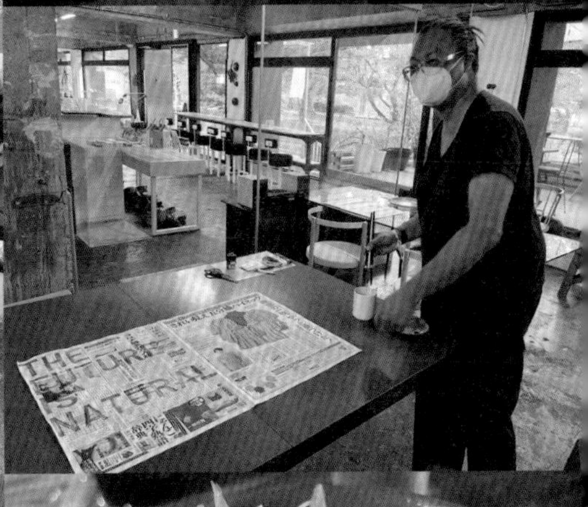
THE
FUTURE
IS
NATURAL
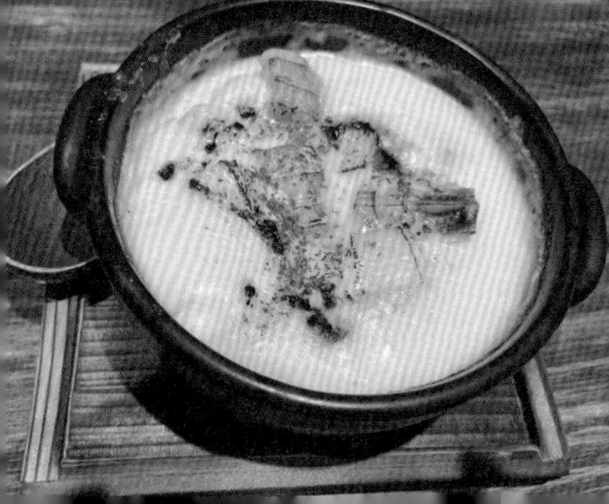
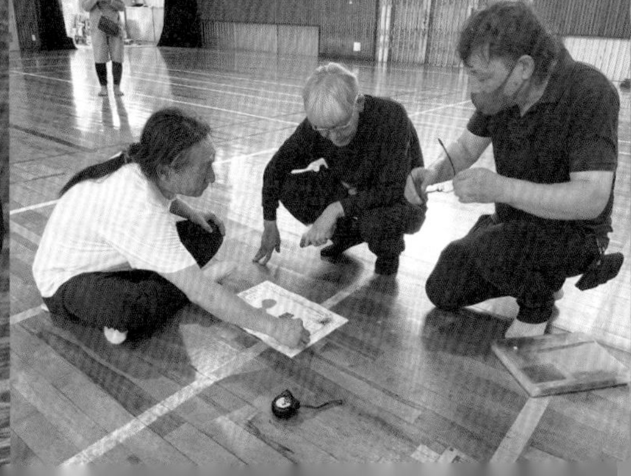
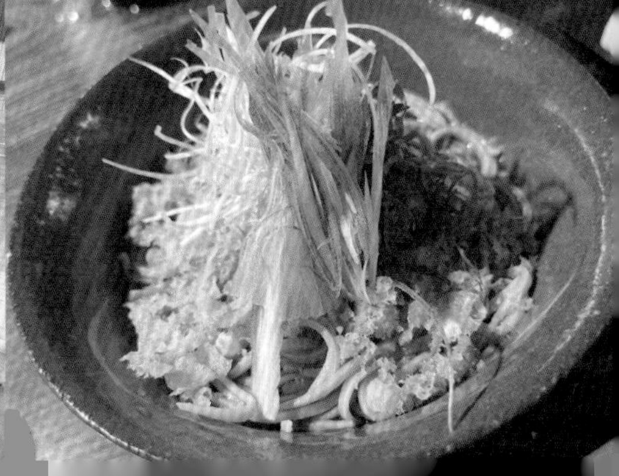

THE WILDERNESS OF MIRRORS

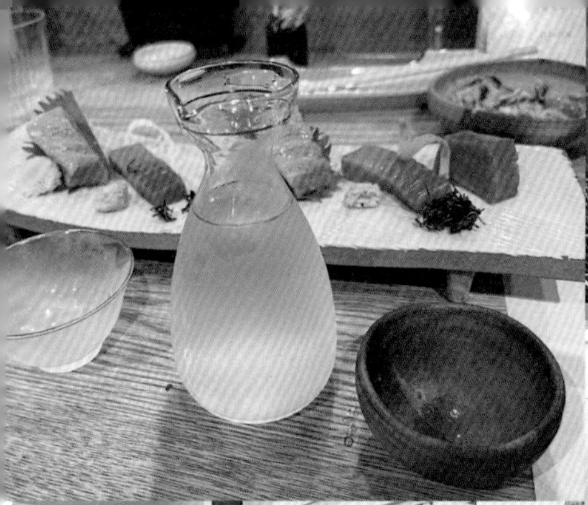

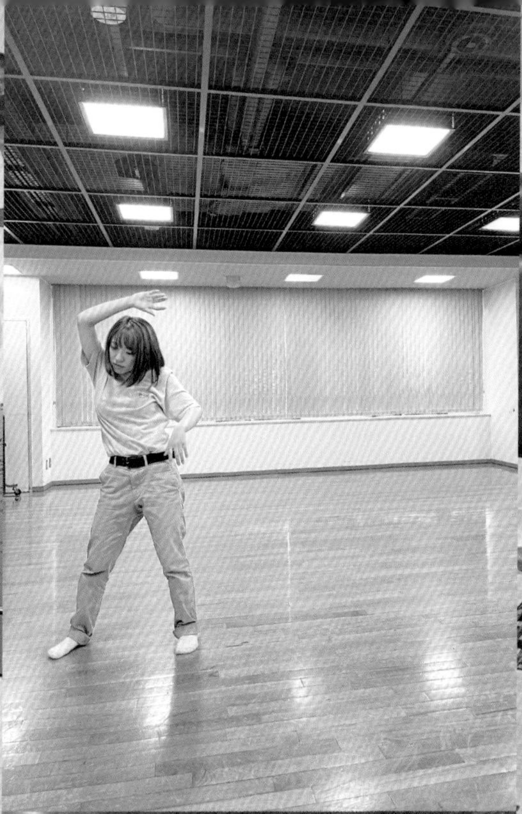

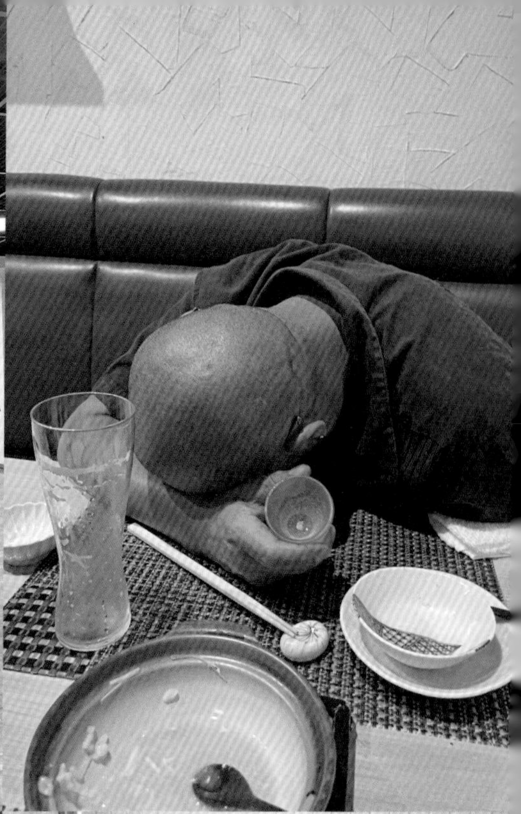

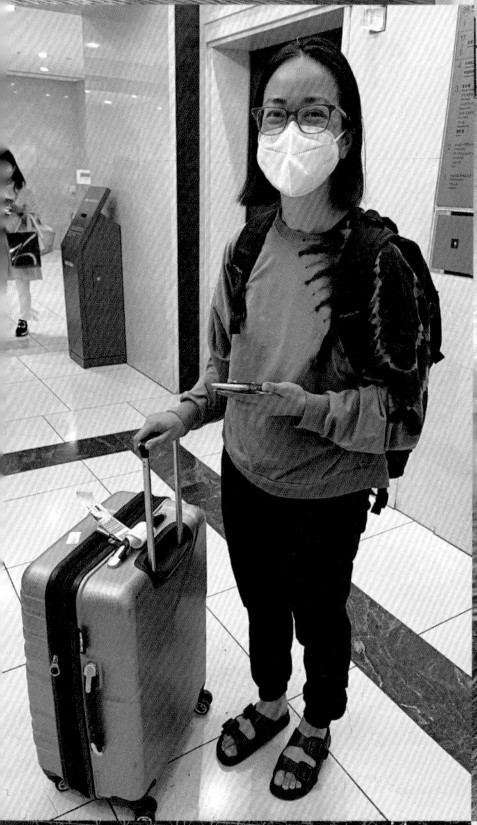

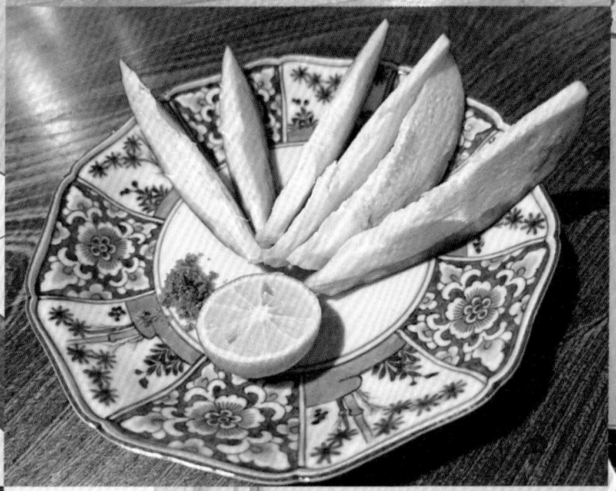

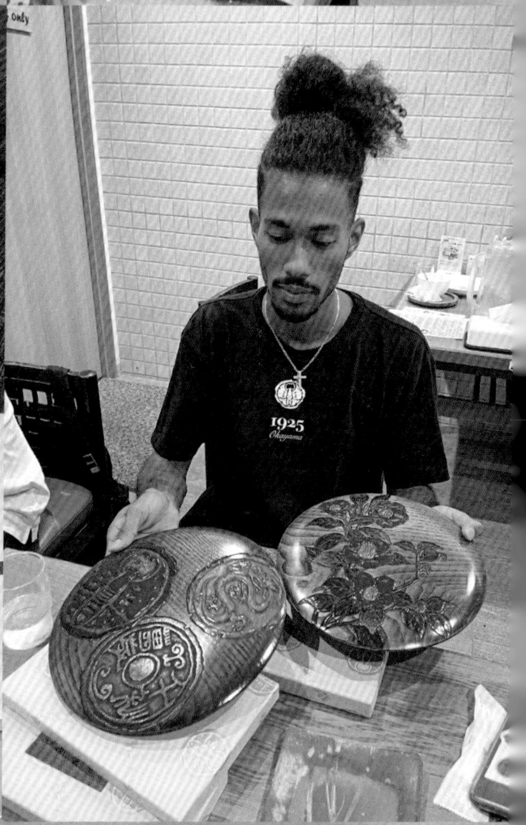
1925
Okayama

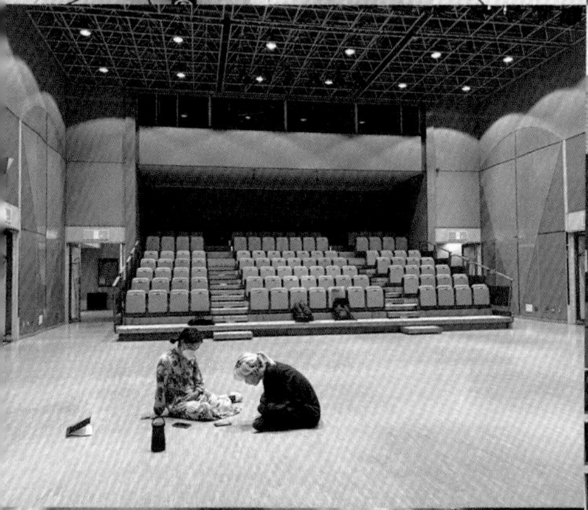

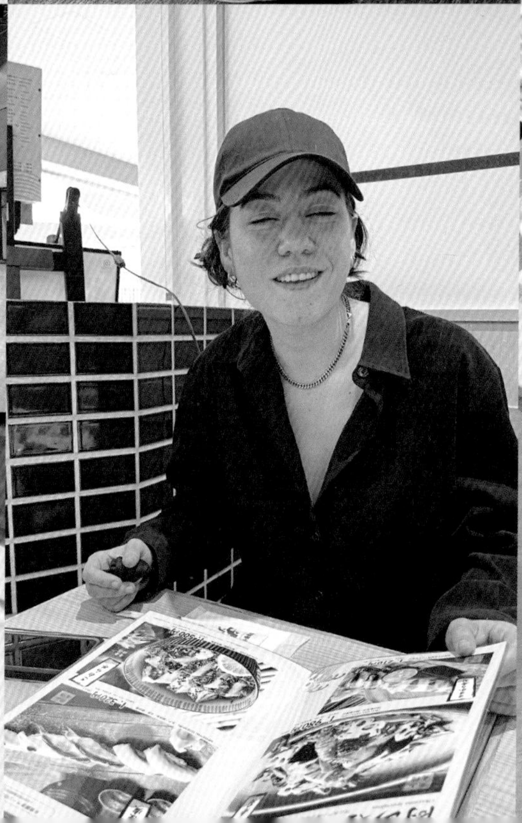

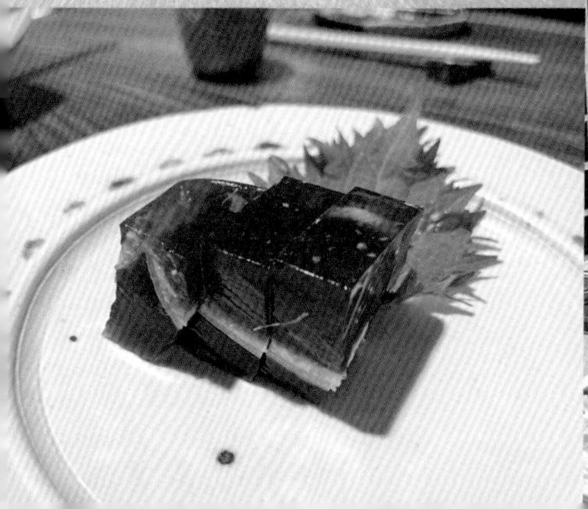

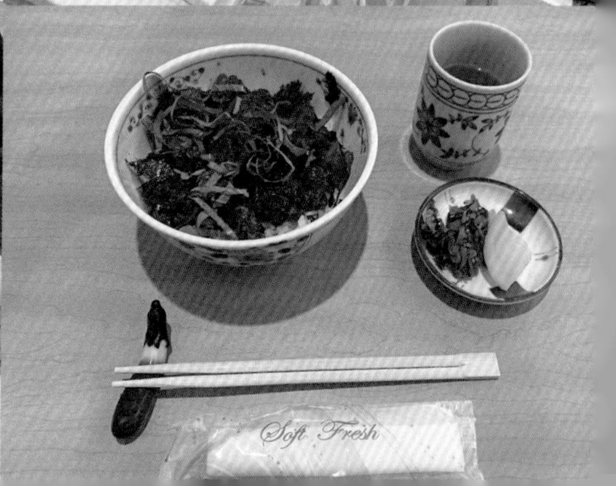
Soft Fresh

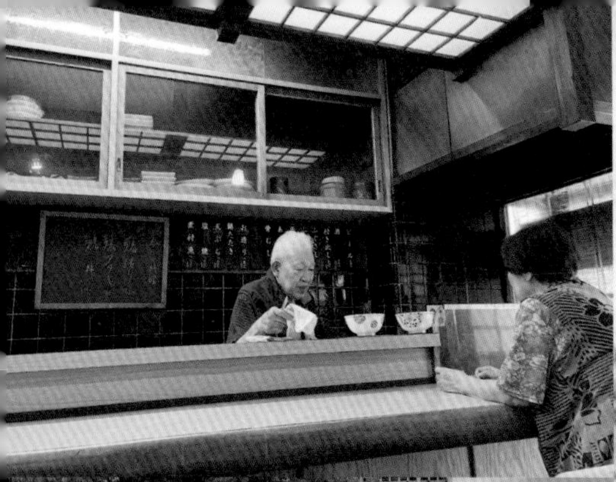

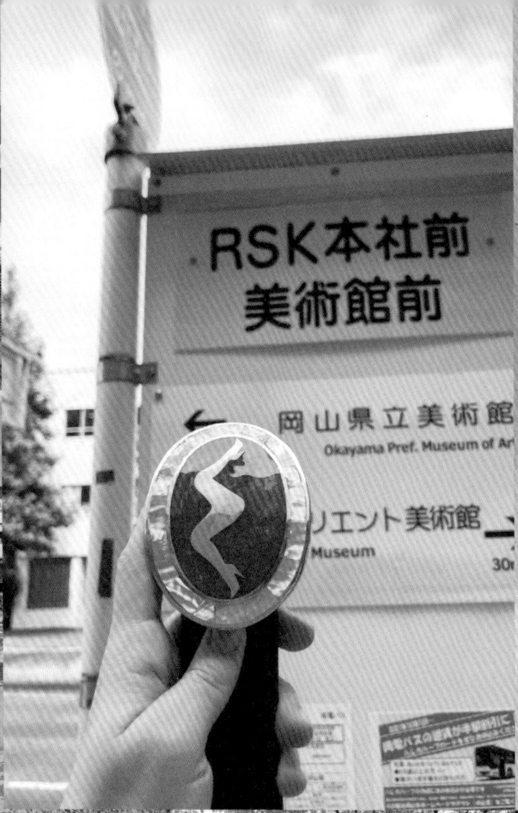

RSK本社前
美術館前
岡山県立美術館
Okayama Pref. Museum of Ar
リエント美術館
Museum

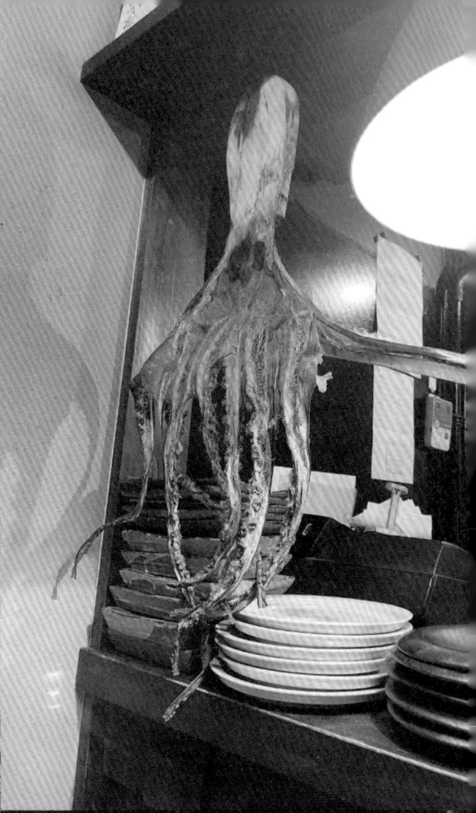

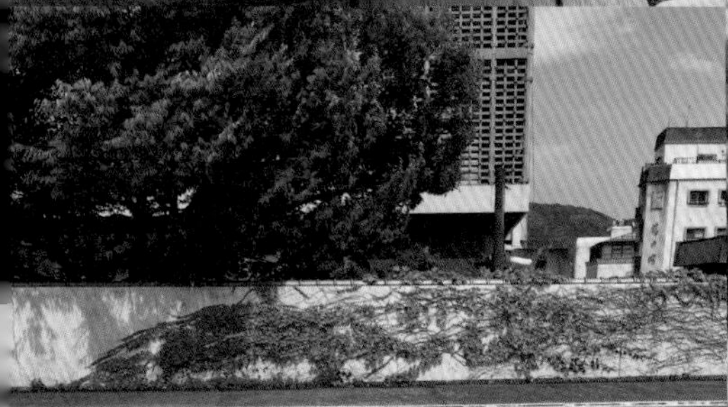

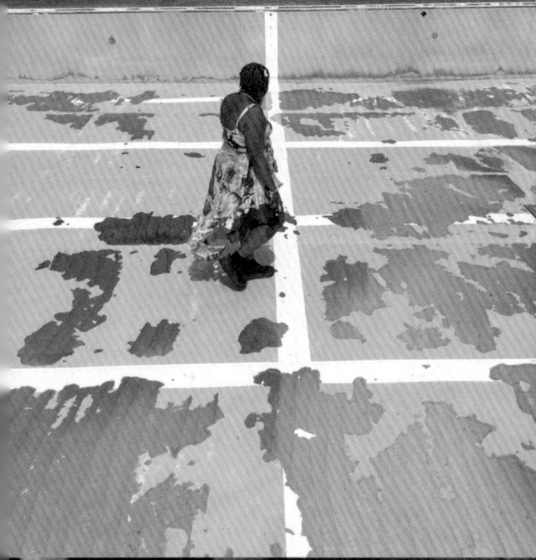

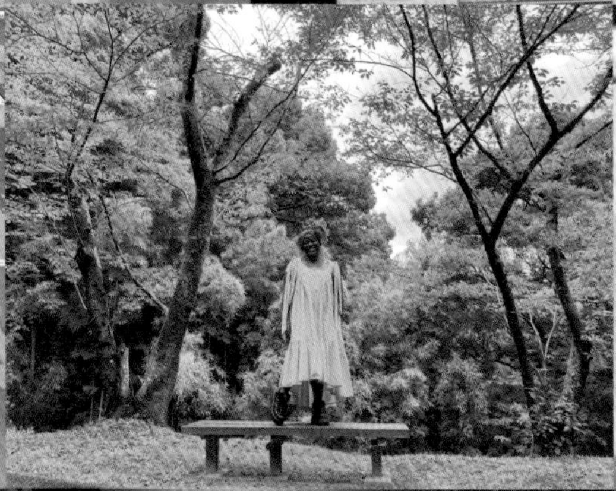

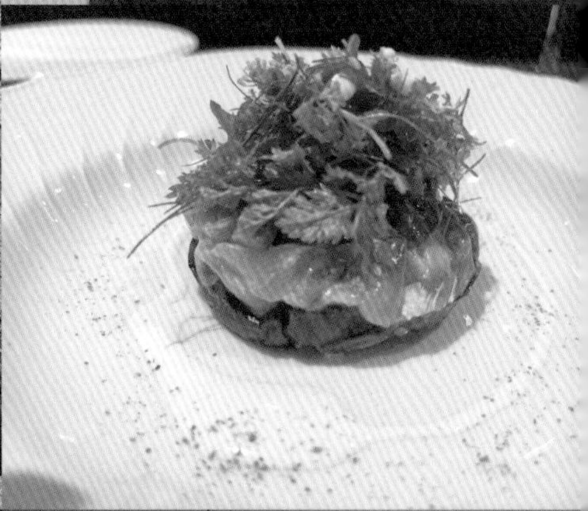

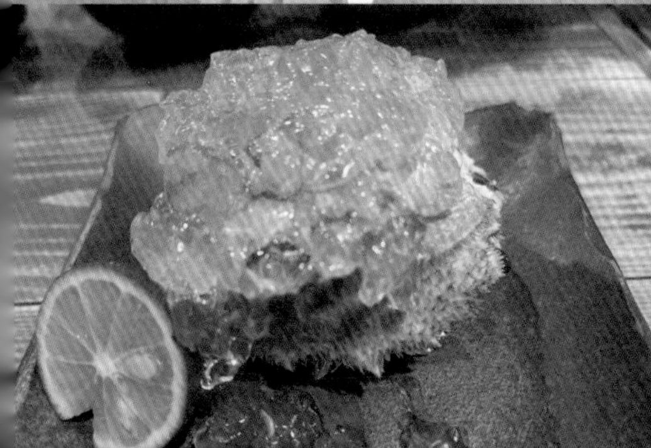

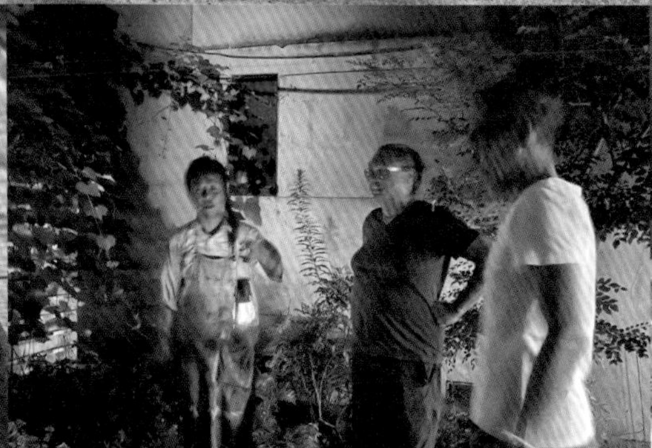

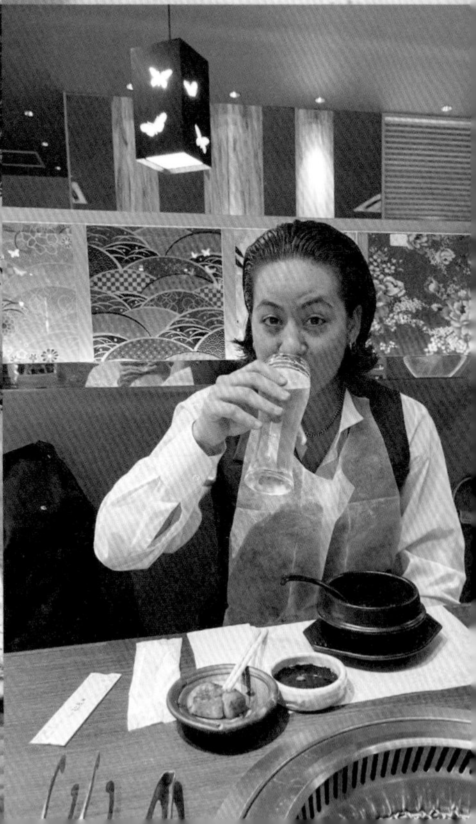

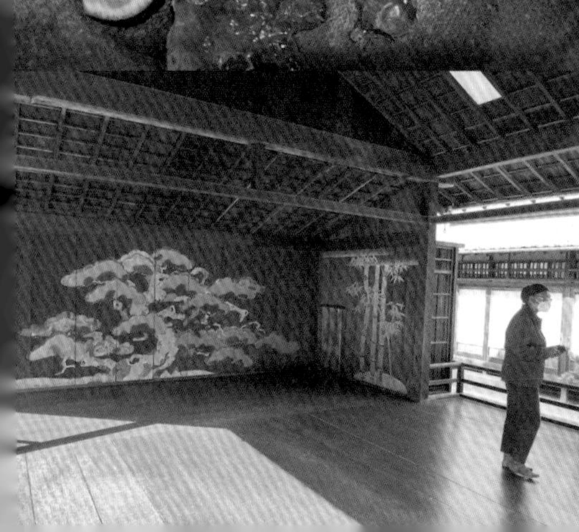

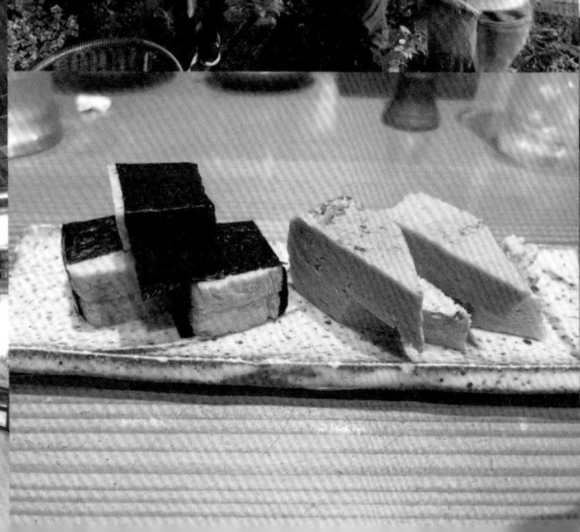

Rasel Ahmed

ラゼル・アハメド

Works in Columbus, Ohio.
His major exhibitions include *Moving Memories*, Hopkins Hall Gallery, Columbus (2022), *Cultivo*, Marli Matsumoto Arte Contemporânea, São Paulo (2022), *Unorthodocs Shorts*, Wexner Center for the Arts, Columbus (2021), The Lenfest Center, NYC (2021), USAID, Washington, D.C. (2018), South Asian Queer Film Festival, Stockholm (2018), British Council, Dhaka (2015), DIALOGUES: Calcutta International LGBT Film & Video Festival, Kolkata (2014).
Rasel is the Assistant Professor in Nonfiction Filmmaking in the Department of Theatre, Film, and Media Arts at The Ohio State University.

オハイオ州コロンバスを拠点に活動。
主な展示に、2022年「Moving Memories」ホプキンス・ホール・ギャラリー（コロンバス）、2022年「Cultivo」Marli Matsumoto Arte Contemporânea（サンパウロ）、2021年「Unorthodocs Shorts」ウェクスナー芸術センター（コロンバス）、2021年レンフェスト・センター（ニューヨーク）、2018年USAID（ワシントンD.C.）、2018年South Asian Queer Film Festival（ストックホルム）、2015年ブリティッシュ・カウンシル（ダッカ）、2014年DIALOGUES Calcutta International LGBT Film & Video Festival（コルカタ）がある。現在、オハイオ州立大学舞台芸術・映画・メディアアーツ科にて助教を務める 。

Do we remember an image the same way we remember a ghost? Isn't the memory of a ghost a trip to imagination? I grapple with questions like this as a moving image maker to find out the potential of the medium in capturing non-indexical moments.

Drawing from history, theory, and memory, I make experimental hybrid films that combine documentary with fantasy. As a displaced person, my work focuses primarily on examining my dialogical relationship with citizenship, queerness, exile, and its intertextual association with body and memory. I use traditional cinematic tropes and formal techniques to combine autoethnographic narratives, archival documents with performances. Characters in my films are flashbacks of memories living on the edge of identities. I also insert myself into the history and memory of other characters to produce unexpected storylines and heterogeneous layers in the film.

Aesthetically, I am curious about identifying the historical impact, function, and characteristics of the involved visual style. I often remove images from the screen and instead use sound cues and digital typography to invite my audience to engage in the mutual deconstruction of reality. Through my practice, I aim to cross-pollinate traditional cinema-making with emerging technologies in ways that unsettle the binaries between fiction and non-fiction and invite the audience to imagine multiple possible realities.

My filmmaking is collaborative and process-oriented; I innovate techniques and methods breaking away from the traditional movie-making workflow. I begin my filmmaking with video editing that informs the writing and layout of the script. Then, I spontaneously develop experimental research models such as participatory documentation, history mapping, and collaborative re-enactment to finalize the performances and movement choices in the film. My participatory research methods involve inviting community members, actors, and film technicians to analyze the visual metaphor, iconography, and psychogeography of characters. Finally, the interaction of the film with the spatial arrangements of the gallery informs the installation that allows multiple visual interpretations. Together, these processes result in an assemblage of actions, relations, and ephemeral moments in flux that create an alternative archive of memory and intimacy.

Rasel Ahmed

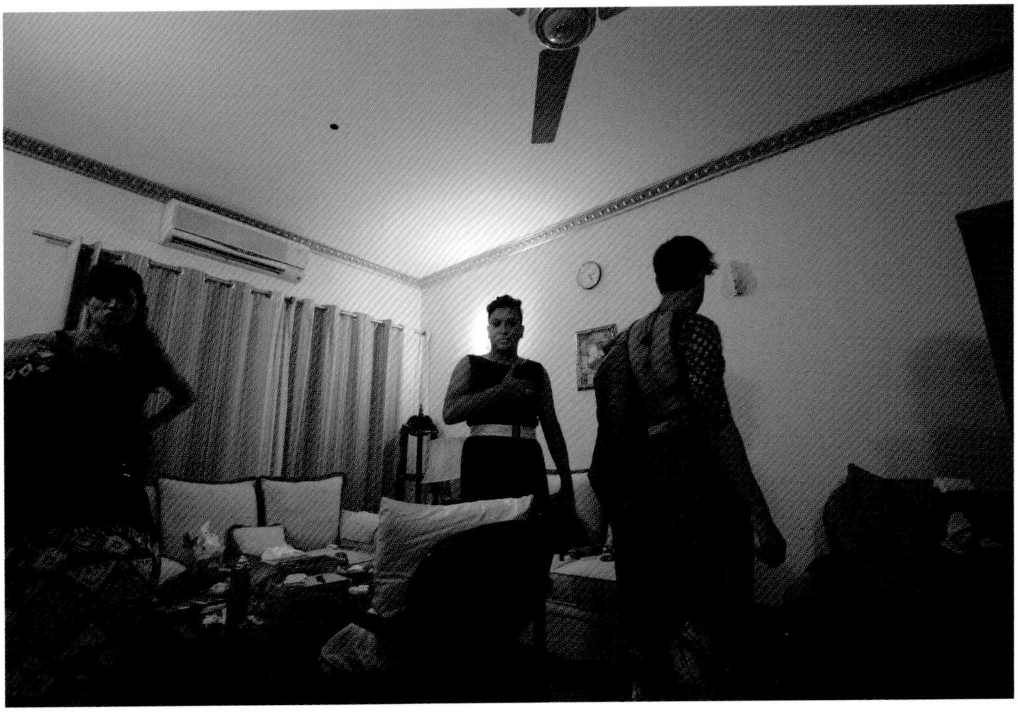

DragOnBall preparation in Dhaka, Bangladesh (2015)
Who Killed Taniya is an imaginary recreation of this drag show.
Credit: Shams
バングラデシュ、ダッカで2015年に行われたドラァグショー「DragOnBall」準備の様子。
《Who Killed Taniya》はこのドラァグショーの空想的再現である

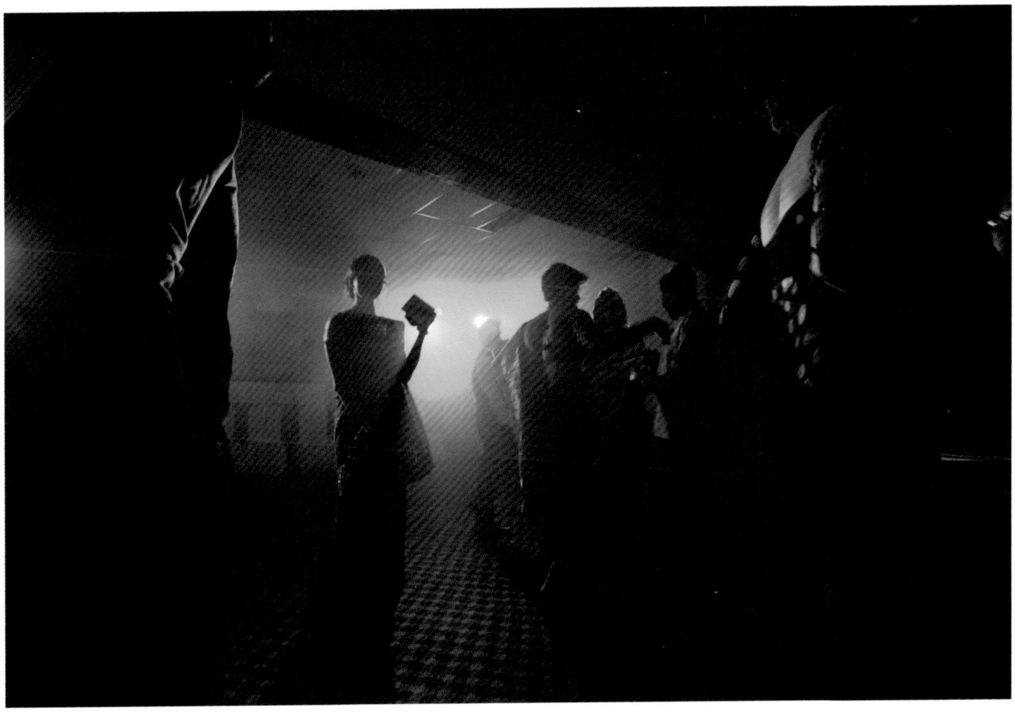

DragOnBall in Dhaka, Bangladesh (2015)
Credit: Shams
ドラァグショー「DragOnBall」の様子

幽霊を記憶するのと同じように、イメージを記憶するのだろうか？　幽霊の記憶は想像への旅ではないのか？　そんな疑問をもちながら、映像作家として、指標とならない瞬間を切り取る映像メディアの可能性を探っている。

歴史、理論、記憶をもとに、ドキュメンタリーとファンタジーを融合させたハイブリッドな実験映画を制作している。難民として、作品は主に、市民権、クィアネス、追放との対話関係、そして身体や記憶との間テクスト的関連性を検証することに重点を置いている。伝統的な映画の手法（比喩）と形式的なテクニックを使い、自伝的な物語、記録文書やパフォーマンスを組み合わせている。映像の登場人物は、アイデンティティの端で生きている記憶のフラッシュバックである。また、ほかの登場人物の歴史や記憶に自分自身を挿入し、予期せぬストーリー展開や異質な層を映画のなかに生み出している。

美学的には、関係する視覚的スタイルの歴史的な影響、機能、特徴を特定することに興味がある。しばしばスクリーンから画像を取り除き、代わりに音の合図やデジタルタイポグラフィーを使い、鑑賞者を現実の相互脱構築に参加するよう招く。実践を通し、フィクションとノンフィクションの間を曖昧にし、鑑賞者が複数の可能な現実を想像するよう促す方法で、従来の映画づくりと新しいテクノロジーを掛け合わせることを目指している。

私の映画制作は、共同作業とプロセス指向であり、従来の映画制作のワークフローから脱却した技術や方法を導入している。まずヴィデオ編集から映画制作を始め、それを脚本の執筆とレイアウトに反映する。その後、参加型ドキュメンテーション、ヒストリーマッピング、共同再演などの実験的なリサーチモデルを自発的に開発し、映画のなかでのパフォーマンスや動きの選択を最終的に決定する。参加型調査では、地域住民、俳優、映画技術者を招き、登場人物の視覚的隠喩、図像学、心理地理学を分析する。最後に、ギャラリーの空間配置と映画の相互作用から、複数の視覚的解釈を可能にするインスタレーションが生まれる。これらのプロセスは、行動、関係、そして流動的ではかない瞬間の集合体となり、記憶と親密さの代替的なアーカイヴをつくり出す。

ラゼル・アハメド

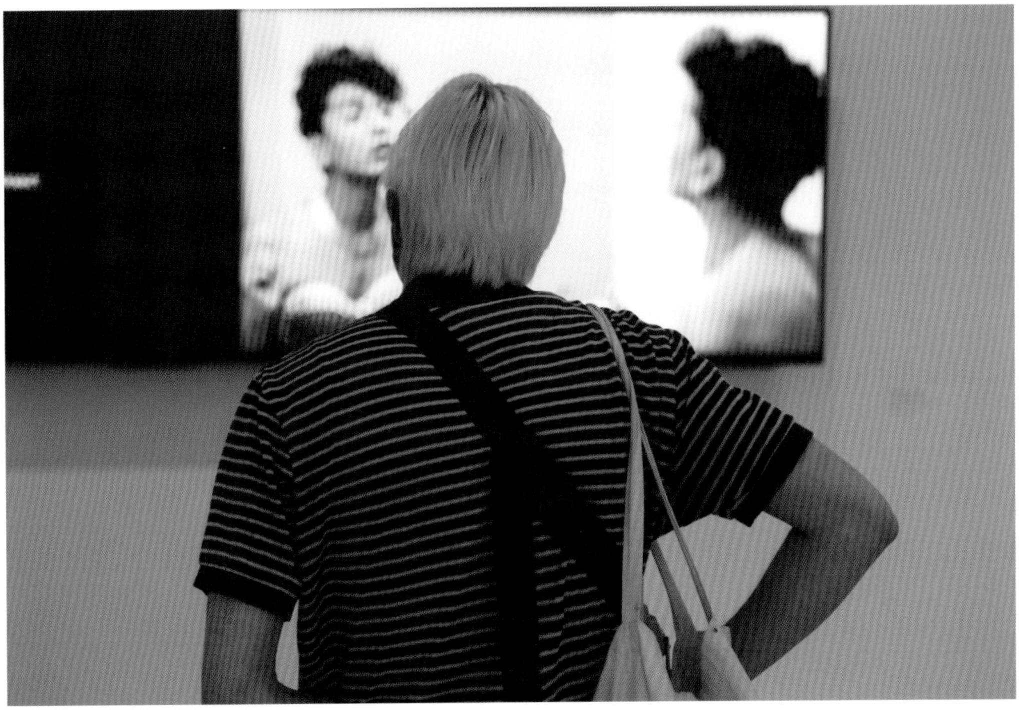

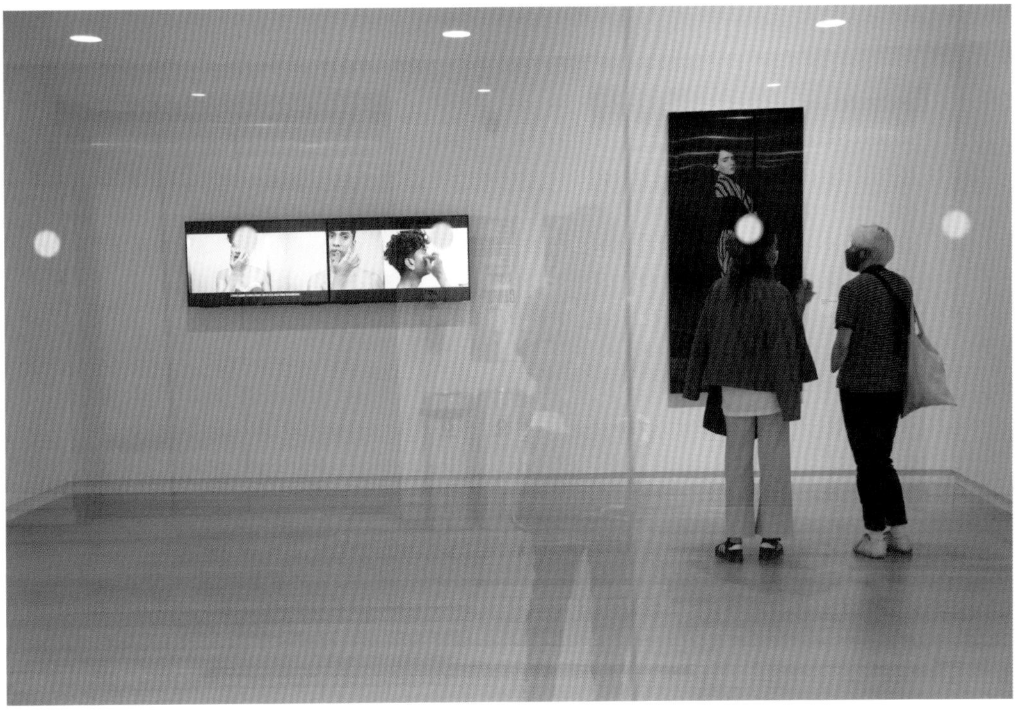

Two channel exhibition of *Who Killed Taniya* in Lenfest Art Center, NYC
Credit: Rasel Ahmed
《Who Killed Taniya》レンフェスト・センター（ニューヨーク）での展示風景

Who Killed Taniya

Episode 1: 2015, Two channel video, 18 min.
Episode 2: 2022, Single channel video, 15 min.

Who Killed Taniya is inspired by a video from my personal archive. The video is from an underground drag show organized in Dhaka, Bangladesh. There are five performers dancing to Bollywood item songs (a musical number inserted into a Hindi film that may or may not have any relevance to the plot). The video is celebratory, joyus, and full of color. The lead performer of this drag show, Mahbub Tonoy, was killed by an Al-Qaeda attack a couple of months later.

When I revisited the video in 2018, I started asking questions like why was Tonoy murdered? Was it because he was dancing? Or because he was playing with his gender? Who killed Tonoy? Was it Al-Qaeda or the state that failed to protect him? All these questions prompted months long research on the nature of post-colonial violence and heteronormative surveillance. The conclusion of my research led me to develop a fictional plot line based on those five performances.

Who Killed Taniya is an experimental murder mystery set in the future that explores the social, emotional, and political nature of murder. It's a story of five fictional drag characters who gather in a makeup room to perform in a community drag event. While wearing makeup, they unpack their complicated relationships with the main character Taniya. I weave together a fictional murder fantasy which is emerging from my research on genocidal trauma, deportation anxiety, gender dysphoria, and political biases.

My primary research material was an archival journal produced by an early 19th century colonial geographer named Francis Buchanan. He was documenting topography, history, antiquities, the condition of the inhabitants, religion, and politics of East Bengal. He spent seven years surveying the region from 1807. I was particularly interested in the description of early forced displacement in the Eastern border that Bangladesh shares with Myanmar. This research inspired me to create the character of Taniya and Hena. Hena's relationship with drag is an examination of the performative aspects of citizenship and border through the lens of drag and makeup.

The framework of murder mystery helped me to explore the oppressive nature of postcolonial state. In neoliberal secular states like Bangladesh, enforced disappearance, killing, abduction, and torture of citizens are often framed with fantasy fiction plots and fabricated stories. Queer bodies and their public/private spaces are subject to surveillence and censorship. The story in *Who Killed Taniya* explores how state violence trickles down and reproduces authoritarian violence within the queer community. In a critical moment like this, queer murder is not a mystery, but a revelation.

《Who Killed Taniya（誰がタニヤを殺したか）》は、私の個人的なアーカイヴヴィデオに端を発している。そのヴィデオは、バングラデシュのダッカで行われたクィア・ドラァグショーを撮影したもの。5人のパフォーマーがボリウッド・アイテムソング（インド映画に挿入される、筋書きと関係があるのかないのかわからないミュージカルナンバー）に合わせて踊っている。映像は、祝祭的で、愉快で、色彩に満ちている。このドラァグショーの主役、マブブ・トノイは、数ヵ月後、アルカイダの襲撃で殺された。

2018年にこのヴィデオを見直したとき、なぜトノイは暗殺されたのかという疑問をもつようになった。彼が踊っていたから？　それとも、彼が自分のジェンダーをもてあそんでいたから？　トノイを殺したのは誰なのか？　アルカイダなのか、それとも彼を保護できなかった国家なのか？　これらすべての疑問は、ポストコロニアルの暴力や異性愛規範監視の本質に関する数ヵ月にわたる調査へと駆り立てた。その結果、私は5つの演目をもとにしたフィクションの筋書きを作成することにした。

《Who Killed Taniya》は、未来を舞台に、社会的、感情的、政治的本質を探る実験的な殺人ミステリー。地域のドラァグイベントに出演するため、メイクルームに集まった5人の架空のドラァグキャラクターたちの物語だ。メイクをしながら、登場人物は主人公のタニヤとの複雑な関係を解きほぐしていく。大量虐殺のトラウマ、国外追放への不安、性別違和、政治的偏見に関する調査から生まれた、架空の殺人ファンタジーを織り込んでいる。

最重要の研究材料は、19世紀初頭の植民地時代の地理学者、フランシス・ブキャナンが作成した記録誌である。彼は、東ベンガルの地形、歴史、古代の遺物、住民の状況、宗教、政治を記録していた。そして、1807年から7年間、この地域の調査を行った。バングラデシュがミャンマーと共有している東部国境での初期の強制移住の記述が特に興味深い。この調査から、タニヤとヘナというキャラクターをつくろうと思った。ヘナとドラァグの関係は、ドラァグとメイクアップというレンズを通して、市民権や国境のパフォーマティヴな側面を考察する。

殺人ミステリーという枠組みは、ポストコロニアルの国家の抑圧的な性質を探るのに役立った。バングラデシュのような新自由主義的世俗国家では、市民の強制失踪、殺害、誘拐、拷問は、しばしばファンタジー小説の筋書きや虚構の物語で切り取られる。クィアな身体とその公的／私的空間は、監視と検閲の対象となる。《Who Killed Taniya》のストーリーは、国家の暴力がどのようにクィアコミュニティのなかで権威主義的暴力を浸透させ、再生産していくかを探るものだ。非常に重要な瞬間において、クィア殺人はミステリーではなく、啓示なのだ。

Rasel Ahmed

SYNOPSIS

Who Killed Taniya is a story of broken relationships and trauma. Five drag performers gather in a makeup room to prepare for an underground community event in Dhaka, 2050. Drag is a temporary escape from their class, ethnic, and immigration crisis. Jewelleries and makeup essentials provide refuge from insecurities and heartbreaks. For a brief period of time, the makeup room becomes a sanctuary outside normative gender practice. But it's an illusion of utopia that slowly dissolves into anxiety and chaos. A melodramatic unpacking of past relationships brings their fear, jealousy, and greed to the surface. A desire for violence emerges with the exchange of silent gaze and hostile gestures. The metaphorical space of pleasure and freedom transforms into a murder fantasy.

あらすじ

《Who Killed Taniya》は、壊れた人間関係とトラウマの物語である。2050年のダッカで行われるアンダーグラウンド・コミュニティのイベントのために、5人のドラァグパフォーマーがメイクルームに集まってくる。ドラァグは階級、民族、移民危機からの一時的な逃避。ジュエリーやメイクアップ用品は、不安や心の傷からの避難場所となる。ほんの短い時間、化粧室は規範的なジェンダーの慣習から外れた聖域となる。しかし、それはユートピアの幻想であり、徐々に不安と混沌に溶けていく。過去の人間関係をメロドラマ風にひもとくと、彼らの恐怖、嫉妬、欲望が表面化する。無言の視線と敵対的な身振りの応酬で、暴力への欲望が浮かび上がる。快楽と自由のメタファー空間は、殺人ファンタジーへと変貌していく。

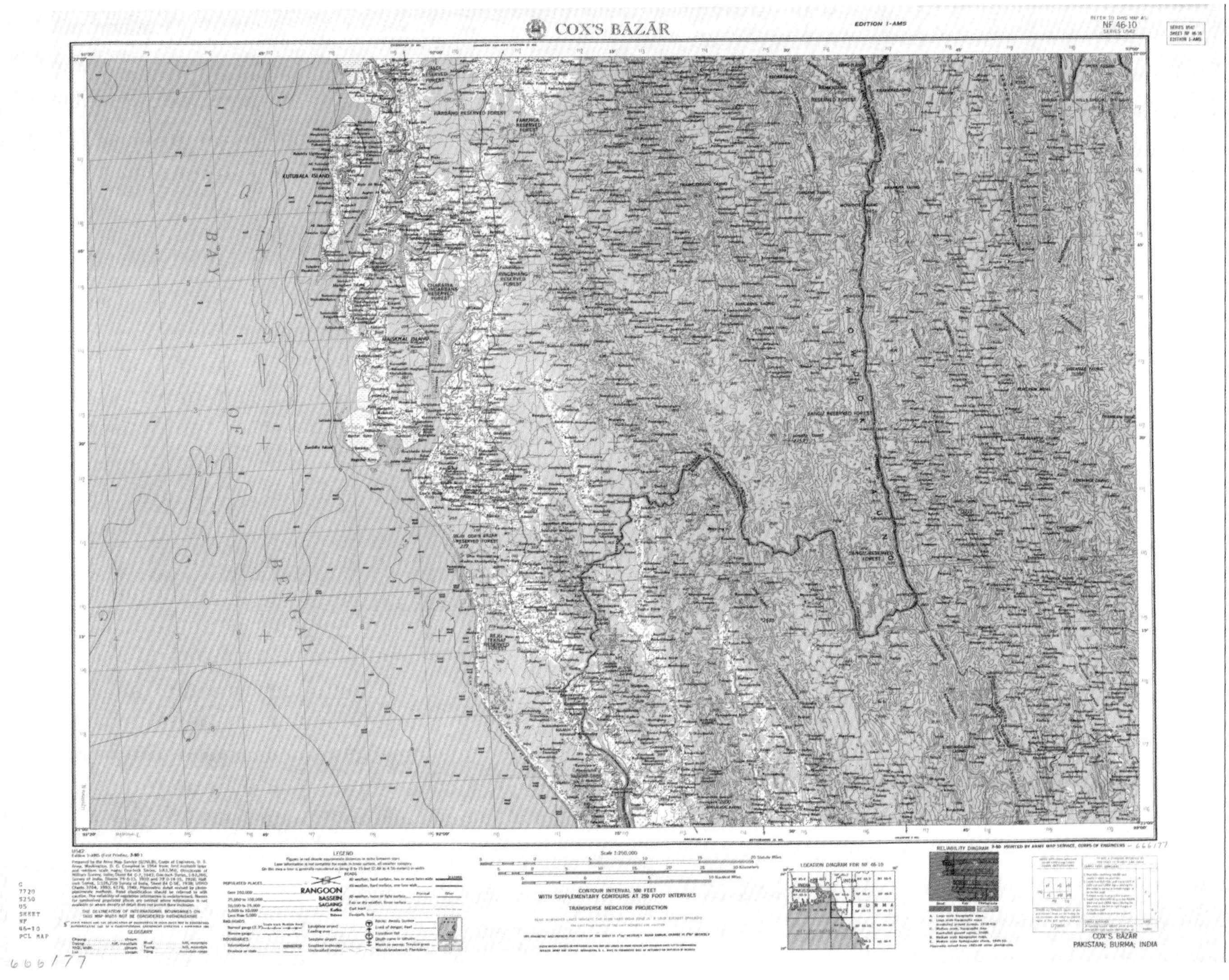

Research Map
1955 Map of Cox's Bazar
Credit: US Army Map Services
調査地図（1955年のバングラデシュ、コックスバザールの地図）

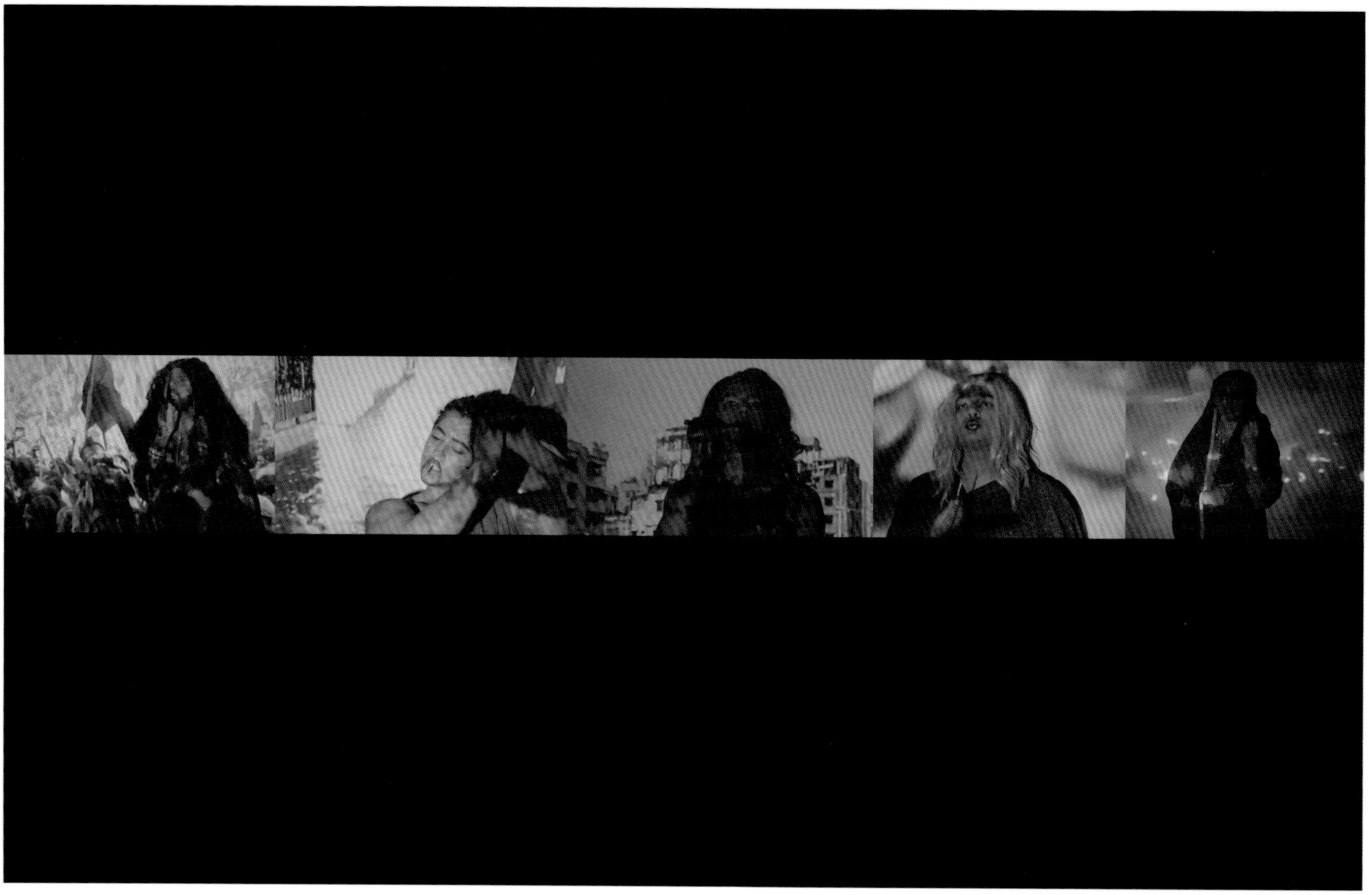

Still from the 1st episode (two channel) of *Who Killed Taniya*
Artists: Kamani, Pallavi, Tausif, Shabab, Sandeep
Credit: Rasel Ahmed
《Who Killed Taniya》 エピソード1より

Art Labor in collaboration with Jrai artists

アート・レーバーとジャライ族のアーティストたち

Art Labor Collective including Thao Nguyen Phan, Truong Cong Tung & Arlette Quynh-Anh Tran is an artist collective based in Ho Chi Minh City, who work in between visual arts, social and life sciences in various public contexts and locales.

They do not produce single artwork but develop many-year-long journey during which one inspiration is a seed to cultivate. The seed grows—the inspiration expands and bears into rhizome of projects and artworks.

Their previous journeys include *Unconditional Belief* (2012–2015), *Jrai Dew* (2016–ongoing) and *JUA* (2019–ongoing).

They have been exhibited widely in Vietnam and international, notably such as Paradise Kortrijk, Triennial for contemporary art (2021); Carnegie International 57th, Pittsburgh; Bangkok Art Biennale; *A beast, a god, and a line* at Dhaka Art Summit, Para Site, Hong Kong and Museum of Modern Art in Warsaw (2018); *Cosmopolis #1: Collective Intelligence* at Centre Pompidou, Paris; Asian Art Biennial, Taichung; *Salt of the Jungle* at KF Gallery, Seoul (2017); *Jrai Dew Sculpture Garden* in Central Highlands of Vietnam (2016–2017); *The Adventure of Color Wheel* at Pediatrics Department, Eye Hospital HCMC, Ho Chi Minh City (2015); *Unconditional Belief* at Sàn Art, Ho Chi Minh City (2014).

ベトナム、ホーチミン市を拠点とするタオ・グエン・ファン、チュオン・コン・トゥン、アルレット・クイン=アイン・チャンの3人によるアーティストグループ。

様々な公共的文脈や場所にアプローチしながら、ヴィジュアルアーツや社会／自然科学の中間地点で活動する。

単体としての作品ではなく、数年をかけてひとつのインスピレーションを種にアイディアを育んでいくスタイルを展開。種が成長することで、発想が広がり、やがてプロジェクトや作品という「根」を張っていく。これまで手がけたプロジェクトに《Unconditional Belief》（2012–2015年）、《Jrai Dew》（2016年–）、《JUA》（2019年–）などがある。

主な展示に、2021年コルトレイク・トリエンナーレ、2018年第57回カーネギー・インターナショナル（ピッツバーグ）、2018年バンコク・アート・ビエンナーレ、2018年「A beast, a god, and a line」ダッカ・アート・サミット／パラ・サイト（香港）／ワルシャワ近代美術館、2017年「Cosmopolis #1: Collective Intelligence」ポンピドゥー・センター（パリ）、2017年アジア・アート・ビエンナーレ（台中）、2017年「Salt of the Jungle」KF Gallery（ソウル）、2016–2017年「Jrai Dew Sculpture Garden」（ベトナム・中部高原地帯）、2015年「The Adventure of Color Wheel」ホーチミン市眼科病院小児科、2014年「Unconditional Belief」Sàn Art（ホーチミン）など、ベトナム・海外で多数紹介されている。

JUA - SOUND IN THE SOUNDSCAPE

In collaboration with Rcham Jeh, Kpuih Gloh, Rahlan Loh, Puih Han,
Siu Lon, Rolan Aleo and Siu Kin
Interactive installation

Art Labor would like to present the project *JUA - SOUND IN THE SOUNDSCAPE*, through its context, inspiration, and collaborative agents.

JUA is a beautiful word in Jrai language—the minority ethnic living among Viet people in Central Highlands. It indicates a dynamic state varying in between water and air, which can be a stream of water, rainy cloud, a breeze, a breath or wind. It represents climate and nature. Minutely it can describe how the leaves breath. Allegorically it can imply the vaporization of things: land, forest, human, capital, labor, etc.

JUA is a continuation of *Jrai Dew* in the Central Highlands of Vietnam, a journey that we form the connection with our Jrai neighbors through the traditional wood carving collaboration. From the Jrai cosmology of the interminable movement between water and air, JUA extends it allegorically to the constant transformation of the ecology and society of the Central Highlands. We view the soundscape upon the entire territory as a platform for human and non-human agents to explore, challenge each other and create hybrid resonance.

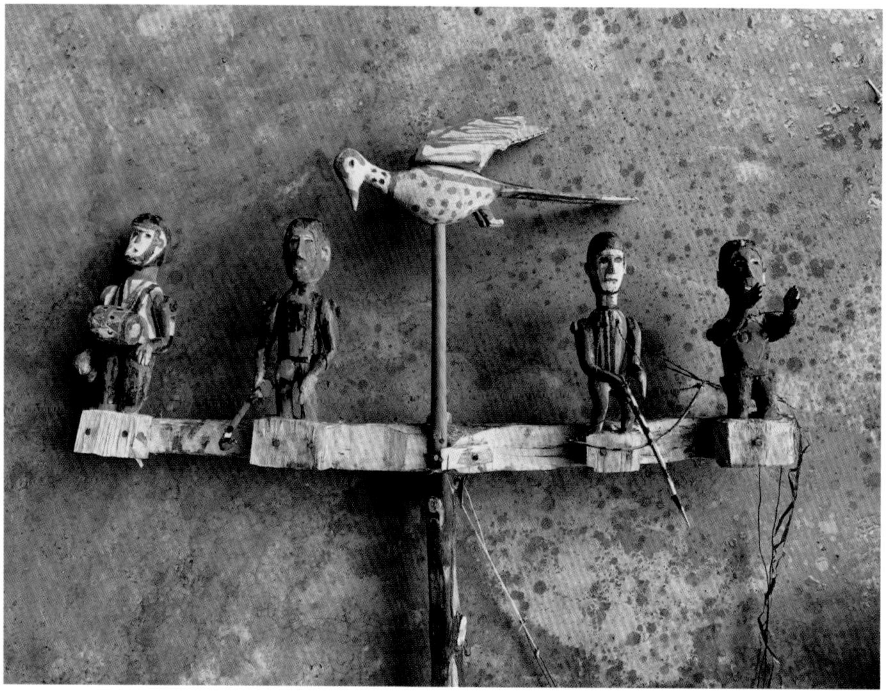

Kinetic sculpture created by Jrai artist Kpuih Gloh
August 2022
ジャライ族のアーティストによる動く彫刻（2022年8月）

アート・レーバーは、プロジェクト《JUA - SOUND IN THE SOUNDSCAPE》を、その背景、インスピレーション、協力者を通して展示したい。

「JUA」は、中部高原に住むベト族の少数民族であるジャライ族の美しい言葉。水と空気の間で変化する動的な状態を指し、水の流れ、雨雲、そよ風、息づかい、風なども含む。また、気候や自然を表すこともある。細かく言えば、葉の息づかいを表現することができる。比喩的には、土地、森林、人間、資本、労働など、ものごとの蒸発を意味することがある。

《JUA》は、ベトナム中部高原の作品《Jrai Dew》に続くもので、伝統的な木彫りのコラボレーションを通じて、ジャライ族の隣人とのつながりを形成する旅である。そして、水と空気の絶え間ない動きというジャライ族の宇宙観から、中部高原の生態系と社会の絶え間ない変容を寓意的に拡張している。人間と非人間的な主体が探求し、互いに挑戦し、ハイブリッドな共鳴を生み出すためのプラットフォームとして、全領域におけるサウンドスケープをとらえているのである。

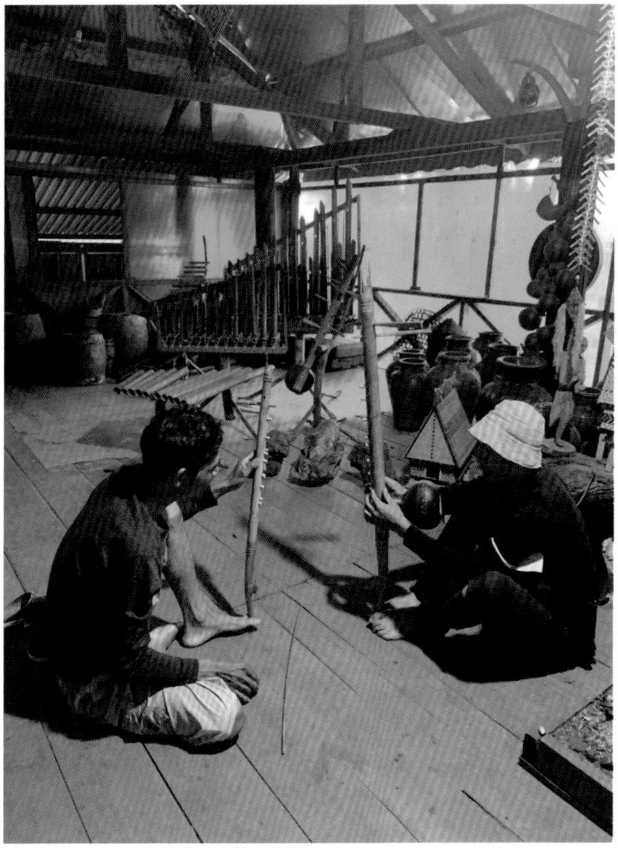

Research photograph at the home of the Jrai musician Rcham Tih
Photo: Thao Nguyen Phan, July 2022
ジャライ族のミュージシャンの自宅での調査

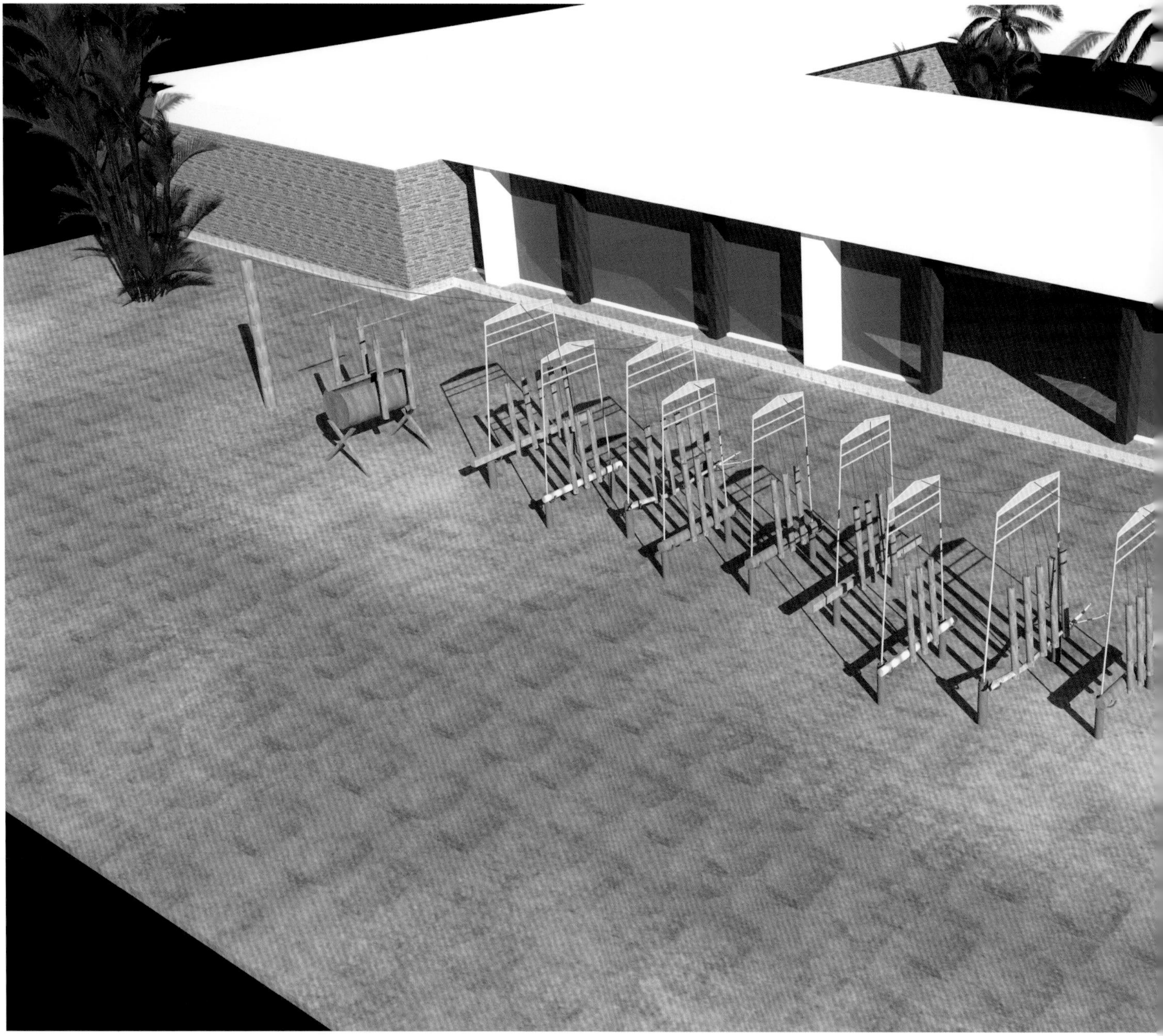

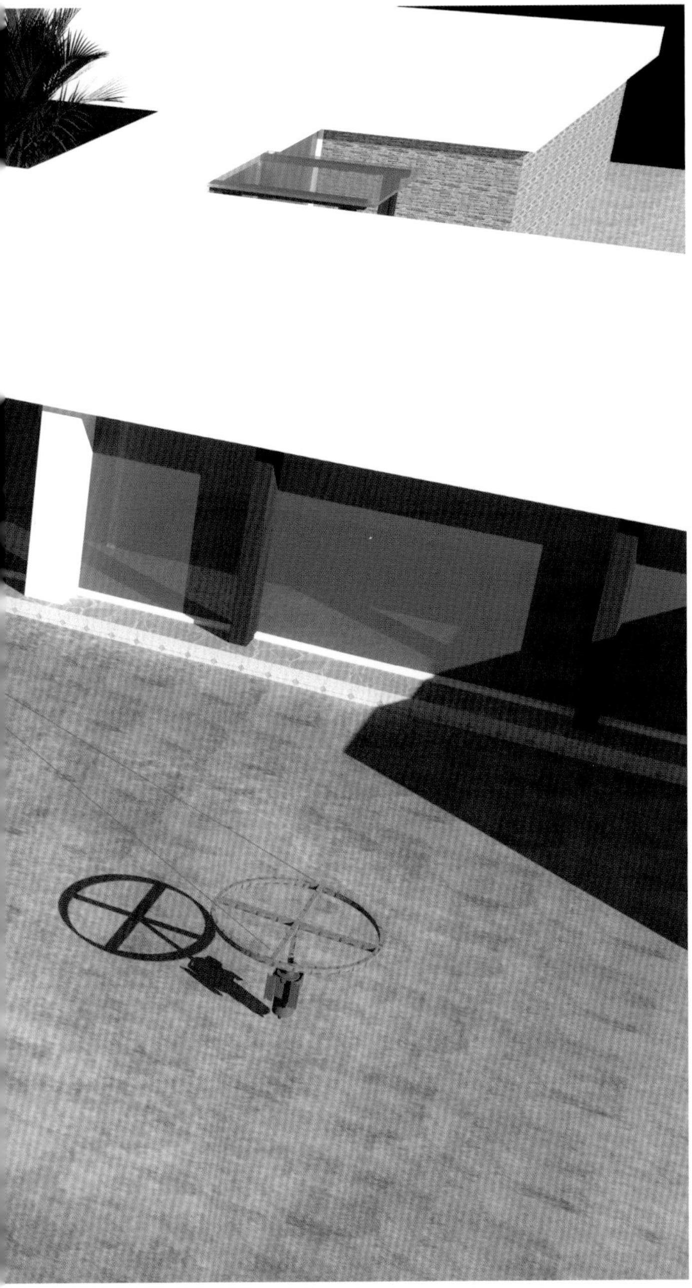

Sketch for *JUA-SOUND IN THE SOUND SCAPE* in the courtyard of the Hayashibara museum
2022–ongoing
Bamboo, steel, found object installation and sound
林原美術館での《JUA-SOUND IN THE SOUND SCAPE》のためのスケッチ

This soundscape is a combination of both traditional materials: bamboo, stone... and new materials such corrugated iron or plastic. These are usually installed in the rice paddies to chase away wide birds that come for the young crops. The installation of a musical instrument by bamboo, played not by human but by the air, the water and the wind.

このサウンドスケープは、竹や石など、天然の素材とトタンの波板やプラスチックなど、近年の素材が組み合わされたもの。水田に設置し、農作物の苗を狙う野鳥を追い払う。竹でつくられた楽器のインスタレーション。人ではなく、空気、水、風により奏でられる。

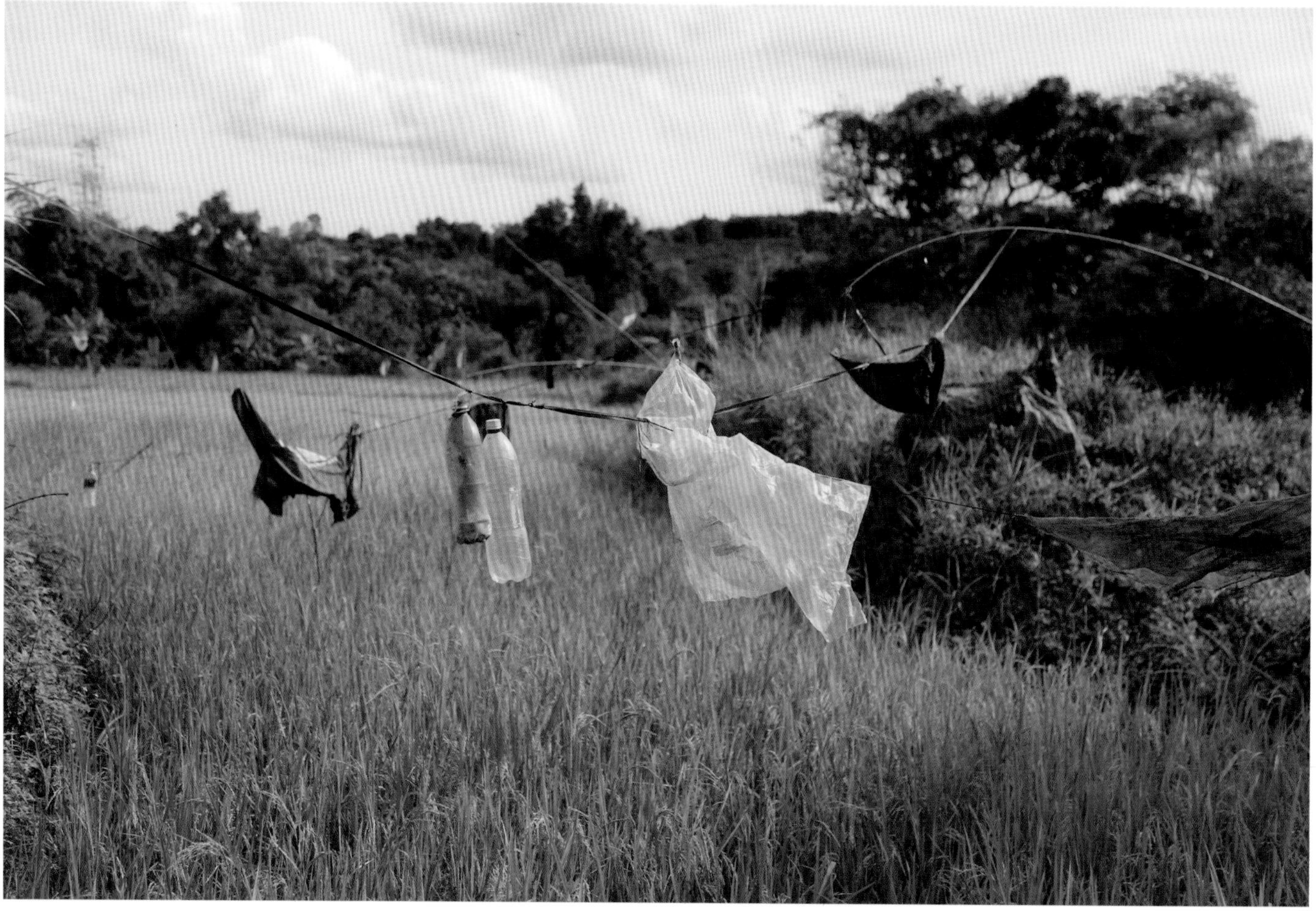

Research photograph of the sonic system created by the Jrai coummunity in the Central Highland, Vietnam
2021
Photo: Truong Cong Tung
ベトナム中部高原、ジャライ族がつくる音の装置の調査

Wang Bing

王兵（ワン・ビン）

Born in 1967, in Xi'an, Shaanxi Province, China.
Lives and works in France and China.
In 1992, Wang Bing graduated in photography from the Luxum Arts University in Shenyang. For his photography work, he watched at length workers of the Tie Xi facility. In 1995, he studied at the Beijing Film Academy, then worked for some time on television before starting a career as an independent film director in 1998. *West of the Tracks* is Wang Bing's first documentary, filmed in 2002, for which he received numerous awards and grants.
In his films, Wang Bing depicts, with rare beauty and uncompromising gravity, people who are often excluded from the recent economic transformation in China. Wang Bing gives his films a beautiful and tragic cinematic intensity in which he seeks to transform the temporality of his characters' lives into allegory. He puts forward a deep reflection on history, paradoxes and sufferings caused by the inexorable progress of modern China, pushing to the extreme a cinema of observation and reality.
In 2009, Galerie Chantal Crousel presented his first solo exhibition in Paris, with the projection of the two documentary films: *Fengming* and *Man with No Name*. Since then, Wang Bing has produced many documentaries such as *Three Sisters* (2012), *TA'ANG* (2016), *Coal Money* (2009), as well as *Mrs Fang* (2017), *15 Hours* (2017), both exhibited during documenta14 in Athens and Kassel in 2017 and *Beauty Lives in Freedom* (2018).
Wang Bing was a visiting artist-professor at Le Fresnoy – contemporary arts national studio, France between 2018 and 2019.
In 2017, he was awarded the Golden Leopard, highest award of the Concorso Internazionale of the Locarno Festival for the film *Mrs Fang*. That same year, he was also the recipient of the EYE Art & Film Prize in Amsterdam, honouring his entire filmography.
Wang Bing notable solo exhibitions include LE BAL, Paris (2021); Kunsthalle Zürich (2018–2019); CCA Wattis Institute, San Francisco (2016); Musée National d'Art Moderne, Centre Pompidou, Paris (2014). In 2018, the Museo Reina Sofía and Filmoteca Española, Madrid have shown his work for a major survey exhibition.
Group exhibitions include the Marta Herford gGmbH (2021); Textile Museum, Washington D.C. (2020); Bowdoin College Museum of Art (2019); Bi-City Biennale of Urbanism\Architecture, Shenzhen (2017); Brunswick Centre Culturel de Strombeek, Brussels (2017); Jeonju International Film Festival (2015); Shanghai Biennale (2014); Milano Filmmaker Film Festival (2010).
His works have joined the collections of the Museo Nacional Centro de Arte Reina Sofía, Madrid; M+, Hong Kong; Musée National d'Art Moderne, Centre Pompidou; the National Museum of Contemporary Art Athens (EMST); CNAP, Paris.

1967年、中国陝西省西安生まれ。現在はフランスと中国を拠点に活動。

1992年、瀋陽の魯迅芸術大学写真専攻を卒業。制作のため、鉄西工場で働く労働者を長期にわたって観察し撮影を続けた。1995年、北京電影学院に入学。テレビ局勤務の経験を経て、1998年から映画監督としての活動を開始。2002年に撮影した初のドキュメンタリー映画『鉄西区』は数々の賞や助成金を獲得した。

王兵の映像作品は、近年の中国の経済変革から排除された人々を無二の美しさと妥協のない厳粛さをもって鮮やかに描き出す。登場人物の人生の一瞬、そのはかなさを寓話に転換しようと試みることで、美しくまた悲哀に満ちた、心を揺さぶる映画をつくり出している。歴史の深い考察と、止めようのない現代中国の発展がもたらす矛盾と苦悩を打ち出し、観察とリアリティを極限まで追及し、映像に昇華している。

2009年、パリのGalerie Chantal Crouselで初の個展を開催し、ドキュメンタリー映画『鳳鳴（フォンミン）　中国の記憶』と『名前のない男』を上映。以来、『三姉妹～雲南の子』(2012年)、『タアン』(2016年)、『石炭、金』(2009年) をはじめ、2017年にアテネとカッセルのドクメンタ14で上映された『ファンさん』(2017年)、『15時間』(2017年)、『Beauty Lives in Freedom』(2018年) など多くのドキュメンタリーを制作している。

2018年から2019年にかけて、フランスのル・フレノア国立現代芸術スタジオの客員アーティスト／教授を務める。

2017年、『ファンさん』でロカルノ国際映画祭最高賞の金豹賞を受賞。同年、これまでの作品実績が評され、EYE Art & Film 賞を受賞（アムステルダム）。

主な個展に、2021年 LE BAL (パリ)、2018–2019年クンストハレ・チューリッヒ、2016年CCA Wattis Institute（サンフランシスコ）、2014年ポンピドゥー・センター（パリ）など。2018年には、マドリードのソフィア王妃芸術センターとFilmoteca Españolaで大規模な回顧展が開催された。

グループ展に、2021年Marta Herford（ドイツ・ヘルフォルト）、2020年織物博物館（ワシントンD.C.)、2019年ボードイン大学美術館（アメリカ・メイン）、2017年Bi-City Biennale of Urbanism/Architecture(深圳)、2017年Brunswick Centre Culturel de Strombeek（ブリュッセル)、2015年全州国際映画祭、2014年上海ビエンナーレ、2010年Filmmaker Festival（ミラノ）などがある。

これまでに、ソフィア王妃芸術センター、M+（香港)、ポンピドゥー・センター、アテネ国立現代美術館EMST、国立造形センターCNAP(パリ）に作品が収蔵されている。

A
LOT
OF
PEOPLE

THE
SUN
IS GONE
BUT
WE HAVE
THE LIGHT

Man with No Name

2009
Digital video, 96 min., edition of 6

"*Man with No Name* is a metaphor based on a real person, whom Wang Bing has been filming since 2007. The man lives in a cave, isolated from Chinese society, and deals with his survival with dignity and determination. He never speaks, refuses his country's system and assumes his marginalization. Living away from the worlds of matter and spirit, he constructs his own conditions of survival."
– Quote from https://www.crousel.com/en/exhibition/wang-bing-2009

「『名前のない男』は、王兵が2007年から撮影してきた実在の人物を題材にしたひとつのメタファーである。この男は中国の社会から隔絶された洞穴で暮らし、生き続けるということに尊厳と決意をもって取り組んでいる。言葉を発することは決してなく、自国の制度を拒絶し、疎外を受け入れている。物質的な世界からも精神的な世界からもひとり離れて暮らす彼は、自らの生存条件を自らのやり方で決めているのだ」
—引用元：https://www.crousel.com/en/exhibition/wang-bing-2009

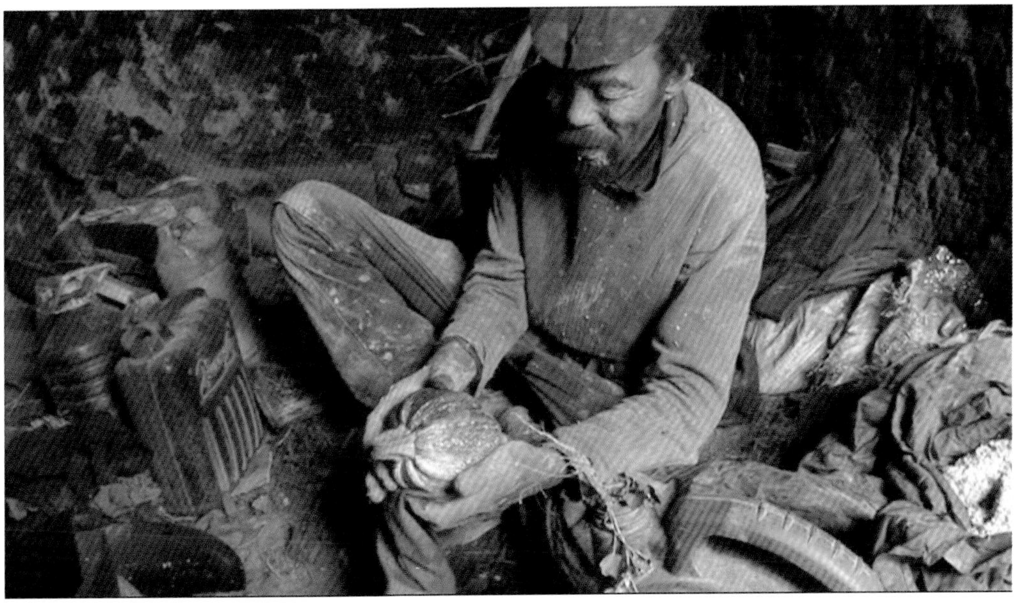

Crude Oil

2009

Digital video, 14 h. (in two parts, each part: 7 h.), edition of 6

The Story:

The 21st century means global competition for the black gold and power of oil. The West in China used to be the poorest region in the country. It consists mostly of the Gobi Desert and hilly country. Today this region relies on oil exports, coal and metal ores for its income. Mined areas are constantly expanding and at an accelerating speed. The Gobi Desert, hilly areas and adverse natural climate prove no match to the power of man and machine.

The film was shot at a high altitude in the Gobi Desert in northwestern China. It shows the heavy industry of crude oil being extracted and the work of groups of laborers who do tiring and dirty work and make long days. Wang Bing follows the workers in their canteens and dormitories, while they play cards and he also listens to them talking about women and money.

ストーリー

21世紀は、石油というブラックゴールドとその力を巡るグローバルな競争の時代だ。中国の西部は、かつて国内で最も貧しい地域だった。そのほとんどが、ゴビ砂漠と丘陵地帯からなっている。現在のこの地域は、石油の輸出、そして石炭と金属鉱石を収入源とする。採掘地域はどんどん拡大し、その開発スピードは加速度的に増している。ゴビ砂漠、丘陵地帯、そして厳しい自然の気候をもってしても、人間や機械の力にはおよばないことがわかる。

この映像は、中国北西部に位置するゴビ砂漠の高地で撮影された。原油の採掘という重工業と、疲労困憊たる汚れ作業をしながら長い日々を過ごす労働者集団の仕事ぶりを映し出す。食堂や寮で過ごす労働者たちの姿を追う王兵は、彼らがカードゲームに興じる姿を写しながら、女や金について語る彼らの話にも耳を傾けている。

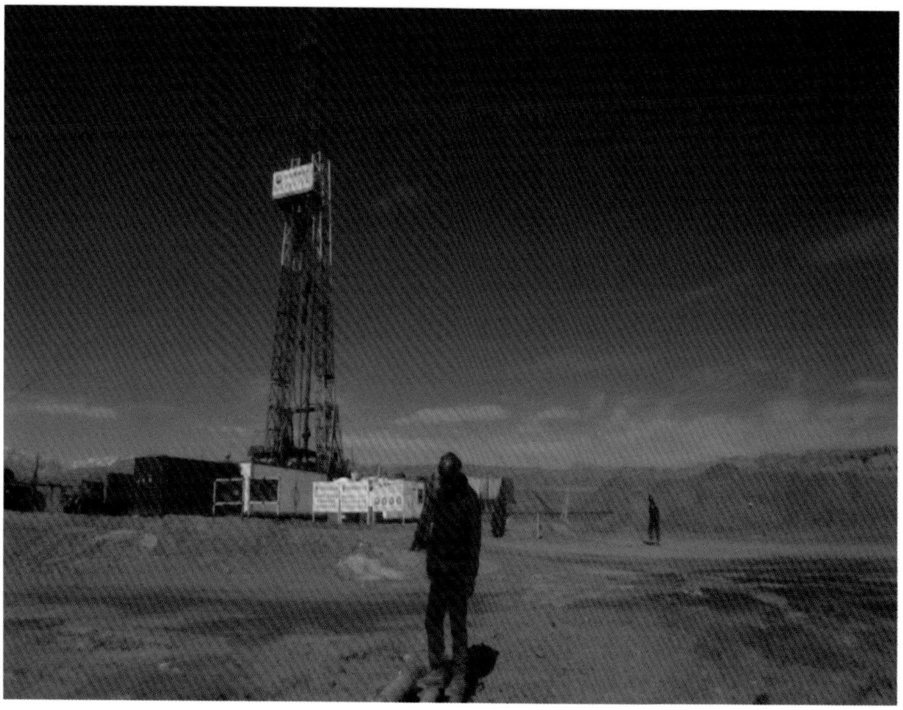

15 Hours

2017
Digital video, 15 h. 48 min. (in two parts, each part: 7 h. 54 min.), edition of 6

The Story:
The film is shot in a centralized garment processing facility consisting of 18 000 small production units employing a total of around 300 000 migrant workers. They start work every day at 8 am, break from 11 to 12 for a lunch of beef and rice, then work from 12 to 5, and again after dinner through to 11 pm. They usually also work on Saturdays and Sundays. Pay is on a piecework basis. Every worker, like every machine, works at top speed. We plan to shoot the entire 15-hr film on a digital HD camera as a single long take, starting at 8 am on the first day and following one group of workers until they clock off at night, faithfully recording their life and work through this one day.

ストーリー
この映像の撮影は、総計約30万人の移民労働者が1万8000の小さな作業グループに分かれて働く集約型の裁縫工場で行われた。労働者は毎朝8時に仕事を始め、11時から12時の間に牛肉と米飯の昼食をとり、12時から午後5時まで仕事をし、さらに夕食後、夜の11時まで仕事を続ける。土曜、日曜も働くのが普通で、給料は出来高制だ。すべての作業員は、あらゆる機械と同じように、全速力で作業に勤しんでいる。今回は、デジタルHDカメラ1台を用い、全15時間のフィルムを長回しのワンテイクで撮影する。初日の朝8時から、あるひとつの労働者グループを夜の退勤時間まで追い続け、労働者たちの一日の生活と仕事を忠実に記録するという計画である。

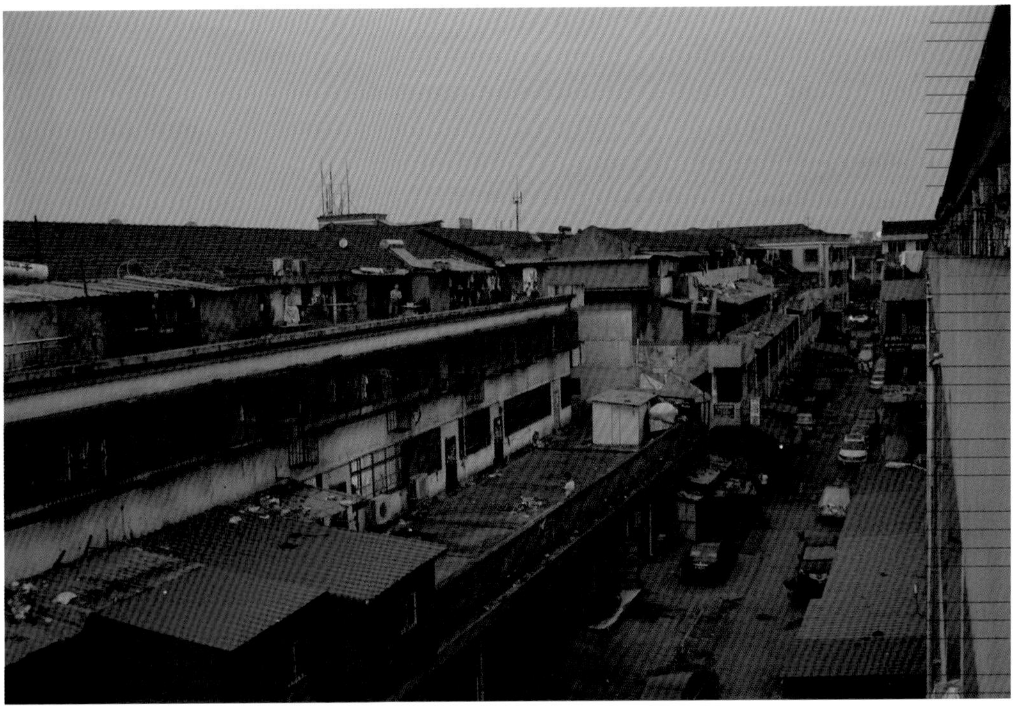

Mrs. Fang

2017

Digital video, 102 min., edition of 6

"Fang Xiuying was a farm worker born in Huzhou, Zhejiang in 1948. For the last eight years of her life she suffered from Alzheimer's. By 2015 the symptoms were quite advanced. She received an ineffective treatment in a convalescent home and few months later she returned home to die. Wang Bing filmed some scenes of her everyday life in 2015, then returned in June 2016 and filmed the last ten days of her life."
– Quote from https://www.crousel.com/en/exhibition/wang-bing-2018

Wang Bing said:
In 2015 I met Fang Xiuying, the mother of a friend of mine. At that time she was still autonomous, but due to Alzheimer's, she could often not recognise people and sometimes lost her way. Her family members were living and working in another town and could only come to visit occasionally, so her children entrusted her to the care of a neighbour who would come to help her wash, dress and cook and generally look after her. For part of each day, she was confined to her house and not allowed to wander freely outside.

The pure, innocent look in Xiuying's eyes when she met someone new appealed to me immediately, and a plan to film her began to take shape in my mind. In the area where she lived, economic conditions were changing fast. The young people had gone to work in the towns, and her once-bustling village had become a desolate and lonely dwelling for the old. Some of the surrounding fields had been requisitioned for factories; a few remaining plots were still farmed by the old folk, or left untended.

Memory loss seems to be a general phenomenon amongst our contemporaries. People no longer feel nostalgia about their past life, but think only about making money to fulfil their material desires. Most people do nothing but rush around at random looking for business opportunities. Pain, disease and death are things to be swept out of sight as quickly as possible. The days when people cared about each other's lives seem gone for ever.

Fang Xiuying lies in bed and watches her visiting friends and relations come and go. But they all seem to be in a hurry, as if they've just dropped to see if she's still alive. No-one tries to understand her, or even comfort her. Most people's feelings towards the dying are very confused; they seem to be here just to accomplish a ritual that is imposed on them, unavoidable; a formality that must be completed.

By following Xiuying's facial expressions at close range, using nuances of imagery to capture her mood and feelings up to the very moment of her death, and simultaneously filming the steady flow of people coming to her bedside, we hope to compose a work that will reflect changing contemporary attitudes towards life and death.

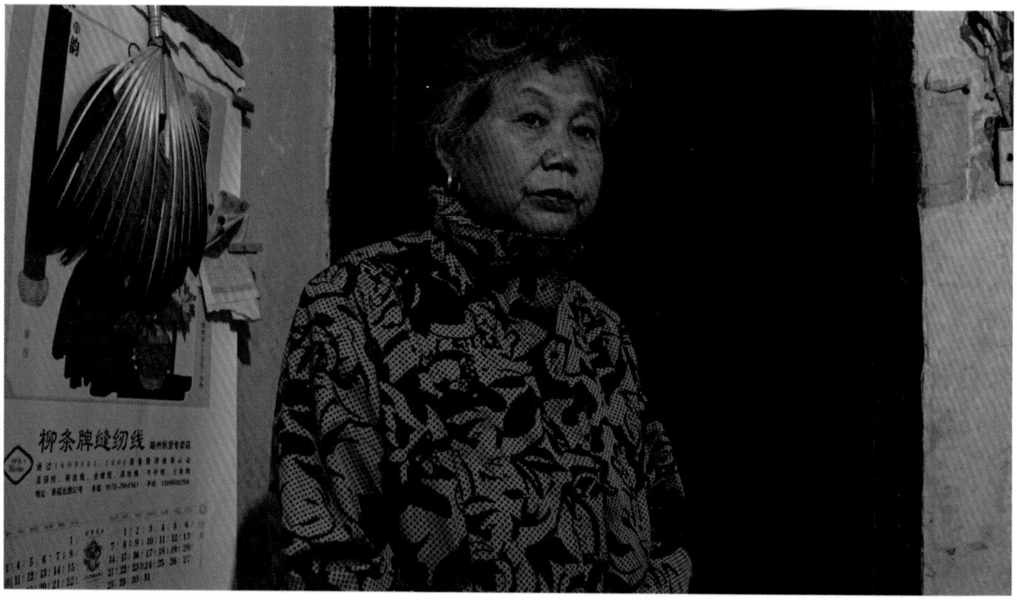

「方繡英（ファン・シウイン）は、1948年に浙江省の湖州で生まれた農民だった。人生の最後の8年間、彼女はアルツハイマー型の認知症を患った。2015年には、症状はかなり進行していた。療養施設で治療を受けたが効果はなく、数ヵ月後に自宅に戻って亡くなった。王兵は2015年に彼女の日常生活のシーンをいくらか撮り、それから2016年6月に再び訪れ、その人生の最期の10日間を撮影した」
—引用元：https://www.crousel.com/en/exhibition/wang-bing-2018

王兵のコメント
2015年、私は友人の母親である方繡英と出会った。その頃、彼女はまだひとりで暮らしていたが、アルツハイマー病のため、相手が誰だかわからなくなることが多く、道に迷うこともあった。家族は別の町に住み、仕事をしていたため、たまにしか会いに来ることができなかった。そこで子どもたちは母親のことを隣人に託し、洗濯や着替え、料理の介助も含めて全般的な世話を任せた。そのため、彼女は毎日のかなりの時間、家のなかに閉じこもることとなり、外を自由に歩き回ることもできなかった。

初対面の人と出会ったときの繡英の純粋無垢な眼差しにたちまち惹かれ、私のなかで彼女を撮影する計画が形をとり始めた。彼女の住む地域では、経済状況が急速に変化していた。若者たちは仕事のために街へと出て行き、かつては賑やかだった村は、老人たちが暮らす寂れた孤独な村と化していた。村の周りの田畑は工場用地として徴用され、わずかに残った田畑は老人たちが耕すか、あるいはそのまま放置されていた。

記憶喪失は、私たち現代人の間では一般的な現象のように思われる。人々はもはや昔の自分の生活を懐かしく思うこともなく、物欲を満たすための金儲けばかりを考えている。多くの人々は、ビジネスチャンスを求めて、ただ漫然と走り回るだけだ。痛み、病気、死は、できるだけ早く視界から消し去るべきものになった。人々が互いの生活を気にかけていた時代は、永遠に終わったようだ。

繡英はベッドに横たわり、訪ねて来る友人たちや親戚が行き交うのを眺めている。だが、こうした人々は皆、一様に急いて見える。まるで、彼女がまだ生きているかどうかを確かめるためだけに立ち寄ったかのようだ。誰も彼女を理解しようとしないし、慰めようとすらしない。死期が迫った人に対する多くの人々の気持ちは、ひどく混乱している。この人たちは、自らに課せられた避けられない儀式を終わらせるためだけに、そこにいるようだ。必要な手続きは完了させなくてはならないのだ。

繡英の表情をクローズアップで追いかけ、死の瞬間に至るまで、彼女の気持ちや感情をとらえるように映像のニュアンスを用いること。と同時に、彼女の枕元を次々と訪れる人々の流れを撮影すること。これによって、生と死に対する現代の意識の変化を映し出す作品にしたいと望んでいる。

Fengming, A Chinese Memoir

2007
Digital video, 226 min., edition of 6

The Story:
Winter in China. A town in the snow. Night is falling. Wrapped in her black coat, an old woman walks slowly through a housing complex to her simple apartment. Inside, Fengming settles into her armchair and remembers. Her memories take us back to 1949 — to the beginning of a journey that will take us through 30 years of her life and of the New China...

Wang Bing Said:
I first met He Fengming in the beginning of this century. I learned how she and her family, and many others with destinies similar to her own, lived through the successive political movements that swept China over those long years. Those memories cannot fade, but live on in her today, like a spectre constantly returning to take us back to that time of extremism and terror, filling me with a growing anxiety.

ストーリー
冬の中国。雪の残る町。夜の帷が下りてくる。黒いコートに身を包んだひとりの老女が、集合住宅が並ぶ地区をゆっくりと通り抜け、質素なアパートへと帰っていく。その部屋で、鳳鳴（フォンミン）はソファーに座り、思い出を語る。記憶は1949年にまで遡る。彼女の人生と「新しい中国」の30年間を巡る私たちの旅の始まりである……。

王兵のコメント
私が和鳳鳴（ホー・フォンミン）と初めて会ったのは、今世紀初頭のことだった。彼女とその家族、そして彼女と同じ運命をたどった多くの人々が、その長い年月の間に中国を席巻した一連の政治的な動乱のなかをどのように生きてきたかを知った。その記憶は褪せることなく、今も彼女のなかに生き続ける。まるであの過激主義と恐怖に満ちた時代へと、私たちを連れ戻そうと絶えずつきまとう亡霊のように、その記憶はますます高まる不安の気持ちで私をいっぱいにする。

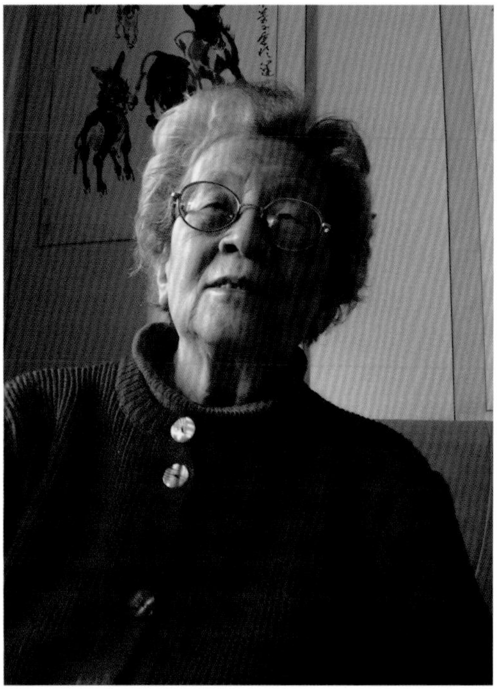

Father and Sons

2014
Digital video, 87 min., edition of 6

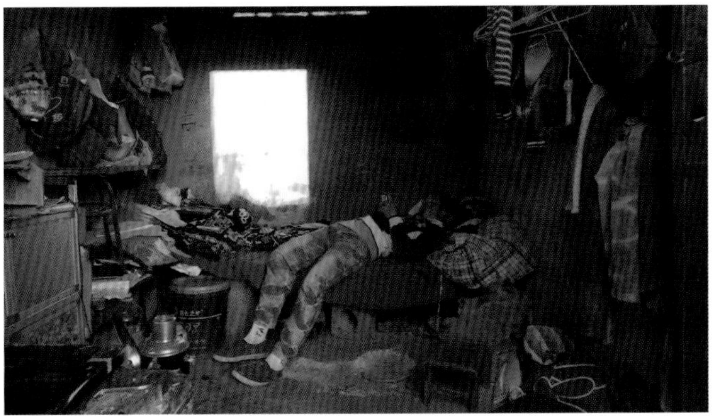

"For several days, Wang Bing filmed and photographed the wretched daily life of Mr. Cai, who left the countryside to work as a stonemason in a factory in the city of Fuming, in the province of Yunnan. His two sons have joined him and the three of them live in a four square-meter room, containing only one bed and an oven. At night, the father goes to work and leaves the bed to his sons."
– Quote from http://www.galerieparisbeijing.com/exhibition/wang-bing-father-and-sons/

「田舎を出て、雲南省の地方にある富民県の町の工場で石工として働く蔡氏の惨めな日常生活を、王兵は数日かけて映像と写真で撮影した。息子2人も加わったこの家族3人は、ベッドもオーヴンもひとつしかない4メートル四方の狭い部屋で暮らしている。夜、父親が仕事に出かけると、息子たちがベッドを使うのだ」
—引用元：http://www.galerieparisbeijing.com/exhibition/wang-bing-father-and-sons/

Scenes, Chapter One

2020– (work in progress)
Digital video, 54 min., edition of 6

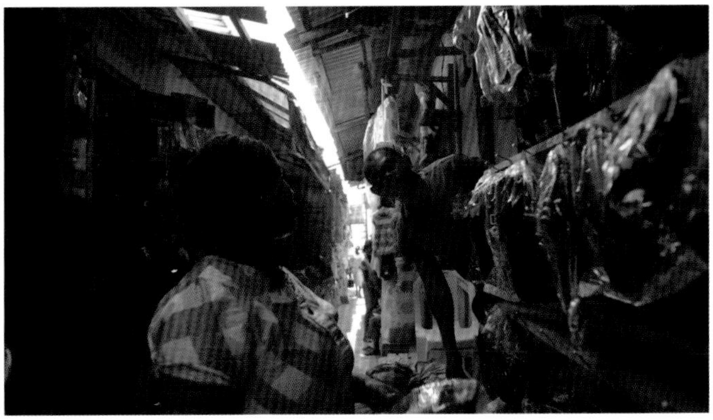

"*Scenes* is the first chapter of Wang Bing's filmic exploration into the ongoing and nuanced exchanges between China and Africa. It began with Wang's encounter with Kingsley, he moved between his hometown Lagos and Guangzhou in search of business opportunities. Intrigued by Kingsley's experiences, Wang decided to go and film in Lagos even though he was unsure if his outsider status would become an intrusive force. Yet, once there, the scenery of waves of green-helmeted motorbike couriers providing shuttle and delivery service though the busy streets and alleys of the city offered Wang a sense of familiarity, which allowed him to capture the daily lives of Kingsley and others in this otherwise foreign land."
– By Yung Ma, from http://magician.space/news/wang-bing-zui-xin-ying-xiang-zuo-pin-can-jia-peng-pi-du-yi-shu-zhong-xin-zhong-guo-fei-zhou-zhan-lan/

「『Scenes』は、中国とアフリカの間で進行中のニュアンスをはらんだ交流について、王兵が追いかけている一連の映像の第一章だ。この作品は、ビジネスチャンスを探して故郷のナイジェリアの都市ラゴスと中国の広州の間を行き来していたキングズレーという人物との出会いによって始まった。キングズレーの経験に興味をそそられた王兵は、部外者としての自分の立場は歓迎されないかもしれないと疑いながらも、ラゴスに行って撮影をしようと決めた。だが、ひとたび現地に到着してみると、緑色のヘルメットをかぶってバイクに乗った大勢のメッセンジャーたちが、混み合った繁華街や路地を行き交いながら配達サービスに勤しむ情景は、王兵にとって親近感の感じられるものだった。そのおかげで、さもなければまったくの異国の地だったその街で、キングズレーをはじめとした人々の日々の生活をとらえることができたのだった」
—馬容元によるテキスト　http://magician.space/news/wang-bing-zui-xin-ying-xiang-zuo-pin-can-jia-peng-pi-du-yi-shu-zhong-xin-zhong-guo-fei-zhou-zhan-lan/

Traces

2014
35 mm film transfered later into a digital video, 29 min., edition of 6

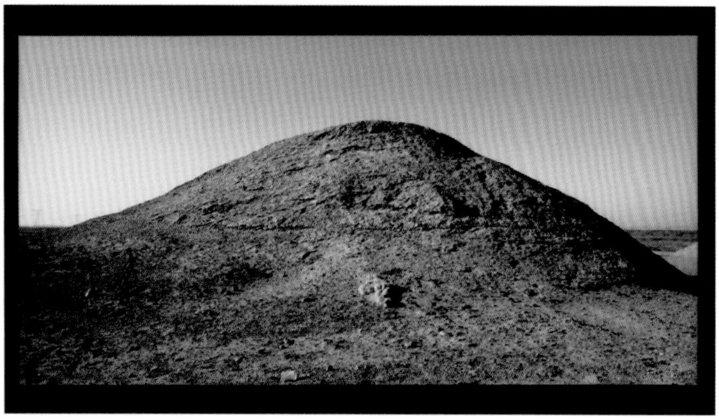

The Story:
In 2005, while doing preparatory on his film, *The Ditch*, Wang Bing travelled to the Gobi Desert, to the exact same places where thousands of people lived and died in the "re-education-through-labour" camps set up by the communist regime in the late fifties. He shot the site with a 35 mm camera for about one hour, with scenes of desert and abandoned bones — a landscape doomed to disappear. Now digitized and revised, these images provide excellent evidence of the events of those times, which have been virtually buried until now.

ストーリー
2005年、映画『無言歌』の準備中にゴビ砂漠を訪れた王兵は、1950年代後半に共産主義政権によって設置された収容所「労働教養所」の跡地に立った。何千人もの人々が暮らし、死んでいった、まさにその場所である。彼は35ミリフィルムのカメラを回し、この場所を約1時間撮影した。砂漠と打ち捨てられた骨が映った、消えゆく運命にある風景だった。今ではデジタル化され、改訂がなされているその映像は、今日ではほとんど埋められてしまったこの場所でかつて起こった出来事を伝える貴重な証拠となっている。

Beauty Lives in Freedom

2018
Digital video, 4 h. 25 min., edition of 6

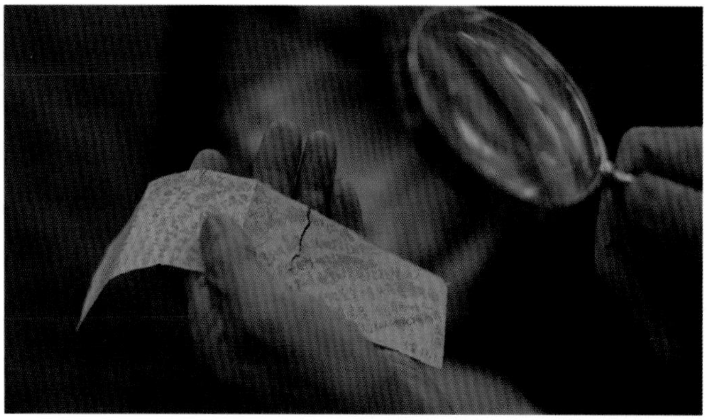

"Gao Ertai, 83, lives with his wife Pu Xiaoyu in Las Vegas. Based on his personal experience of over 50 years under a totalitarian system, Gao Ertai's works on aesthetics and alienation provide a piercing analysis of how an individual is coercively alienated and turned into a tool of a political regime. Driven by an ordinary man's urge to be free, an oppressed body uses himself as an alienated tool to demonstrate that beauty is the symbol of freedom."
— Quote from https://www.crousel.com/en/exhibition/wang-bing-2018

「83歳の美学者、高爾泰（ガオ・エァータイ）は、妻の浦小雨（プー・シャオユー）と共にラスベガスに居住している。全体主義体制のもとで50年以上を生きてきた個人的な経験をもとに、高爾泰が著した美学と疎外に関する著作は、個人がいかにして強制的に疎外され、政治体制の道具へと変えられるかについて、鋭い分析を提示している。ごく普通の人間が自由を求める衝動に駆り立てられたとき、その抑圧された身体は、自身を疎外された道具として見ることによって、美は自由のなかにしか存在しないことを論証しているのだ」
—引用元：https://www.crousel.com/en/exhibition/wang-bing-2018

All images on pp. 35–42: Courtesy of the artist, Galerie Chantal Crousel, Gallery Take Ninagawa, Magician Space

Daniel Boyd

ダニエル・ボイド

Born in 1982, Gimuy/Cairns, Australia. Lives and works in Warrang/Sydney, Australia. Boyd's practice engages with the pluralities of time, space, culture and personal experience. At once intimate, historical and metaphysical in its scope, his paintings, video works and installations mine the complexity of perspectives through which we—individually and collectively—assemble cultural and personal memory. Boyd's practice has lead him to participate in major biennales and exhibitions including Kathmandu Triennale 2077 (2022) curated by Cosmin Costinas and Co-Curators Sheelasha Rajbhandari and Hit Man Gurung; *Treasure Island*, Art Gallery of New South Wales, Sydney (2022) curated by Isobel Parker Phillip and Erin Vink; *Mondialité*, the Boghossian Foundation, Villa Empain, Brussels (2017), curated by Hans Ulrich Obrist and Asad Raza; *All the World's Futures*, 56th Venice Biennale (2015) curated by Okwui Enwezor; *A Time for Dreams*, Moscow International Biennale for Young Arts (2014) curated by David Elliot; The 7th Asia Pacific Triennial of Contemporary Art, Queensland Art Gallery | Gallery of Modern Art, Brisbane (2012); Kochi-Muziris Biennale: *Whorled Explorations*, Kochi (2014) curated by Jitish Kallat; *Culture Warriors*: National Indigenous Art Triennial, National Gallery of Australia, Canberra (2007) curated by Brenda L Croft.

1982年、オーストラリア、ケアンズ生まれ。現在はシドニーを拠点に活動。
時間、空間、文化、個人的体験の複数性に関する作品制作を行う。ボイドの絵画、映像、インスタレーション作品は私的でありながら同時に歴史的、形而上学的広がりをもち、私たちが個人あるいは集団として文化的・個人的記憶を構築する際にともなう複雑な視点を掘り下げている。2022年カトマンズ・トリエンナーレ2077や、2022年「Treasure Island」ニューサウスウェールズ州立美術館（シドニー）、2017年「Mondialité」ヴィラ・アンパン（ブリュッセル）、2015年第56回ヴェネツィア・ビエンナーレ、2014年モスクワ国際ヤングアート・ビエンナーレ、2012年第7回アジア・パシフィック・トリエンナーレ、クイーンズランド州立美術館（ブリスベン）、2014年コチ=ムジリス・ビエンナーレ（コチ）、2007年先住民アート・トリエンナーレ、オーストラリア国立美術館（キャンベラ）など、その活動実績から、これまでに多数の主要なビエンナーレ・展示に参加。

AND THE HORIZON SWALLOWED THE TORTOISE

Not long ago I knew how to explain things, but at this moment I don't feel that I do. I sat down and tried to explain some pictures that were yet to be made and ended with disparate notes. Make of these as you will for now. I'll explain another day.

Australian history...does not read like history, but like the most beautiful lies. [MT.DB.1897]

Perhaps it is I who knows best why it is only man that laughs. Only he suffers so deeply that he was forced to invent laughter. The most unfortunate and most melancholic animal is, quite rightly, the most elated. [FN.JR.1885]

The people are happy not to say anything against the social structures they enjoy. [DB>JR2020]

On the day that news of Fanon's death reached Paris, all copies of The Wretched of the Earth were seized by police because it was believed that the book was a threat to national security. [SC.2008]

That won't give me my bone marrow back. [FF.1961]

When Orpheus descends to Eurydice, art is the power that causes the night to open. Because of the power of art, the night welcomes him; it becomes the welcoming intimacy, the understanding and the harmony of the first night [MB<DB&AA.1981(44)]

Blackbird singing in the dead of night
Take your broken wing and learn to fly
All your life
You were only waiting for this moment to arise

I thought I saw a black sun in the deserted sky and a red ball of blood over the Tuileries. I said to myself: "The internal night begins, and it will be terrible. What will happen when people realise that there no longer is a sun?" [GdN<DD&AA(45)]

A diagnosis of "multiple trauma" implies the presence of two or more separate injuries, at least one or a combination of which endangers the [person's] life. [NCBI.2020]

There are also these birds called Curlews, they bring bad news when they call at night. It's more like a scream. [DB>JR.2020]

Zeno of Elea was involved in a plot to overthrow Nearchus. The plot was discovered and he was arrested. During his interrogation, Zeno said that he had something to tell Nearchus about people but only in his private ear. When Nearchus was summoned, Zeno laid hold of the tyrant's ear with his teeth and would not let go until he was stabbed to death. [SC. 2008]

We do not explain pictures: we explain remarks about pictures – or rather, we explain pictures only in so far as we have considered them under some verbal description or specification. [MB.1985(1)]

Every evolved explanation of a picture includes or implies an elaborate description of that picture. The explanation of the picture then in turn becomes part of the larger description of the picture, a way of describing things about it that would be difficult to describe another way. [MB.1985(1)]

At this moment things are difficult to describe another way.

Jarrod Rawlins, 2020

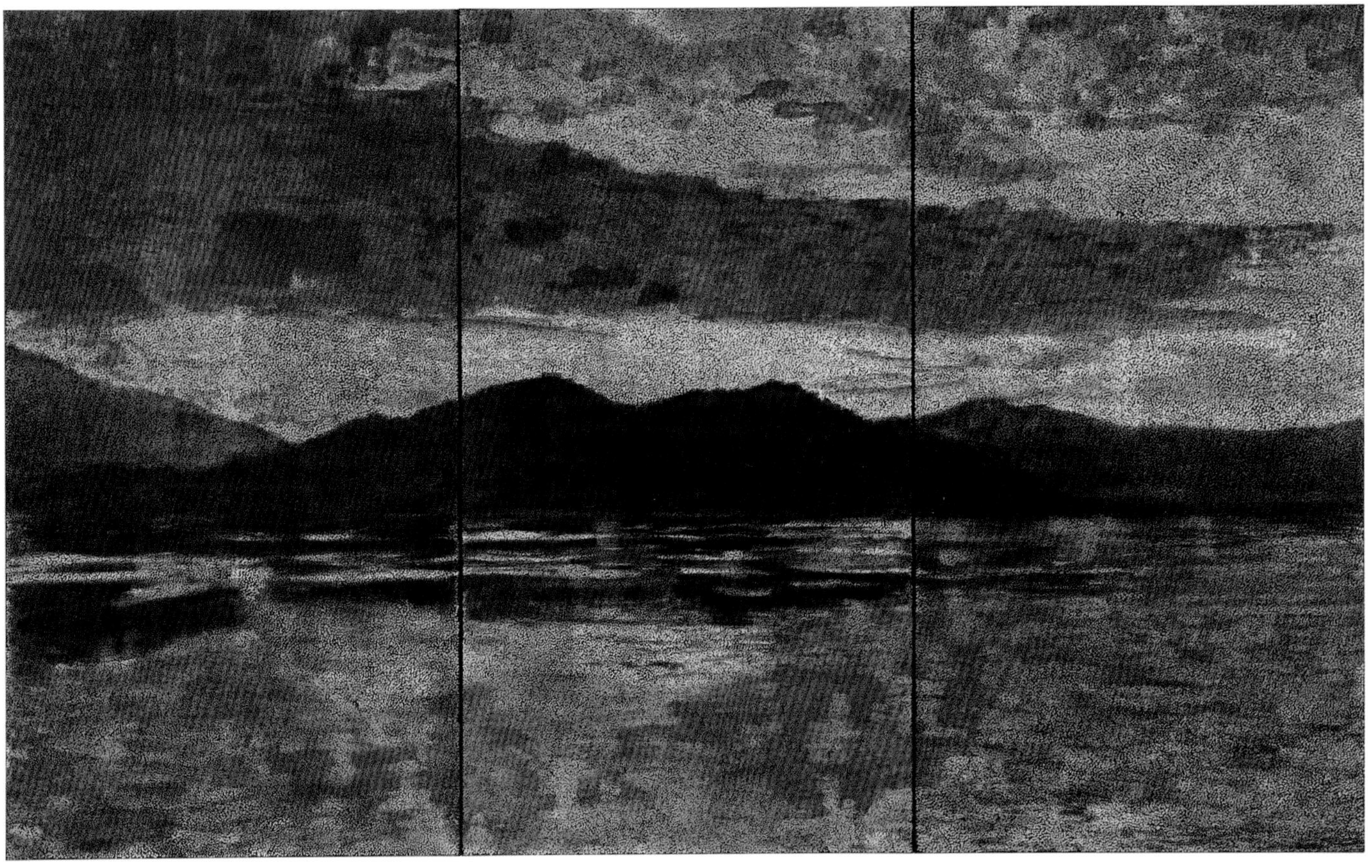

untitled (SOAGS), 2020
Oil, acrylic, charcoal and archival glue on canvas
350 × 570 cm

Recalcitrant Radiance

Oscillating for a brief mystical moment, in the form of a
wave – her wave –
augments two distant points, a cave and a cave
yamani forged by the kiss of dawar, witness to the
archaeologist
enters a synthesis
the crystal ball is split.

そして水平線は亀を飲み込んだ

少し前までは説明の仕方がわかっていたが、今はその実感がない。まだつくっていない絵を説明しようとして、異なるメモに終始してしまった。とりあえず、これを好きなように使ってください。またの機会に説明します。

オーストラリアの歴史は…歴史のようには読めず、最も美しい嘘のように読める。[MT.DB.1897]

なぜ人間だけが笑うのか、その理由を一番よく知っているのは私かもしれない。彼だけがあまりに深く苦しんでいるので、笑いを考案せざるを得なかったのだ。最も不幸で最も憂鬱な動物が、当然のことながら、最も高揚している。[FN.JR.1885]

人々は、自分たちが享受している社会構造に対して何も言わないことが幸せなのだ。[DB>JR2020]

ファノンの訃報がパリに届いた日、『The Wretched of the Earth』は国家の安全を脅かすものとして全巻を警察に押収された。[SC.2008]

それでは骨髄は元に戻らない。[FF.1961]

オルフェウスがエウリュディケのもとに降り立つとき、芸術は夜を開かせる力である。芸術の力のために、夜は彼を歓迎し、最初の夜の歓迎する親密さ、理解、調和となる［MB<DB&AA.1981(44)]

真夜中に歌うクロウタドリ
壊れた翼で飛ぶことを学べ
人生のすべて
ただこの瞬間が来るのを待っていた

荒れ果てた空に黒い太陽、チュイルリー宮殿に赤い血の球を見た気がした。私は自分に言い聞かせた、「内なる夜が始まる、恐ろしいことになる。人々が、もはや太陽がないことに気づいたら、どうなるのだろう？」[GdN<DD&AA(45)]

「多発外傷」の診断は、2つ以上の別々の傷害の存在を意味し、少なくとも1つまたはその組み合わせは、［人の］生命を危険にさらす。[NCBI.2020]

シャクシギという鳥がいて、夜に鳴くと悪い知らせをもたらす。それは悲鳴のようなもの。[DB>JR.2020]

エレアのゼノンは、ネアルコス打倒の陰謀に関与した。その陰謀が発覚し、彼は逮捕された。ゼノンは取り調べの際、ネアルコスに人のことを話すことがあるが、それは内密の話だと言った。ネアルコスが呼び出されると、ゼノンは歯で暴君の耳を押さえ、刺し殺されるまで離さなかった。[SC. 2008]

絵画の説明をするのではない。絵画についての意見を説明するのだ—むしろ、何らかの口頭での説明や仕様の下でそれらを考慮する場合にのみ、絵画を説明するのである。[MB.1985(1)]

絵画の進化した説明には、その絵画の精巧な説明が含まれているか、暗示されている。そして、絵画の説明は、より大きな説明の一部となり、他の方法では説明するのが難しいことを説明する方法になる。[MB.1985(1)]

この瞬間は、別の方法で表現するのは難しい。

ジャロッド・ローリンズ、2020年のテキストより引用

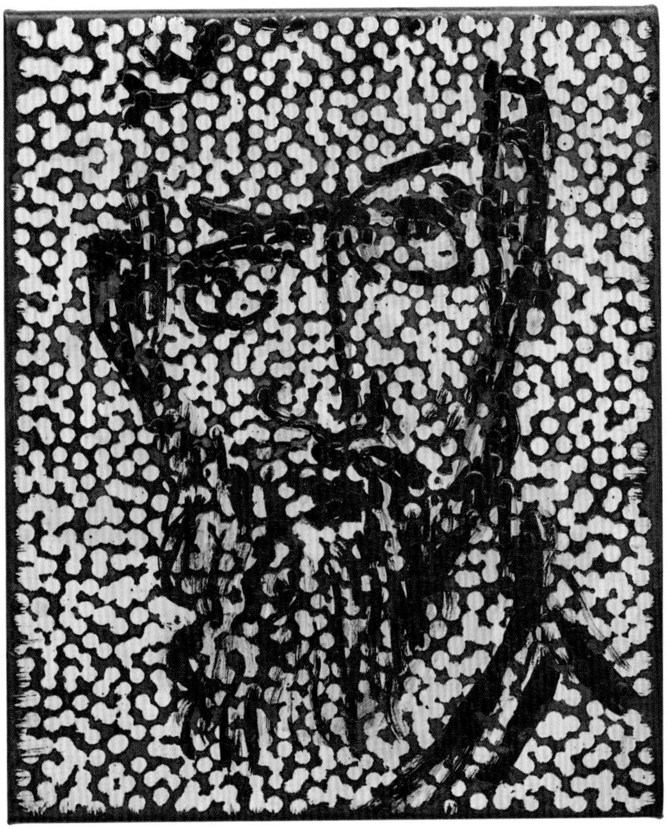

untitled (DOWM), 2021
Oil, acrylic and archival glue on canvas
30.5 × 25 cm

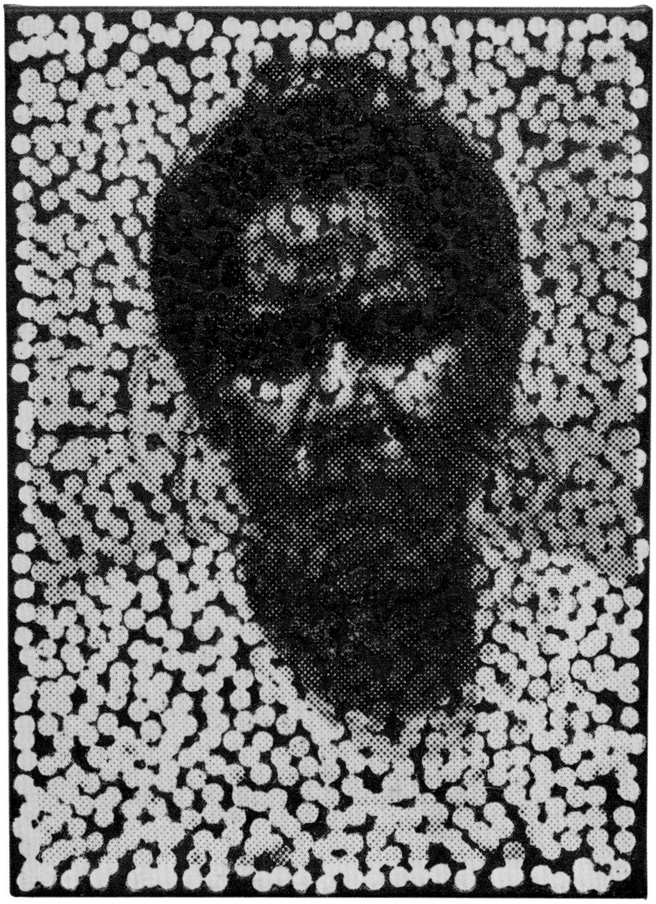

untitled (FJ), 2019
Oil, screenprint, archival glue on canvas
40 × 30 cm

反抗的な輝き

つかの間の神秘的な瞬間のために振動する、波の形をした
―彼女の波―
遠く離れた二つの点、洞窟と洞窟
を補強する
ダワールのキスによってつくられたヤマニは、考古学者の証人として
合成に入る
水晶玉が割れる。

46–47

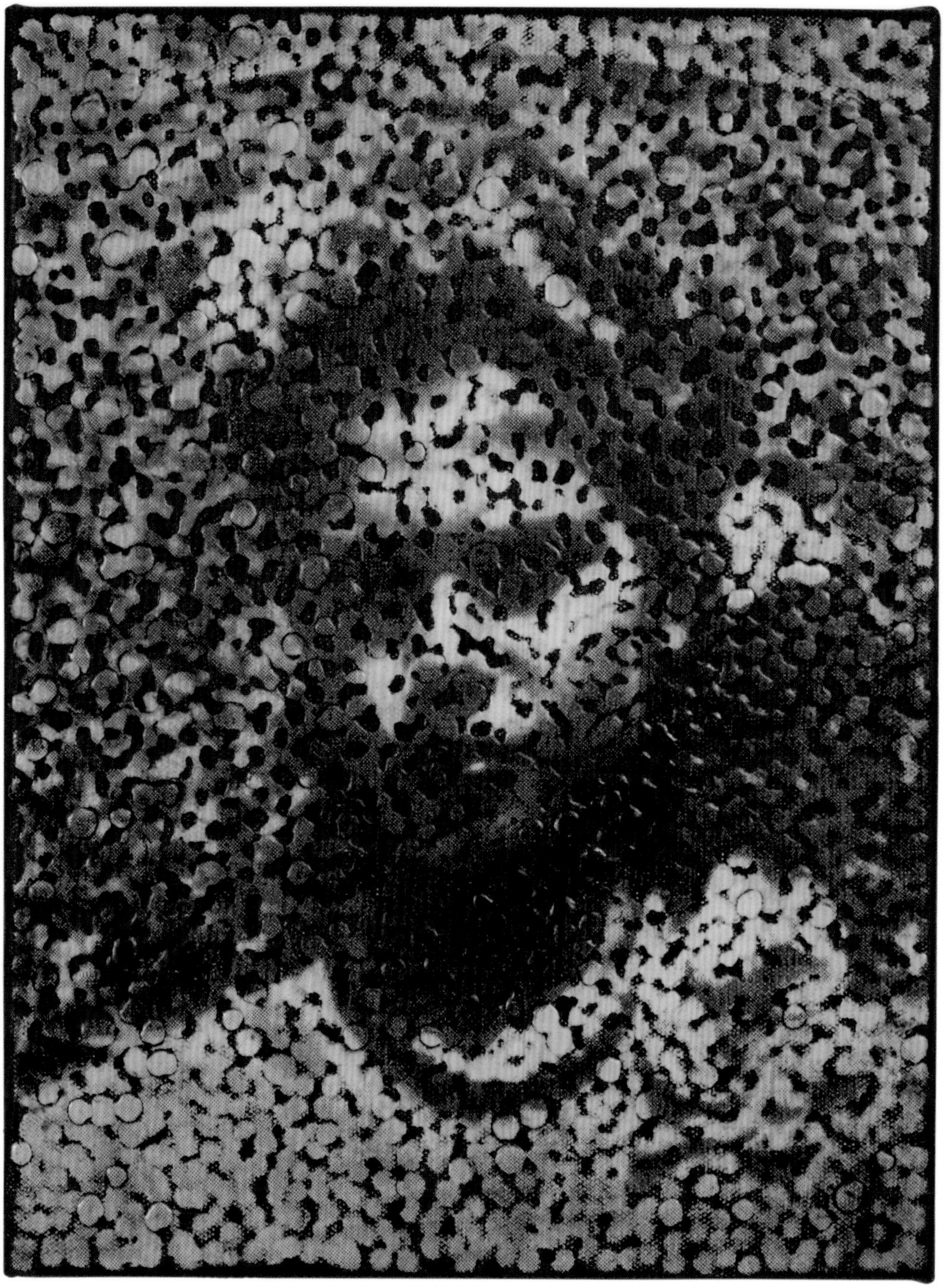

untitled (GB5), 2015
Oil, screen print, watercolour and archival glue on canvas
41 × 31 cm

Lygia Clark

リジア・クラーク

For more than three decades, Lygia Clark (1920–1988) created works that proposed a radical reassessment of the role and function of art. Primarily working in painting, sculpture, performance and, later, psychoanalytical experiences, Clark intended to break down traditional ideas concerning the artist, artwork and viewer. Her pioneering practice questioned the relationship between art object and spectator, through corporeal and organic forms that encouraged physical encounters and sensorial experiences.

Clark's formal training began in Rio de Janeiro in the 1940s where she was taught by Roberto Burle Marx and Zélia Ferreira Salgado, key figures in Brazilian modernism. Her interest in European painting, particularly the work of Paul Klee and Piet Mondrian, led her to Paris (1950–1952) where she made her first oil paintings under the mentorship of Fernand Léger and Árpád Szenes. In 1954, following her return to Brazil, Clark joined the Grupo Frente which enabled her to associate and exhibit with other avant-garde artists, including Hélio Oiticica and Lygia Pape. By 1959, Clark had played a critical part in establishing Neo-Concretism. This movement had evolved from the prevailing trend of Concrete Art, which favoured precise, geometric forms detached from reality. The Neo-Concretists pursued a more personal form of abstraction, that allowed for sensuality, colour and expression.

During the 1950s, Clark continued to develop her intimate, geometric paintings but was already beginning to question the notion of space. Her preoccupation with creating a dynamic environment was first evident in a series of gouaches titled *Planes in Modulated Surface* (1954–1958). In these intimate compositions, forms are placed together at various angles, emphasising the significance of the canvas as a structural component in itself. Clark also started to make architectural models of interior settings that looked like paintings to be entered, indicating her desire to rupture the two-dimensional surface. The artist's intricate series *Estruturas de Caixas de Fósforos* (Matchbox Structures), created a few years later, resemble models for imaginary modernist buildings. Describing her goals during this period, Clark reflected: 'What I seek is to compose a space and not compose in it.' The artist would cease painting by the end of the decade. This important transitional moment was marked in 1959 by an imaginary letter Clark wrote to Mondrian, whose consideration of space and structure had influenced Clark's own vision. 'You are more alive today for me than all the people who understand me, up to a point.'

By the early 1960s, Clark's interest to 'find an organic space - places that open up to the viewer' resulted in a series of small metal and wood sculptures. Her *Bichos*, meaning 'critters', revealed hinged plates that could be manipulated into various arrangements. Reminiscent of insect-like creatures, these were the artist's first wholly participatory works, intended to be realised through physical interaction. 'It is a living organism', Clark wrote. 'What happens is a body-to-body between two living entities.'

In 1963, the artist created *Caminhando*, a breakthrough work that led Clark from the art object to what she called a 'proposition'—an artwork, or 'act', that would be conceived through action and process—in this case, cutting a twisted cylindrical strip of paper with a pair of scissors. 'From there on I attribute an absolute importance to the immanent act carried out by the participant [...] It allows choice, the unpredictable, and the transformation of a virtuality into a concrete event.'

Clark's practice would eventually conclude with her abandoning art altogether. Questioning the purpose of conventional works of art, Clark spent the 1970s developing collective activities and ritualised interactions that relied on others, after being invited to teach a course on gestural communication at the Sorbonne, Paris, in 1972. Upon her return to Rio de Janeiro in 1976, Clark devised her own method, termed *Estruturacao do self* (Structuring of the Self). Informed by items such as plastic bags and balls, these therapeutic tools were used for evolving her artistic processes. This final episode in the artist's career signals how vital the human body was to her practice overall, and underlines Clark's belief in the value of art as social practice.

Clark has had solo exhibitions at Guggenheim Bilbao (2020); Tate Modern, London (with Hélio Oiticica, 2020); Alison Jacques Gallery, London (2016); MoMA, New York (2014); Henry Moore Institute, Leeds (2014); and Itaú Cultural, São Paulo (2012).

Her work has been included in recent group shows at Centre Pompidou, Paris (2021); MASP, São Paulo (2019); MoMA (2019); ZKM, Karlsruhe (2019); Haus der Kulturen der Welt, Berlin (2019); Garage Museum of Contemporary Art, Moscow (2018); MAMBA, Buenos Aires (2018); Brooklyn Museum, New York (2018); and Museum of Modern Art, Warsaw (2017).

Clark's work is held in the collections of Centre Pompidou; Museo Nacional Centro de Arte Reina Sofia, Madrid; Museum of Fine Arts, Houston, Texas; MoMA; MAM Museu de Arte Moderna, Rio de Janeiro; Museu de Arte Moderna de São Paulo; San Francisco Museum of Modern Art; and Tate Modern.

リジア・クラーク（1920–1988年）は、30年以上にわたり、芸術の役割と機能を根本的に問い直す作品を手がけ、主に絵画、彫刻、パフォーマンス、後に精神分析理論を展開しながら、アーティスト、作品、鑑賞者に対する固定概念の解体を目指した。物理的な交流と感覚的な体験を促す身体的・有機的な形態を通じて、作品と鑑賞者の関係性に疑問を呈する先駆的な活動を続けた。

1940年代に本格的なアート活動を開始し、リオデジャネイロでブラジルのモダニズムの中心人物であったロバート・ブール・マルクスとゼリア・フェレイラ・サルガドに師事。ヨーロッパの絵画、特にパウル・クレーやピート・モンドリアンの作品に傾倒し、1950年から1952年の間パリに移る。そこでフェルナン・レジェとアルパド・スゼンヌの指導のもと、最初の油彩画を制作した。ブラジルに帰国後の1954年にグループ・フレンチに加入し、エリオ・オイチシカやリジア・パペら前衛芸術家たちと交流、展示を行い、1959年には新具体主義確立の中心的な担い手となった。これは、現実から切り離された厳密で幾何学的な形態を貴ぶコンクリート・アートの台頭から発展し、身体感覚、色彩、表現を通じてより個人的な抽象表現を追求した運動である。

1950年代にかけて、内省的・幾何学的な絵画をさらに展開していたが、一方で空間という概念を探求し始めていた。彼女の動的な環境を創出することへのこだわりは、ガッシュ画の連作《Planes in Modulated Surface》（1954–1958年）で初めて顕在化する。この内省的な作品では形が様々な角度で配置され、構成要素としてのカンヴァスの重要性が強調されている。またこの頃から、立体化した絵画のような室内模型の制作も始めており、二次元表現を克服することへの意欲を示している。数年後に制作された連作《Estruturas de Caixas de Fósforos（マッチ箱の構造物）》は、架空のモダニズム建築の模型を思わせる複雑な構造をもった作品である。この時期の制作意図について、クラークは「空間に構成するのではなく、空間を構成したかった」と振り返っている。そして1950年代の終わりに、クラークは絵画から離れた。クラークの空間と構造に対する考え方に影響を与えたモンドリアンに宛てて、（訳注：彼がすでに亡くなっていた）1959年に書かれた架空の手紙が、この重要な転換期を裏づけている。「私を理解してくれるすべての人々より、貴方はある意味、今の私にとって生きた存在なのです」。

1960年代の初めには、有機的な空間・見る人に開かれた場を探ることに着目し、金属と木材による小さな彫刻の連作を発表した。《Bichos（動物）》と名づけられたこの作品は、蝶番のついた金属板を動かして様々な形に変化させることができる。どこか虫のような生き物を思わせる本作はクラークにとって、身体的な操作（インタラクション）によって成立する初の参加型作品だった。「これは生き物です」「ここでは2つの生き物の間で身体的対話が生まれます」とクラークは記している。

1963年の《Caminhando（歩行）》は、作品としてのオブジェをクラークが称した「proposition（提案）」、つまり、行動とプロセスを経て創造される芸術作品または「行為」（本作の場合、筒状にねじれた紙をハサミで切断すること）へと移行させた画期的な作品だ。「私はこれ以降、参加者による内在的な行為を絶対視しています［…］それは選択、不可測性、そして仮想を具体的な出来事へと変えることを可能にするからです」。

クラークは最終的に芸術全般を「放棄」する。1972年にパリのソルボンヌ大学で非言語コミュニケーションの講義を受けもったことをきっかけに従来の芸術作品の意義に疑問を抱き、1970年代は他者を巻き込んだ集団的活動や儀式的な交流を展開した。1976年にリオデジャネイロに戻ると、「Estruturacao do self（自己の構造化）」という独自のメソッドを確立。セラピーに用いられるビニール袋やボールに啓発を受け、自身の創作工程を進化させた。最終ステージで迎えたこの転換は、クラークの活動全般における身体の重要性と、芸術の意義を社会的実践に見出した彼女の信念を強調している。

開催された個展に、2020年ビルバオ・グッゲンハイム美術館、2020年テート・モダン（ロンドン／エリオ・オイチシカと合同）、2016年Alison Jacques Gallery（ロンドン）、2014年ニューヨーク近代美術館、2014年Henry Moore Institute（イギリス・リーズ）、2012年イタウ・カルチュラル・センター（サンパウロ）がある。

近年のグループ展では、2021年ポンピドゥー・センター（パリ）、2019年サンパウロ美術館、2019年ニューヨーク近代美術館、2019年カールスルーエ・アート・アンドメディア・センター、2019年世界文化の家（ベルリン）、2018年ガレージ現代美術館（モスクワ）、2018年ブエノスアイレス現代美術館、2018年ブルックリン美術館（ニューヨーク）、2017年ワルシャワ近代美術館などに出展された。

また、ポンピドゥー・センター、ソフィア王妃芸術センター（マドリード）、ヒューストン美術館、ニューヨーク近代美術館、リオデジャネイロ近代美術館、サンパウロ近代美術館、サンフランシスコ近代美術館、テート・モダンに作品が所蔵されている。

SHADOWS IN PROGRESS

I CAN SEE
THE WHOLE
ROOM
AND
THERE IS
NOBODY
IN IT

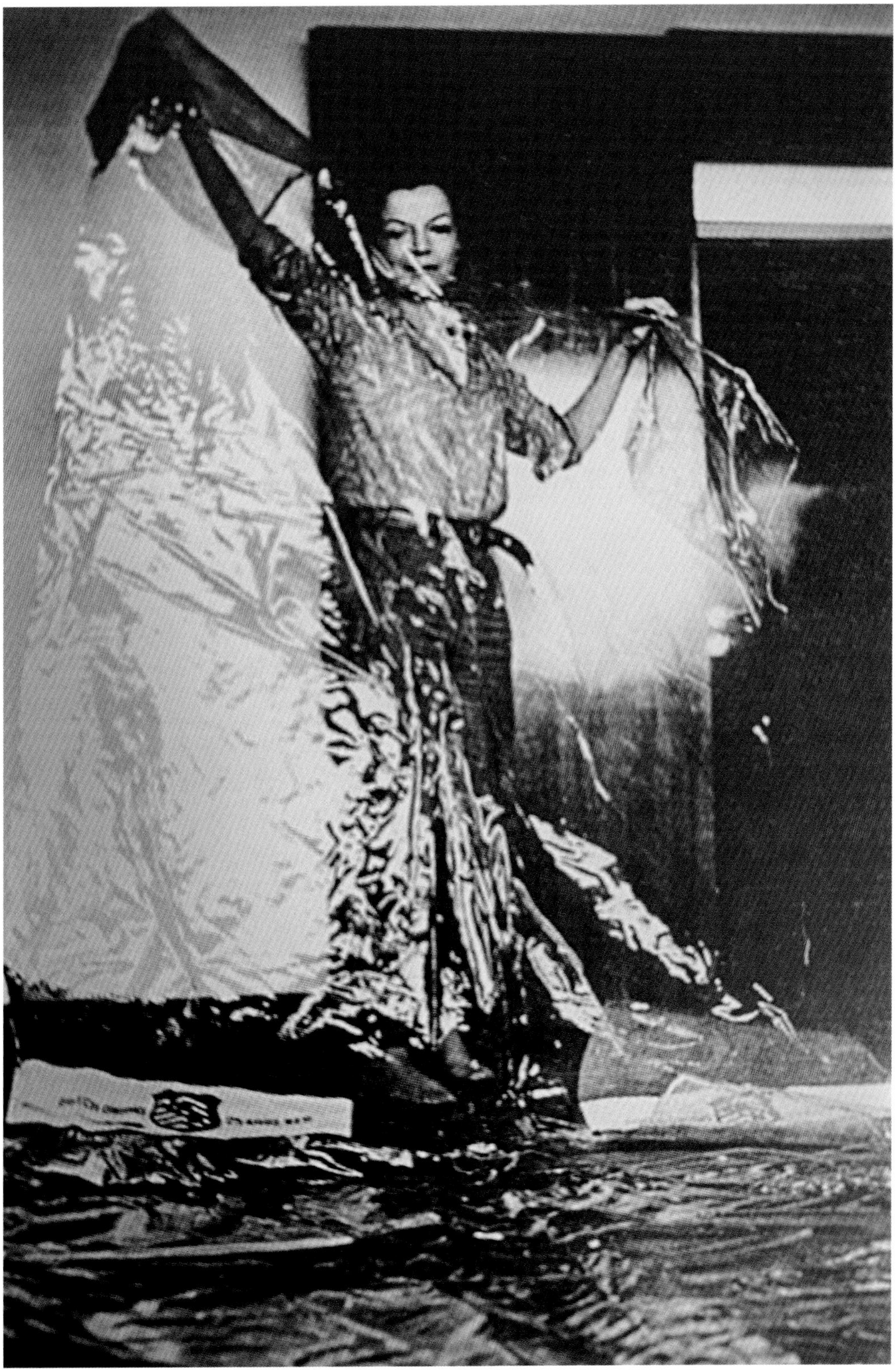

Clark's proposition *Arquitetura biológica I* [Biologic architecture I, 1969], in use probably in Paris in the early 1970s
Courtesy of Associação Cultural "O Mundo de Lygia Clark," Rio de Janeiro
1970年代初頭のパリで使用されたと考えられる、クラークの「提案」
《Arquitetura biológica I［有機的な建築 I］》

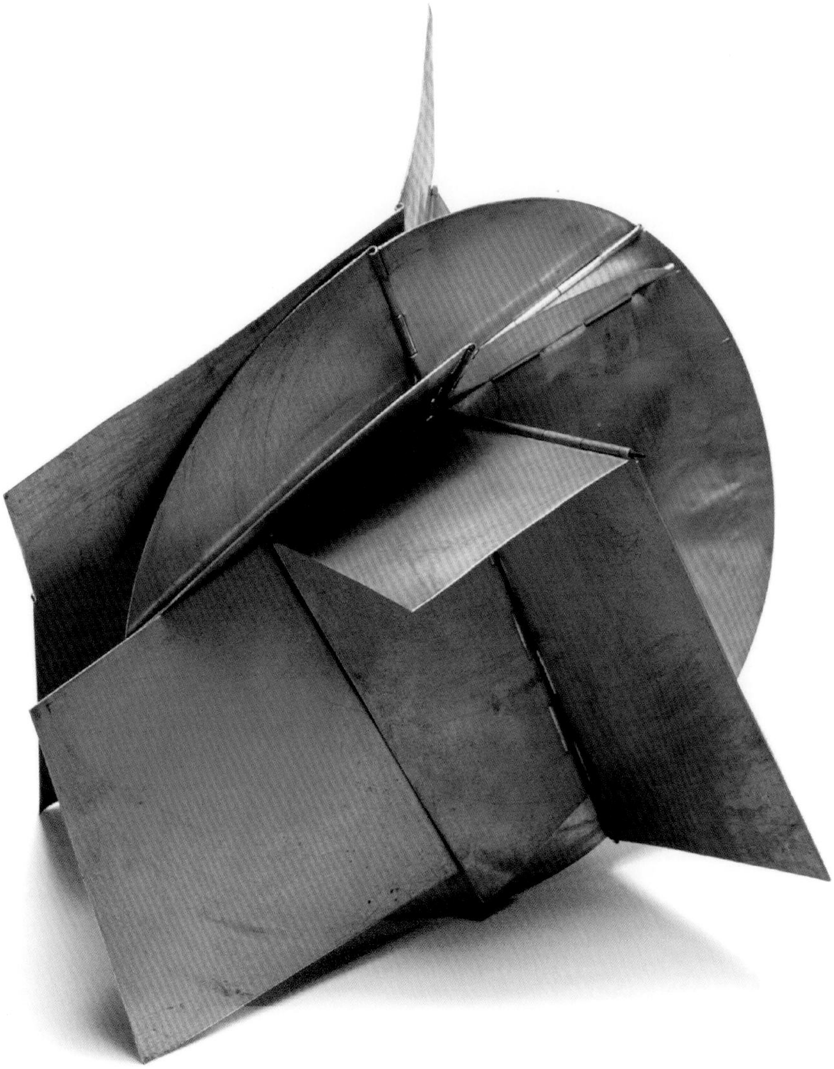

Replica of *Pan Cubismo*, 2022 (original piece was made in 1960)
Aluminum
Dimensions variable (flat size: 62 × 50 cm)
《Pan Cubismo》のレプリカ（2022年、オリジナルは1960年制作）

Lygia Clark

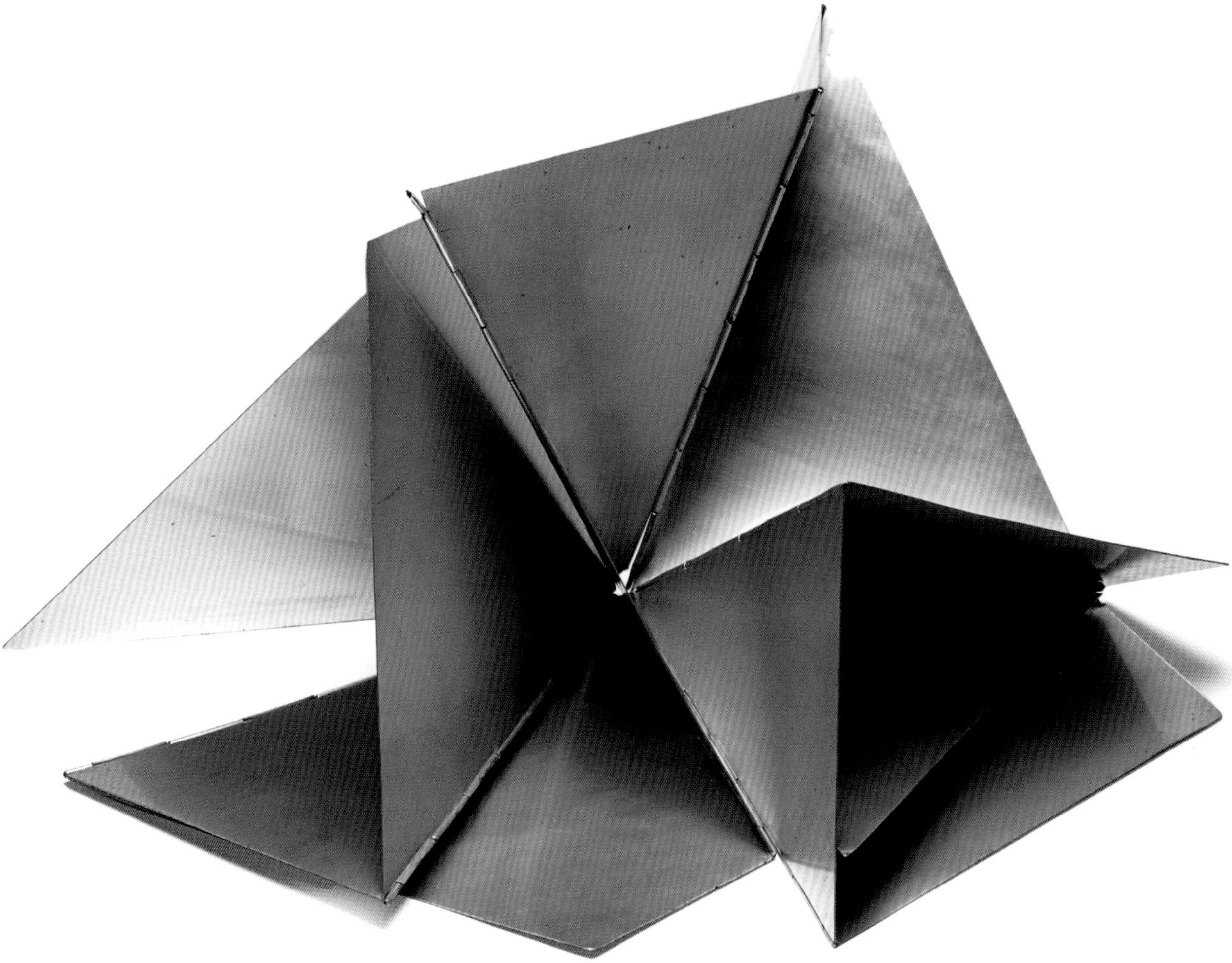

Replica of *Flor* [Flower], 2022 (original piece was made in 1960)
Aluminum
Dimensions variable (flat size: 82 × 74 cm)
《Flor ［Flower］》のレプリカ（2022年、オリジナルは1960年制作）

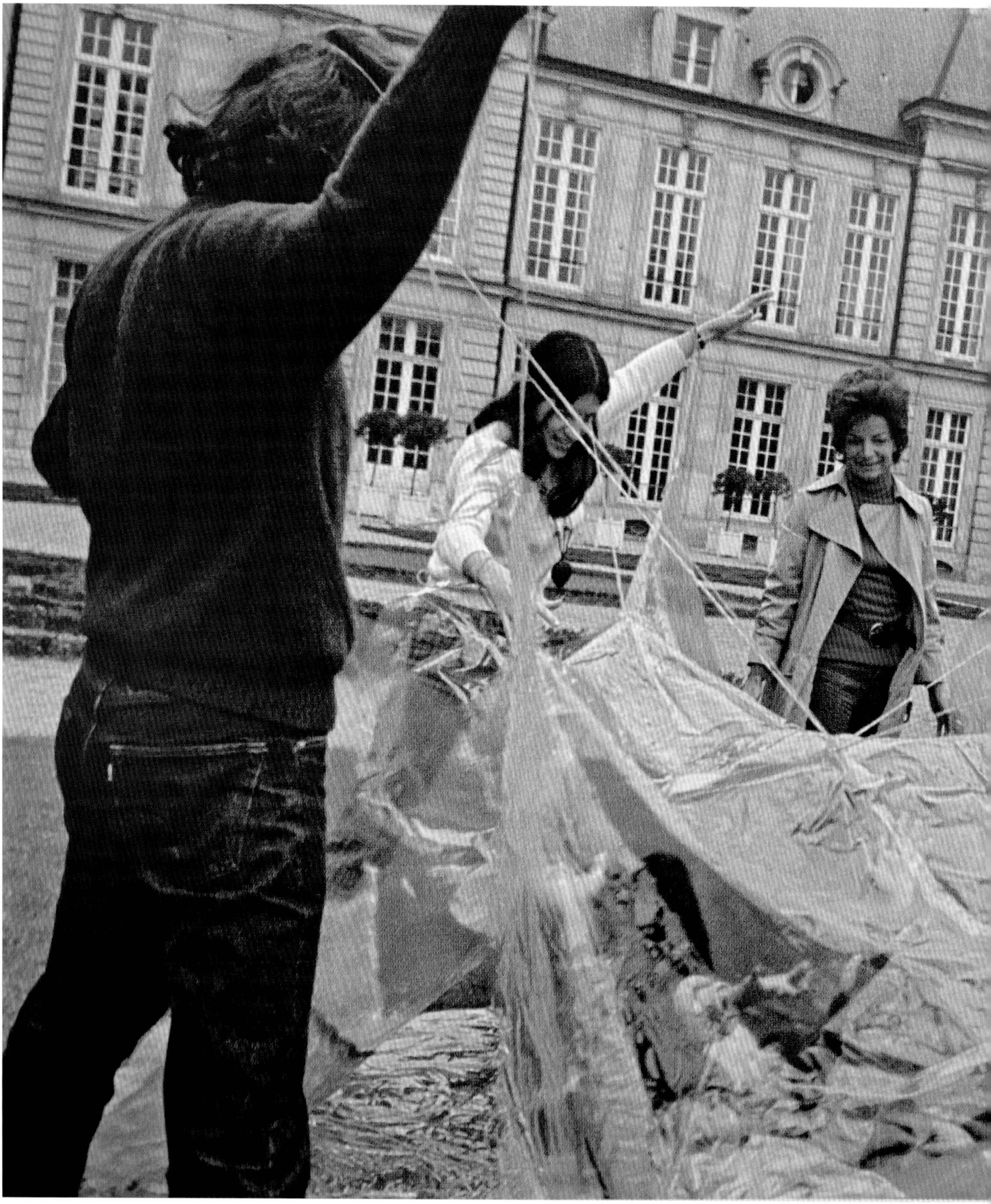

Lygia Clark

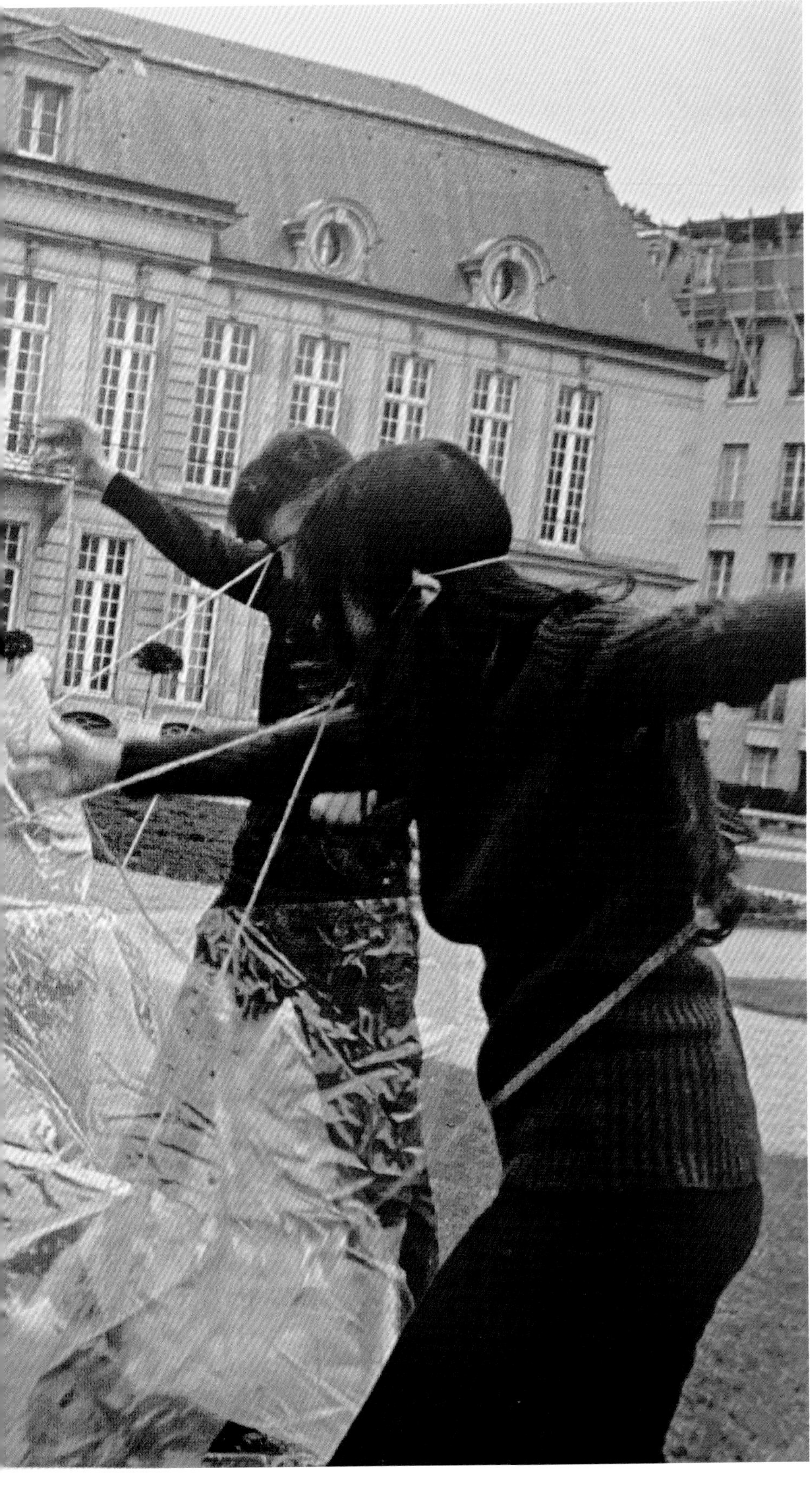

Clark's proposition *Arquitetura biológica II* [Biologic architecture II, 1969], in use outside the Hotel d'Aumont, Paris, in 1969
Photo: Alécio de Andrade
1969年パリのホテルドーモンの屋外にて使用された、クラークの「提案」《Arquitetura biológica II［有機的な建築Ⅱ］》

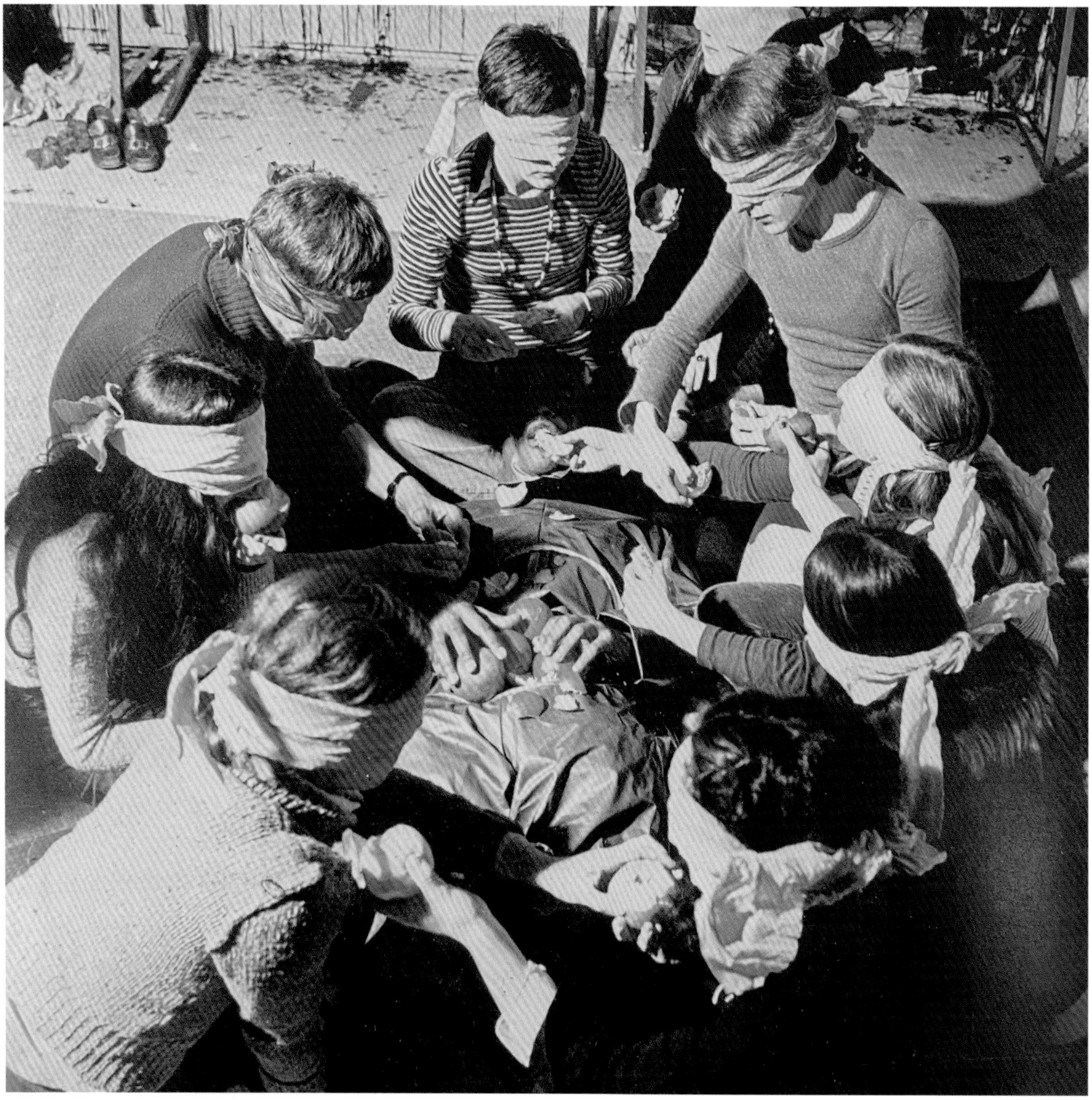

Clark’s proposition *Canibalismo* [Cannibalism, 1973], in use probably in Paris in 1973
Courtesy of Associação Cultural “O Mundo de Lygia Clark,” Rio de Janeiro
1973年のパリで使用されたと考えられる、クラークの「提案」《Canibalismo［カニバリズム］》

Abraham Cruzvillegas

アブラハム・クルズヴィエイガス

Abraham Cruzvillegas (Mexico City, 1968) is a member of The Intergalactic Taoist Tai Chi Society.

1968年、メキシコシティ生まれ。インターギャラクティック・タオイスト・タイチー・ソサエティの現役メンバー。

Installation view, *Abraham Cruzvillegas, Autorreconstrucción: Social Tissue*, Kunsthaus Zürich, Switzerland, February 16 – March 25, 2018

「Abraham Cruzvillegas, Autorreconstrucción: Social Tissue」（2018年2月16日–3月25日、チューリヒ美術館）展示風景

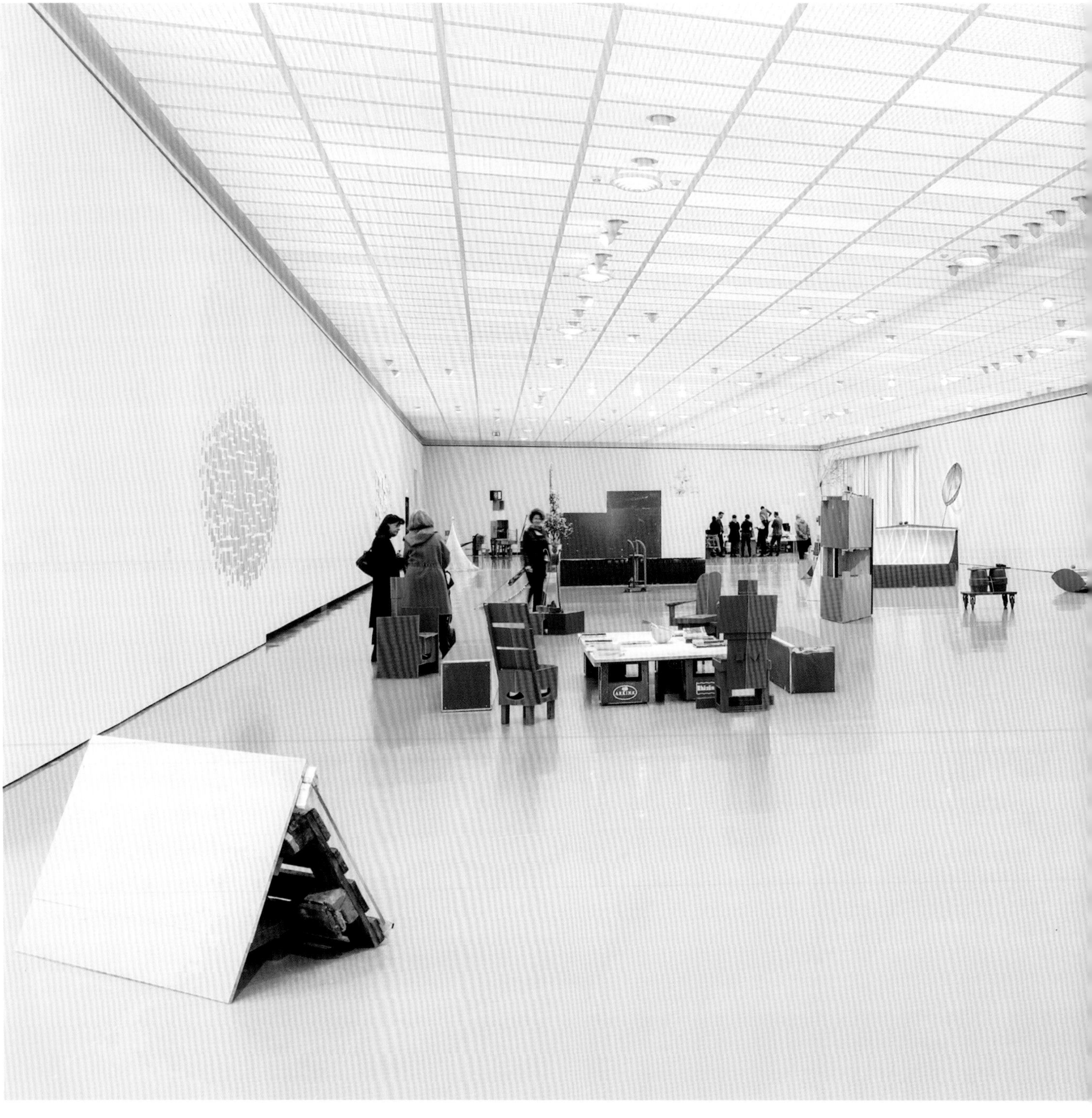

Based in some 35 years of improvising experience, my work for Okayama Art Summit is a smooth test on new possibilities in terms of the construction of my language and discourse, trying not to overrate political or aesthetical consistency, attempting to use as less -or nothing- as I can. Singing, drawing, eating, drinking, being together, would be a technical description…

Abraham Cruzvillegas

岡山芸術交流での私の作品は、35余年にわたる即興制作の経験に基づき、政治的ないし美的な一貫性を重んじ過ぎないようにしながら、最低限の要素で、あるいは何も用いず、自身の言語と言説を構築する新しい可能性を探る、ゆるやかな実験である。厳密には、歌い、描き、食し、飲み、共に過ごす……ということである。

アブラハム・クルズヴィエイガス

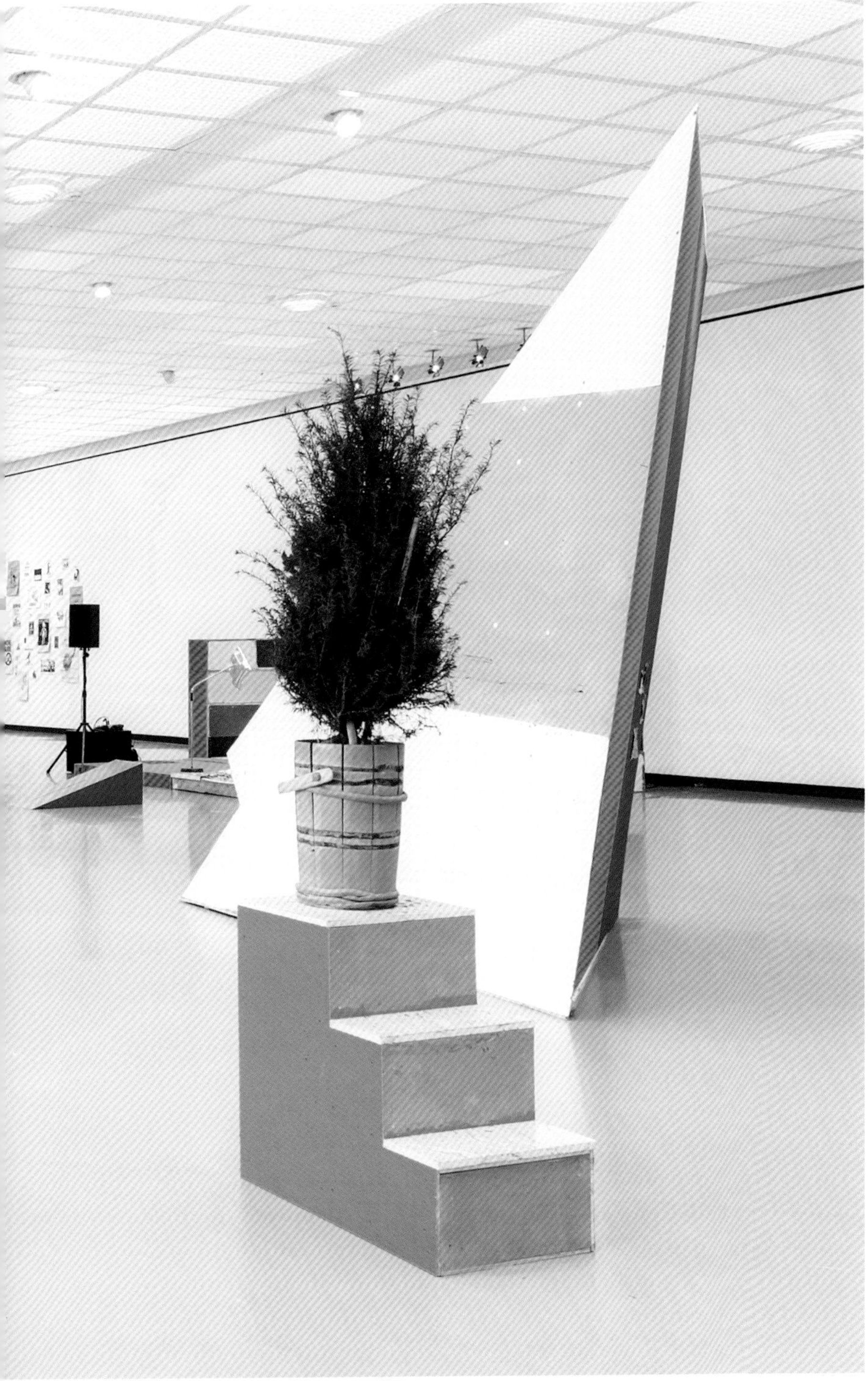

A performance during the exhibition *Abraham Cruzvillegas: Song*, March to April 2020
Performance with Gabriel Kuri and Alberto Cabrera at the drums
Organized by: Lulu, Mexico City. Venue: LA MAISON DE RENDEZ-VOUS, Brussels, Belgium
Photo: Isabelle Arthuis / all images copyright and courtesy of the artist, Lulu and LA MAISON DE RENDEZ-VOUS, Brussels
展覧会「Abraham Cruzvillegas: Song」（2020年3–4月、LA MAISON DE RENDEZ-VOUS、ブリュッセル）会期中に行われたパフォーマンスの様子

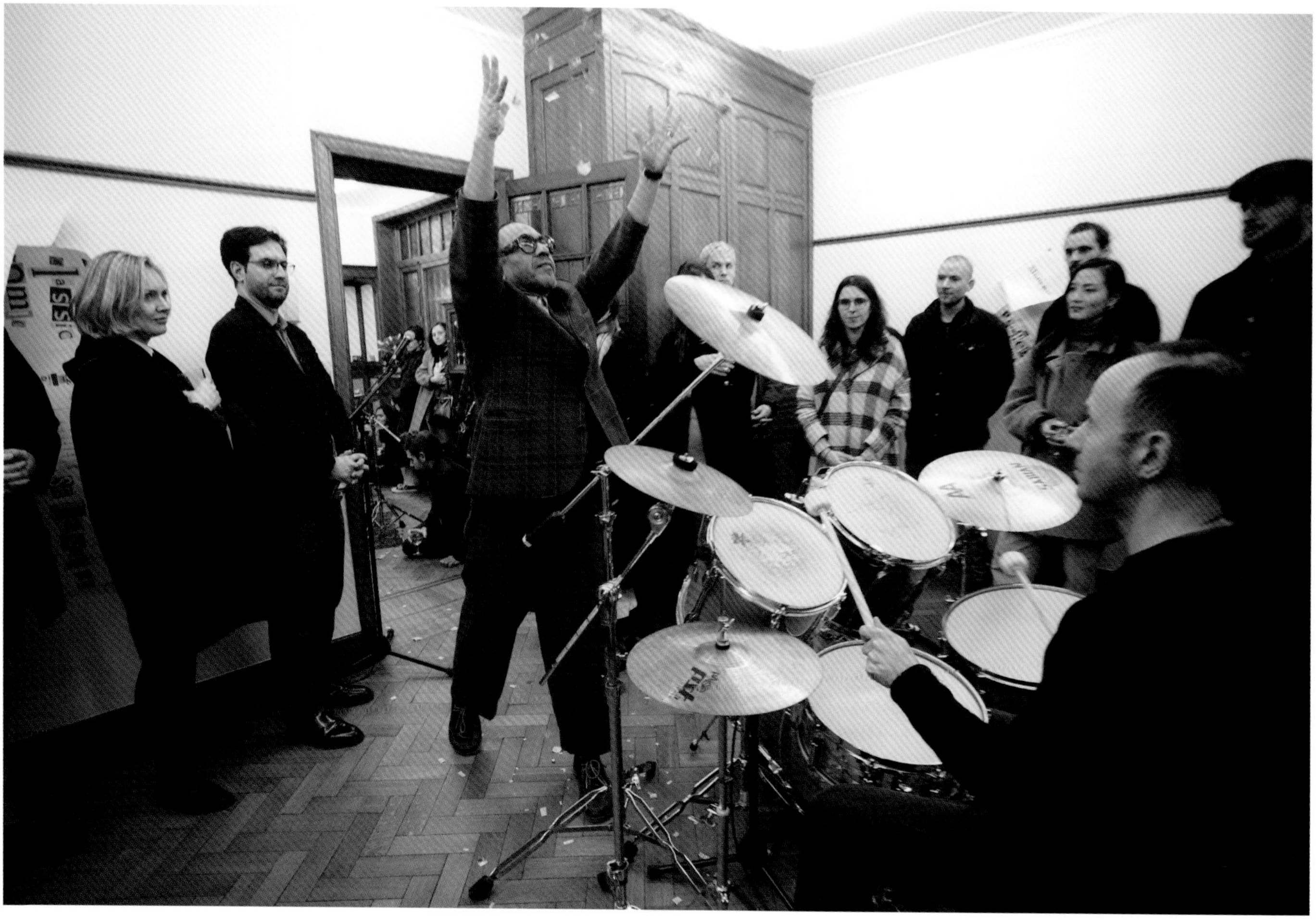

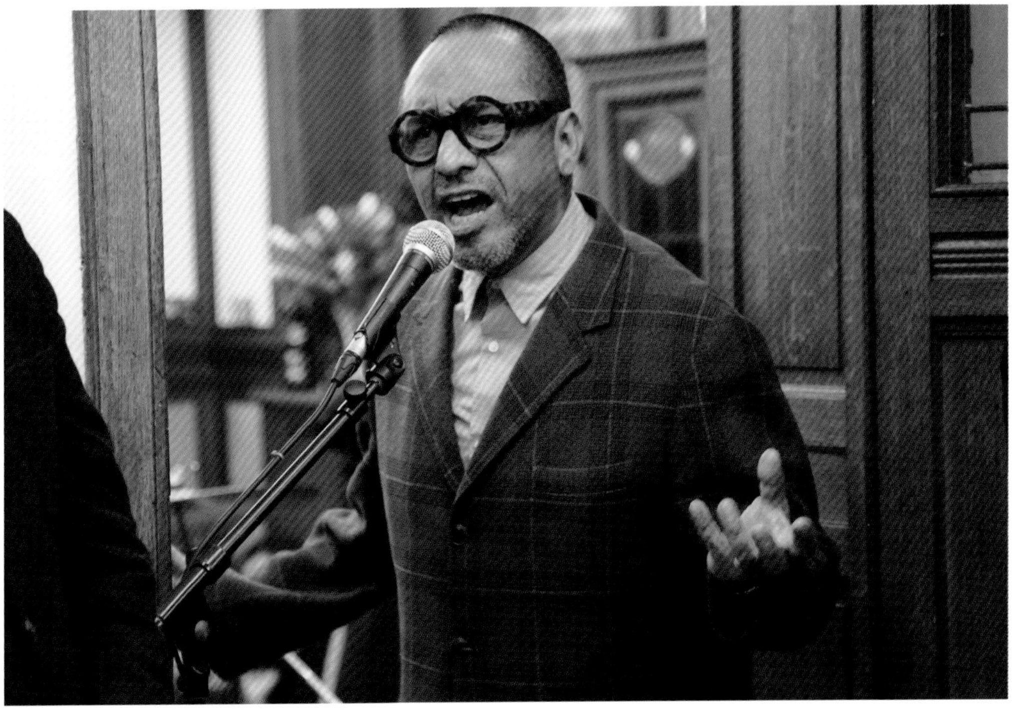

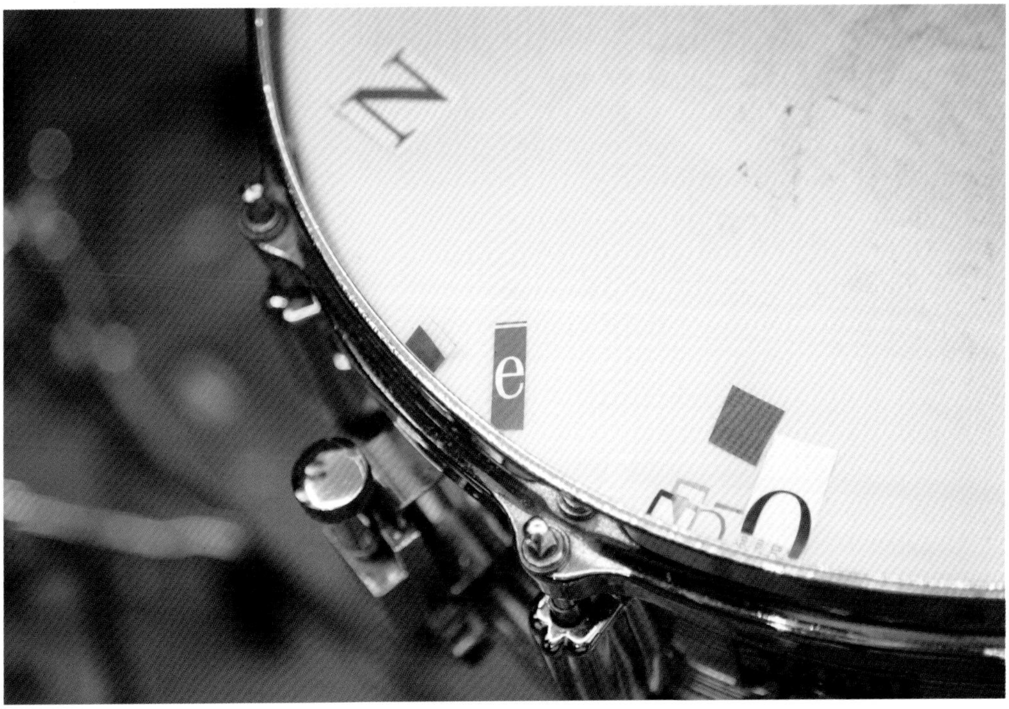

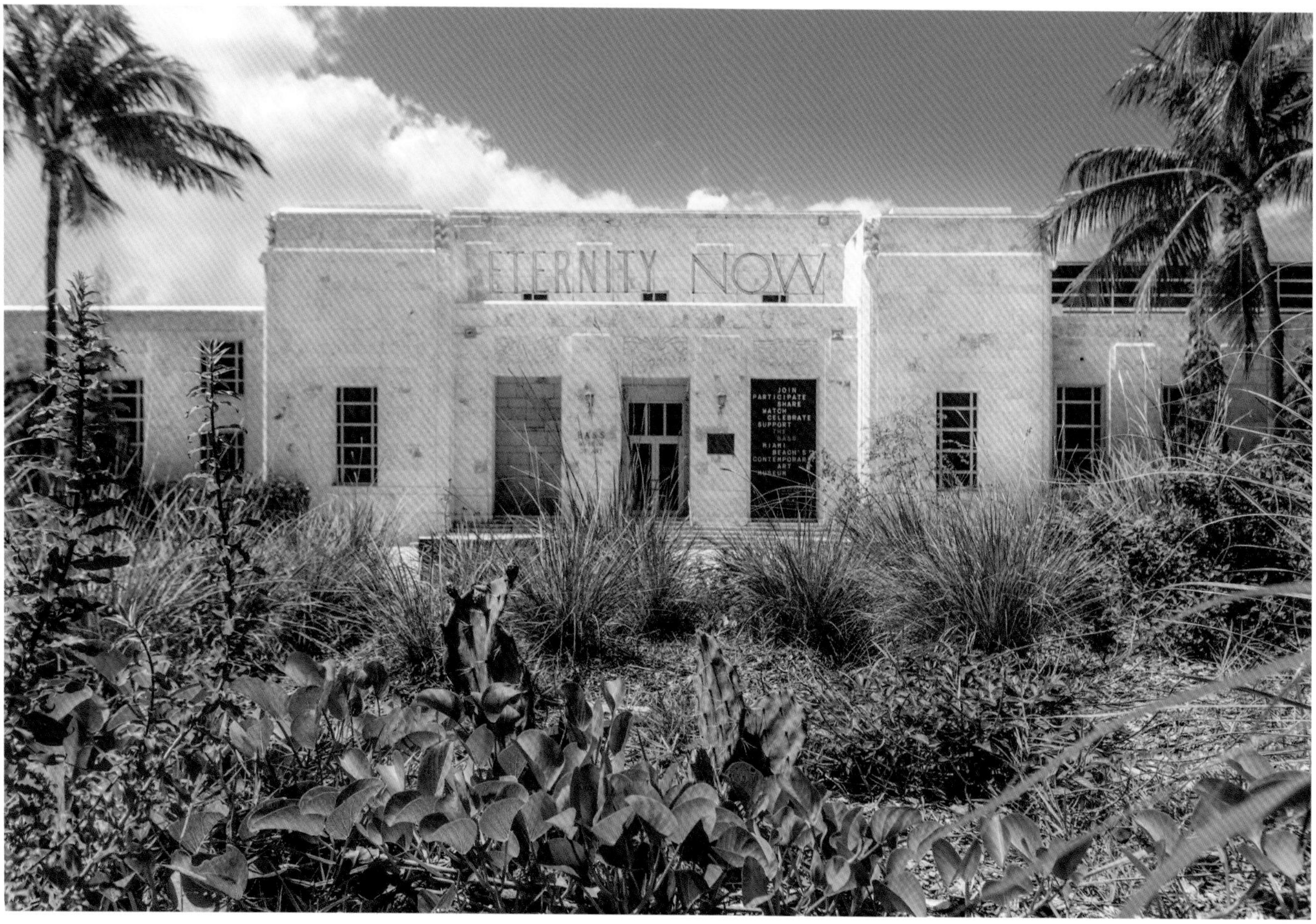

Installation view of *Agua dulce* by Abraham Cruzvillegas at The Bass
Photo: Zaire Kacz
Image courtesy of The Bass, Miami Beach
《Agua dulce》インスタレーション風景（2021年、The Bass、マイアミ）

Enku

円空

Enku (1632–1695) was a Japanese Buddhist monk and sculptor during the early Edo period. He was born in Mino Province (Gifu Prefecture) in 1632, and is thought to have entered the priesthood at a young age, after which he continued his mountain asceticism on Mt. Hakusan and other mountains. Enku left Mino in his early 30s, and traveled through the Hokkaido, Tohoku, Kanto and Kinai regions. By 1663, He began carving statues and is said to have created over 100,000 statues during his lifetime. Enku returned to Mino in 1695 and died at the age of 64 on July 15 of the same year.

Enku's sculptures are known for being crudely carved from a single piece of wood and feature bold, simple forms. Their rustic expression of natural wood texture without color or decoration is often described as 'folksy.' In his early years, some of Enku's works followed the tradition of carving smooth surfaces, but he gradually shifted to a strong, abstract style with chisel marks. Many softly smiling Buddha statues were carved after his style was established.

Enku's numerous Buddha statues must have been made not only to teach Buddhism to the people, but also as part of his way to realize his enlightenment as a Buddhist monk.

Written by
Sadamu Yokoyama, Deputy Director, Okayama Prefectural Museum
Yuki Okazaki, Curator, Okayama Prefectural Museum

円空（1632–1695年）は、江戸時代前期の僧侶、仏師。1632（寛永9）年に美濃国（岐阜県）で生まれる。幼少期に出家したとされ、その後も白山などで山岳修行を重ねた。30歳前半頃に美濃国を離れ、北海道、東北、関東、畿内などを遊行した。また、1663（寛文3）年までには造像を始め、生涯において10万躯以上を制作したと言われている。1695（元禄8）年に美濃国に戻り、同年7月15日64歳で死去した。

円空の彫刻は、一木を粗削りし、造形を大胆に簡略化して彫りだす表現で知られる。彩色や装飾を施さず、木質を生かしたその素朴な描写は、庶民的とも評される。初期には、表面を滑らかに整え、伝統的な表現を踏襲した作品も見られるが、次第に鑿痕を残した、力強く抽象的な作風へと変化していった。作風の確立後は、穏やかな表情の微笑仏も多く造像された。

円空の大量の造像は、僧侶として、民衆への教化と共に自身の修行の一環でもあったと言えよう。

執筆：
横山定（岡山県立博物館副館長）
岡﨑有紀（岡山県立博物館学芸員）

Jizo Bosatsu (Kṣitigarbha)
55 cm　Katsuro Hayashi collection
《地蔵菩薩像》 林克朗 蔵

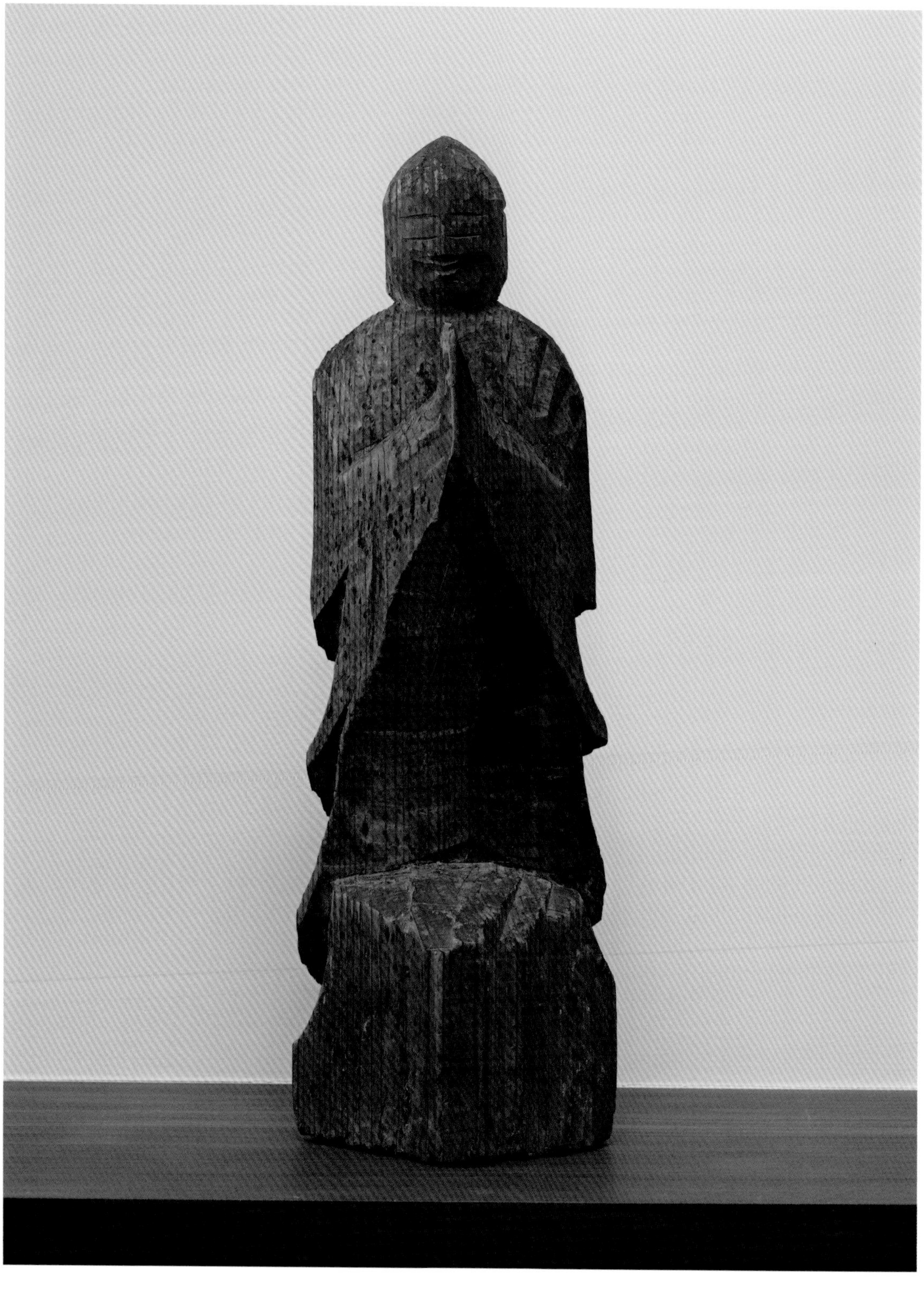

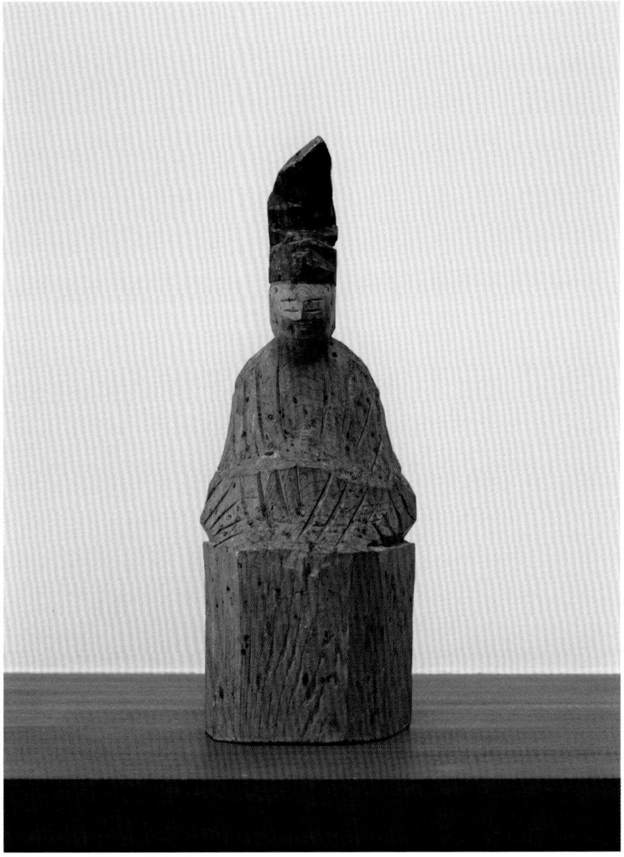

Seated male deity
30.5 cm　Katsuro Hayashi collection
《神像》　林克朗 蔵

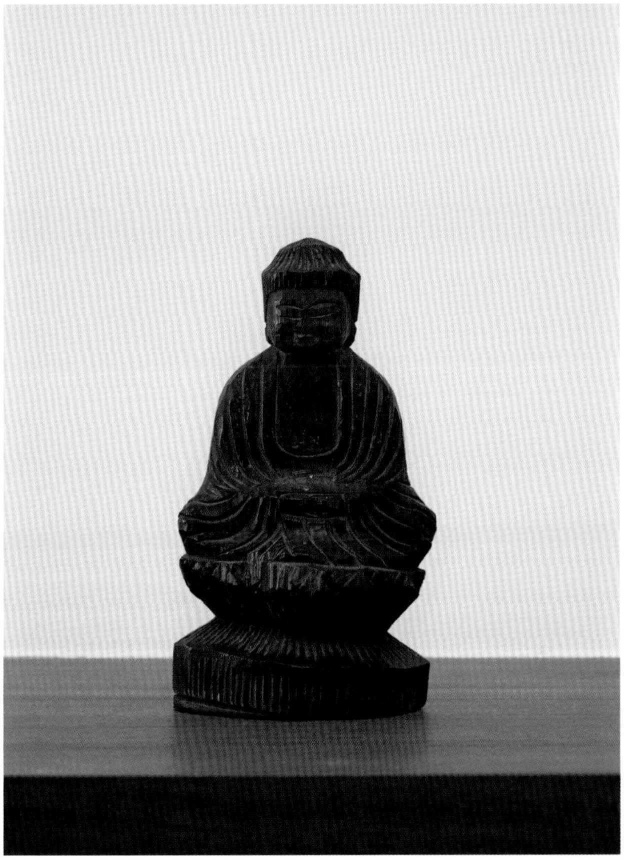

Shaka Nyorai (Śākyamuni)
18.2 cm　Katsuro Hayashi collection
《釈迦如来像》　林克朗 蔵

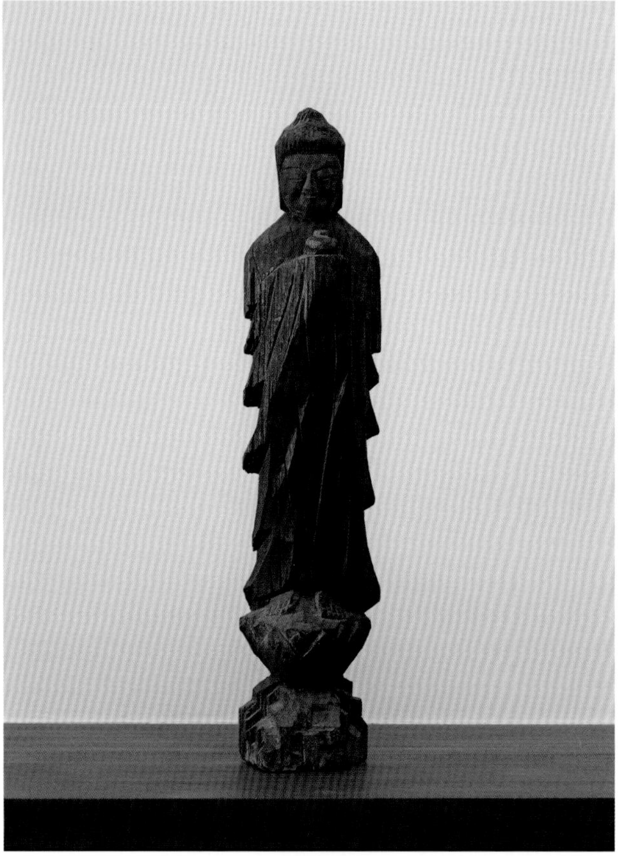

Yakushi Nyorai (Bhaiṣajyaguru)
4.5 cm　Shigeo Tazuke collection
《薬師如来像》　田附滋大 蔵

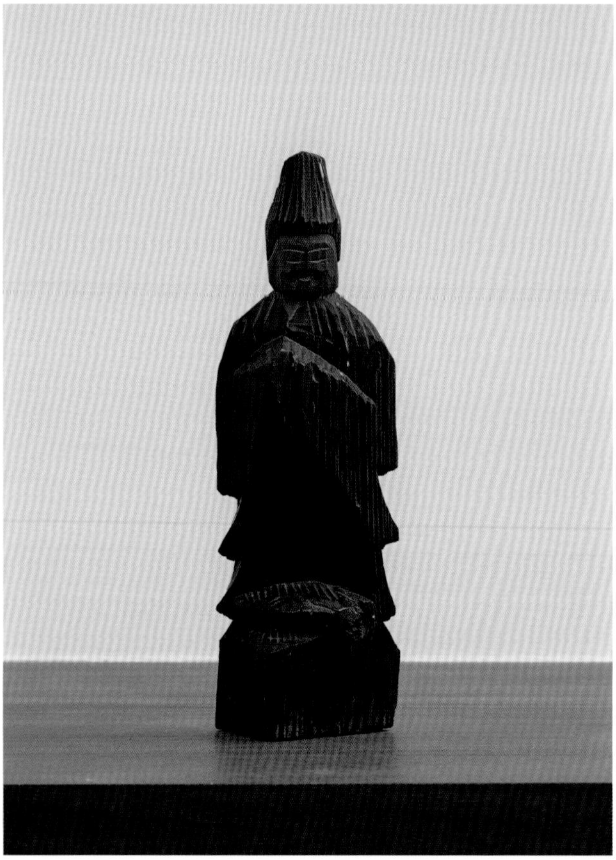

Kannon Bosatsu (Avalokiteśvara)
26.5 cm　Tomoki Imadegawa collection
《観音菩薩像》　今出川朋樹 蔵

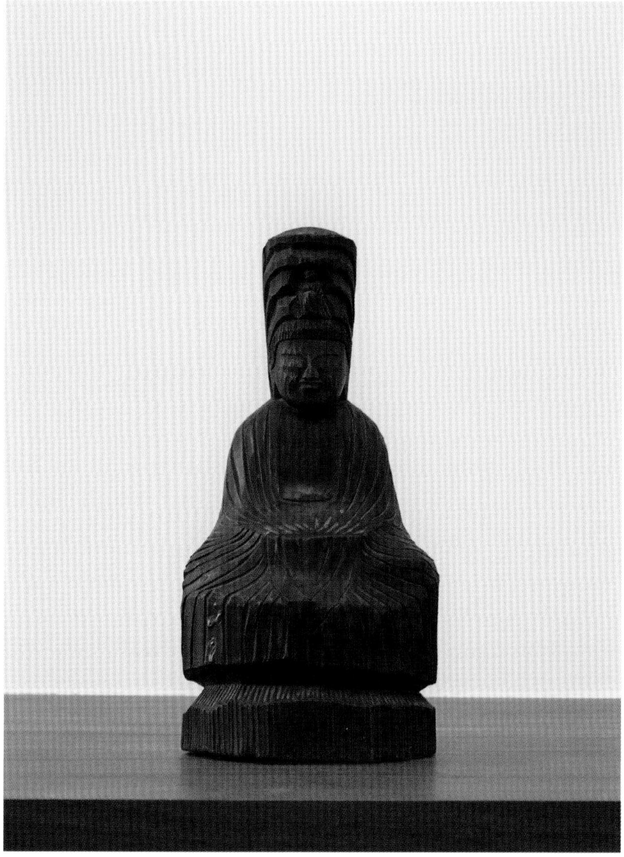

Kannon Bosatsu (Avalokiteśvara)
25 cm　Shigeo Tazuke collection
《観音菩薩像》　田附滋大 蔵

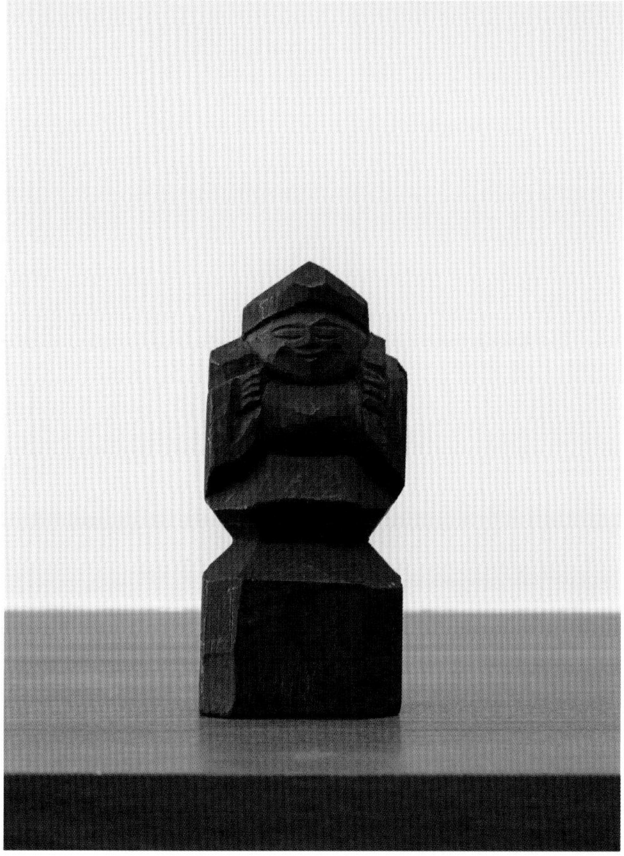

Daikoku Ten (Mahākāla)
11.5 cm　Shigeo Tazuke collection
《大黒天像》　田附滋大 蔵

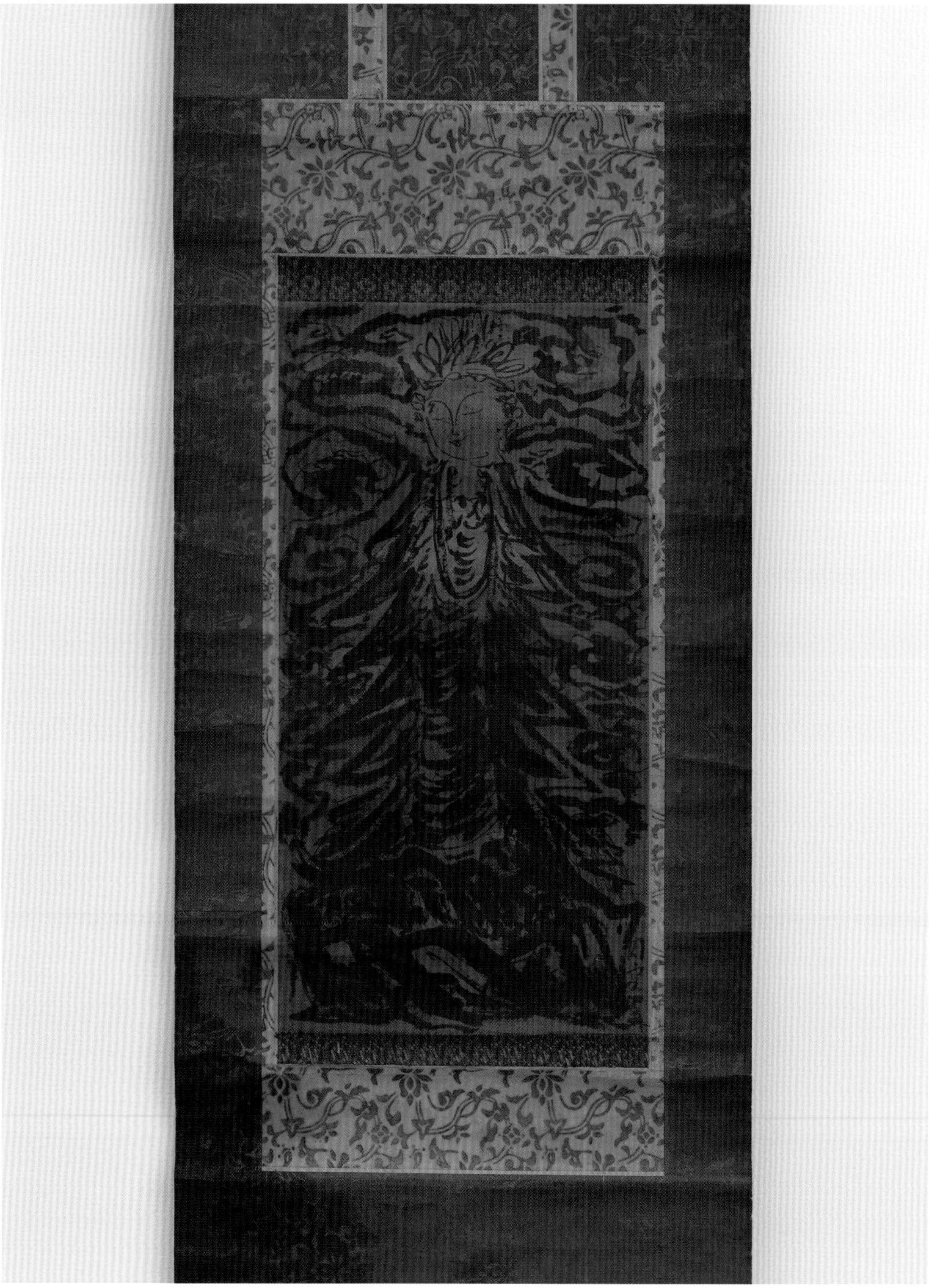

Bosatsu (Bodhisattva)
Hanging scroll: 88 cm　Paper: 35.5 cm
Tomoki Imadegawa collection
《菩薩像》　今出川朋樹 蔵

All photos on pp. 66–70: Yasushi Ichikawa
Special thanks: Kobijutsu Imadegawa
特別協力：古美術 今出川

Ryoji Ikeda

池田亮司

Born in 1966 in Gifu, Ikeda currently lives and works in Paris and Kyoto. While rooted in electronic music, the internationally active composer and artist also produces art as experimentation. Ikeda's immersive live performances and installations employ an elaborate orchestration of sound, visuals, matter, physical phenomena, and mathematical concepts.

Since 2008, he presented solo exhibitions in major institutions worldwide such as Center Pompidou Paris, Carriageworks Sydney, MONA Hobart-Tasmania, Park Avenue Armory New York, Museum of Contemporary art Tokyo, Museo de Arte Bogota, ZKM centre for Art and Media Karlsruhe, Eye Filmmuseum Amsterdam, Taipei Fine Arts Museum, 180 The Strand London amongst others. In 2022, Hirosaki Museum of Contemporary Art presented his first major solo exhibition in Japan since 2009.

Ikeda's long term audiovisual project, *data-verse* commissioned by Audemars Piguet Contemporary was revealed at Venice Biennale 2019, *May You Live in Interesting Times* curated by Ralph Rugoff.

As a composer, Ikeda's audiovisual and acoustic concerts performed at Barbican Center London, Centre Pompidou and Festival d'Automne à Paris, Los Angeles Philharmonic, Concertgebouw Brugge, The MET New York, Kyoto Experiment, Festival Musica Strasbourg, Diaghilev Festival Perm.

Ikeda has received the Prix Ars Electronica Collide@CERN in 2014, and the 70th Japanese Minister of Education Award for Fine Arts (Media Arts Division) in 2020.

1966年、岐阜県生まれ。現在はパリと京都を拠点に活動。電子音楽の作曲家・アーティストとして国際的に活動し、実験的なアート作品も手がける。音、イメージ、物質、物理現象、数学的概念を緻密に編成した没入型のライヴパフォーマンスやインスタレーション作品を発表している。

2008年以来、ポンピドゥー・センター（パリ）、キャリッジワークス（シドニー）、MONA（タスマニア島ホバート）、パーク・アベニュー・アーモリー（ニューヨーク）、東京都現代美術館、コロンビア国立大学美術館（ボゴタ）、カールスルーエ・アート・アンド メディア・センター、アイ・フィルムミュージアム（アムステルダム）、台北市立美術館、180 The Strand（ロンドン）など、世界的に名高い会場で個展を行っている。2022年に弘前れんが倉庫美術館（青森）にて、国内では2009年以来となる大規模な個展を開催。

ラルフ・ルゴフがキュレーションを手がけた2019年の第58回ヴェネツィア・ビエンナーレ「May You Live in Interesting Times」では、オーデマ・ピゲ コンテンポラリーから委託された長期的なオーディオヴィジュアル・プロジェクト《data-verse》が公開された。

またこれまでに、バービカン・センター（ロンドン）、ポンピドゥー・センター、フェスティバル・ドートンヌ（パリ）、ロサンゼルス・フィルハーモニック、コンセルトヘボウ（ブルージュ）、メトロポリタン美術館（ニューヨーク）、Kyoto Experiment京都国際舞台芸術祭、ストラスブール音楽祭、ディアギレフ・フェスティバル（ロシア・ペルミ）などで、アコースティックおよびオーディオヴィジュアル・コンサートを行っている。

2014年、アルス・エレクトロニカのCollide@CERN Award受賞。2020年、第70回芸術選奨文部科学大臣賞（メディア芸術部門）を受賞。

data.flux [LED version]

2021
LED panels, computer, speakers
Concept and composition: Ryoji Ikeda
Computer graphics and programming: Norimichi Hirakawa, Tomonaga Tokuyama
Commissioned by Alternative Kyoto

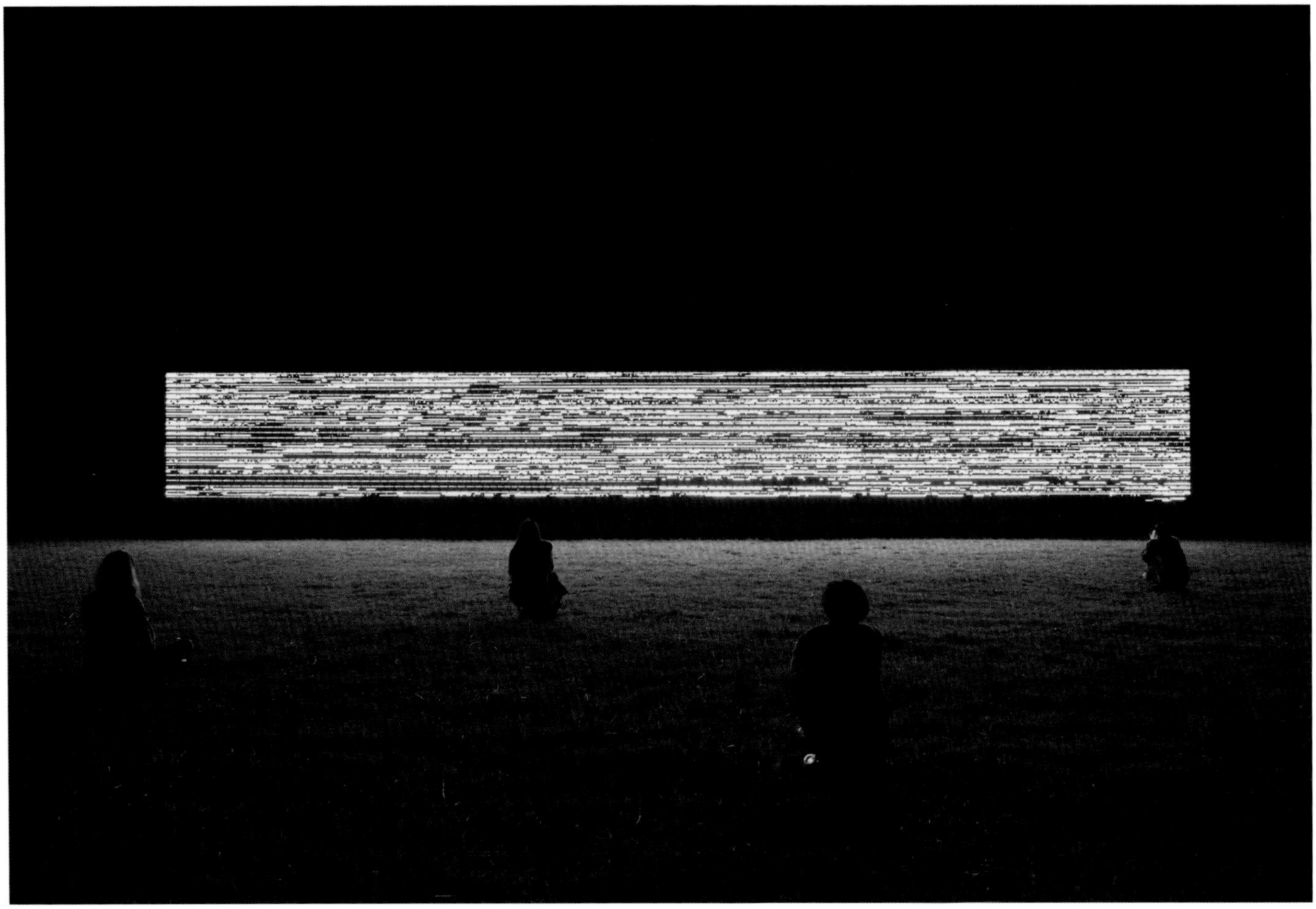

data.flux is a site-specific audiovisual installation by Japan's leading electronic composer/visual artist Ryoji Ikeda.

Data and sounds are fundamentally invisible as entity. The artistic intention of *data.flux* is to make the invisible visible/audible/experienceable and to immerse visitors completely in the site-specific installation.

A video image is displayed on a large LED screen which is a 24-meter long, massive scientific data sets are mathematically depicted on it as maps of the Universe, molecular structures of protein, DNA sequences, 4-dimensional mathematical hypercubes and super-highway of raw data etc.

Both video and sound components are tightly synchronized each other and artistically orchestrated as a whole symphony, which brings "total sensory experiences" to visitors.

data.flux is part of Ikeda's long-term project (since 2006–) called *datamatics* which is an art project that explores the potential to perceive the invisible multi-substance of data that permeates our world. It is a series of experiments in various forms—audiovisual concerts, installations, publications and CD releases—that seek to materialise pure data.

《data.flux》は、日本を代表する作曲家でアーティストでもある池田亮司によるサイトスペシフィックなオーディオヴィジュアル・インスタレーションである。

データとサウンドは、基本的には実体として目に見えるものではない。《data.flux》の芸術的な意図は、不可視なものを可視化、可聴化、体験化し、来場者がその場でしか知覚できないサイトスペシフィックなインスタレーションに完全に没入できるようにすることだ。

全長24メートルの大型LEDスクリーンに映像が映し出され、宇宙の地図、タンパク質の分子構造、DNAの塩基配列、数学的な四次元空間の超立方体「ハイパーキューブ」、生データの情報スーパーハイウェイなど、膨大な科学データ群が数学的に表されていく。

映像と音響の両コンポーネントが緊密に同期し、ひとつの完全なシンフォニーとして芸術的に編成され、来場者に「完全な感覚体験」をもたらすのである。

《data.flux》は、池田が長期にわたって手がけているプロジェクト《datamatics》(2006年–)の一環として制作された。《datamatics》は、我々の世界に浸透しているデータという、目に見えない複雑な実体を知覚する可能性を探るアートプロジェクトだ。純粋なデータの具現化を目指すこの一連の実験は、オーディオヴィジュアル・コンサート、インスタレーション、出版物、CDリリースなど、様々な形で展開されている。

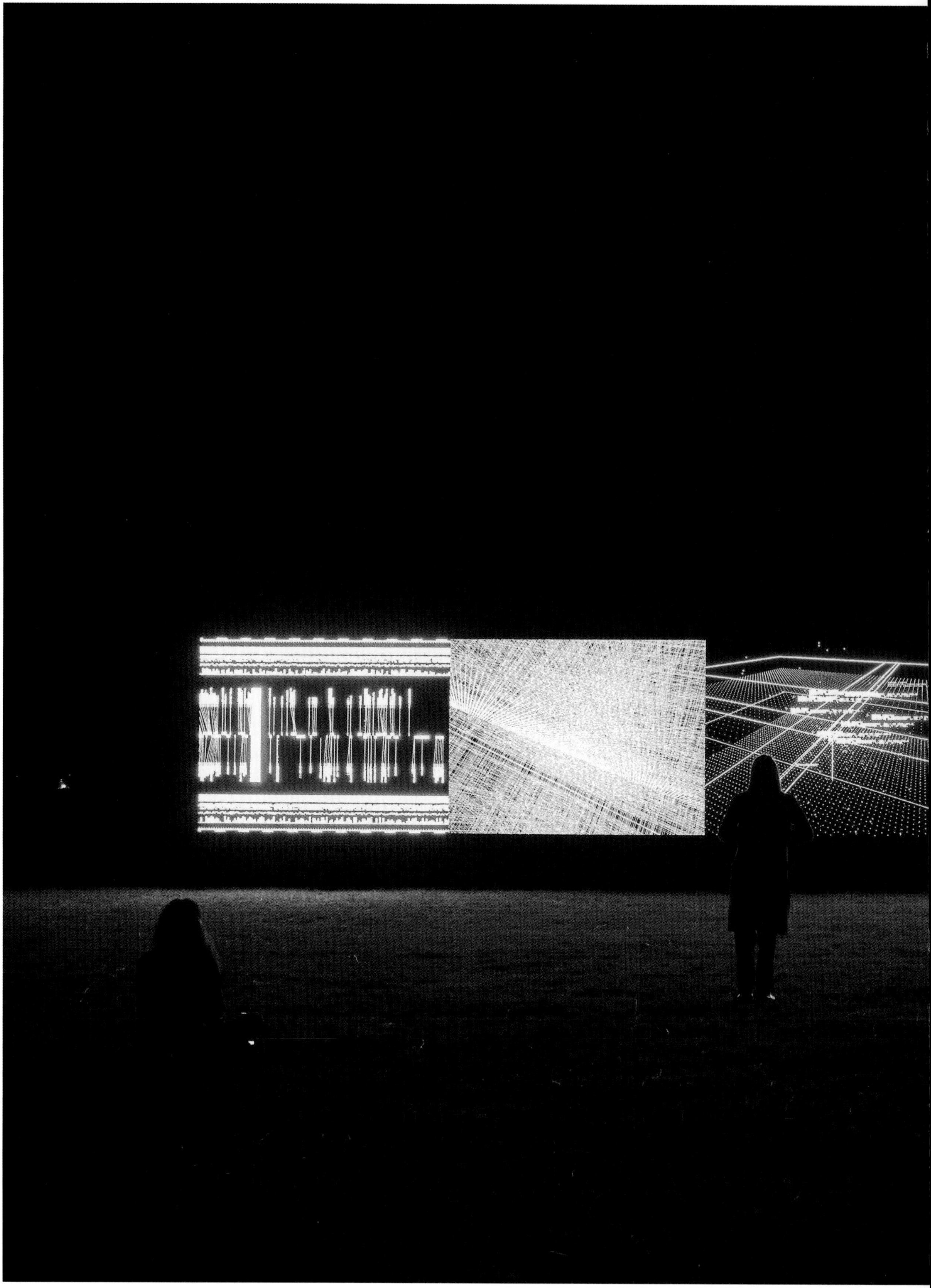

Ryoji Ikeda

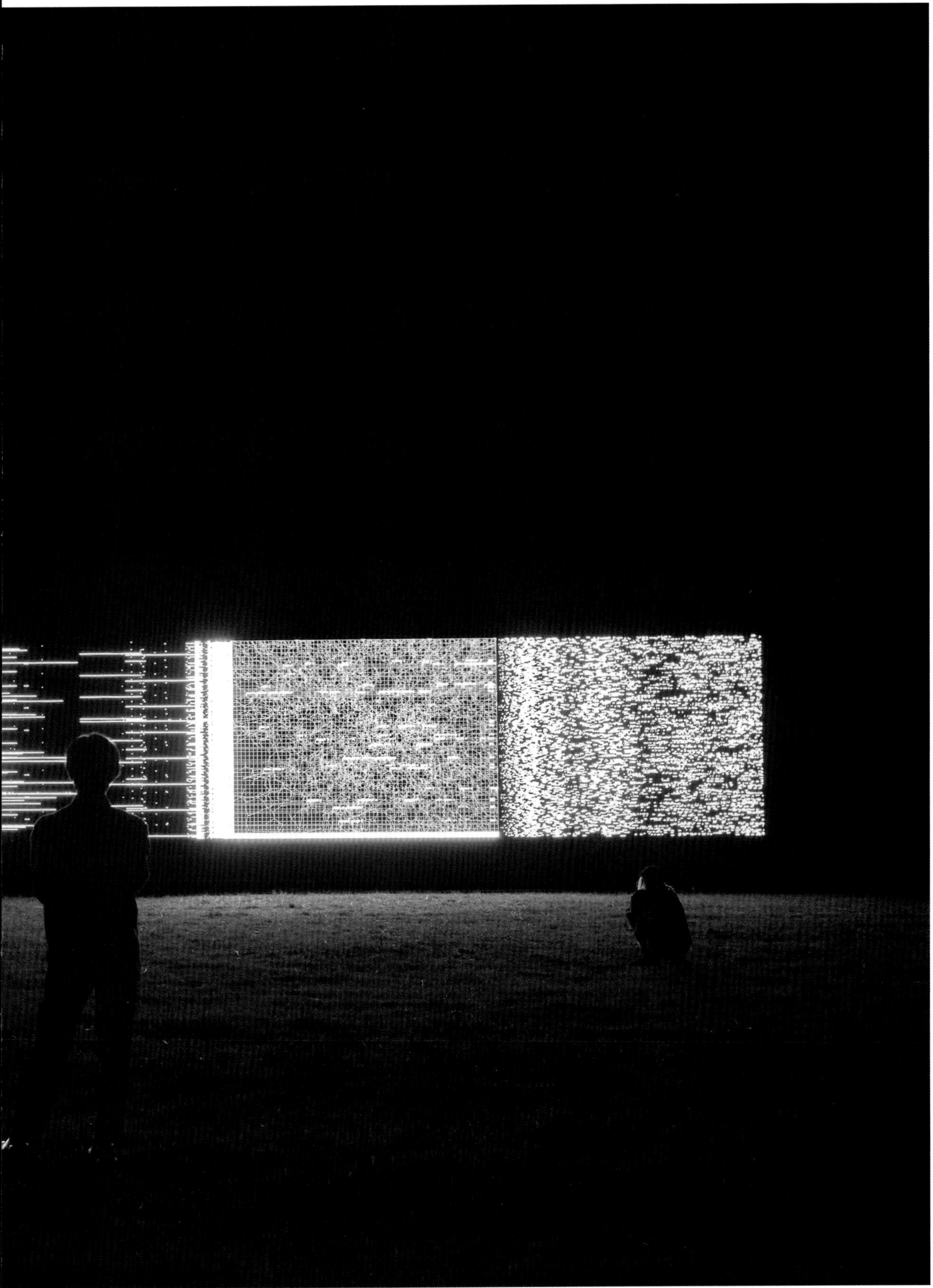

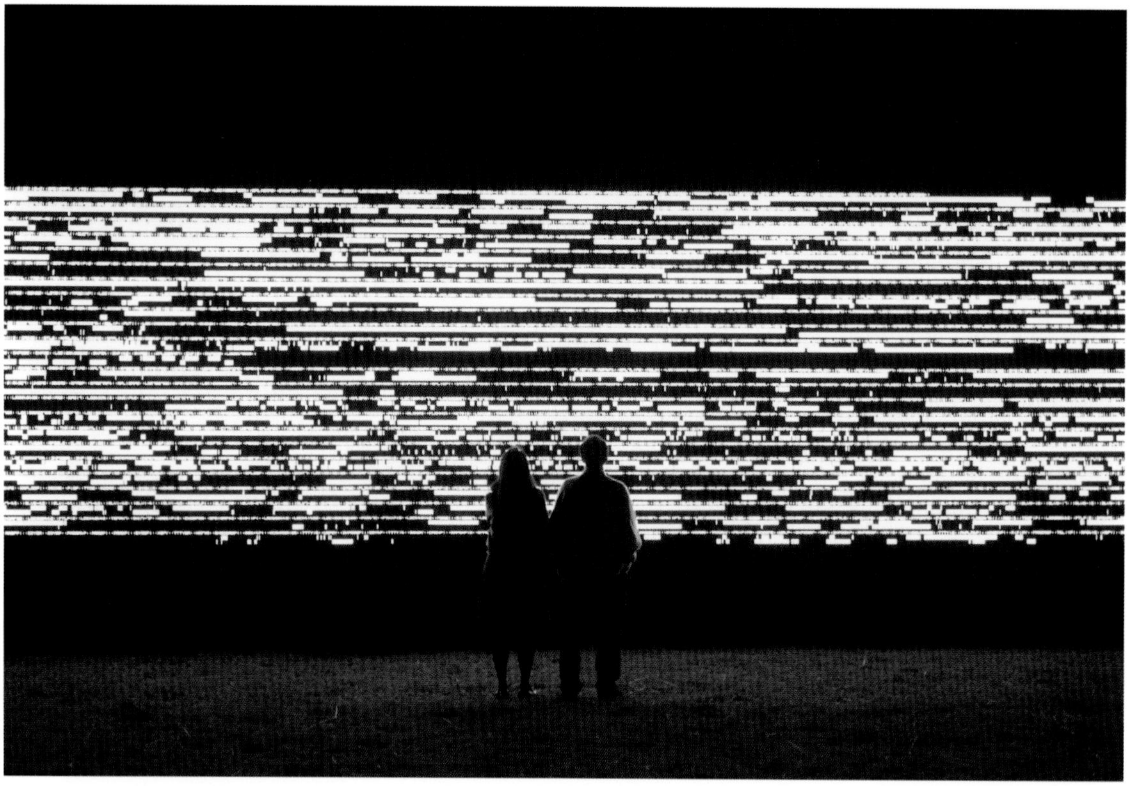

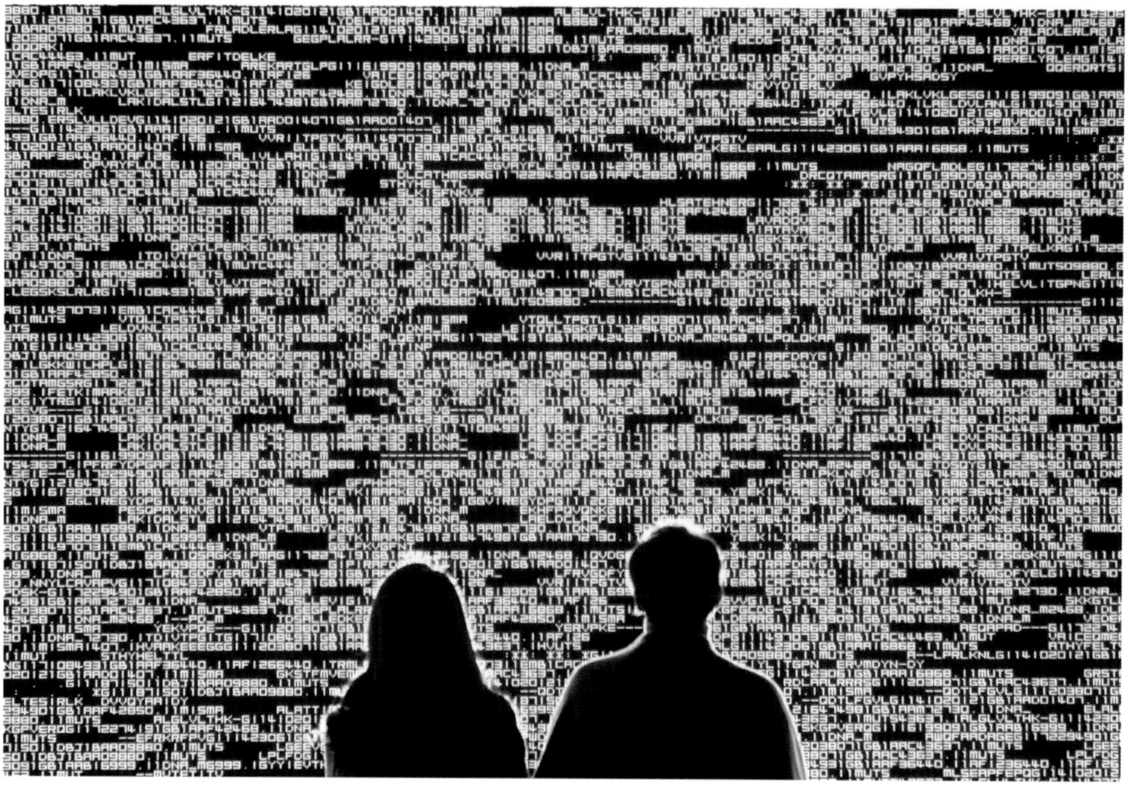

All images on pp. 72–76: *data.flux [LED version]* audiovisual installation, 2021
https://www.ryojiikeda.com/project/datamatics/#data_flux_LED_version

Mari Katayama

片山真理

Born 1987 in Saitama and raised in Gunma, Japan. Graduated with a Master's degree from the Department of Intermedia Art at Tokyo University of the Arts in 2012. Katayama creates hand-sewn objects imitating her body, paintings and collages, intricately arranging them to take self-portraits. In addition to her creative art, she has also worked as singer, fashion model, keynote speaker and writer. Katayama also leads *High Heels Project* in which she wore customized high-heeled shoes specially made for prosthesis to perform on stage.

Her major exhibitions include, *home again*, Maison Européenne de la Photographie, Paris (2021), 58th Venice Biennale, Giardini and Arsenale (2019), *broken heart*, White Rainbow, London (2019), *Photographs of Innocence and of Experience: Contemporary Japanese Photography Vol.14*, Tokyo Photographic Art Museum (2017), *on the way home*, The Museum of Modern Art, Gunma (2017), *Roppongi Crossing: My Body, Your Voice*, Mori Art Museum, Tokyo (2016), Aichi Triennale 2013 (2013). Her major publications include *GIFT* (United Vagabonds, 2019).

She received the Encouraging Prize of Gunma Biennale for Young Artists in 2005, Grand Prix of Art Award Tokyo Marunouchi in 2012, Higashikawa Award for The New Photographer category in 2019 and Kimura Ihei Award in 2020.

1987年、埼玉県生まれ、群馬県育ち。2012年東京藝術大学大学院美術研究科先端芸術表現専攻修士課程修了。自らの身体を模した手縫いのオブジェ、ペインティング、コラージュのほか、それらの作品を用いて細部まで演出を施したセルフポートレイトなど、多彩な作品を制作。アーティストとしての活動に留まらず、歌手、モデル、講演、執筆など、幅広く活動している。作品制作以外の主なプロジェクトとして、2011年より「ハイヒールプロジェクト」を展開。特注の義足用ハイヒールを装着し、ステージに立っている。

主な展示に2021年「home again」ヨーロッパ写真美術館（パリ）、2019年第58回ヴェネツィア・ビエンナーレ、「Broken Heart」White Rainbow（ロンドン）、2017年「無垢と経験の写真 日本の新進作家 vol.14」東京都写真美術館、「帰途—on the way home—」群馬県立近代美術館、2016年「六本木クロッシング 2016展：僕の身体、あなたの声」森美術館（東京）、2013年あいちトリエンナーレ 2013など。主な出版物に2019年『GIFT』(United Vagabonds)がある。

2005年に群馬青年ビエンナーレ奨励賞、2012年アートアワードトーキョー丸の内2012グランプリ、2019年第35回写真の町東川賞新人作家賞、2020年第45回木村伊兵衛写真賞を受賞。

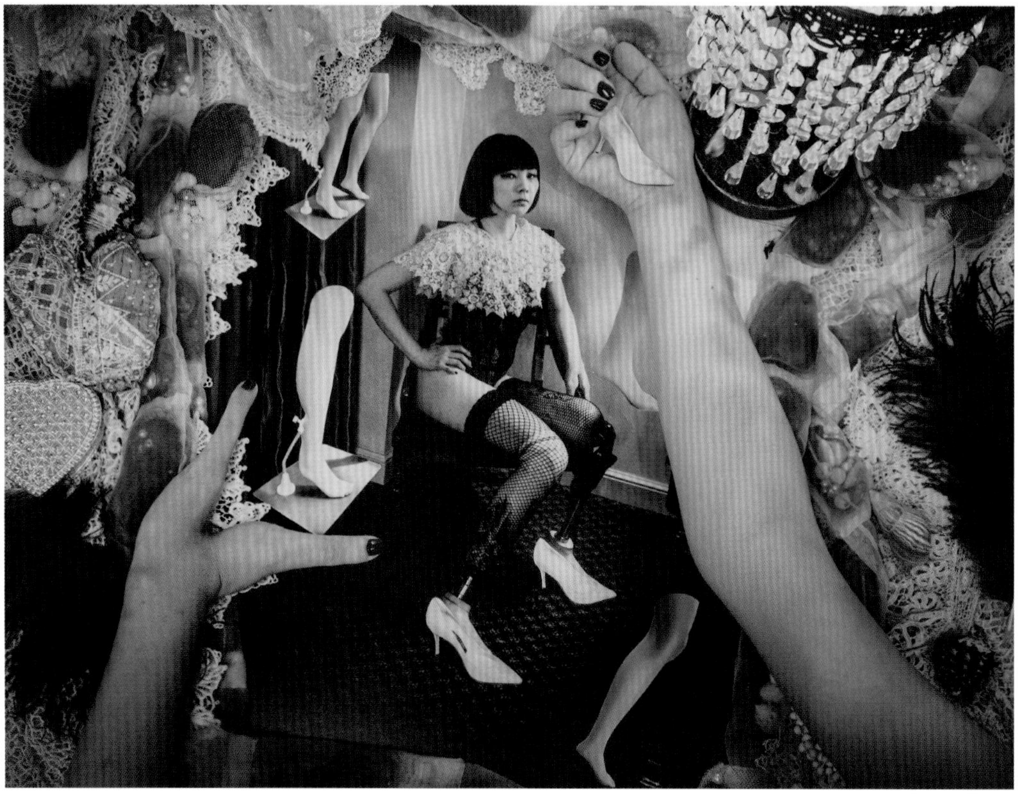

To live as an artist—to be economically active—is to be involved in society, and in this society, I am also a disabled person, a woman, and a mother. In short, I am tagged with various labels.

When I was in my twenties, I often heard people say to me, "If you use your distinctive body as a subject, you will attract attention," or "The reason why your work is highly evaluated is because you are a young disabled girl." Even though I knew that my artwork and myself were two separate things, I strived to live, create, and work "just like a non-disabled person." Sometimes, I acted or pretended to be unfeminine, and sometimes I misrepresented my age.

These days I don't care about that sort of thing, so I don't get depressed on that account anymore. I live a happy life. And I believe that living well is the greatest revenge.

I may be invited to an exhibition and told that "diversity is the theme, so we need artists with disabilities." Or during pregnancy, someone may lecture me that I will bear a child with a disability. Or I may be asked to go to a hotel by someone who says "I'll have sex with you." Or I may be asked to undress in front of a crowd at an airplane inspection or for a portrait shoot without prior warning. But on such occasions, as long as I smile and hold back, I know I'll be fine.

When you are labeled, you effectively become the property of "someone." For example, the "mother" tag doesn't only mark one as the mother of a particular child. For some reason, when people are labeled with the "disabled" tag, they tend to be treated as if they belonged to everyone in society. It reminds me of an "standpoint" I had forgotten about. That realization resonates through my frustrated and yet unprotected body and mind and is not easy to dispel. This sort of experience makes a stronger impression on me than any words of love I might receive, and it is something I am sure I will never forget. That's why I want to use my work as a spear while using this echo as a shield to protect my love.

August 5, 2022
Mari Katayama

just one of those things #002, 2021
C-print
© Mari Katayama

作家として生きること＝経済活動をしていくことは社会に関わることであり、この社会では、私は障害者であり、女であり、母であり、いろんなタグがついている。

20代の頃は、「特異な身体を被写体にすれば注目されるだろう」、「君の作品が評価されるのは君自身が障害者で若い女の子だからだよ」という言葉を投げかけられることがよくあった。作品と私自身は別物だとわかっていても、私自身が「健常者のような」生活や制作、作品ができるよう努力した。時に女性的ではないように振る舞ったり、装ったり、年齢を偽ることもあった。

この頃はそんなこと気にも留めないから、そのせいで落ち込むこともなくなった。幸せな日々を過ごしている。よりよく生きることは最大の復讐だ。

「ダイバーシティがテーマだから障害者が必要なんだ」と展示に誘われたり、妊娠に際して「障害のある子が生まれる」と他人に説教されたり、「セックスしてあげる」とホテルに呼び出されたり、飛行機の検査やポートレートの撮影で突然大勢の前で「脱ぎますか」と言われることもあるけれど、笑顔でぐっと我慢すれば大丈夫。

タグをつけられると、「誰か」の所有物になってしまう。たとえば、「母」のタグはその子のものだけじゃない。「障害者」というタグをつけられるとなぜか社会みんなのものにされがちだ。忘れていた「立場」を思い出させてくれる。その気づきは、悔しいけれど無防備な体と心に響き渡ってなかなか出ていかない。この経験はどんな愛の言葉よりも強く、きっと一生忘れることはないだろう。だからこそ作品を矛にして、この響きを盾にして、愛を守りたい。

2022年8月5日
片山真理

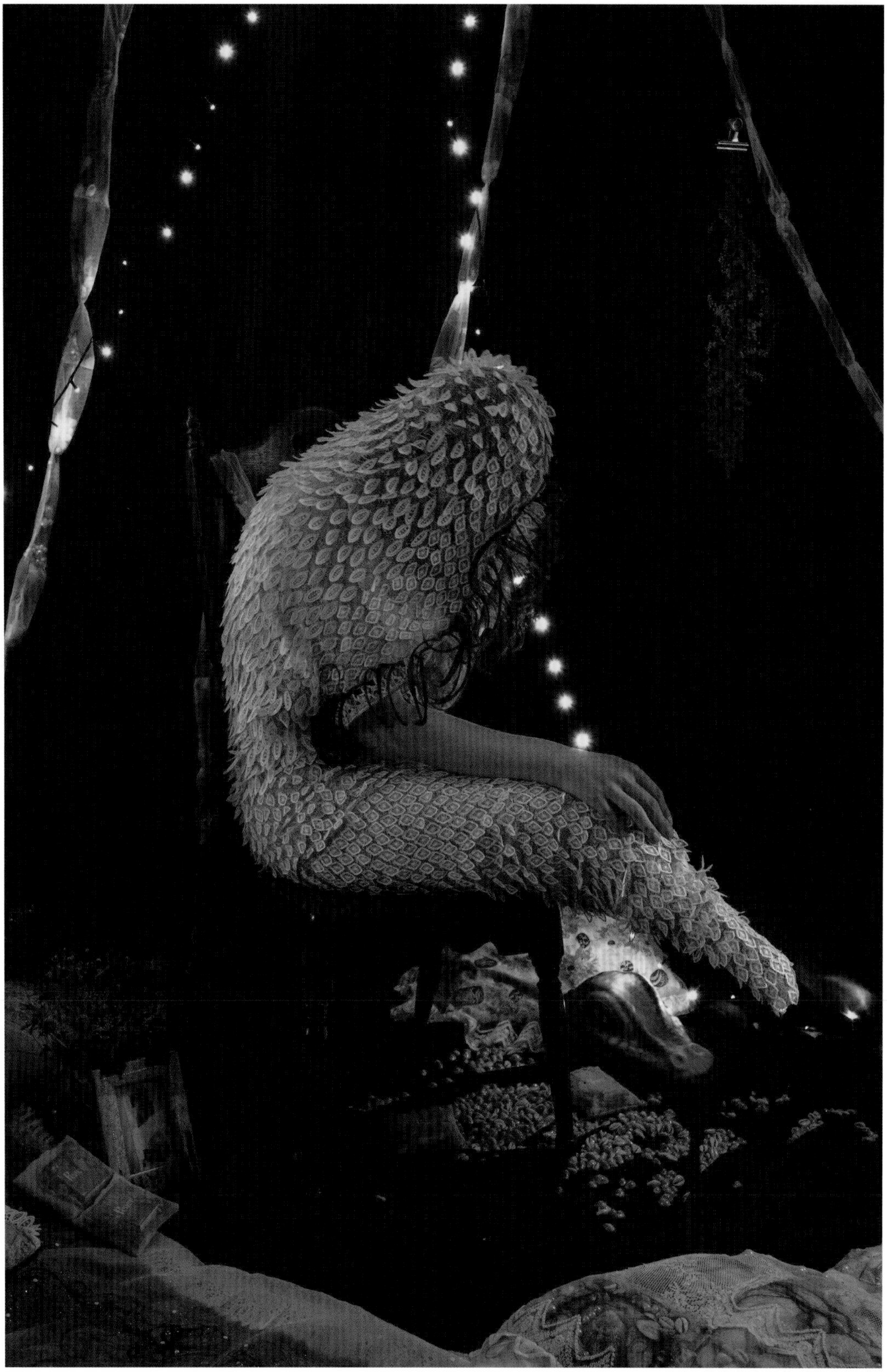

possession #2429, 2022
C-print

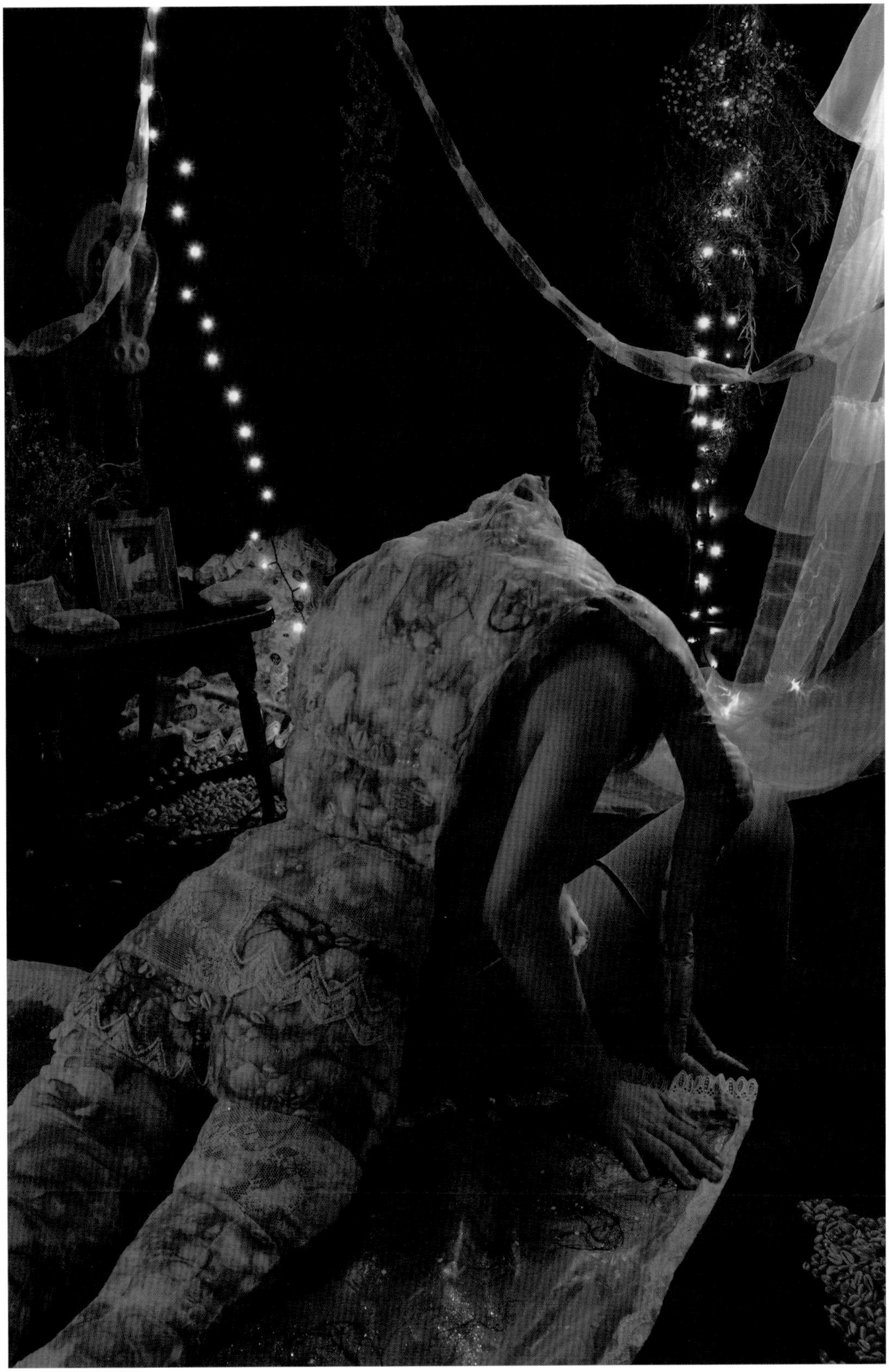

possession #2411, 2022
C-print

cycadopsida, 2016
C-print

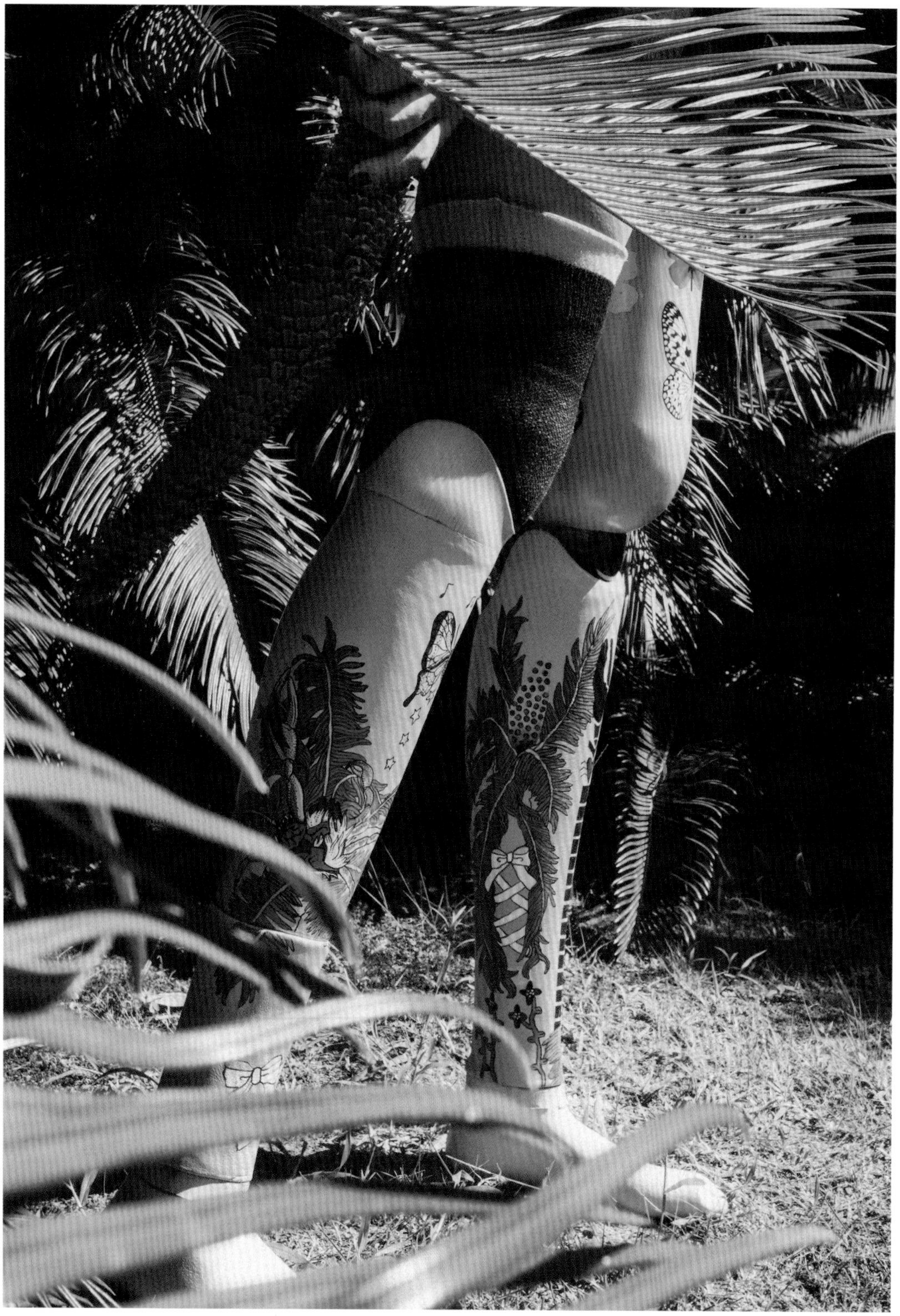

My-Linh Le

ミー・リン・ル

Le grew up in San Jose, California where she began dancing as a teenager in the early 2000s. The Vietnamese-, Mexican-, Black-, Samoan- and Filipino- American street dancers that surrounded her are reflected in her dance crew, Playboyz Inc., which was established in 1981 by a group of Chicanos who popularized the San Jose style of popping. As the first woman ever to represent the globally renowned dance crew, she has taught workshops, competed in and judged dance battles all over the world. Le's experience with various street dance communities throughout the years has been a large influence on her work as an interdisciplinary storyteller. From immersive installations that embolden audiences to explore their own natural dance movement, to films that examine the autoethnographic aspects of dance improvisation, Le's works present dance not only as an artistic medium or form, but as a method of knowing and remembering, as a way of relating and connecting, and as an instrument for liberation and restoration. In 2021, Le received a Special Award in Choreography from the Gerbode Foundation for her work with the turf dance collective she founded in Oakland, known as Mud Water Theatre. She wrote and directed a narrative dance film by the same title, *MUD WATER*, which premiered at the 65th San Francisco International Film Festival (SFFILM).

Her other major works include *ANIMA*, San Francisco (2022), *THE ORIGIN STORY OF NO NAME*, San Francisco (2021), *TRONG NUOC*, Tempe, USA (2020), and *THE REVERSE TURING TEST*, Chiang Mai (2017).

カリフォルニア州サンノゼ育ち。

2000年代初め、10代の頃よりダンスを始める。サンノゼスタイルのポップダンスを広めたチカーノのグループによって1981年に設立されたPlayboyz Inc.に所属。ベトナム系、メキシコ系、アフリカ系、サモア系、フィリピン系アメリカ人から成るストリートダンサーメンバーと共に活動。

世界的なダンスクルーを代表する初の女性ダンサーとして、ワークショップ講師を務めるほか、ダンスバトルに出場者、また審査員として参加するなど、国際的に活躍している。長年にわたる様々なストリートダンス・コミュニティでの経験は、様々な分野にまたがって活躍するストーリーテラーとしての彼女の活動に大きな影響を与えている。

自然に湧き出るダンスの動きを観客から引き出す没入型インスタレーションや、即興ダンスを自己エスノグラフィー的な解釈から探る映像など、ルの作品は、ダンスを単なる表現媒体や形式としてだけではなく、知ることや思い返すこと、相互に関係しつながること、そして解放と回復のための手法として提示している。2021年、オークランドで結成したターフダンス・グループ「Mud Water Theatre」の作品がGerbode財団の振付部門で特別賞を受賞。また、同グループから名前をとったダンス映像作品《MUD WATER》の脚本・監督を務め、本作は第65回サンフランシスコ国際映画祭(SFFILM)で初上映された。その他の代表作に、2022年《ANIMA》(サンフランシスコ)、2021年《THE ORIGIN STORY OF NO NAME》(サンフランシスコ)、2020年《TRONG NUOC》(アメリカ・テンピ)、2017年《THE REVERSE TURING TEST》(チェンマイ)などがある。

demons of good dreams

2022
Performance, video installation

Momotaro appeared *everywhere* in Okayama, from the moment I arrived at the airport, and all throughout my visit. However, it was not until I was introduced to the Urajya Odori Festival dancers at the Okayama sports ground, where various teams rehearsed their choreography, that I became interested in Momotaro's history, what he meant to them, and more broadly, the modernization and transformation of mythological symbols into tools to construct and reinforce political narratives. However, *demons of good dreams* looks beyond the folktale as allegory for Japanese nationalism and imperial militarism, using personal movement practices as a vehicle to dive further into the personal myths and dreams of the featured dancers, and the demons that reside there. *demons of good dreams* is a collection of screen dances and live performances that collage material from life and myth based on a series of private workshops that were held in Okayama during my first site visit, and that will carry on in my second site visit, which is also when the screen dances will be filmed and edited.

岡山では、あらゆる場所に「桃太郎」が現れる。空港に到着した瞬間から、それこそ私の滞在期間を通じて至るところで目にしてきた。だが、私が桃太郎の歴史に興味をもつようになったのは、「おかやま桃太郎まつり うらじゃ」で踊るダンサーたち「うらじゃ踊り連」を紹介され、岡山のスポーツグラウンドで行われていた様々なチームの振付練習に接したときだった。桃太郎は、このダンサーたちにとってどのような存在なのか。さらに話を広げれば、昔話の象徴的な存在が近代化され、また変容され、政治的な物語の構築やその強化のための道具となったのはどういうことなのか。だが、《demons of good dreams》は、日本の国家主義や帝国時代の軍国主義の寓意（アレゴリー）としての昔話を超え、その先へと目をやる作品である。主役となるダンサーたち個々人の動きの鍛錬を見ることを通じて、そのダンサーたちの私的な神話と夢を、さらにはそこに棲まう鬼たちを深く探っていこうとしているのだ。スクリーンダンスとライヴパフォーマンスを組み合わせる《demons of good dreams》は、一連のプライヴェートなワークショップをもとにして、現実のダンサーたちと神話から集めた素材をコラージュする作品だ。ワークショップは、私が最初に岡山を訪れた際に開催したものだが、2度目となる滞在時にも継続し、その際にスクリーンダンスの撮影・編集も行う予定だ。

My-Linh Le

COME
TOGETHER

SMALL
DROPLETS
OF WATER
MAKE
A
BEAUTIFUL
OCEAN

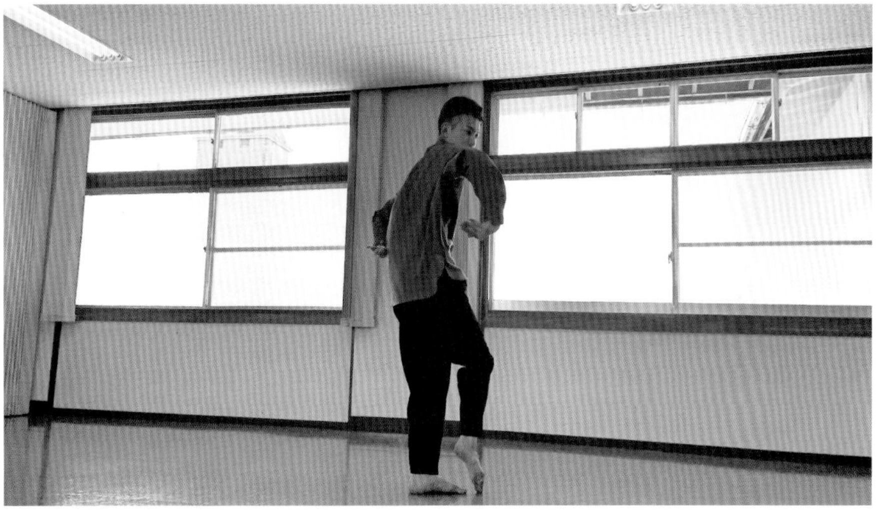

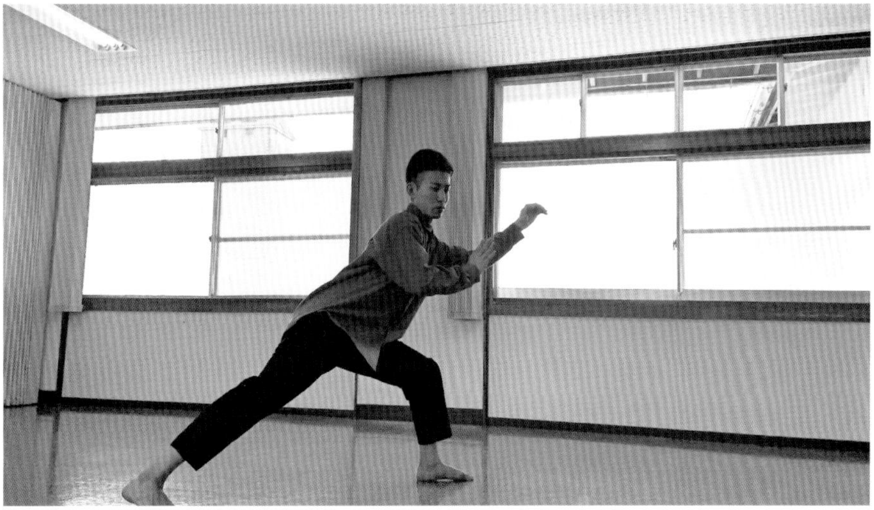

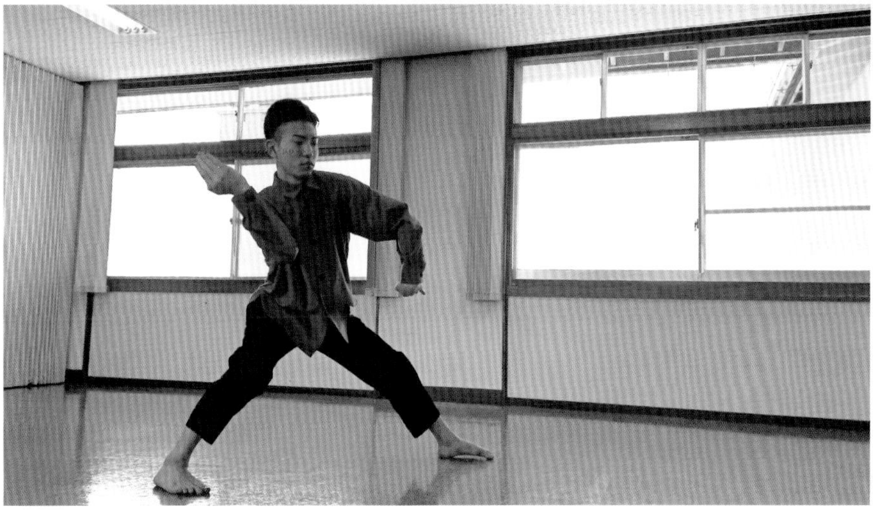

Still taken from the video *demons of good dreams*, courtesy of My-Linh Le.
《demons of good dreams》のヴィデオより

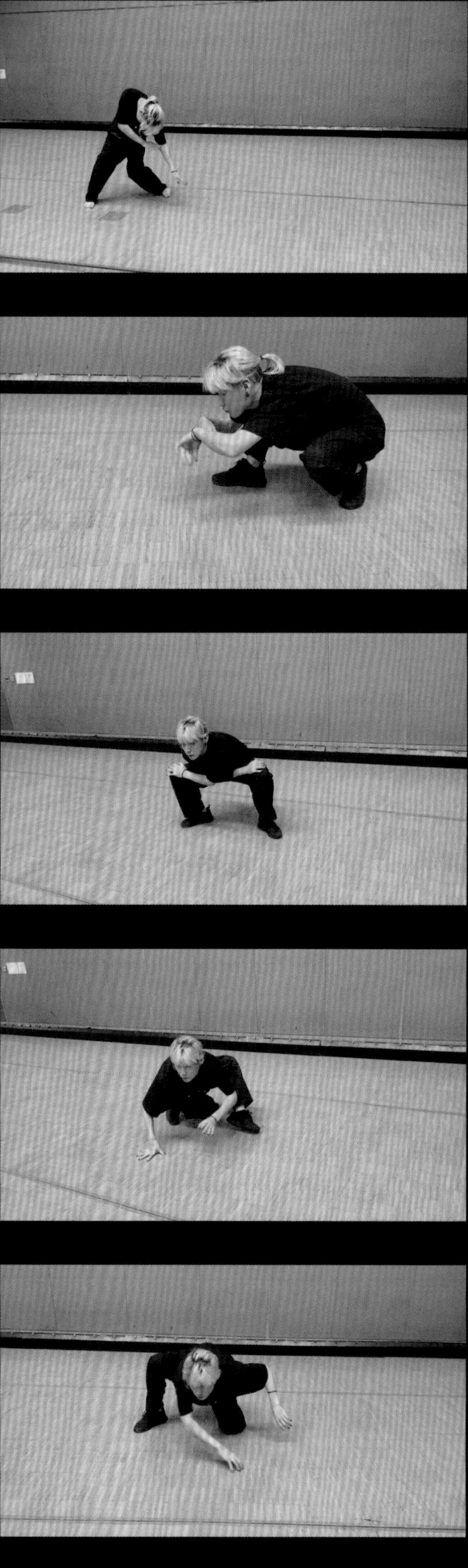

Still taken from the video *demons of good dreams*, courtesy of My-Linh Le.

MUD WATER

2022
Video
30 min.

Turfing is a dance style that originated in Oakland, California in the early 2000s. But for us, it's much more than a dance trend—it's also an entire community, a living, breathing culture. As a dancer born and raised in the Bay to war refugees from Vietnam, I found in turfing a kinetic archive of stories and histories that had long been left out of our libraries.

Mud Water is a film by dancers for dancers, the result of a 5-year-long collaboration between the cast and myself. I initially founded Mud Water Theatre as a performance collective based in Oakland, with the mission of expanding the contexts in which turfing is usually seen: rather than in subway cars and public sidewalks, we insisted that turfing also belonged in the theater.

More than a film about dancers, it is a meditative exploration of the hidden or abandoned parts of ourselves, told through two simultaneous plot lines: one is the story of how everything came to have a shadow, the other is the story of the kinship bonds of one's "chosen family" and the journey of self-discovery. As a dancer first and filmmaker second, it was important to me to broaden the existing body of dance films, beyond the documentaries that portray strange, underground dance worlds, and beyond the flashy hip hop dance films that center white celebrity actors in action-packed choreography. I wanted to make the kind of film that I have longed to see: one that recognizes dance as metaphor, as mythology, as narrative poetry, rather than as gimmick. *Mud Water* is thus a way of filmmaking that incorporates the movement, breath, suspension and flow of dance-making.

ターフィングは、2000年代初頭にカリフォルニア州オークランドで生まれたダンスのスタイルだ。しかし、我々にとっては、ダンスのトレンドという以上のもので、コミュニティ全体であり、生きて、呼吸をしている文化でもある。ベトナム難民の親の元、ベイエリア（カリフォルニア）に生まれ育ったダンサーとして、ターフィングは、長い間図書館に取り残されていた物語や歴史の動的なアーカイヴだと感じる。

《Mud Water》はダンサーによるダンサーのための映画で、出演者と私自身の5年にわたるコラボレーションにより制作した。まず、ターフィングがいつも見られる状況を広めることを目標として、オークランドを拠点とするパフォーマンスグループ、Mud Water Theatre（マッド・ウォーター・シアター）を結成した。つまり、地下鉄の電車内や公共の歩道に限らず、劇場もターフィングの場であると主張したのだ。

本作は、ダンサーを描いた映画というよりも、我々自身の隠された、もしくは見捨てられた部分についての瞑想的な探求であり、2つの筋書きが同時進行で語られている。ひとつは、すべてのものが影をもつようになった物語で、もうひとつは、「選ばれし家族」の親族の絆と自分探しの旅の物語だ。ダンサーであることが第一で、映像作家は第二とする私にとって、既存のダンス映画の幅を広げること——奇妙でアンダーグラウンドなダンスの世界を描くドキュメンタリーや、著名な白人俳優を中心にアクション満載の振付で派手に踊るヒップホップダンス映画の枠を超えること——が重要だった。私自身が見たいと思っていたような映画、つまり、ダンスをギミック（人目を引くための仕掛けや道具）としてではなく、隠喩や神話、物語詩として認めるような作品をつくりたかった。ゆえに、《Mud Water》は、動作、呼吸、ゆっくりと浮遊するような状態やダンスを構成するフローを取り入れた映画制作の方法である。

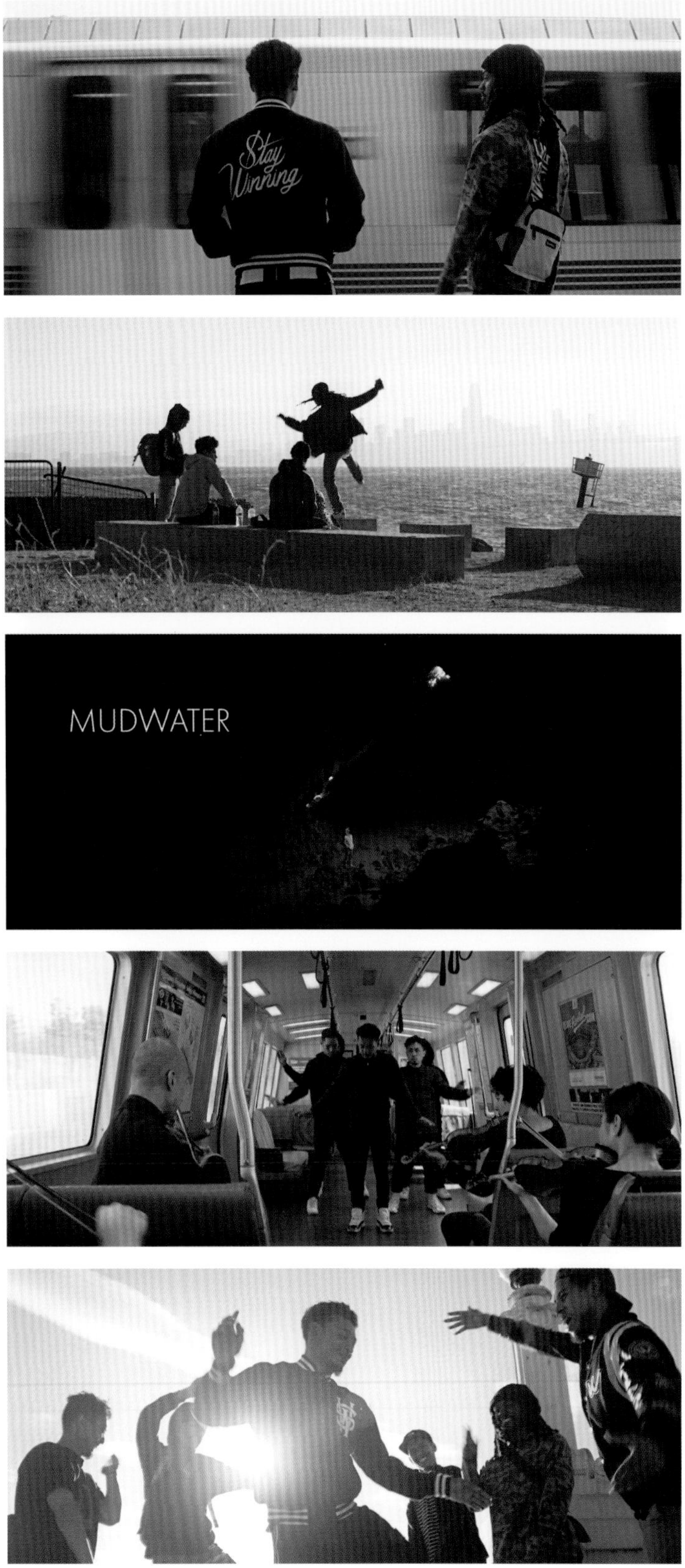

Still from the short film *Mud Water* (2022) which premiered at the 65th San Francisco International Film Festival
Courtesy of the artist
第65回サンフランシスコ国際映画祭で初上映された《Mud Water》より

David Medalla

デヴィッド・メダラ

David Medalla (1942–2020) was a Filipino international artist. His work ranged from sculpture and kinetic art to painting, installation and performance art. He lived and worked, amongst other places, in Manila, London, New York City and Paris.

Medalla was born in Manila, the Philippines, in 1942. At the age of 12 he was admitted at Columbia University in New York upon the recommendation of American poet Mark van Doren, and he studied ancient Greek drama with Moses Hadas, modern drama with Eric Bentley, modern literature with Lionel Trilling, modern philosophy with John Randall and attended the poetry workshops of Léonie Adams.

Strongly influenced by 19th and 20th century European art and literature, and an active figure in postwar London avant garde communities, Medalla was instrumental in the brief but pioneering experience of London's Signals Gallery (1962–1964), the experimental performance collective The Exploding Galaxy (1967–1968) and the politically engaged Artists for Democracy, of which he was president (1974–1977). In collaboration with the artist Adam Nankervis (1994) he founded The Mondrian Fan Club and the London Biennale (2000), where processes of collaboration and exchange continued to take centre stage.

His work was included in Harald Szeemann's exhibition *Weiss auf Weiss* (1966), *Live in Your Head: When Attitudes Become Form* (1969), and in the documenta 5 (1972).

During many years, Medalla remained a prolific artist and engaged in numerous biennials, such as the Biennale of Sydney, London Biennale, Johannesburg Biennale and the 8th Asia Pacific Triennial of Contemporary Art, as well as being a part of international exhibitions at renowned institutions, such as Tate Liverpool, Centre Pompidou, Paris, the New Museum, New York, Institute of Contemporary Arts London, Secession Vienna, and DAAD Galerie in Berlin, to only name a few.

In 2017 he took part in in *Viva Arte Viva*, the 57th International Art Exhibition of the Venice Biennale, curated by Christine Macel, with the reactivation of the performance *A Stitch in Time* and *the Mondrian Fan Club* with Adam Nankervis. David Medalla passed away in December 2020 in Manila. His archive is kept in Berlin by another vacant space.

デヴィッド・メダラ（1942–2020年）は、フィリピン出身の国際的アーティスト。作品は彫刻やキネティックアート、絵画、インスタレーション、パフォーマンスアートまで多岐にわたる。生前はマニラのほか、ロンドン、ニューヨーク、パリにも滞在し、芸術活動を行った。1942年、マニラに生まれ、アメリカの詩人、マーク・ヴァン・ドーレンの推薦により、12歳でニューヨークのコロンビア大学への入学が認められる。また、モーゼズ・ハダスのもとで古代ギリシャ演劇を学んだほか、現代演劇をエリック・ベントレー、現代文学をライオネル・トリリング、現代哲学をジョン・ランドールに師事し、またレオニー・アダムズによる詩のワークショップにも参加。

19世紀および20世紀のヨーロッパの芸術や文学に強く影響を受け、戦後ロンドンの前衛芸術界でも活躍。ロンドンのSignals Gallery（1962–1964年）での短期ながらも先駆的な取り組みや、実験的パフォーマンス集団「The Exploding Galaxy」（1967–1968年）で中心的役割を果たし、政治的活動を展開する「Artists for Democracy」では1974年から1977年にかけて会長を務めた。また芸術家のアダム・ナンカービスと共に1994年に「モンドリアン・ファンクラブ」を、さらに2000年には「ロンドン・ビエンナーレ」を創設し、コラボレーションや交流を主軸とした継続的な活動を展開した。

作品は、ハラルド・ゼーマンのキュレーションによる「Weiss auf Weiss」（1966年）、「Live in Your Head: When Attitudes Become Form（態度が形になるとき）」（1969年）、ドクメンタ5（1972年）などで展示されている。

加えて、シドニー・ビエンナーレ、ロンドン・ビエンナーレ、ヨハネスブルグ・ビエンナーレ、第8回アジア・パシフィック・トリエンナーレなどの国際芸術祭をはじめ、テート・リヴァプール、ポンピドゥー・センター（パリ）、ニュー・ミュージアム（ニューヨーク）、インスティテュート・オブ・コンテンポラリー・アート（ロンドン）、セセッション館（ウィーン）、DAADギャラリー（ベルリン）を含む著名な美術館や施設での国際展示にも出展するなど、長年にわたり多数の作品を発表し続けた。

2017年には、クリスティーヌ・マセルがキュレーションを務めた第57回ヴェネツィア・ビエンナーレ企画展「Viva Arte Viva」にて、自身のパフォーマンス作品「A Stitch in Time」の再演および、ナンカービスとの共同作品である「モンドリアン・ファンクラブ」を披露。2020年12月、マニラにて死去。作品のアーカイヴはベルリンのanother vacant space.に収蔵されている。

"The initial inspiration for my first sand machine came from my memories of the rice terraces of the mountain provinces of the Philippines, where I spent one year of my boyhood as a student at St. Mary's School in Sagada. I also witnessed a sandstorm in the Sahara desert [sic] on my way to Europe in the spring of 1960.

I gave the title Lament to my first sand machine because I thought of the death of metal. The other sand machines I made, for the exhibition *Force Fields* curated by Guy Brett at MACBA in Barcelona, and at the Hayward Gallery in London in 2000, were of a more festive nature and reminded me of the happy times I spent on the beaches in the Philippine Islands, like the island of Cebu where my mother came from."

David Medalla

—Quote from Guy Brett, *Exploding Galaxies – The Art of David Medalla* (London: Kala Press, 1995), 56.

「サンド・マシンはフィリピンのマウンテン州の棚田から着想を得ました。サガダ村のセント・メアリー・スクールで一年を過ごした少年時代の思い出です。1960年の春にヨーロッパへ向かう途中、サハラ砂漠で砂嵐を見たこともあります。

金属の死という連想から、最初のサンド・マシンは『Lament（嘆き）』と名づけました。2000年にバルセロナ現代美術館とロンドンのヘイワード・ギャラリーでガイ・ブレット氏のキュレーションによる展覧会『Force Fields』が行われましたが、それに向けて制作したサンド・マシンはより祝祭的で、母の故郷であるセブ島やフィリピン諸島のビーチでの幸せな時間を思い起こさせるものとなりました。」

デヴィッド・メダラ

引用元：ガイ・ブレッド『Exploding Galaxies – The Art of David Medalla』（ロンドン：Kala Press、1995年）、56頁。

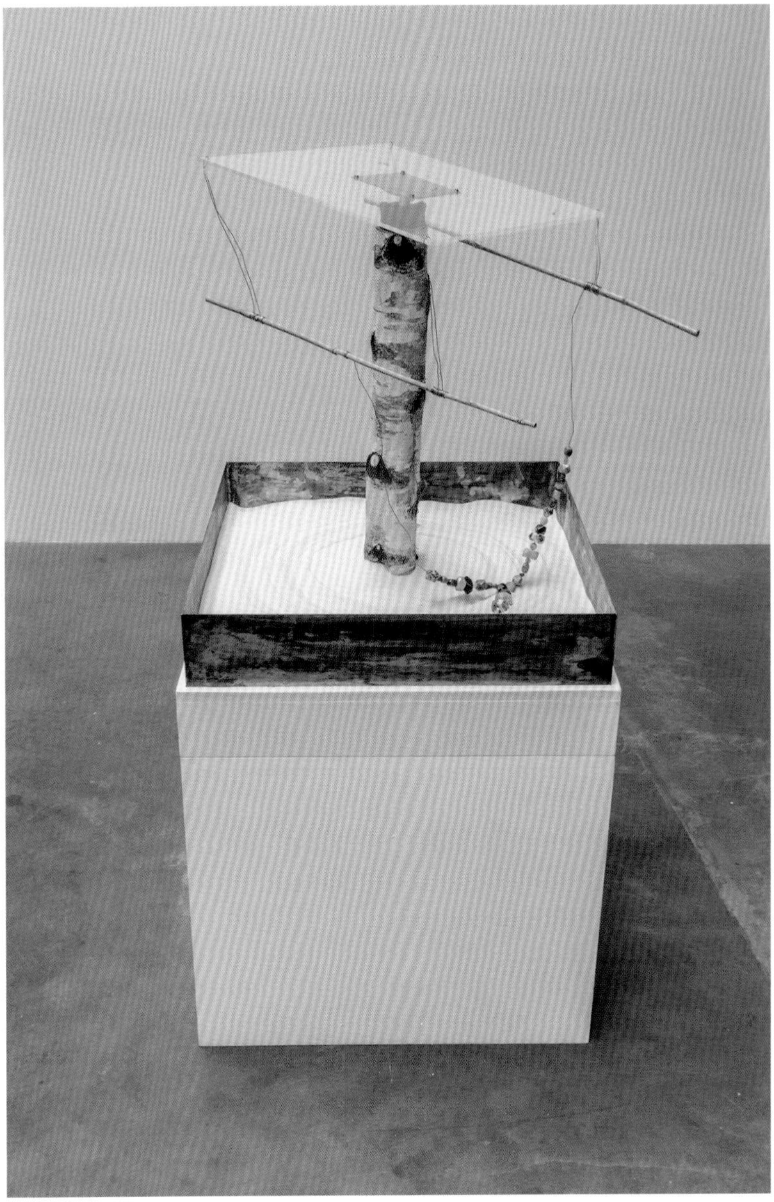

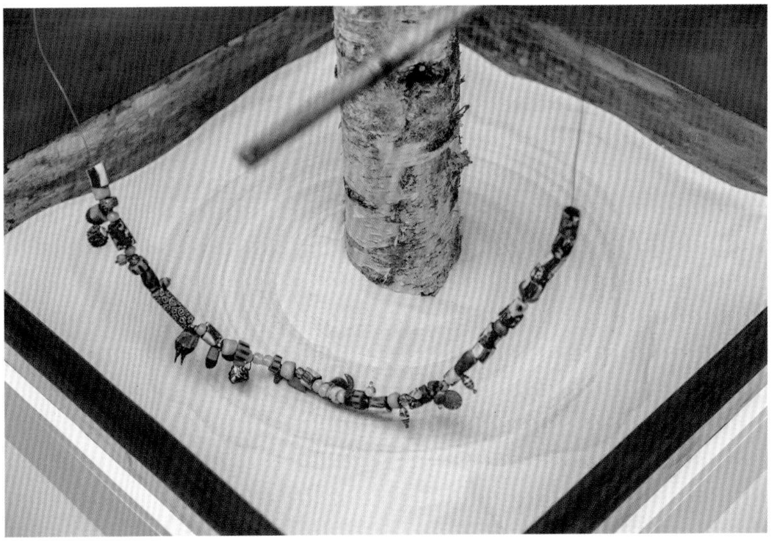

Sand Machine Bahag- Hari Trance #1, 1963–2015
Wood, copper, brass, sand, glass, electrical timers
124 × 60 × 60 cm
Image courtesy of kurimanzutto, Mexico City/New York
Photo: Omar Luis Olguín

Mohole Flower, 1968
Graphite on paper
Paper size: 26 × 20 cm
Framed dimensions: 43 × 36.3 × 3.5 cm
Signed by David Medalla

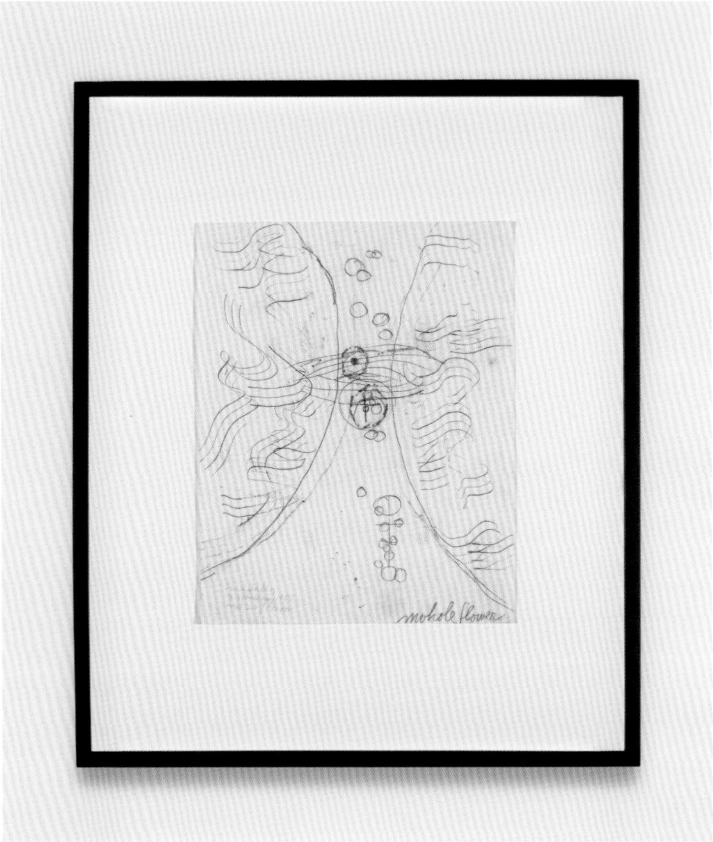

Mohole Sculpture, 1968 Paris
Ink on paper
Paper size: 32 × 20.5 cm
Framed dimensions: 43 × 36.3 × 3.5 cm
Signed by David Medalla

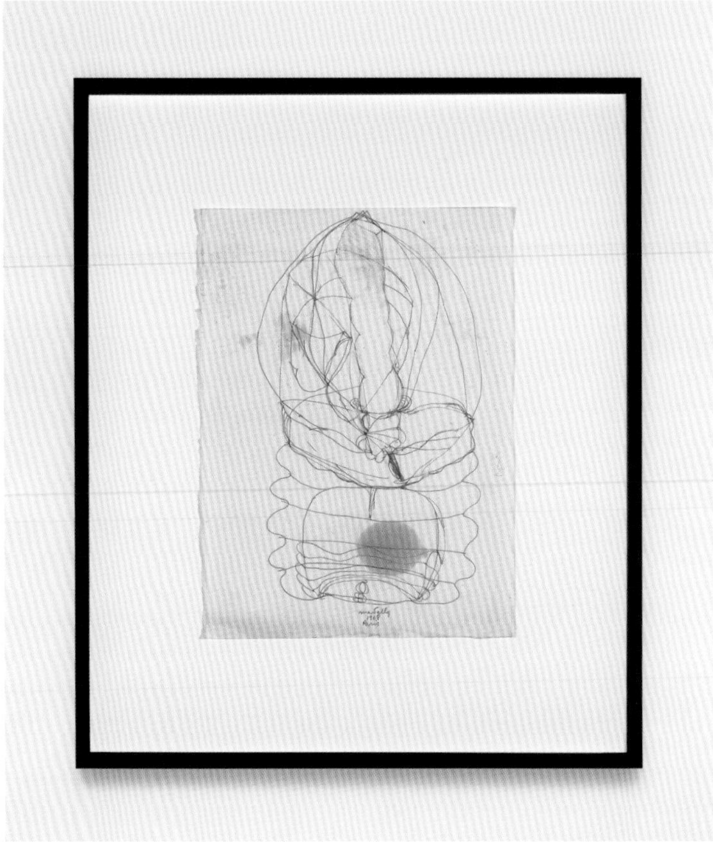

Study for a Monumental Peelable Sculpture, 1967
Ink on paper
Paper size: 25.4 × 20.3 cm
Framed dimensions: 43 × 36.3 × 3.5 cm
for francís /ponge poet,/ with admiration/and/affection,/ David Medalla

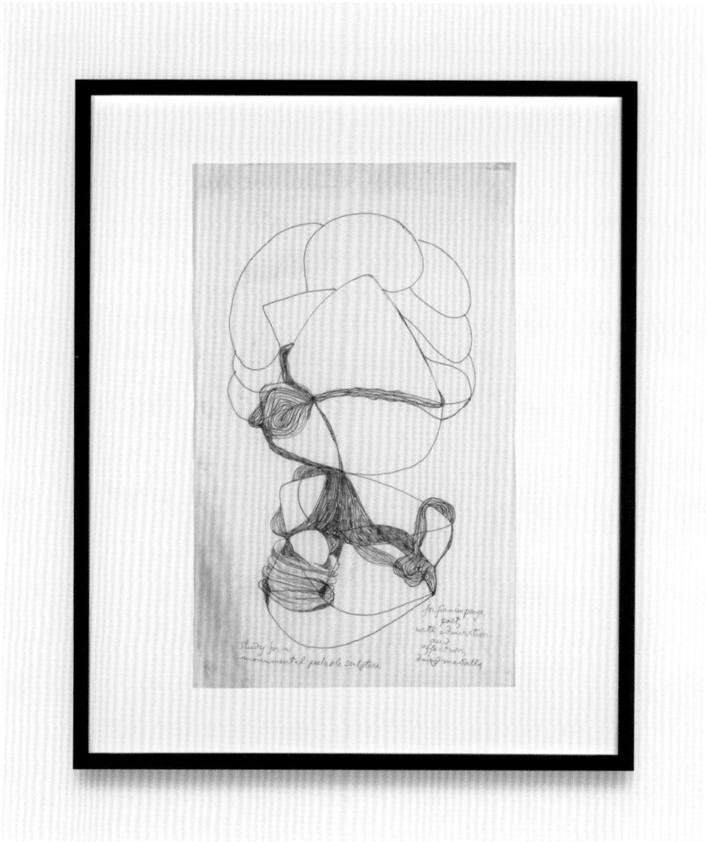

The Mountain, 1975
Collage
Paper size: 25.4 × 20.3 cm
Framed dimensions: 43 × 36.3 × 3.5 cm
Signed by David Medalla

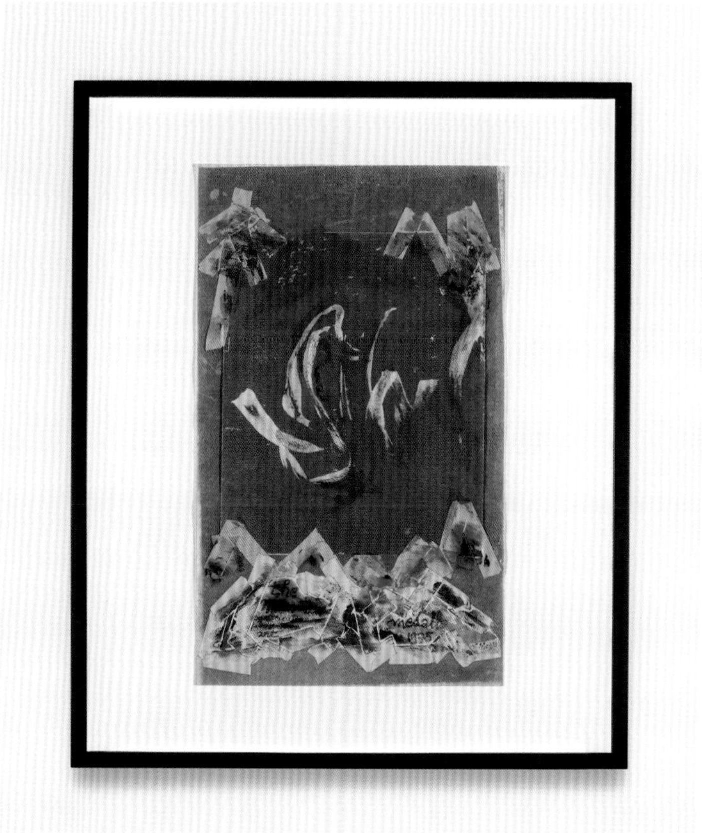

Chartres Cathedral – Homage to Arthur Rimbaud, 1960
China ink on paper
Paper size: 50.5 × 34.5 cm

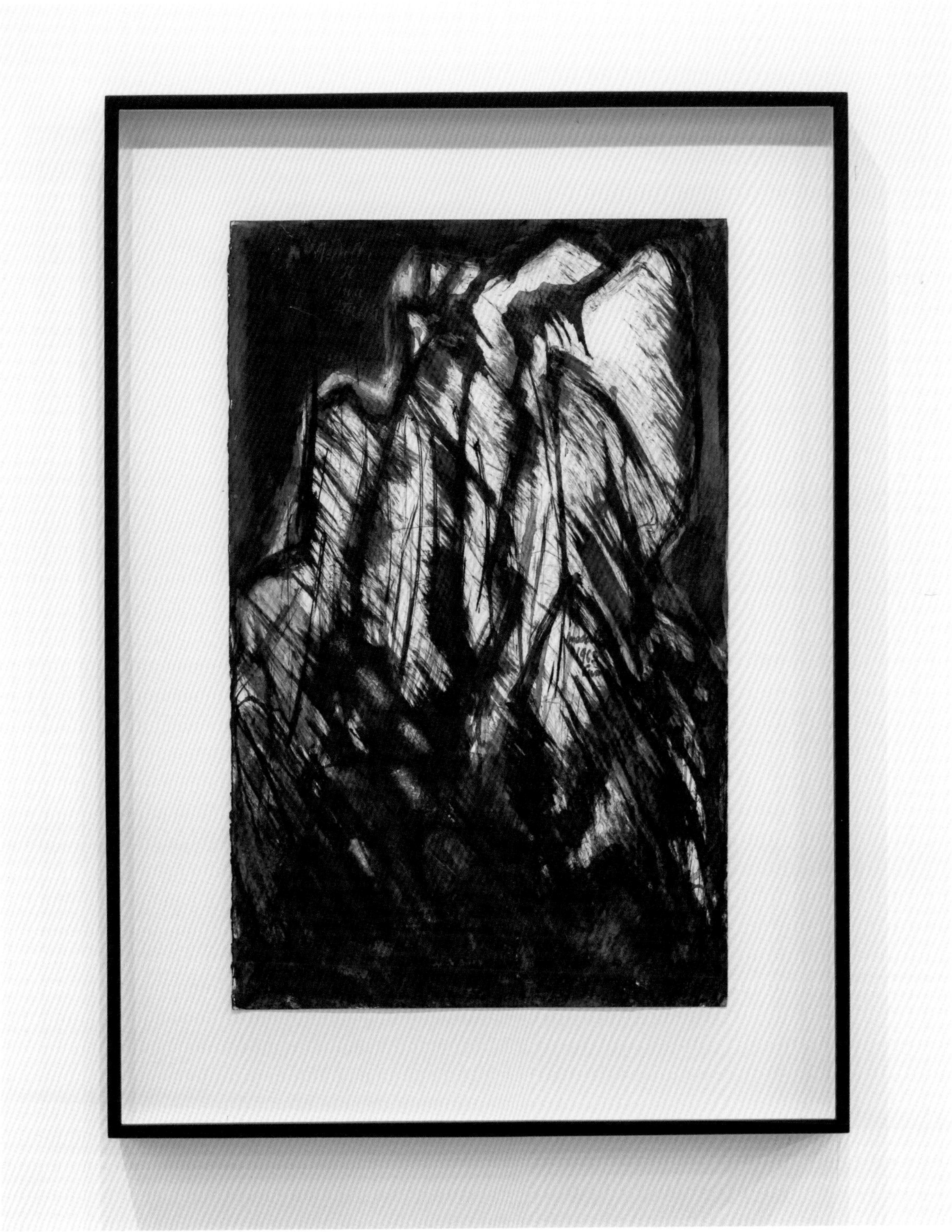

Cuma – Studies for Lava Machine, 1963
China ink, graphite pencil, felt pen on paper
Paper size: 49.9 × 32.5 cm

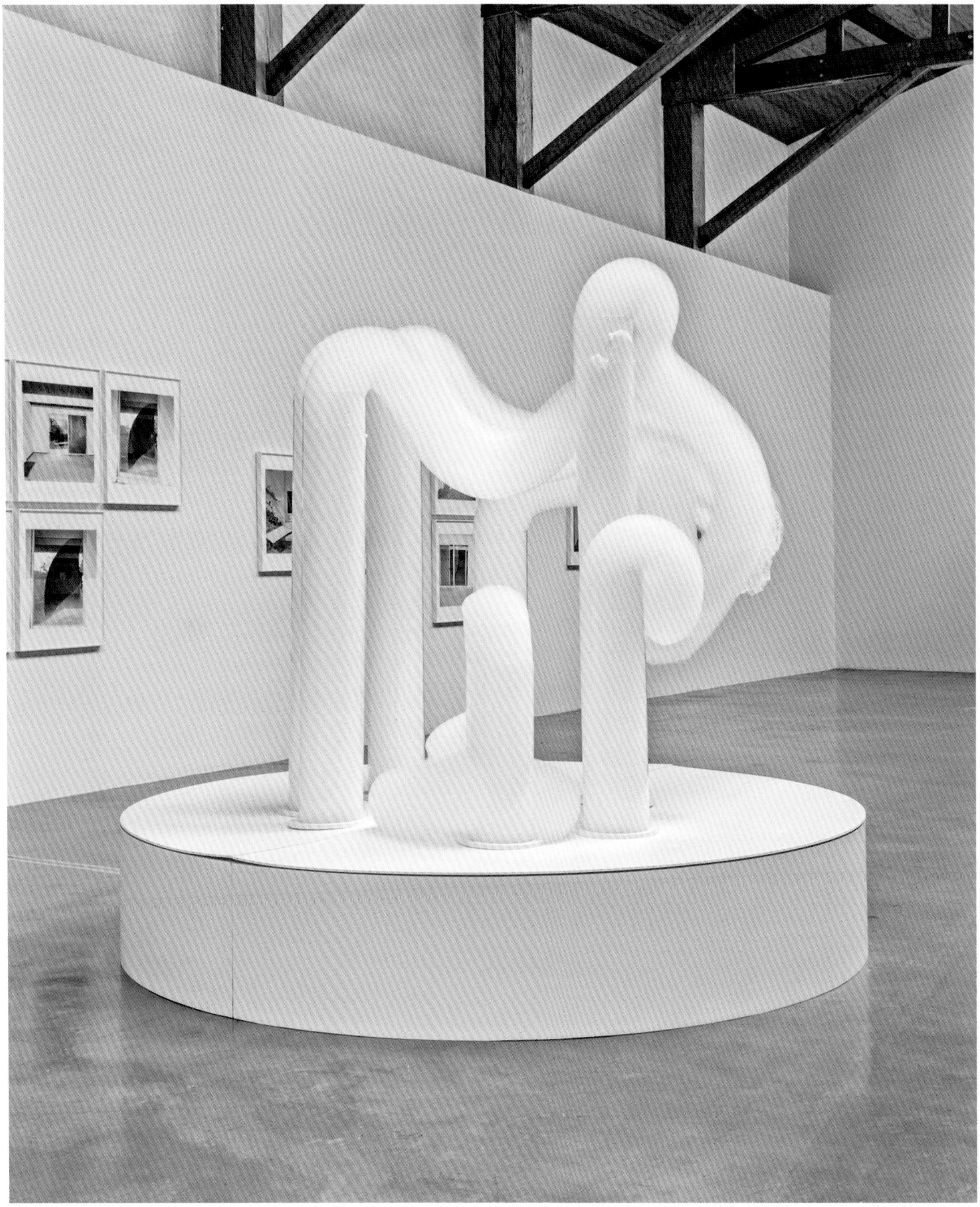

Cloud Canyons, 1963–2014
Metal, perspex, compressors, timers, water, soap
241.3 × 243.8 cm bubble dimensions variable
Image courtesy of kurimanzutto, Mexico City/New York
Photo: Omar Luis Olguín

Asif Mian

アジフ・ミアン

Asif Mian (b. 1978) is a New York City based artist working at the intersection of drawing, sculpture, video, and performance. Drawing on personal and collective experiences, Mian psychologically shifts everyday objects and practices through metabolization, embedding, and hybridization. His varied methods employ the splicing of rugs together as 'event sculptures,' modifying intimidation rituals for performance, and subverting drone thermal cameras for video installations.

Mian was a finalist for the 2022 Artadia New York Award, and winner of the 2020 Queens Museum-Jerome Foundation Fellowship with the solo exhibition, *RAF: Prosthetic Location* at Queens Museum, New York (2021). His work has also been featured in group exhibitions including *Always, Already, Haunting, "disss-co," Haunt* curated by Whitney Independent Study Program (ISP) fellows at The Kitchen, New York (2019); Open Call at The Shed, New York (2019); *Beyond Geographies: Contemporary Art and Muslim Experience* at BRIC, New York (2019); and the *Queens International Biennial: Volumes* at Queens Museum, New York (2018).

1978年生まれ。ニューヨークを拠点に活動。ドローイング、彫刻、ビデオ、パフォーマンスなどの作品を制作。個人的・集団的体験を引き合いに、「交換」「同化」「混成」を通じて日常の物や行為を心理的に転換させている。「イベント・スカルプチャー（出来事の彫刻）」と称して絨毯をつなぎ合わせた立体作品や、威嚇行為をパフォーマンスに変容させた作品、ドローンの赤外線カメラの映像を用いたヴィデオインスタレーションなど、その表現手法は多岐にわたる。

2022年Artadia New York Awardのファイナリストに選出。2020年度Queens Museum-Jerome Foundation Fellowshipを受賞し、2021年にクイーンズ美術館（ニューヨーク）で個展「RAF: Prosthetic Location」を開催。その他、2019年にはザ・キッチン（ニューヨーク）にてホイットニー美術館のIndependent Study Program（ISP）が企画した「Always, Already, Haunting, "disss-co," Haunt」、ザ・シェッド（ニューヨーク）が主催する「Open Call」プログラムや、ブルックリンのBRIC（ニューヨーク）での「Beyond Geographies: Contemporary Art and Muslim Experience」、2018年のクイーンズ美術館のクイーンズ国際ビエンナーレなど、数々のグループ展で作品が紹介されている。

Smokeless Fire

2022
Video installation
Thermal infrared video and HD video, projection screens, black dyed pond water

Nothingness & Specter

2022
Live video installation
Polyethylene plastic bags, heat guns, clear acrylic, chromed steel, hardware, electronic controllers, and live video feed from thermal infrared camera onto flatscreen monitors

The prefix *infra* means "below."
Infrared radiation oscillates at a lower frequency than red light.
This technology detects thermal energy and heat, converting it into an electronic signal that produces an image, allowing for the surveillance or capture of a scene beyond what is visible to the naked eye.

I read a news article describing how a police helicopter was searching for a fugitive.
The fugitive was running and hiding in the woods near a body of water.
The helicopter used an infrared thermal camera to find him inside a boat.

The camera could see him *through* a plastic tarp covering the boat's hull.
He thought he was safe under the white tarp, but his thermal form was clearly seen.
Through the camera, the polyethylene tarp became transmissive and transparent.

What if he wrapped himself in the tarp, and etherealized into a ghostly shape?
Not to escape, but to transform for the camera.
Allowing technology to create the mythological.

There and not there.
Like the figure of a ghost.
That which is neither present nor absent, neither dead nor alive.

We created figures from technological traces of heat, the thermal scannings of bodies,
Seen through material interfaces while embodying liminal performances.
Like the characters woven into traditional South Asian rugs, the figures perform as part of mythology.

Shrouded in a plastic skin that etherealizes under the infrared eye of a flying drone.
Each figure is a unique segment of a serpent,
Segments connect and shapeshift into the monstrous.

Shedding skin, shedding histories that cling.
A remnant of a past someone/someone's past,
The technological translation of the mythological: a transgenerational communication.

The thermal works are two types of seeing:
The actual and the virtual.
Two different states of perception, each contending with the other.

We performed in an unused school in Yonkers, New York, USA.
And present the work at an unused school in Okayama, Japan.
A mirror of mythology, technology, and place.

Asif Mian

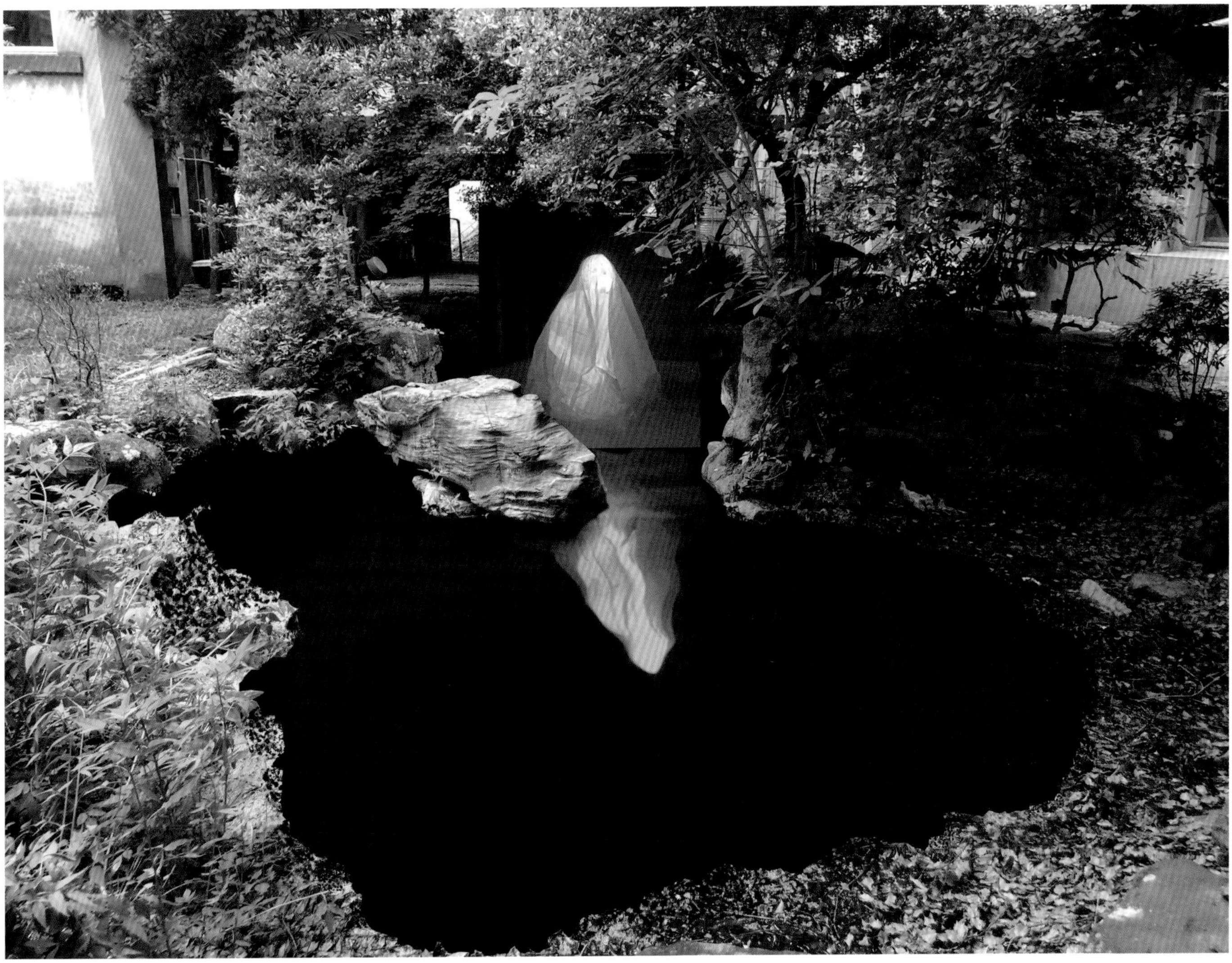

Proposal image for *Smokeless Fire*, 2022
Image courtesy of the artist
《Smokeless Fire》展示イメージ

「infra」という接頭語には「下の」という意味がある。
赤外線（Infrared）は赤色光よりも低い周波数で振動する。
赤外線によって熱エネルギーや熱を検知し、電子信号に変換して画像を生成することで、裸眼では見えない世界を観察し、撮影することができる。

警察のヘリがどのように逃亡者を捜索したのかが書かれた記事を読んだことがある。
容疑者は水辺の森に逃走し身を潜めたため、
ヘリは赤外線サーモカメラを用いてボートのなかにいる逃亡者を発見。

船体を覆うビニールシート越しに「透けて」見える姿をとらえた。
白いシートに隠れていれば安心だと思ったのだろうが、
身体の熱の形がはっきりと映し出されていたそうだ。
カメラによってポリエチレンのビニールシートが透過し、中が見える状態になったのである。

もし彼がシートに身を包み、逃げるのではなく、代わりにカメラに向けて
この世のものでないような姿に変身するとしたら？
テクノロジーが生み出す神話的なもの。

そこにあって、そこにない。
まるで幽霊のように。
存在も不在もなく、生きているのでも死んでいるのでもない。

サーモグラフィによって表出した身体の熱の痕跡から人の姿が生成され、
可視・不可視のはざまで淡く浮かび上がるパフォーマンスが生地の向こう側に透けて知覚される。
南アジアの伝統織物に編まれた人物のように、その姿は神話の一部となる。

飛行ドローンの赤外線の眼を通してビニールの覆いは幽玄な膜となり、
その膜に包まれた人影は異様な蛇の断片として、
やがてつながり化け物のように姿を変える。

脱皮し、まとわりつく歴史を脱ぎ捨てて。
過去の誰か、誰かの過去の名残り。
神話の技術的解釈、すなわち、世代を超えた対話。

これら熱を扱った作品には2つの知覚が存在する。
現実と仮想。
互いに主張し合う2つの異なる認知の状態である。

今回、私たちはアメリカのニューヨーク州ヨンカーズにある廃校でパフォーマンスを行い、
それを日本の岡山の廃校で発表することにした。
それは神話、テクノロジー、そして場を映す鏡となる。

Asif Mian

MAKE
WAR
AGAINST
ABSURDITY

HOPE
HAS
NO
RIGHT
ANGLES

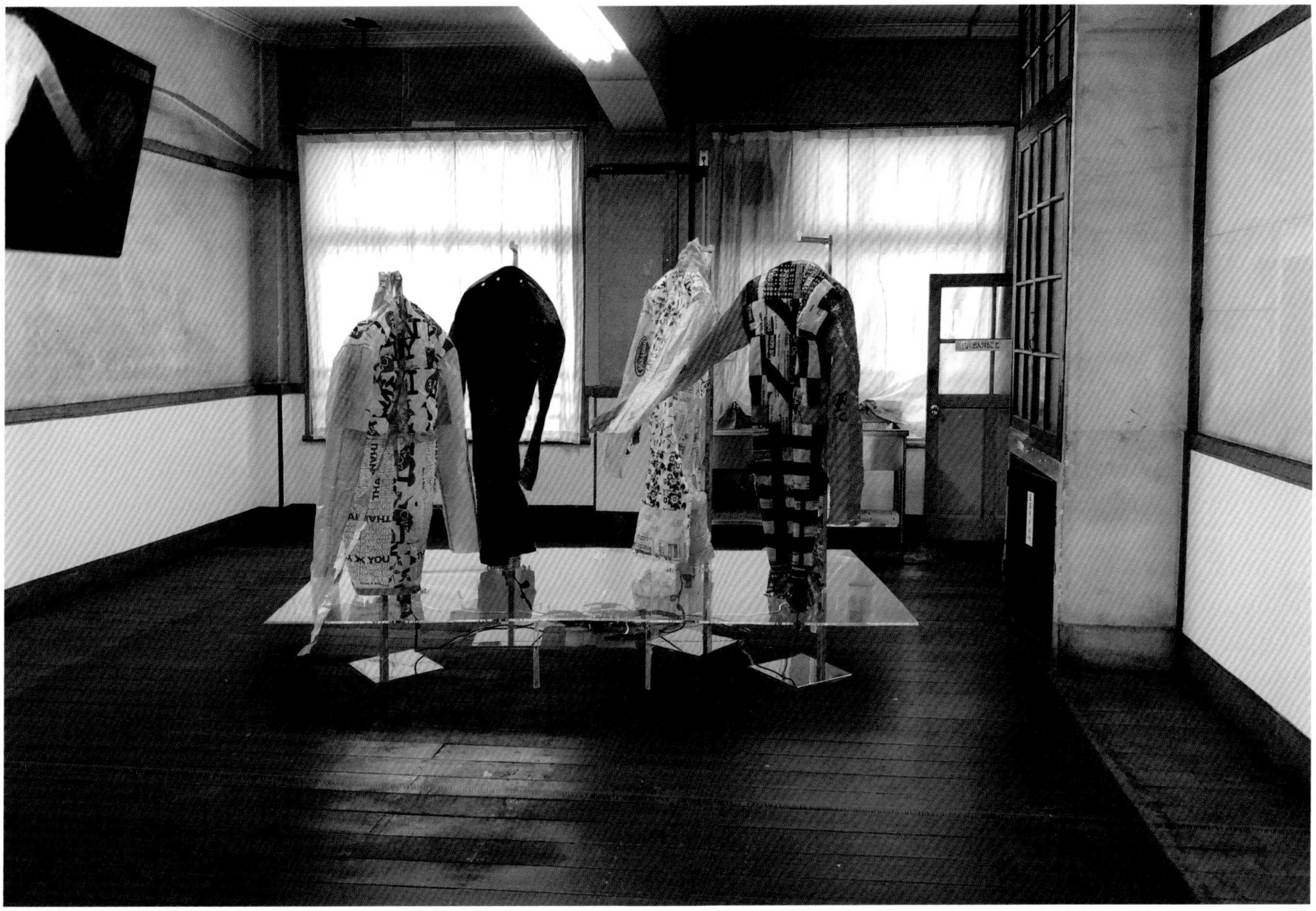

Proposal image for *Nothingness and Specter*, 2022
Image courtesy of the artist
《Nothingness and Specter》展示イメージ

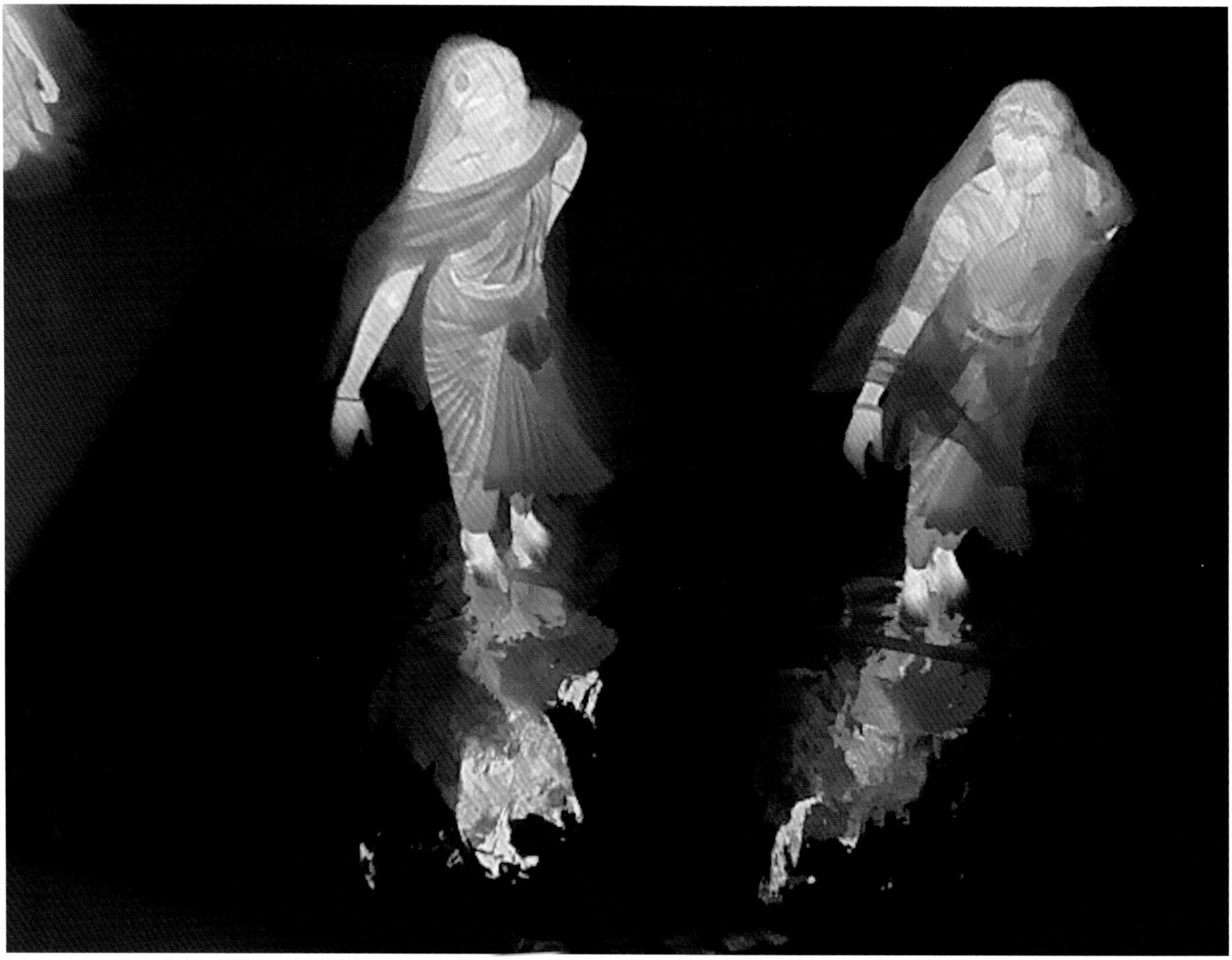

Smokeless Fire, 2022
Video installation
Image courtesy of the artist
《Smokeless Fire》展示イメージ

Asif Mian

Precious Okoyomon

プレシャス・オコヨモン

Precious Okoyomon (b. 1993) is a Nigerian-American poet and artist living and working in New York City. They have had institutional solo exhibitions at Performance Space New York (2021), the Aspen Art Museum (2021), the Museum Für Moderne Kunst in Frankfurt (2020), and the LUMA Westbau in Zurich (2018). They were included in the 59th Venice Biennale, the 58th Belgrade Biennial as well as group exhibitions at the Palais de Tokyo, Paris, and the LUMA Arles, France. Major performances have been commissioned by the Serpentine, London (2019) and the Institute of Contemporary Art, London (2019). Their second book of poetry *But Did U Die?* will be co-published by the Serpentine and Wonder Press in 2022. Okoyomon was a 2020 artist-in-residence at the LUMA Arles. They are the 2021 recipient of the Frieze Art Fair Artist Award, as well as the 2022 CHANEL Next Art Prize.

1993年、ロンドン生まれ。現在はニューヨーク市を拠点に活動。ナイジェリア系アメリカ人詩人およびアーティスト。
これまでに、2021年Performance Space New York、2021年アスペン美術館、2020年フランクフルト現代美術館、2018年LUMA Westbau（チューリッヒ）で個展を開催。また、第59回ヴェネツィア・ビエンナーレ、第58回ベオグラード・ビエンナーレに出展するほか、パレ・ド・トーキョー（パリ）、LUMA Arles（アルル）でグループ展に参加。2019年、ロンドンのサーペンタイン・ギャラリーおよびインスティテュート・オブ・コンテンポラリー・アートから委嘱を受け、パフォーマンス作品を発表。2022年、2作目の詩集『But Did U Die?（でもあなたは死んだの？）』（サーペンタイン・ギャラリー／Wonder Press）を出版予定。2020年LUMA Arlesのアーティスト・イン・レジデンスに参加。2021年Frieze Artist Award、2022年CHANEL Next Prizeを受賞。

it's depressing as fuck

In a room full of white people
trying to manifest the sight of heaven
the rebirth takes place
every ten years

I'm naked
when the cops come
covered in blood
Light makes shift repetition

the world keeps breaking and my head hurts
here is the image of a wounded black body
hanging down like the sun
glass in my braids

glass in my feet
blood in my mouth
angelic raptures in an era of endless exploitation

I get so tired sometimes of feeling everything
Pardon my forgetting how to play the game

Whose shame
is this anyways

think of the body as ash
spilling an orbital road

Something yellow is drowning me again

Precious Okoyomon

ひどく気がめいる

白人だらけの部屋の中
天国の光景を明らかにしようとしている
再生は10年ごとに起こる

私は無防備だ
警官が来たとき
血まみれだった
光はシフトを繰り返す

世界は壊れ続ける、頭が痛い
傷ついた黒い身体のイメージ
太陽のように垂れ下がり
三つ編みの中にガラス

足の中にガラス
口の中の血
終わりのない搾取の時代における天使の歓喜

すべてを感じることで、時々とても疲れる
ゲームの遊び方を忘れてしまったことを許して欲しい

これはいったい
誰の恥なのか

身体を見立てる
軌道道路にこぼれる灰に

何か黄色いものがまた私を溺れさせる

プレシャス・オコヨモン

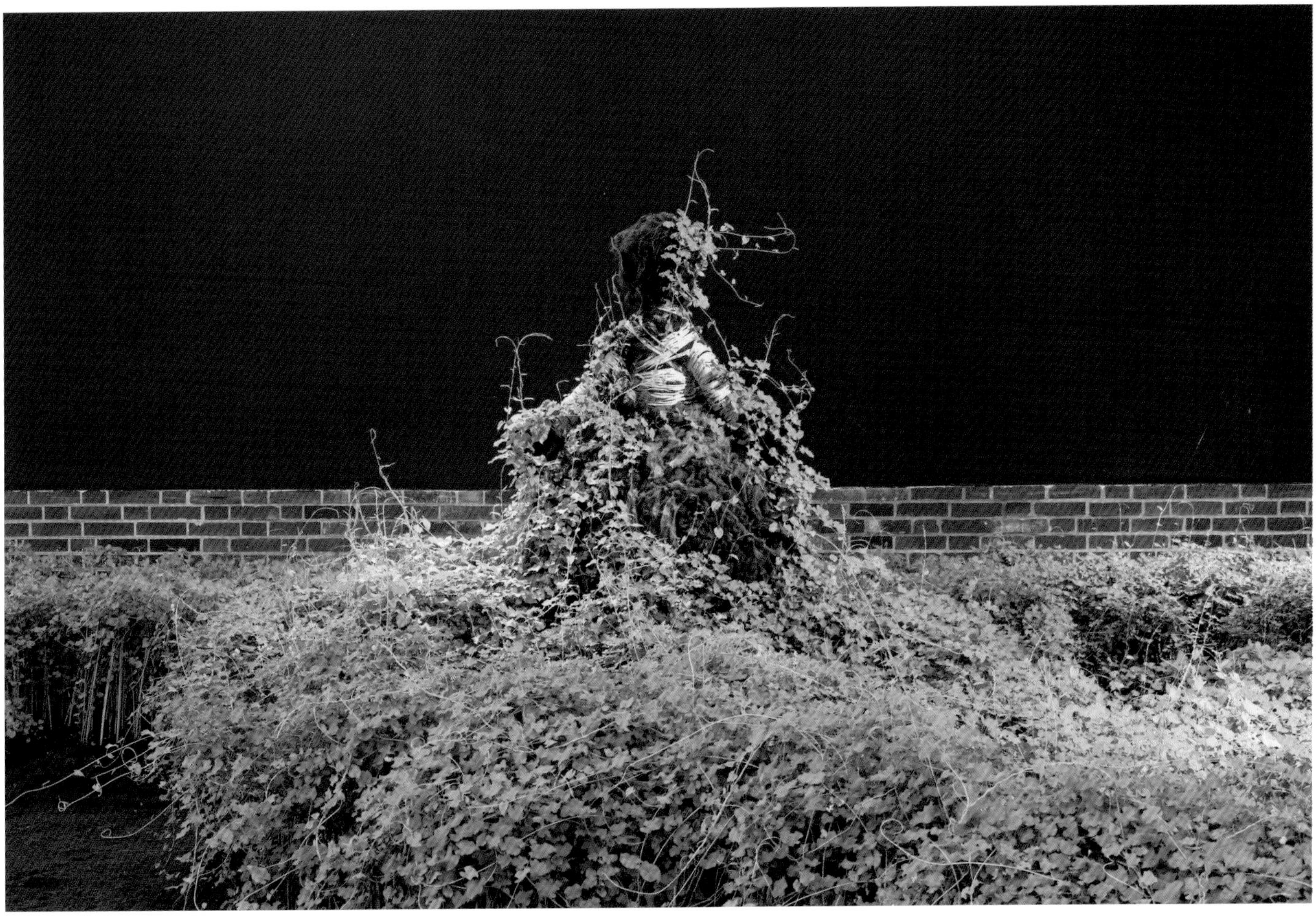

Earthseed, Exhibition view at the Museum Für Moderne Kunst, Frankfurt, 2020
Photo: Axel Schneider. Courtesy of the artist and the Museum Für Moderne Kunst
フランクフルト現代美術館での《Earthseed》展示風景（2020年）

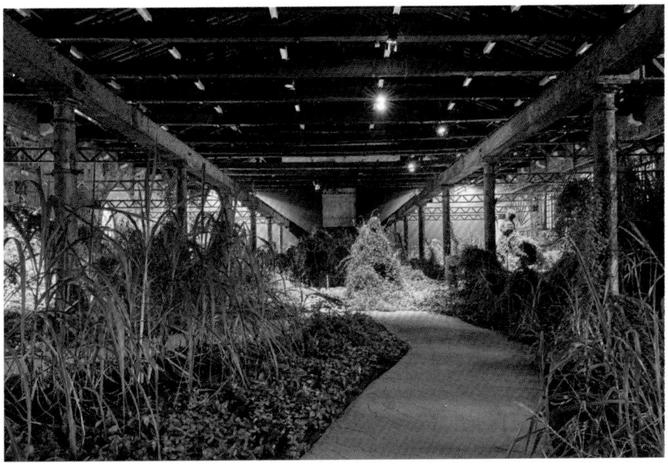

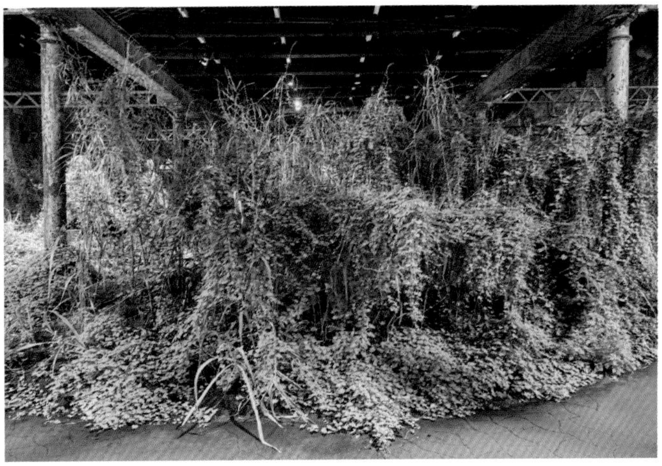

Installation view of *To See The Earth Before the End of the World*, 2022, at the 59th International Art Exhibition – La Biennale di Venezia, *The Milk of Dreams*, 2022
Photo: Clelia Cadamuro. Courtesy of the artist and Quinn Harrelson Gallery
第59回ヴェネツィア・ビエンナーレの展覧会「The Milk of Dreams」（2022年）での《To See The Earth Before the End of the World》展示風景

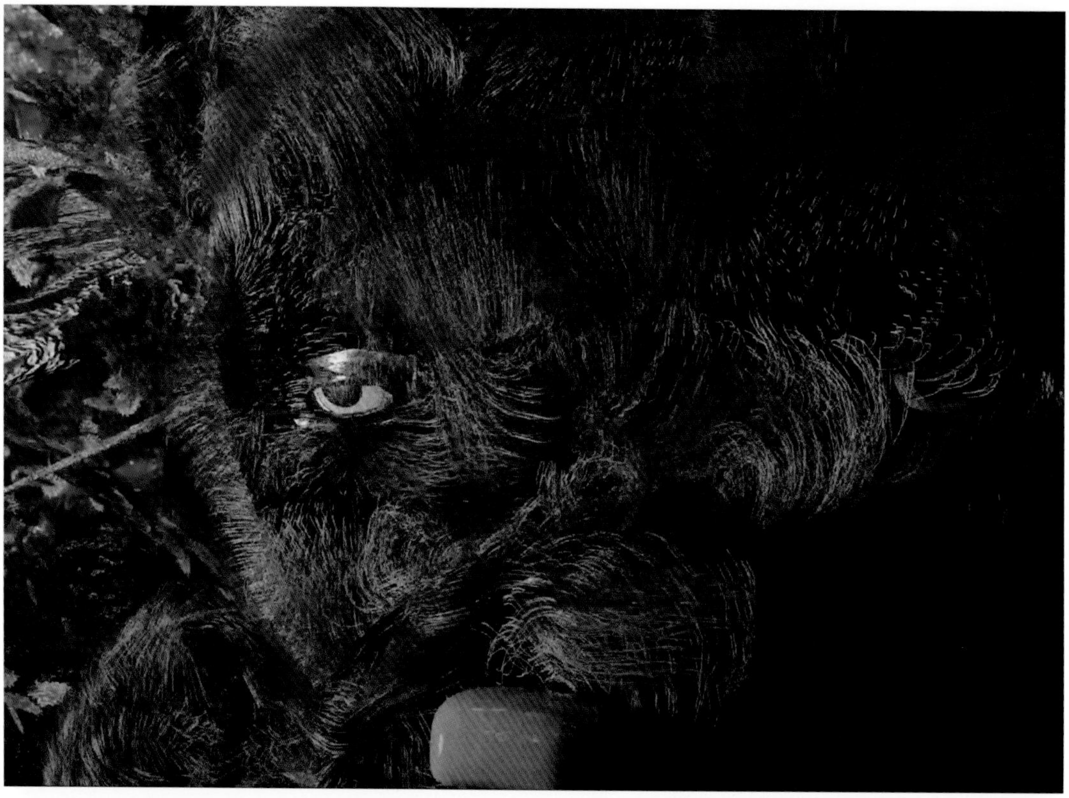

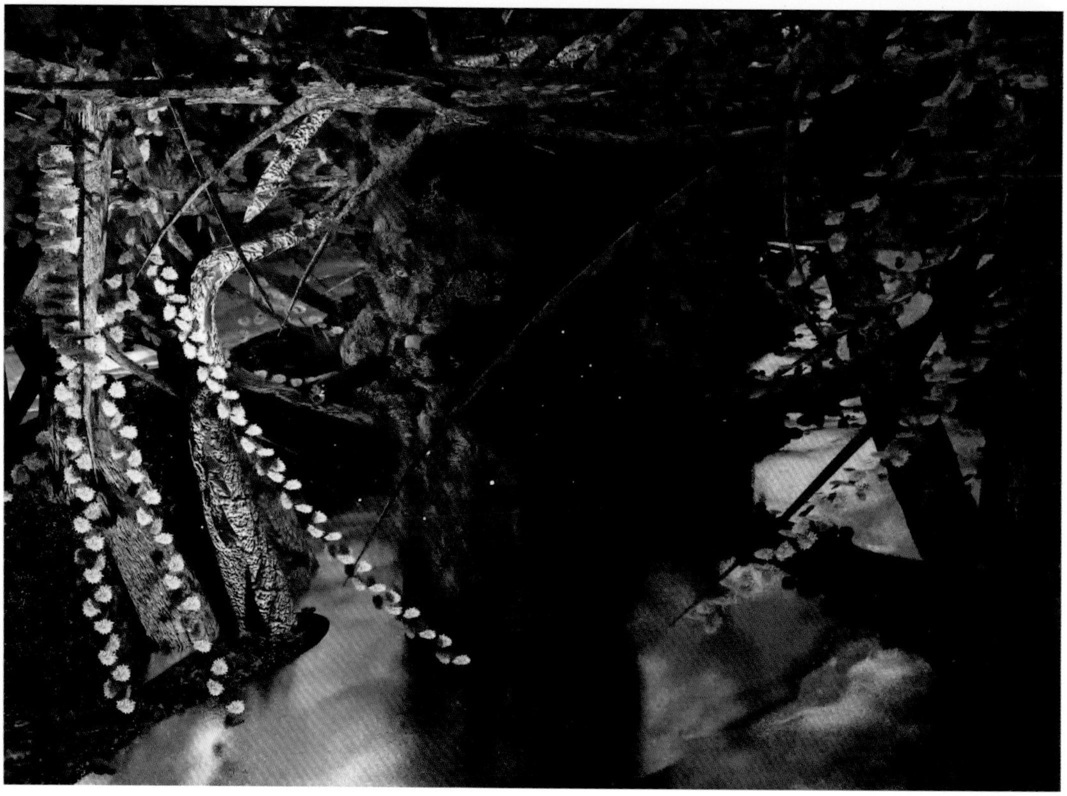

Still from *It's Disassociating Season*, 2019
HD video, 9 min. 51 sec.
Courtesy of the artist and Quinn Harrelson Gallery
《It's Disassociating Season》（2019年）より

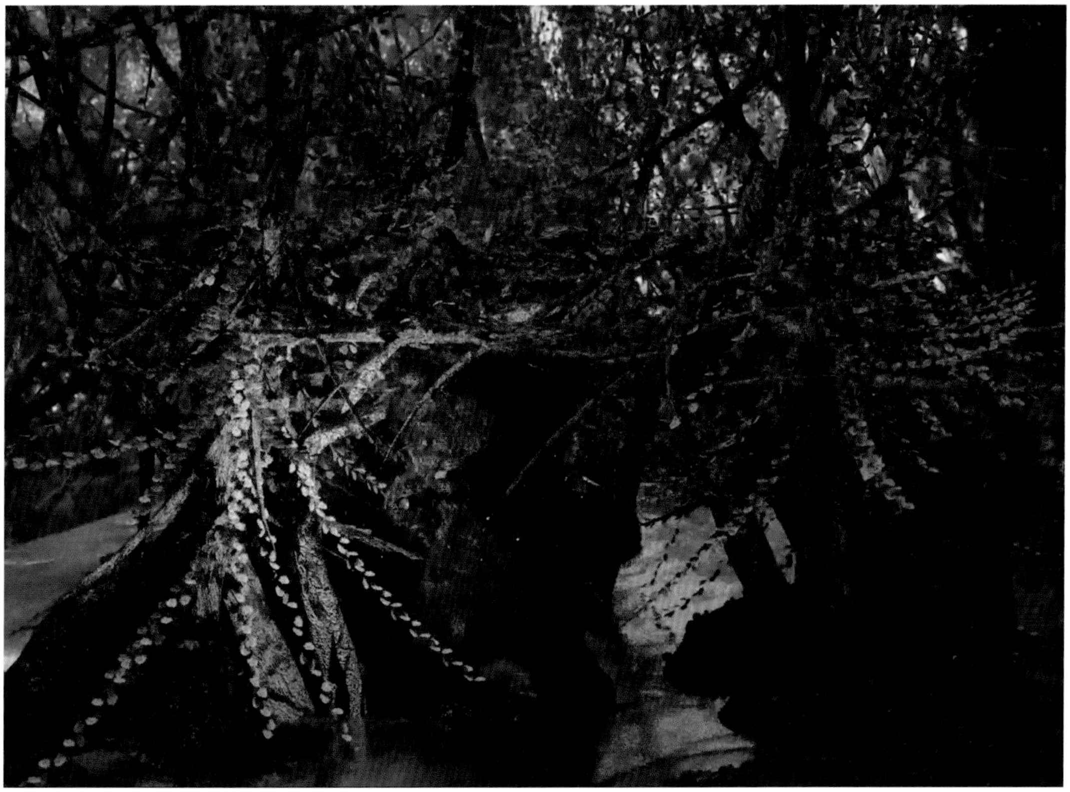

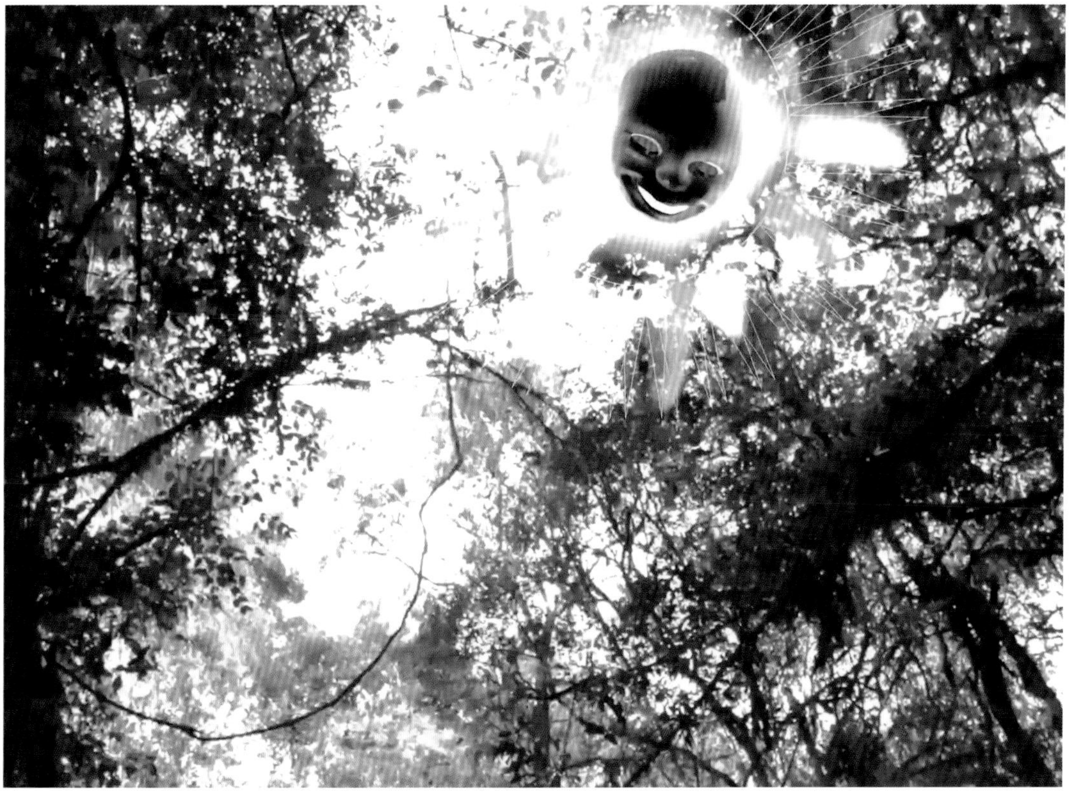

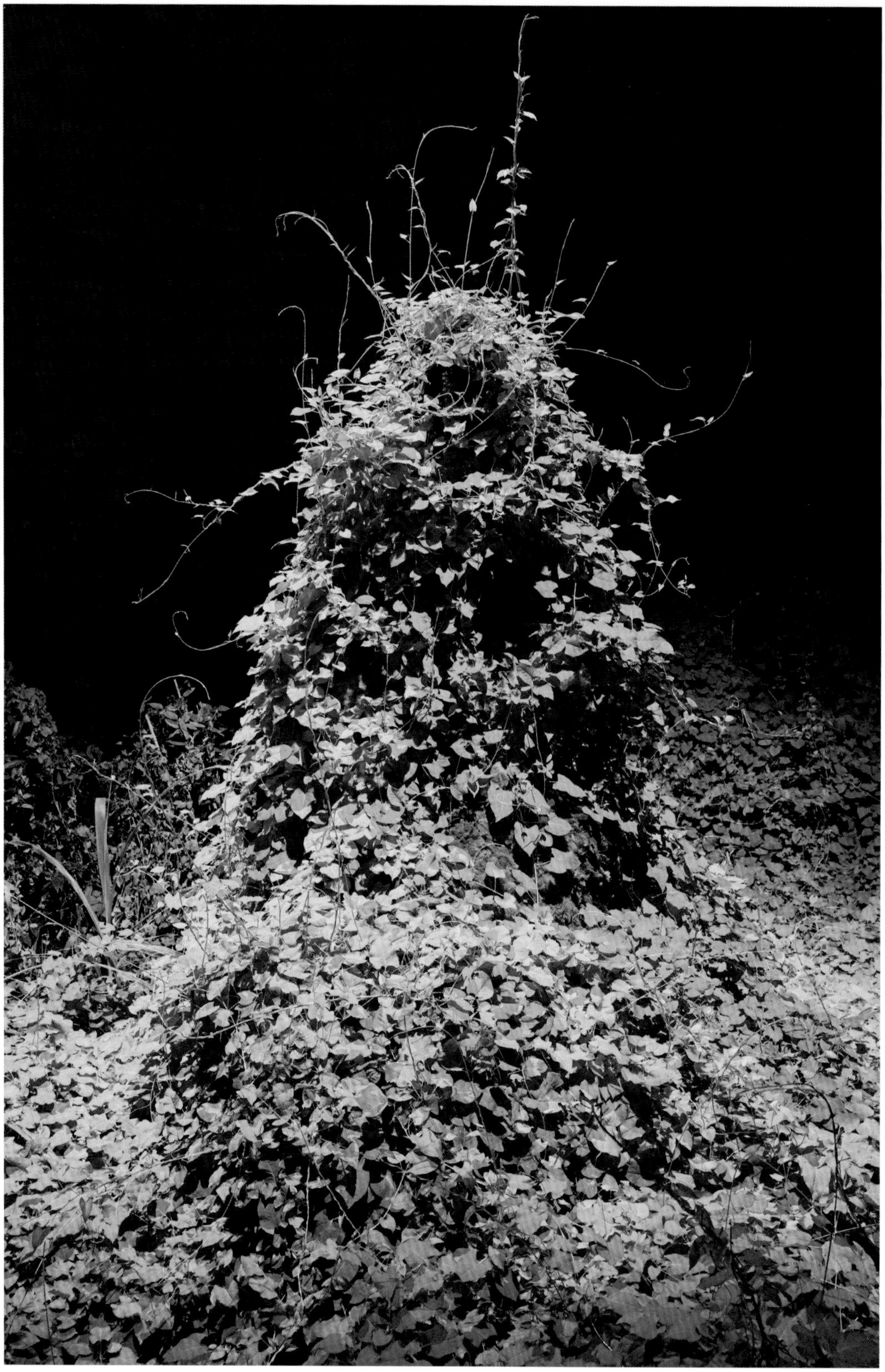

Ihoemoegbe, Memory has Forsaken Me, All the Ties Untangle in my Silence, 2022
Raw wool, yarn, dirt, blood
168 × 98 × 103 cm
Photo: Clelia Cadamuro. Courtesy of the artist and Quinn Harrelson Gallery

Frida Orupabo

フリーダ・オルパボ

Frida Orupabo was born 1986 in Sarpsborg, Norway, and lives and works in Oslo.
Solo exhibitions include Fotomuseum Winterthur (2022); Museu Afro Brasil, São Paulo (2021); Kunsthall Trondheim (2021); Huis Marseille, Amsterdam (2020); Portikus, Frankfurt am Main and Kunstnernes Hus, Oslo (both 2019). Orupabo participated in the 58th Venice Biennale exhibition (2018) as well as the 34th São Paulo Biennial (2021). Together with Ming Smith and Missylanyus, Frida Orupabo presented her work in Arthur Jafa's exhibition *A Series of Utterly Improbable, Yet Extraordinary Renditions* at Moderna Museet in Stockholm, Galerie Rudolfinum in Prague (both 2019), Julia Stoschek Collection, Berlin (2018), and Serpentine Sackler Gallery, London (2017).

1986年、ノルウェー、サルプスボルグ生まれ。現在はオスロを拠点に活動。
これまでに、2022年ヴィンタートゥール写真美術館（スイス）、2021年アフロ・ブラジル博物館（サンパウロ）、2021年Kunsthall Trondheim（ノルウェー・トロンハイム）、2020年ハウス・マルセイユ写真美術館（アムステルダム）、2019年Portikus（フランクフルト）、2019年Kunstnernes Hus（オスロ）などで個展を開催。また、2018年の第58回ヴェネツィア・ビエンナーレおよび2021年の第34回サンパウロ・ビエンナーレに参加したほか、アメリカのヴィデオアーティスト・映画監督のアーサー・ジャファによ「A Series of Utterly Improbable, Yet Extraordinary Renditions」展でミン・スミス、ミッシー・ランヤスと共に作品を発表。同展はストックホルム近代美術館、プラハのルドルフィヌムギャラリー（いずれも2019年）、2018年Julia Stoschek Collection（ベルリン）、2017年サーペンタイン・サックラー・ギャラリー（ロンドン）で開催された。

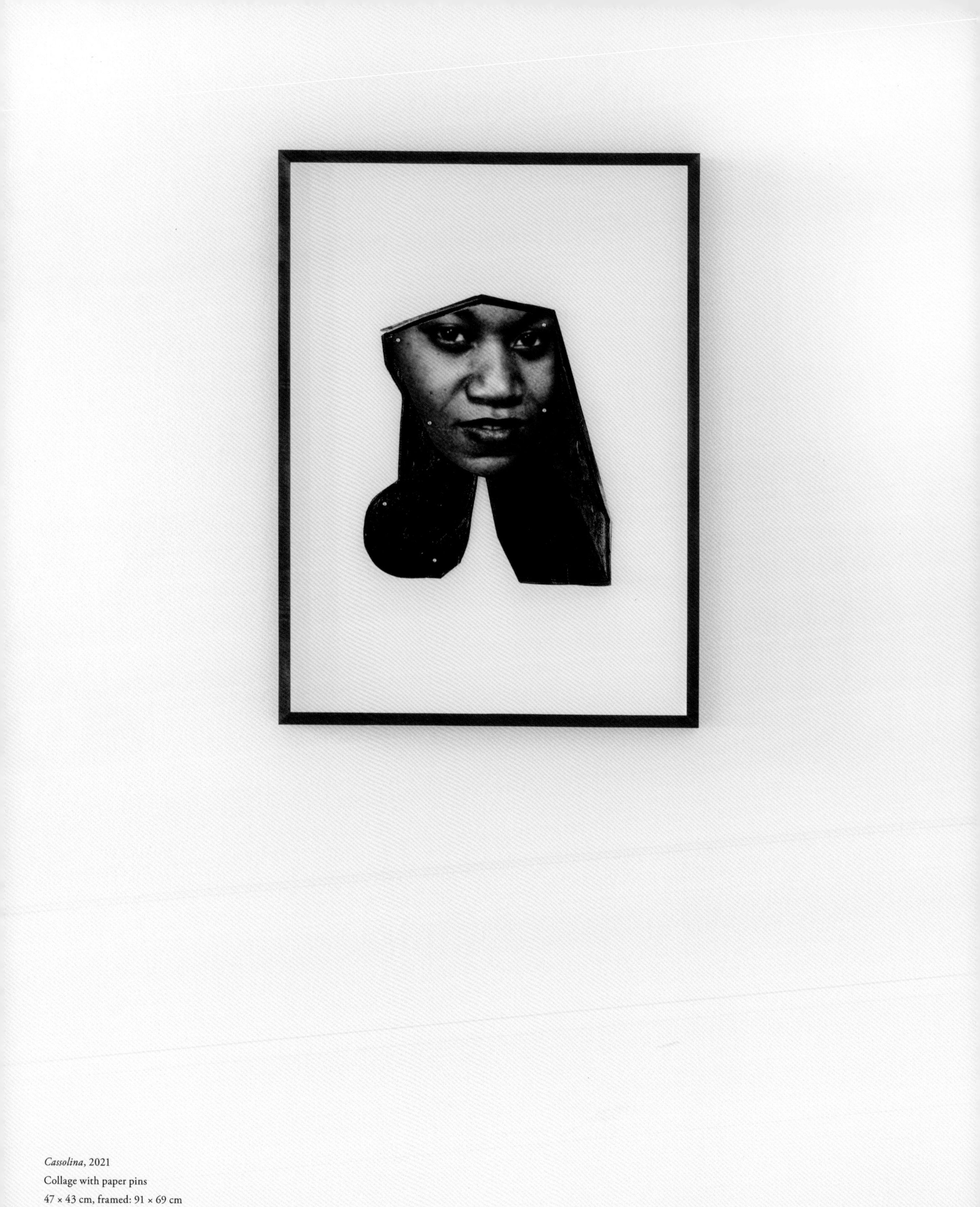

Cassolina, 2021
Collage with paper pins
47 × 43 cm, framed: 91 × 69 cm

Born to a Norwegian mother and Nigerian father, Frida Orupabo explores themes of race, gender, sexuality, violence, the gaze, colonialism and identity in media that in their nature are fragmented and multifarious. She enlists image platforms including Instagram, YouTube and Tumblr as both source and tool, engaging in the simultaneously monolithic and splintered abundance of images of digital platforms and archival sources to create works in a variety of media, including collage, sculpture and video.

Orupabo often uses photographs from colonial sources to investigate the way black women are portrayed as hyper-sexualised, deviant and subjects of curiosity and study. She explores how these loaded images address race and gender relations; pain, abuse, and violence, but also strength, power and resistance. In suites of works Orupabo addresses themes such as childbirth and motherhood, matriarchal relations, childhood and play and discipline.

Orupabo's figures bear the scars of their stories. They are de-formed and re-formed, unshackled from the confines of their photographic likenesses. The figures that populate Orupabo's physical collages and digital montages are mainly found on the internet. The artist trawls material from thematic and arcane archives as well as the wider, more diffuse flotsam and jetsam of online imagery. Orupabo relocates her matriarchal figures in anachronistic conditions, clothes and reposes. The possibilities of corporeal dislocation and reassembly inherent to collage restores them to sovereign protagonists of their own stories.

ノルウェー人の母とナイジェリア人の父の間に生まれたフリーダ・オルパボは、人種、ジェンダー、セクシュアリティ、暴力、視線、植民地主義、アイデンティティといったテーマを、断片的で多種多様な性質をもつメディアを通じて探究している。Instagram、YouTube、Tumblrをはじめとした画像プラットフォームを着想や制作の源泉かつツールとして用いる彼女は、デジタル・プラットフォームとアーカイヴから得られる画一的であると同時に分裂的でもある豊富な画像に取り組み、コラージュや立体、ヴィデオなど、様々なメディアを用いて作品化してきた。

オルパボがしばしば用いるのは、植民地時代の資料にある写真である。どのようにして黒人女性が性的特徴を過剰に付加され、逸脱した存在として、好奇心や研究の対象として表されてきたかを探るためだ。こうした誘導的なイメージが、人種とジェンダーの関係にどのように関わるのか、そこにある苦痛や迫害、暴力、だが同時に強さや力、抵抗について探究しているのである。一連の作品のなかでオルパボは、出産や母性、母権制との関係、幼年期、遊びや規律といったテーマを扱っている。

オルパボが取り上げる人物たちは、自らの物語が残した傷を負っている。こうした人物たちは、オルパボによって姿を変えられ、また整え直され、写真のなかの肖像という制約から解き放たれる。オルパボが制作した物質的なコラージュ作品やデジタルによるモンタージュ作品に登場する人物たちの画像は、主にインターネット上で見つけてきたものだ。テーマ別の閉ざされたアーカイヴや、より広範で拡散的なオンライン上に漂うイメージから、彼女は素材を渉猟している。そうして選んだ女家長のような強さを見せる女性たちに、オルパボは時代錯誤な状況や衣装、新たなポーズを与えて再配置する。コラージュという手法に特有の身体的な転移や再構築の可能性が、その人物たちを、自らの物語を生きる自立した主人公として蘇らせているのだ。

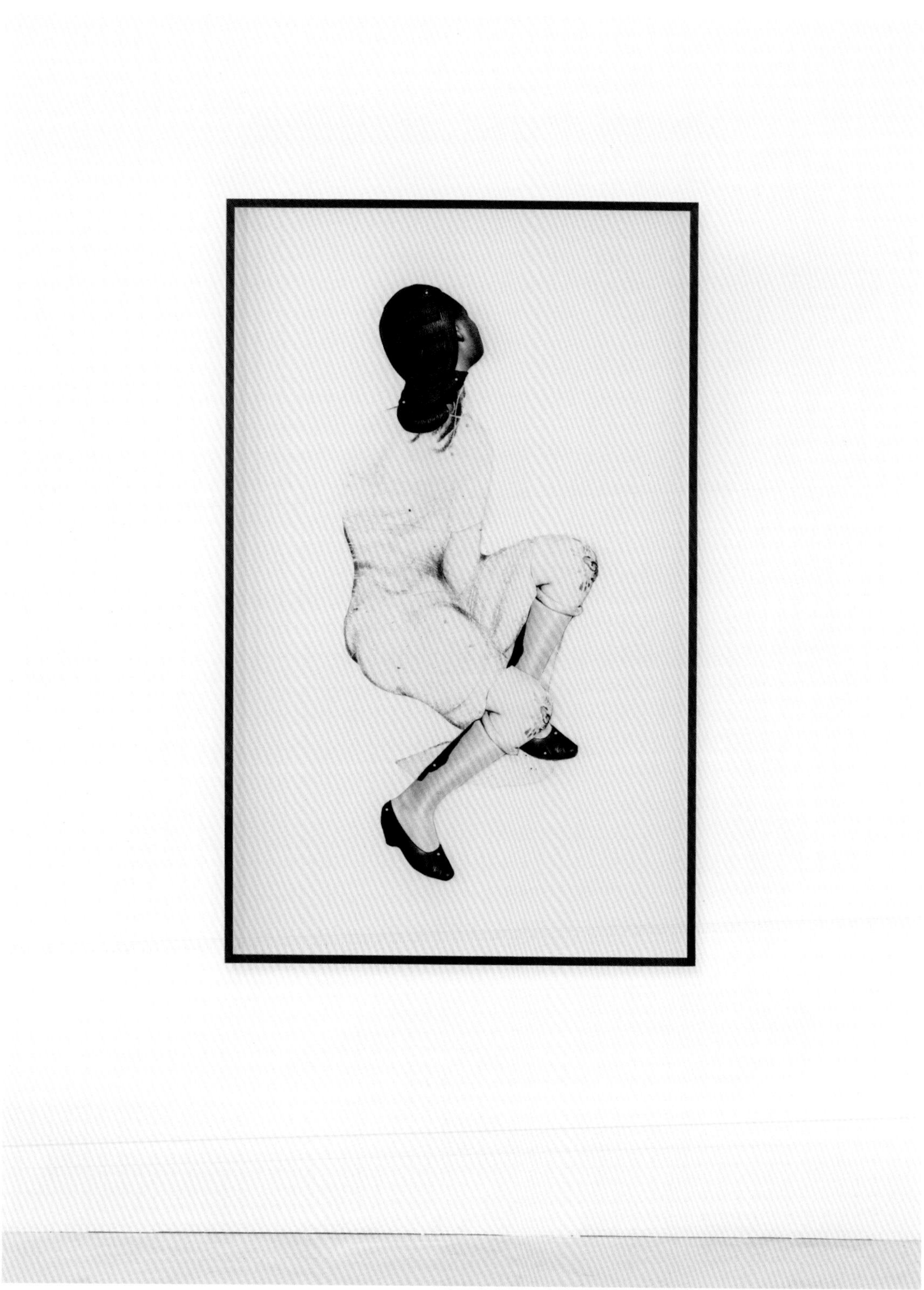

Longing / woman, 2021
Collage with paper pins
140 × 64 cm, framed: 177 × 113 cm

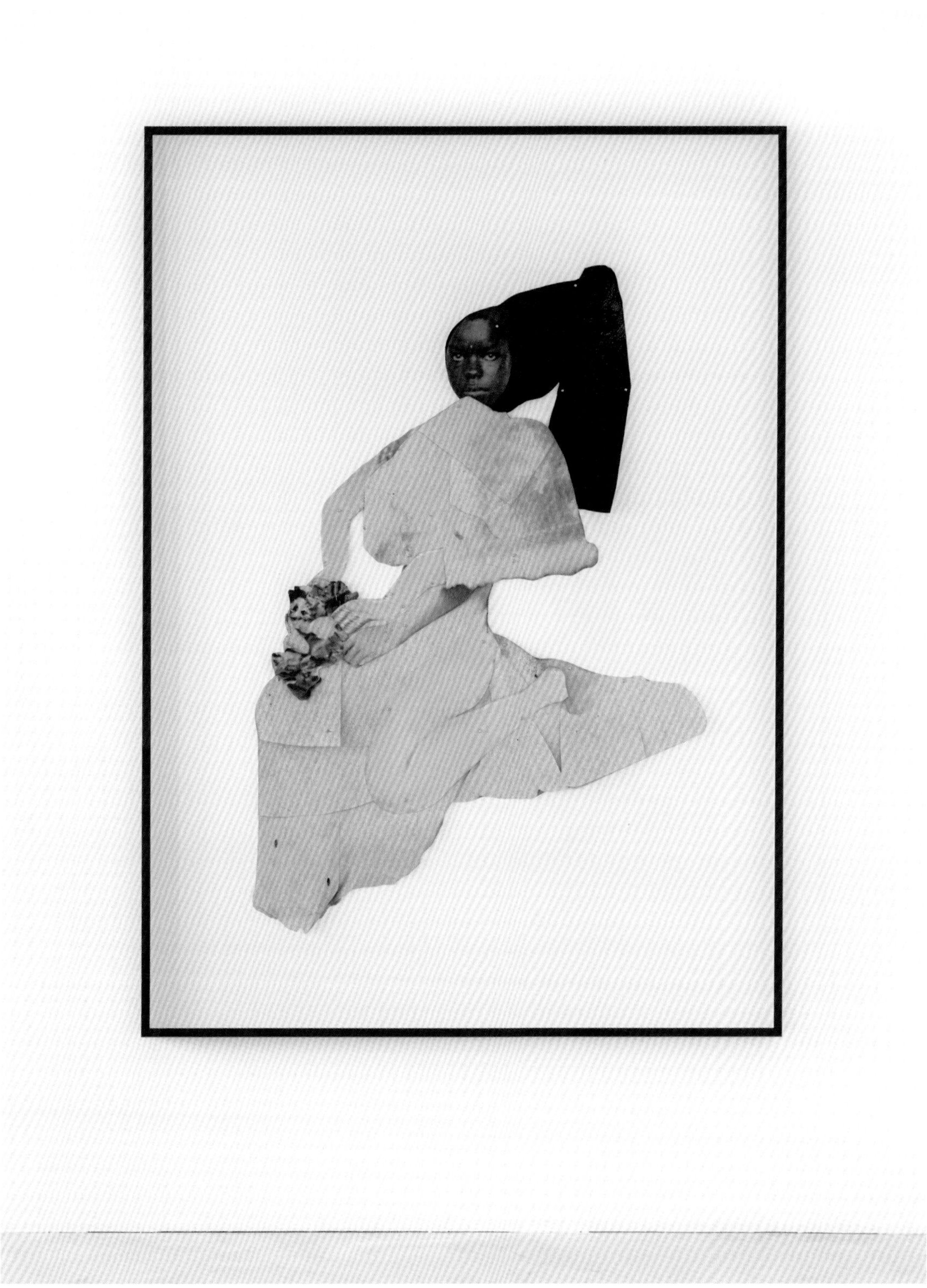

Woman with bouquet, 2021
Collage with paper pins
160 × 118 cm, framed: 209 × 152 cm

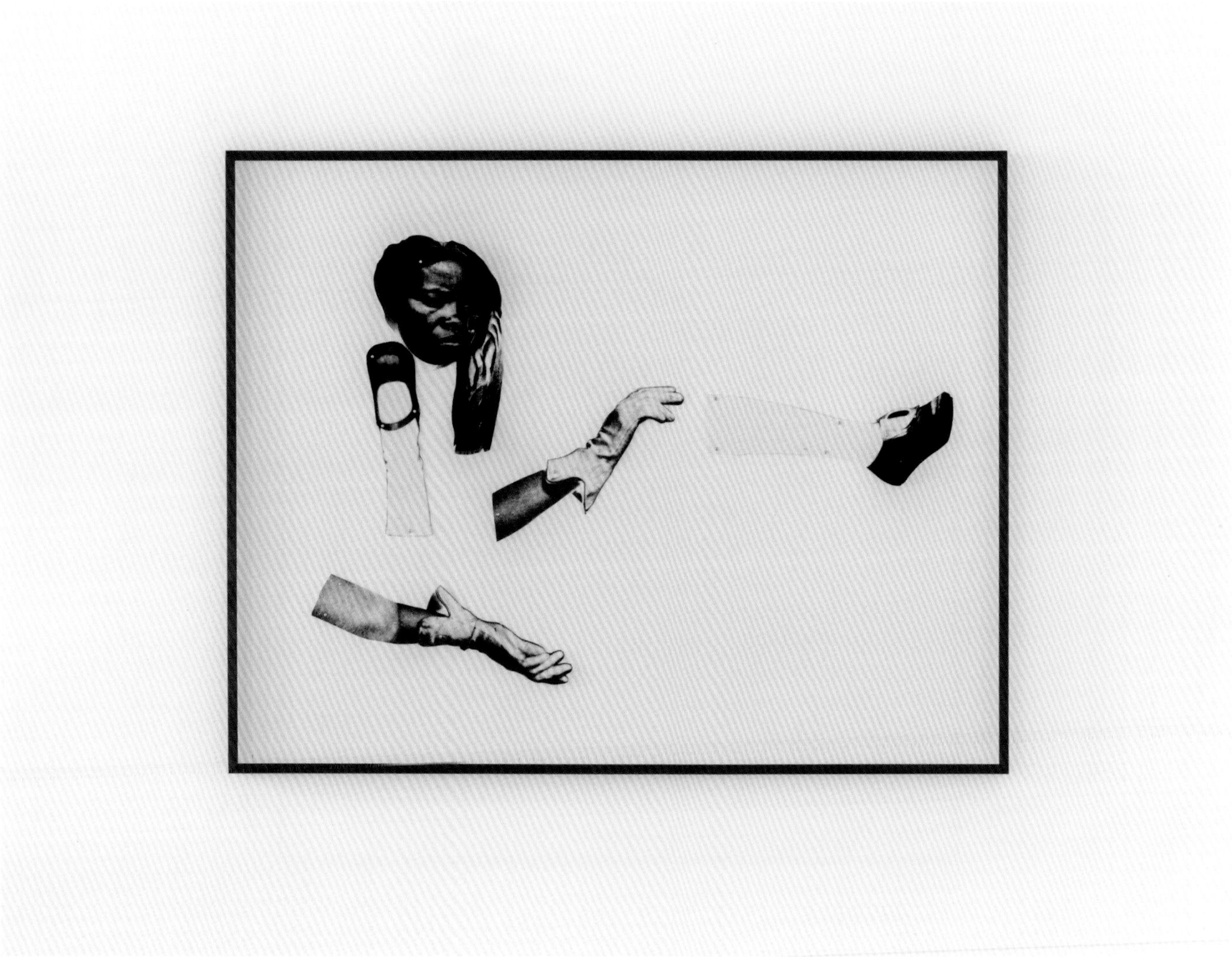

Limbs, 2021
Collage with paper pins
132 × 90 cm, framed: 124 × 161 cm

All images on pp. 114–118:
Photographer: Gerhard Kassner
Courtesy of the artist and Galerie Nordenhake Berlin/Stockholm/Mexico City

Vandy Rattana

ヴァンディー・ラッタナ

Born in 1980. Currently lives and works in Taipei, Taiwan. Born in Cambodia in the aftermath of the Khmer Rouge and having grown up in Phnom Penh, Vandy Rattana portrays episodes of historical violence through understated and tranquil images. He began his photography practice in 2005. His serial work employed a range of analog cameras and formats, straddling the line between strict photojournalism and artistic practice. His recent works mark a shift in philosophy surrounding the relationship between historiography and image making. For Vandy Rattana, photographs are now fictional constructions, abstract and poetic surfaces, histories of their own.

Since the photographic work and documentary *Bomb Ponds* (2009), in which his photos of bomb craters articulate the psychological wounds of Cambodians who survived American carpet bombing between 1964 and 1973, Vandy Rattana has been scanning the idyllic Cambodian countryside with his viewfinders and revealing its traumatic past. After his first short-film *MONOLOGUE* (2015), he released the short-film *Funeral* in 2018 and *...far away, over there, the ocean* (2019).

His major solo exhibitions include Taipei National University of the Arts (2020), Galerie Chateau d'Eau, Toulouse (2018), CAPC, Bordeaux (2015), Asia Society Museum, New York (2013). His major group exhibitions include Busan Biennale (2020), Singapore Biennale (2019), Jewish Museum, Frankfurt (2019), Yamaguchi Center for Arts and Media (2019), Kaohsiung Museum of Fine Arts (KMFA) (2019), Galerie Faux Mouvement, Metz (2017), Mori Art Museum, Tokyo (2017), Museum of contemporary art, Tokyo (2015), Yokohama Museum of Art (2013), documenta 13, Kassel (2012).

1980年生まれ。現在は台湾の台北を拠点に活動。

クメール・ルージュ後のカンボジアに生まれ、プノンペンで育つ。穏やかで静的なイメージを通して暴力の歴史を表現する。2005年に写真家としての活動を開始。様々なアナログカメラとフィルム・フォーマットを用いて、厳格なフォトジャーナリズムと芸術的実践の境界をまたぐ連作を発表している。近作では、史学とイメージ構築の関係性を巡る哲学へ視点を向けている。ラッタナにとっての写真とは虚構の構築物であり、抽象的かつ詩的な表層、かつそれ自身の歴史の語り手でもある。

爆弾跡（クレーター）を収めた写真およびドキュメンタリー作品《Bomb Ponds》(2009年) では、1964年から1973年にかけてのアメリカの絨毯爆撃を生き延びたカンボジア人の心の傷を表現。以降、カンボジアの地方の牧歌的な風景をファインダーでとらえ、悲惨な過去を暴き続けている。初の短編映像作品《MONOLOGUE》(2015年) を経て、2018年には《Funeral》、2019年には《...far away, over there, the ocean》を発表。

主な個展に、2020年国立台北芸術大学、2018年Galerie Chateau d'Eau（トゥールーズ）、2015年ボルドー現代美術館、2013年アジア・ソサエティミュージアム（ニューヨーク）など。

主なグループ展に、2020年釜山ビエンナーレ、2019年シンガポール・ビエンナーレ、2019年ユダヤ博物館（フランクフルト）、2019年山口情報芸術センター、2019年高雄市立美術館（KMFA)、2017年Galerie Faux Mouvement（メッス）、2017年森美術館（東京）、2015年東京都現代美術館、2013年横浜美術館、2012年ドクメンタ13（カッセル）などがある。

The MONOLOGUE Trilogy

2015–2019

MONOLOGUE
Full HD, 18 min. 53 sec.
© Vandy Rattana

...far away, over there, the ocean
Full HD, 35 min. 07 sec.
A Singapore Biennale 2019 Commission
© Vandy Rattana

Funeral
Full HD, 45 min. 08 sec.
© Vandy Rattana

The MONOLOGUE Trilogy, produced between 2015 and 2019, includes three films: *MONOLOGUE* (co-produced by Jeu de Paume and the CAPC Bordeaux), ... *far away, over there, the ocean* (produced by the Singapore Art Biennale), and *Funeral* (self-produced). This trilogy reflects Cambodian artist Vandy Rattana's unique vision of historical trauma and resilience.

The eponymous first part of the trilogy, *MONOLOGUE*, stem from the flood of emotions and reflections of the artist when he found the place where his sister, whom he never knew, lies, alongside five thousand other victims of the Khmer Rouge. The main witnesses of this painful "encounter" are two mango trees, under which his sister is buried. Echoing his previous work *Bomb Ponds* on the bomb craters of the Vietnam War, leaving traces that have become almost invisible, the landscape appears as one of the main protagonists of *MONOLOGUE*. A simple rice field, cultivated by almost amnesiac villagers, without any indication reminding that thousands of deceased lie there. As everywhere in the world, landscapes carry the scars of history. Vandy Rattana gives this silent landscape a subjective voice, through the history of his family, which intertwines with the great History.

The landscape is also prominent in the other two films of the trilogy, which extend the first film through fiction. In ... *far away, over there, the ocean*, a young painter is searching for the essence of landscape, without ever succeeding. Along the way, he witnesses both the beauty of the forest, which nevertheless continues to recede, and the unbridled urbanization of Phnom Penh, sweeping away the traces of the past. It can be seen as an extension of Vandy Rattana's photographic series on the first skyscraper in Phnom Penh and the urban evictions ten years earlier. This film is also a reflection on post-Khmer Rouge youth, between the traumas inherited from history and a future paved with illusions. "The landscape is nowhere to be found, I'm looking at myself, that's it. Why am I looking for myself? Maybe the landscape is the mirror in which I can see myself through the light particles. My image in the mirror has no flavor, no smell, no warmth. Rather, it is the pain of wanting to become something. I'm always wondering if the landscape is an infinite dream (excerpt)."

Funeral opens with the sound of footsteps of freed slaves. "I am building a refuge (...) a refuge that is so high I will meet the gods. This is what my dream has told me. The others are also dreaming, dreams that will destroy mine. The civilization born of dreams is fading away (...), it is disintegrating until it becomes ashes (...). Little by little, my dream is withering, my memory is falling into abyss, into an inconceivable void. I still remember all the things, what I have built. My voice has completely faded. This is where my dream ends (excerpt)." Last part of the trilogy, *Funeral*, through emotions, questions our existence. Aren't human beings slaves to their illusions, to their myths? Perhaps the ashes of the past are incubating a rebirth, although every act of creation also contains within itself its own end.

Facing the cruelty that crosses places and times—thousands of dead buried under rice paddies, the destruction of landscapes under the steamroller of land speculation, ambitious dreams that turn out to be dead ends—Vandy Rattana, echoing Albert Camus, appeals us to face the reality, to accept the absurdity of our existence, and to continually question ourselves about our place in this changing world.

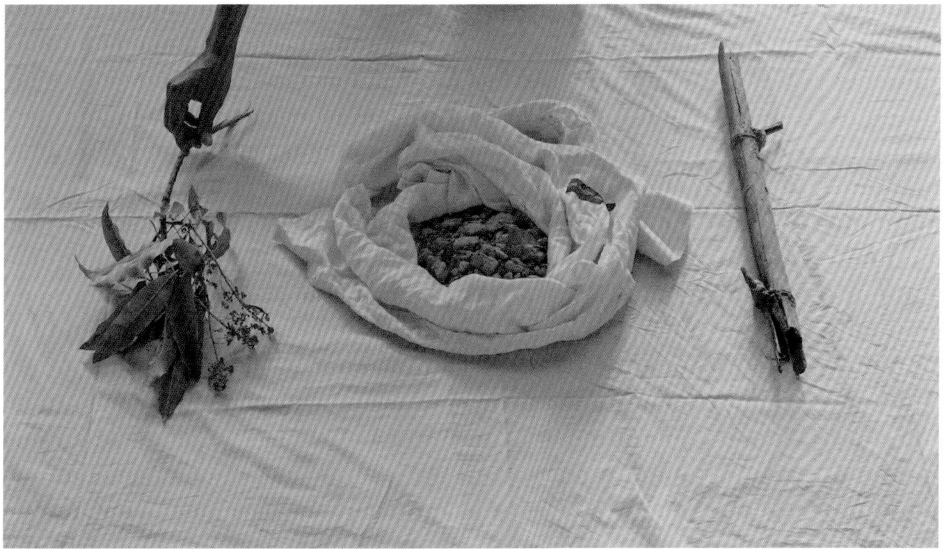

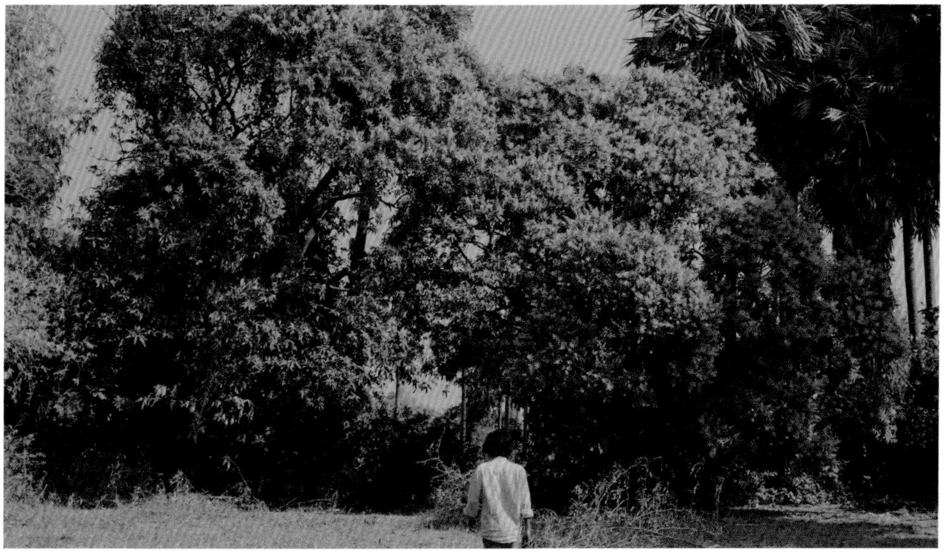

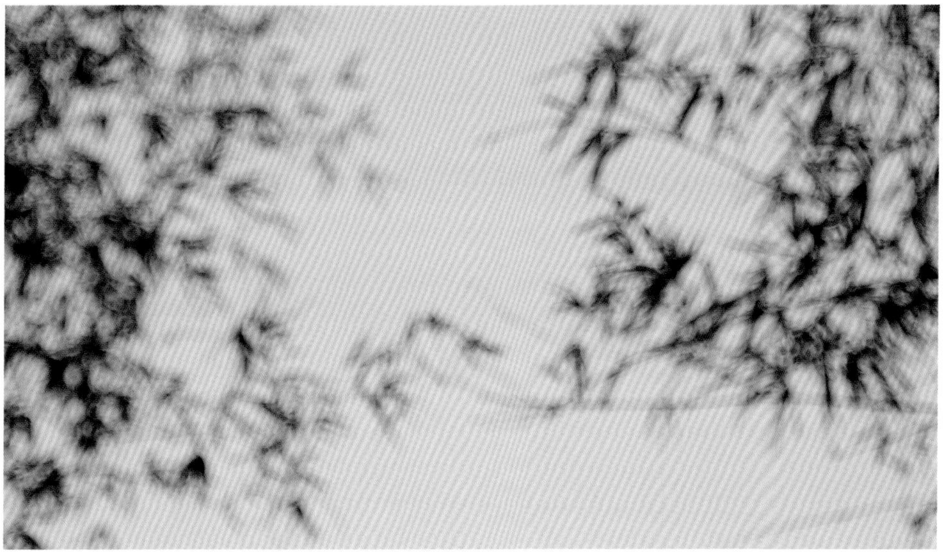

2015年から2019年にかけて制作された《The MONOLOGUE Trilogy》には、3つの映像が含まれている。《MONOLOGUE》（パリのアート・センター、ジュ・ド・ポームとボルドー現代美術館との共同制作）、《...far away, over there, the ocean》（シンガポール・アート・ビエンナーレによる制作）、《Funeral》（自主制作）だ。この三部作には、カンボジア人アーティスト、ヴァンディー・ラッタナの歴史的なトラウマと回復力に関する独自のヴィジョンが映し出されている。

三部作全体のタイトルのもとともなっている第1作《MONOLOGUE》は、カンボジアの共産党政権クメール・ルージュ（ポル・ポト政権、1975–1979年）に虐殺されたほかの5千人の犠牲者と共に、この作家自身が一度も会うことのかなわなかった姉が眠る場所を訪れた際に、心の内に溢れ出た激しい感情と内省から生まれた作品である。この痛ましい「出会い」の主たる目撃者は、姉が葬られた場所に植えられた2本のマンゴーの樹だった。ベトナム戦争の爆撃の跡をテーマとした前作の《Bomb Ponds》と同じように、過去の痕跡がほとんど見えなくなってしまった風景が《MONOLOGUE》でも主役として登場する。ありきたりの水田は、過去の記憶をほとんど喪失したかのような村人たちによって耕され、その土地に何千人もの死者が眠っていることを思い出させるようなものは何もない。だが、世界のどこでもそうであるように、風景には歴史の傷跡が残っている。ヴァンディー・ラッタナは、大きな歴史と絡み合う彼自身の家族の歴史を通じて、この静かな風景に主観的な声を与えているのだ。

第1作をフィクションによって展開したほかの2作でも、風景は際立っている。《...far away, over there, the ocean》では、ひとりの若い画家が風景の本質を探求しているが、一度もうまくとらえることができないでいる。彼はその過程で、衰退し続けながらもなおも美しい森の魅力と、過去の痕跡を一掃しつつある首都プノンペンの野放図な都市化の両方を目撃する。この作品は、ヴァンディー・ラッタナが10年前に撮影したプノンペン初の超高層建築と都市部での立ち退きをとらえた写真シリーズの延長線上にあるとも言えるだろう。この映像作品はまた、歴史から受け継いだトラウマと幻想に満ちた未来との狭間で、クメール・ルージュ以降の世代の若者たちを省みるものでもある。「風景はどこにも見つからない。僕は僕自身を見ている、ただそれだけだ。なぜ自分自身を探しているのだろう？　たぶん、風景とは、光の粒子を通して自分自身を見ることのできる鏡なのかもしれない。鏡に映る僕の姿には、風味も匂いも温もりもない。むしろ、何者かになりたいと欲する痛みがある。風景は果てしない夢なのだろうかと、いつも考えている」（抜粋）。

《Funeral》は、解放された奴隷たちの足音で始まる。「僕は避難所を建てている（…）神々に会えるほど高い避難所だ。これが僕の見た夢のお告げだ。ほかの人たちも夢を見ている。僕の夢を破壊するだろう夢だ。夢から生まれた文明は廃れていく（…）、崩壊して、ついには灰になる（…）。僕の夢は少しずつしぼんでいき、記憶は奈落の底へ、想像を絶する空虚へと落ちていく。僕はまだすべてのことを、自分が築いたもののことを覚えている。僕の声はひどく弱まってきた。ここで僕の夢は終わるのだ」（抜粋）。三部作の最後となる《Funeral》は、いくつもの感情を通して私たちの存在を問いかける。人間とは、自分でつくり出した幻想や神話の奴隷なのではないか。あらゆる創造行為は、それ自体のうちに終わりを含んでいるとはいえ、もしかしたら過去の灰は、再び生まれてくる命を温めているのではなかろうか。

水田の下に埋められた何千人もの死者たち、土地投機の強行による景観の破壊、袋小路に陥ることがわかっている野心的な夢など――場所や時代を超えた残酷さに直面するヴァンディー・ラッタナは、フランスの作家アルベール・カミュと同じように、私たちにこう訴えかけているのかもしれない。現実と向き合い、私たちの存在という不条理を受け入れ、そしてこの変わりゆく世界における自らの立ち位置について、常に自分自身に問いかけるように、と。

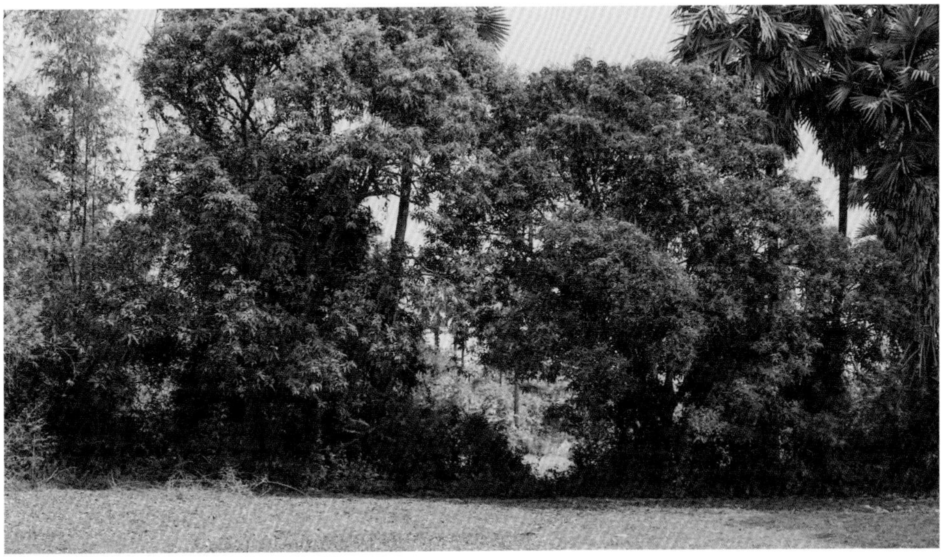

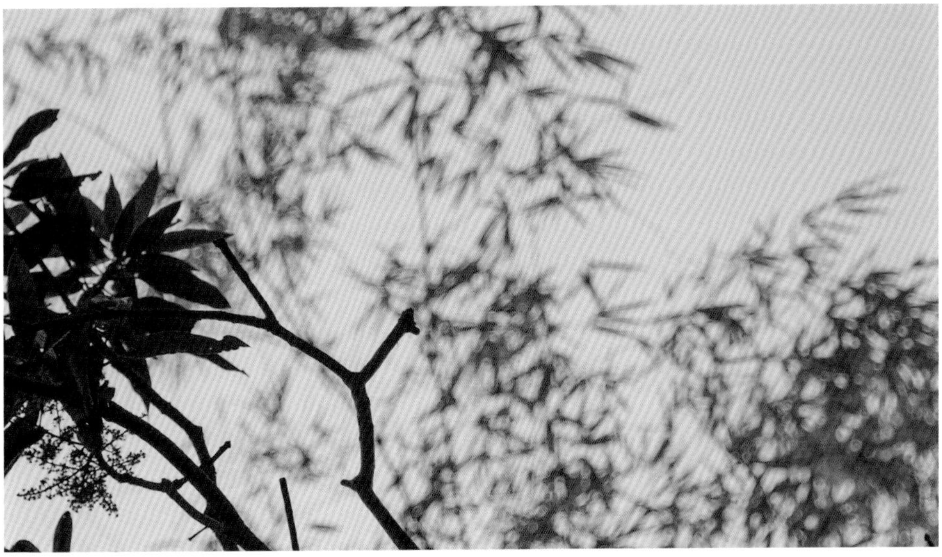

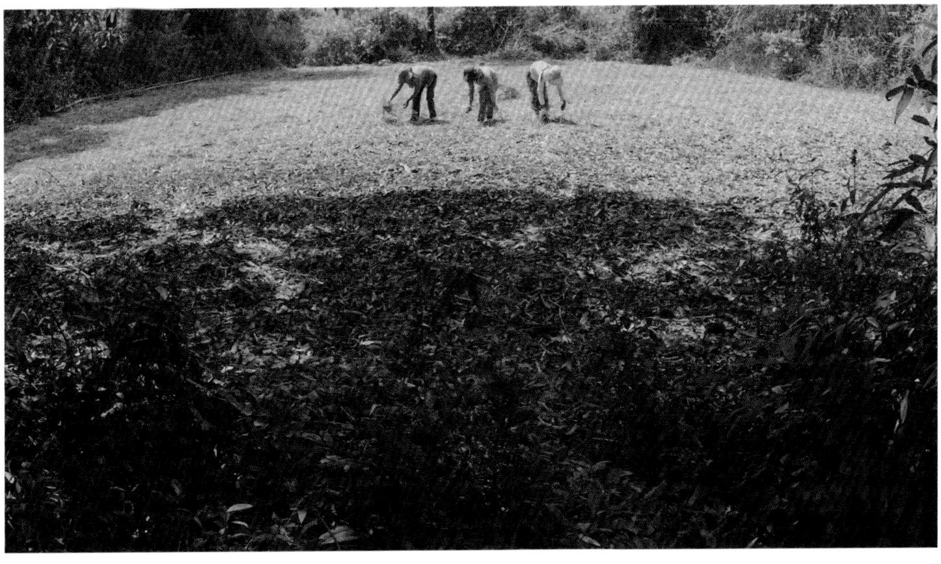

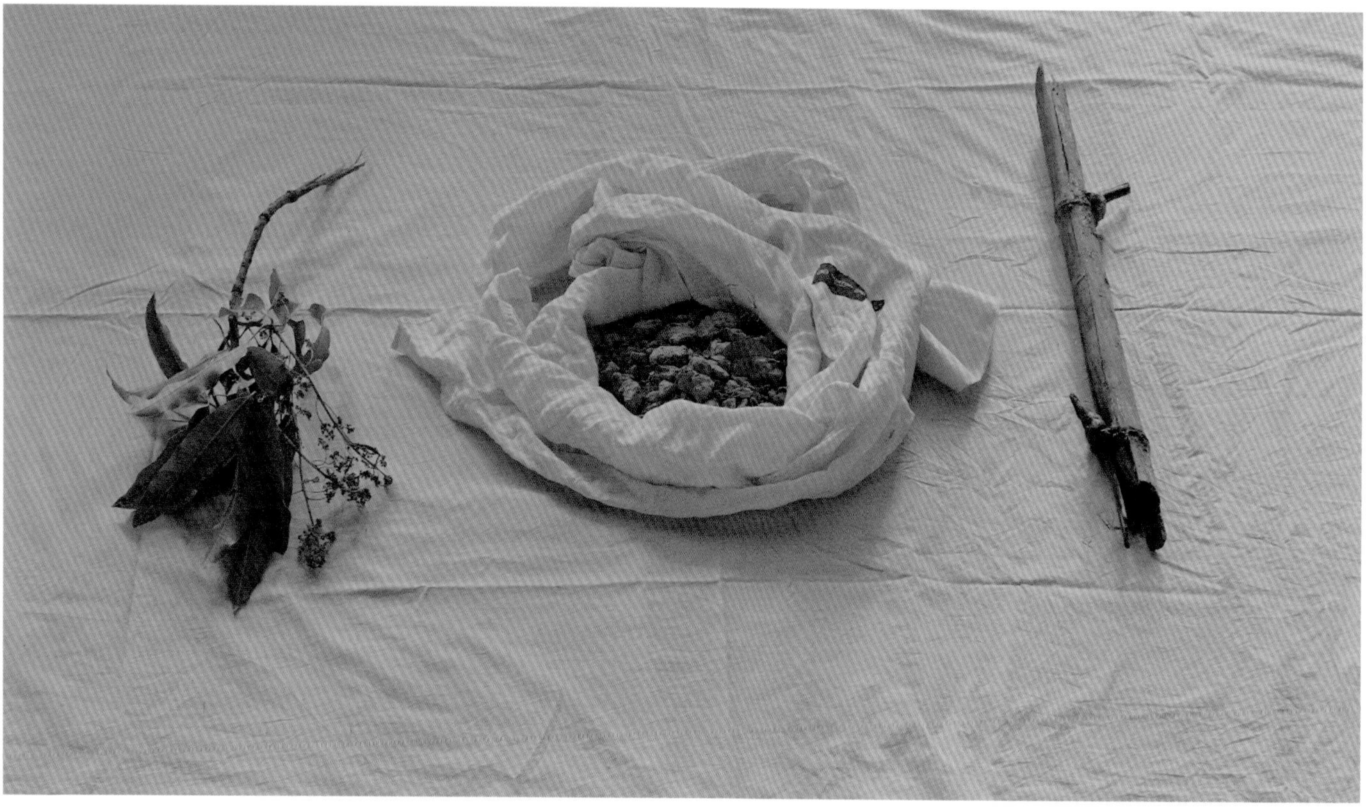

All images on pp. 121–124:
MONOLOGUE
Co-Production: Jeu de Paume, Paris and CAPC musé d'art contemporain de Bordeaux

Bárbara Sánchez-Kane

バルバラ・サンチェス・カネ

1987, Mérida, Mexico.
Bárbara Sánchez-Kane lives and works in Mexico City.
Under the figure of the *macho sentimental*, Sánchez-Kane resists the traditional notions of *mexicanidad* and its relationship with the feminine and masculine. It does not matter if it is through fashion design, painting, performance or installation, the work is the same, going through anxiety and fear, to question pleasure and domination.
Some of the most notable solo exhibitions and performances by the artist include: *Sánchezkaneismo*, kurimanzutto, Mexico City (2022); *Prêt-à-Patria* (as part of *Siembra*), kurimanzutto (2021); *Latino Couture*, Museo Experimental El ECO, Mexico City (2020); *Macho Sentimental vol. II*, Palais de Tokyo, Paris (2019); *Las Puertas al Sentimentalismo*, Licenciado Gallery, Mexico City (2019); *Macho Sentimental vol. I*, Grand Tour Studio, Milan (2018); and *Vast Graveyard of the Missing*, Institute of Contemporary Art, Los Angeles (2017). Among her most recent group exhibitions are *De por Vida*, Company Gallery, New York (2021); *en llamas*, LLANO, Mexico City, (2021); *Otrxs Mundxs*, Museo Tamayo, Mexico City (2020); *Señora*, Galerie Meyer Kainer, Vienna (2020); and *Prince·sse·s des villes*, Palais de Tokyo (2019).

1987年、メキシコ、メリダ生まれ。現在はメキシコシティを拠点に活動。
独自に提唱する「macho sentimental（マッチョ・センチメンタル）」の考えに基づき、メキシコに対する伝統的なイメージ、およびその女性性や男性性との関係に抵抗する。ファッションデザイン、絵画、パフォーマンス、インスタレーションなどの手法を用いて、不安と恐れ、そして快楽と支配に対する問いを一貫して表現している。
主な個展・パフォーマンスに、2022年「Sánchezkaneismo」kurimanzutto（メキシコシティ）、2021年「Prêt-à-Patria」（「Siembra」展示企画の一環として）kurimanzutto、2020年「Latino Couture」エコ現代美術館（メキシコシティ）、2019年「Macho Sentimental vol. II」パレ・ド・トーキョー（パリ）、2019年「Las Puertas al Sentimentalismo」Licenciado Gallery（メキシコシティ）、2018年「Macho Sentimental vol. I」Grand Tour Studio（ミラノ）、2017年「Vast Graveyard of the Missing」インスティテュート・オブ・コンテンポラリーアート・ロサンゼルスなど。
近年の主なグループ展に、2021年「De por Vida」Company Gallery（ニューヨーク）、2021年「en llamas」LLANO（メキシコシティ）、2020年「Otrxs Mundxs」ルフィーノ・タマヨ博物館（メキシコシティ）、2020年「Señora」Galerie Meyer Kainer（ウィーン）、2019年「Prince.sse.s des villes」パレ・ド・トーキョーがある。

Versos Rancios [Rancid verse]

2022
Installation
Bronze and rawhide sculpture, 6 wood school desks, 6 rawhide shirts, chalks, green chalkboard paint
235 cm height
Dimensions variable
On site installation
Courtesy of the artist and kurimanzutto, Mexico City/New York

The skin, our biggest organ, is also what separates and divides us by its aesthetic attributes. Anchored to our identity as a tool of differentiation.

In addition, it shows the reflection of what it covers, what lays in it, what we honor as invisible and inaccessible.

Working as a shield to protect those displays of history of violence, of fragility and mortality of emptiness. Of what was forced upon us and its symbolic reinterpretation.

Society's violent sapiential dogmas and paradigms revitalized and in permanent re-creation.

How do we break through those thinking schemes when those become such a fundamental part of us? The rotten lineage is worn on our skin, a power that is not earned but instead given to ourselves. Who was born first, the belief or the believer?

With all differentiation attributes removed, a neutral body image is put forward, enrolled in a life and death cycle, condemned to rottenness, from which only will survive its mental model evolution, inherited from its ancestors, engraved in a fossilized room of wounded bodies.

私たちの身体の最大の器官である皮膚は、その審美的な特性によって人間を分け隔て、また引き離すものでもある。それは人を差別するツールとして、私たちのアイデンティティに根づいている。

さらに皮膚は、それが覆っているもの、その内側にあるもの、見ることも触れることもできないものとして私たちが守っているものを映し出す。

暴力の歴史を、虚弱性を、そして儚い生き物の死すべき運命を表すものを守るために、皮膚はその盾として機能している。私たちに押しつけられたものを守り、そしてその押しつけられたものの象徴的な再解釈を守るための盾となっているのだ。

社会の暴力的な知の教義《ドグマ》とパラダイムが再生し、永遠に再創造され続ける。

こうした思考回路が私たちの根本を占めるようになってしまったとき、どうしたらそれを打破できるのだろうか？　腐った血統は、私たちの皮膚にまとわりつく。その力は、私たち自身が獲得したものではなく、私たちに与えられたものだ。信条とそれを信ずる者、どちらが先に生まれたのだろうか？

あらゆる差別的な属性を取り除けば、現れるのはニュートラルな身体イメージだ。それは生と死のサイクルに組み込まれ、やがては腐敗へと至る。そこに残るのはただ、祖先から受け継いだそのメンタルモデルの進化のみ。それが、傷んだ身体の化石化した部屋に刻まれるのだろう。

Bárbara Sánchez-Kane

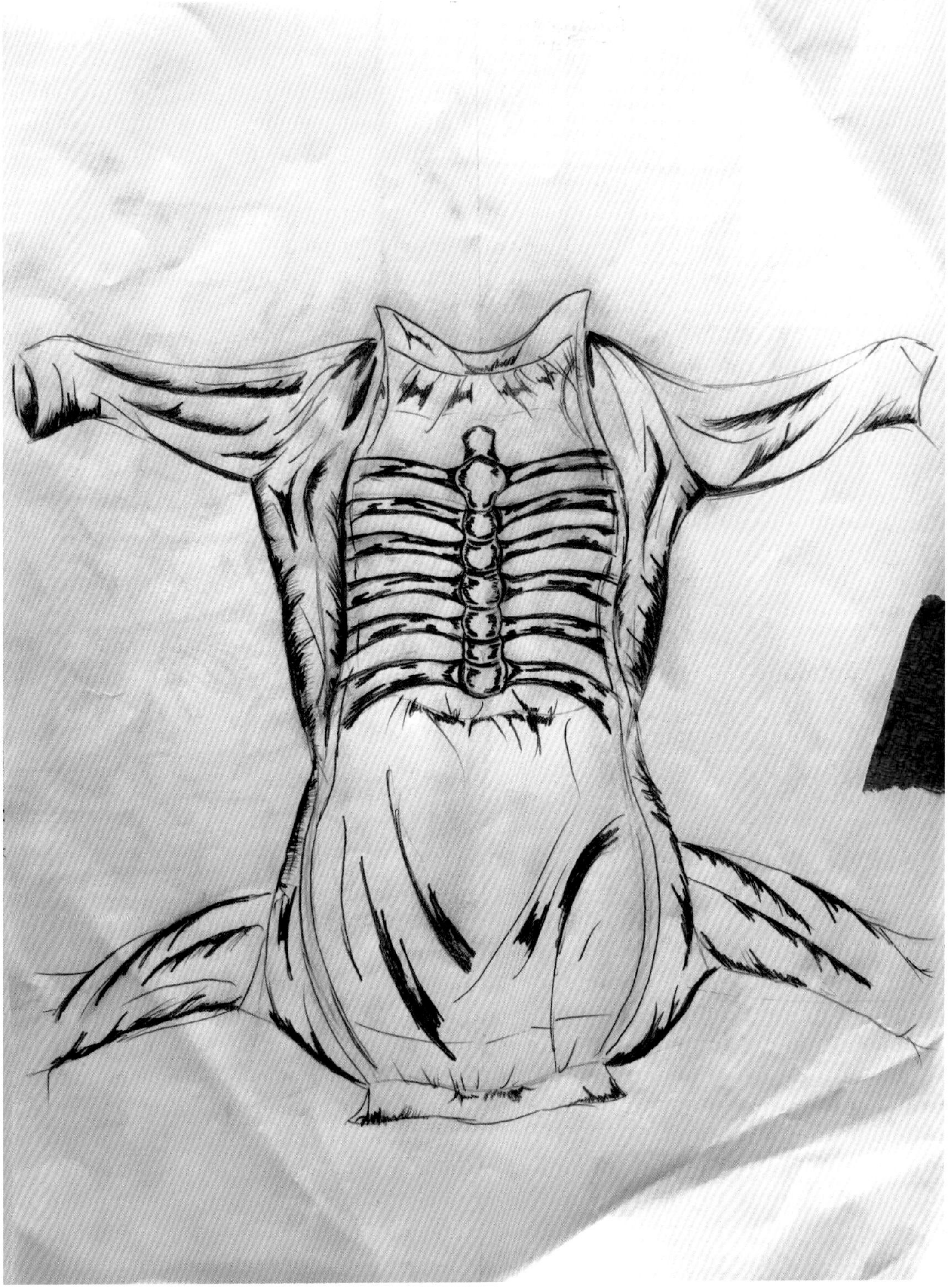

Sketch image for *Versos Rancios* [Rancid verse]
© Studio Sánchez-Kane
《Versos Rancios [Rancid verse]》のためのスケッチ

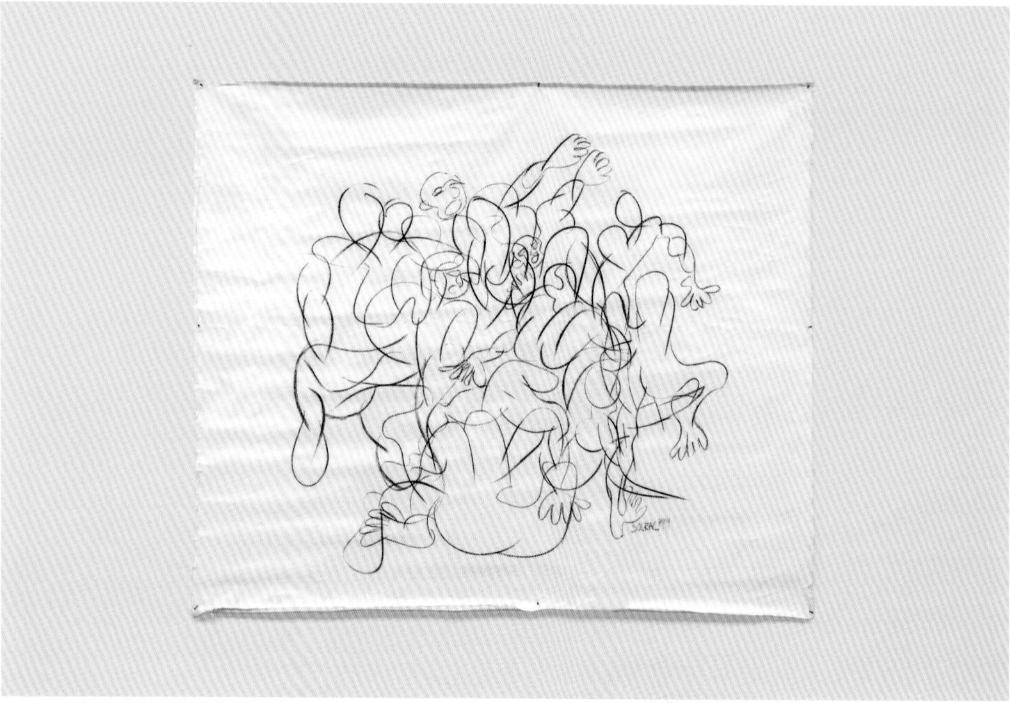

Formando barricadas para retrasar nuestro adios, 2022
Charcoal on canvas
260 × 303 cm
Photo: kurimanzutto

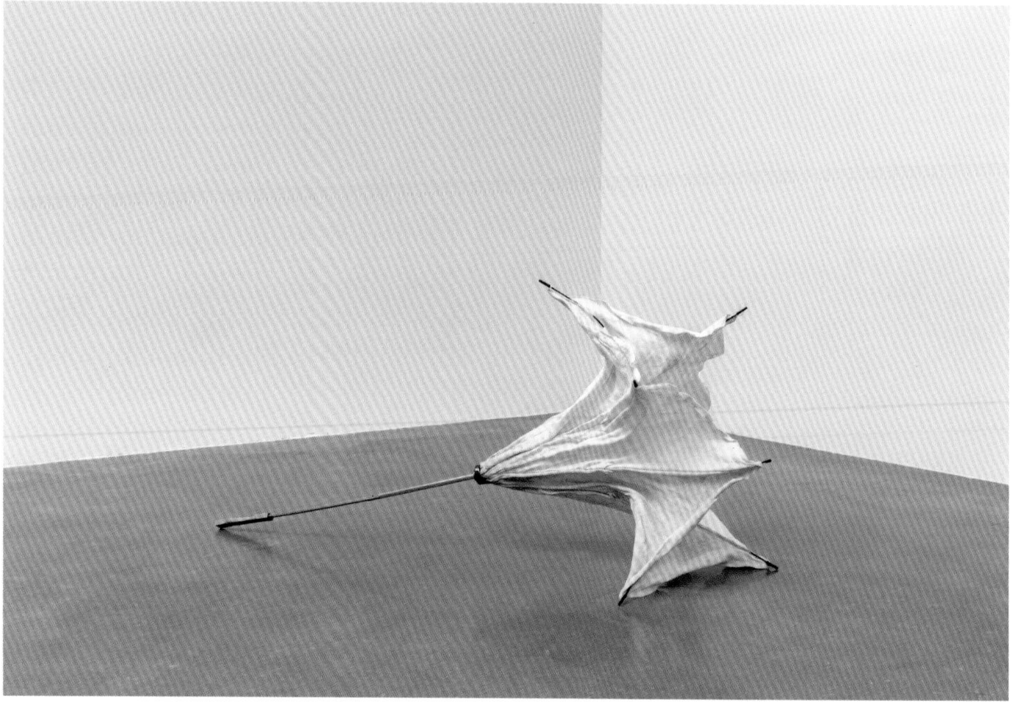

La lluvia ya no es gozo cuando se carga el desierto dentro, 2022
Rawhide and copper
86 × 143 × 86 cm
Photo: kurimanzutto

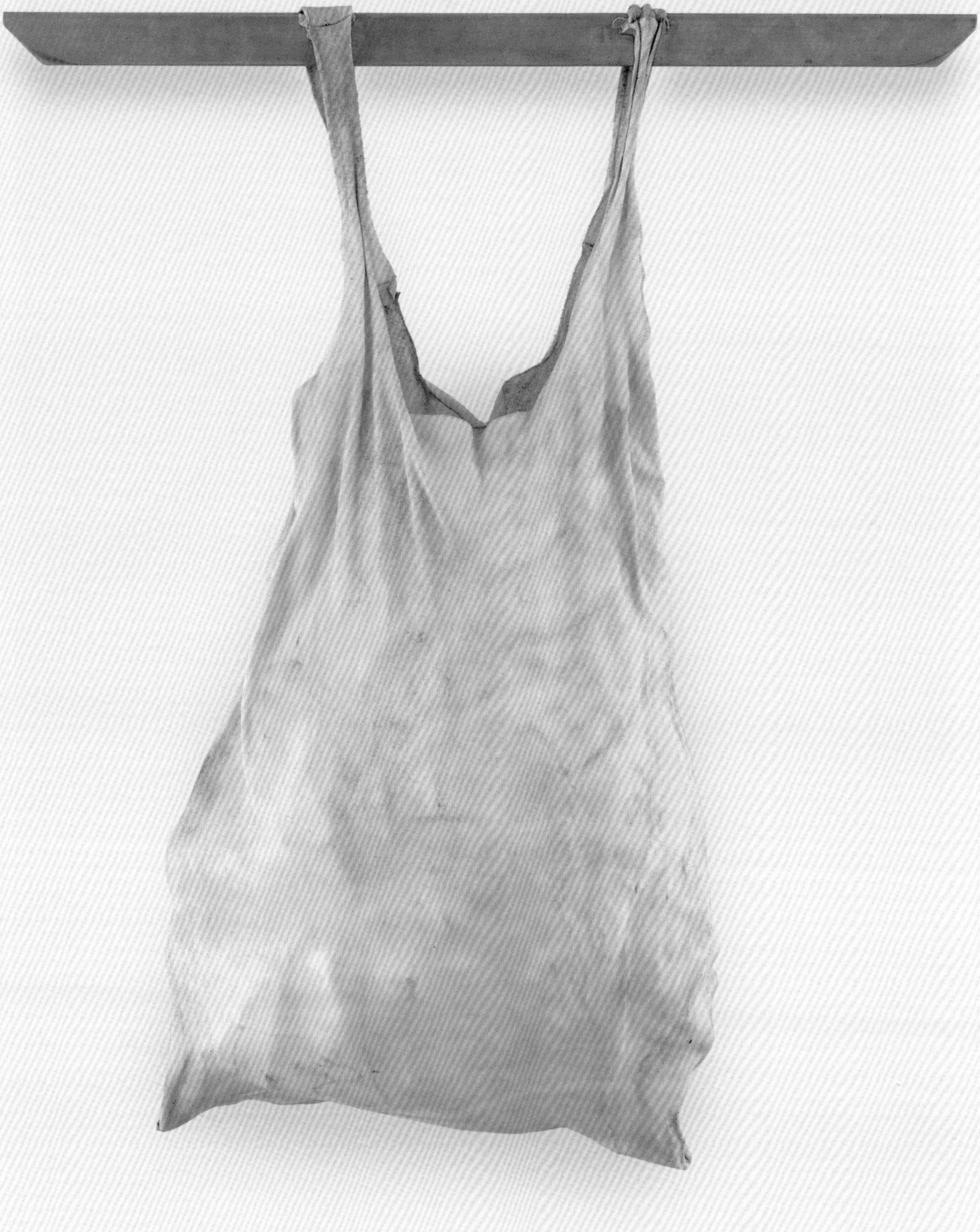

Mercado Rawhide, 2022
57 × 49 × 26 cm
Rawhide and copper
Photo: kurimanzutto

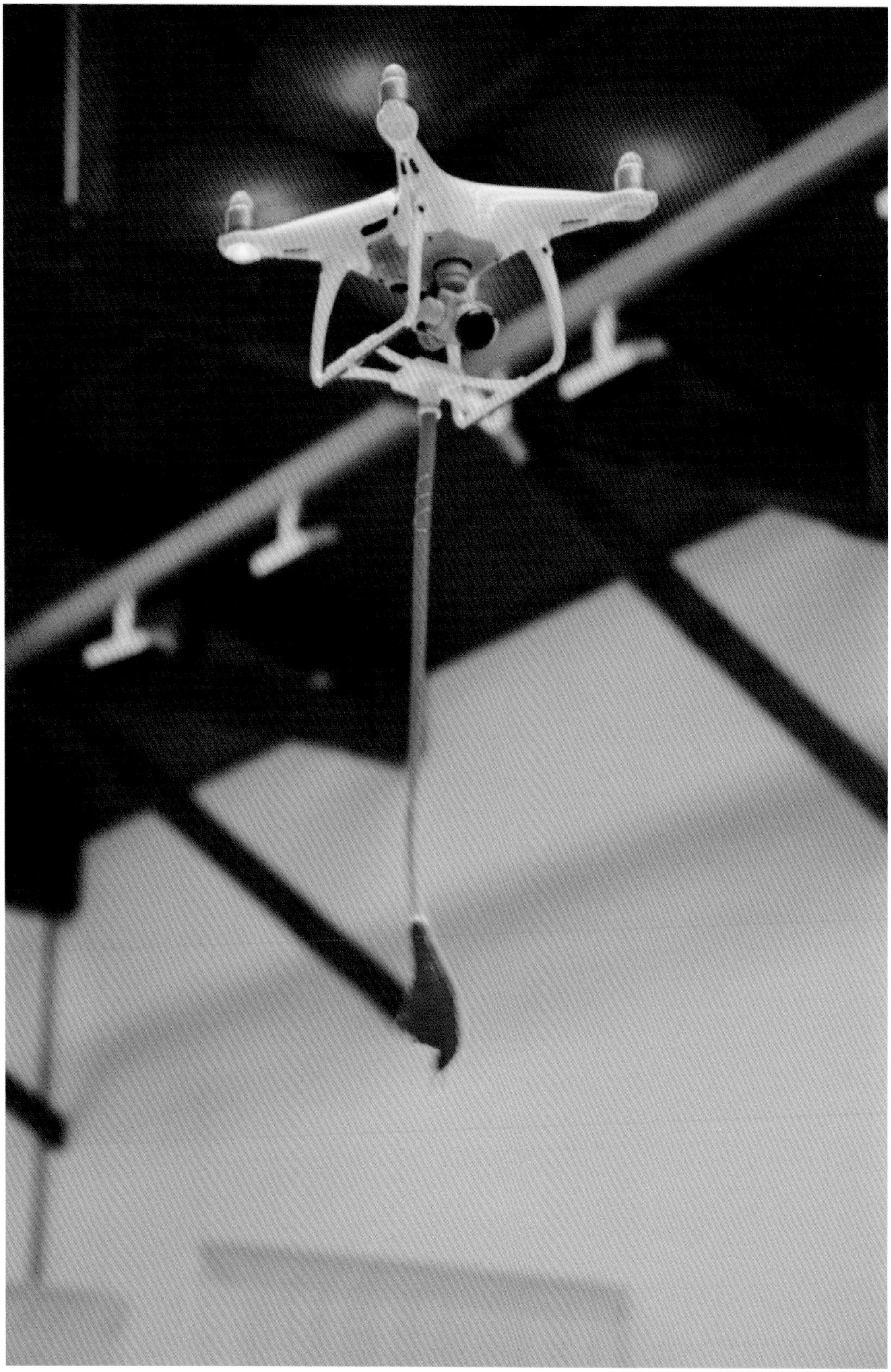

Sánchez Kaneismo
© Studio Sánchez-Kane

Aki Sasamoto

笹本晃

Aki Sasamoto is a New York-based, Japanese artist, who works in performance, sculpture, dance, and video. Her works have been shown both in performing art and visual art venues in New York and abroad. Besides her own works, she has collaborated with musicians, choreographers, scientists and scholars, and she plays multiple roles of dancer, sculptor, or director. Sasamoto's performance/installation works revolve around gestures on nothing and everything. Her installations are careful arrangements of sculpturally altered found objects, and the decisive gestures in her improvisational performances create feedback, responding to sound, objects, and moving bodies. The constructed stories seem personal at first, yet oddly open to variant degrees of access, relation, and reflection.
Solo exhibitions include *Yield Point*, The Kitchen, New York (2017) and *Delicate Cycle*, SculptureCenter, New York (2016). Group exhibitions include Aichi Triennale 2022 (2022); 59th Venice Biennale (2022); Kunsthal Rotterdam (2021); UCCA Edge, Shanghai (2021); Tai Kwun, Hong Kong (2018); Reykjavik Art Museum (2017); Yebisu International Festival for Art & Alternative Visions, Tokyo (2017); 3rd Kochi-Muziris Biennale, Kochi (2016); 11th Shanghai Biennale (2016); Dojima River Biennale, Osaka (2015); Parasophia: Kyoto International Festival of Contemporary Culture (2015); High Line Art, New York (2014); Mori Art Museum, Tokyo (2013); Gwangju Biennale (2012); MoMA PS1, New York (2010); Whitney Bienniale, New York (2010); and Yokohama Triennale (2008).

笹本晃はパフォーマンス、彫刻、ダンス、映像作品などを手がけ、ニューヨークをはじめ世界各国のパフォーミングアーツやヴィジュアルアートの美術館・ギャラリー・施設などで作品を発表している。ミュージシャン、振付師、科学者、学者など幅広い分野の人間とのコラボレーションも多数展開し、自他の作品のなかでダンサー、彫刻家、ディレクターとして様々な役割を演じている。笹本のパフォーマンス／インスタレーション作品は、何気ない、ありとあらゆるしぐさを中心に展開している。彫刻的に編集した物（ファウンド・オブジェ）を緻密に構成したインスタレーション、また即興パフォーマンスで展開するきつ然とした身振りがフィードバックを生み、音や物、身体動作と呼応する。そこで組み立てられた物語は一見すると個人的なものに見えるが、その背景には様々な社会との関係性や考察への可能性がある。
主な個展に、2017年「Yield Point」ザ・キッチン（ニューヨーク）、2016年「Delicate Cycle」スカルプチャー・センター（ニューヨーク）がある。主なグループ展に、2022年国際芸術祭「あいち2022」、2022年第59回ヴェネツィア・ビエンナーレ、2021年ロッテルダム芸術ホール、2021年UCCA Edge（上海）、2018年大館（香港）、2017年レイキャビク美術館、2017年第9回恵比寿映像祭（東京）、2016年の第3回コチ=ムジリス・ビエンナーレ（コチ）、2016年第11回上海ビエンナーレ、2015年堂島リバービエンナーレ2015（大阪）、2015年Parasophia: 京都国際現代芸術祭、2014年High Line Art（ニューヨーク）、2013年森美術館（東京）、2012年光州ビエンナーレ、2010年MoMA PS1（ニューヨーク）、2010年ホイットニー・ビエンナーレ2010（ニューヨーク）、2008年横浜トリエンナーレなどがある。

Weather Bar

2022
Site-specific video installation

Inserting a bar set up in the school building, this installation invites the audience member to watch (=drink) weather forecasts. Inspired by a transitional location like an airport corridor, the weather bar in a classroom may extend the meaning of transition into life. It will be a part lecture, a part sports bar, and infuse the surrealistic mixture of fear and beauty that weathers present.

This bar is to serve a lonesome customer, one person or a small group. The bar will serve a "drink," a phenomenon of spinning of a whiskey glass. Some other possible drinks are presented in the weather forecast videos, in its making as demonstration.
As the forecasts unfold, science and mystery are fused with much satire for the recent abnormal world events and climate changes.

Transcription from Weather Bar Forecast #1

Hi, thanks for joining me for the weather forecast. Fluctuating conditions across the map.
No two days are the same really over the next few days and you can see that on the city forecast for London and Paris. Some rain, and some sunshine. We got some heavier rain, quite torrential. This rain is moving through the Balkans out of Italy. But it won't be long before another storm develops through the Mediterranean, affecting Corsica and Sardinia.
Now to the east of that we've actually got some warmth. Temperatures way higher than they should be for this time of the year across Iran up into Kazakhstan. You can see quite clearly the Middle East will see the rain easing as the stormy weather is set to arrive back into the Black Sea.
Now we've got a little bit of wintry flavor across the Himalayas as that colder air continues to dominate across China, Burma, and over into Thailand, the Philippines as well really seeing those temperature tumbling away.
So this is the story into Monday—pretty unsettled through the Mediterranean. Another weather front moving through, leaving dryer and brighter conditions behind. The best of the sunshine and warmth for Athens.

Now let's look at the local weather in your body. Expect some travel delays, it's going to be a mess. Keep those travel plans flexible. Inside your gastrointestinal tract, some dry interlude, sandwiched between the east and the west. The liquid will move along the dry front against the gust at 30 miles per hour, prolonging the process through the esophagus. The whiskey vapor will quickly evaporate to form a cloud full of heavy gastric acid rain. In the stomach, 45 miles per hour. It may experience sporadic burst as the spleen adds its angry gust. 60 miles per hour. Now when this hot air mixes with Kidney's chill, the air shrinks rapidly at the speed of 70 miles per hour. This will cause the cloud full of hail, radiating throughout the small intestines. In the big intestines, it will be a storm you have never expected. Definitely bring an umbrella.

After the storm you will see sunshine with slight breeze at 5 to 7 miles per hour, smooth sailing for the next few days. Good days for moving and for kids to roll on the ground in the park. I recommend doing all your laundry while you can before the next cloud rolls in.

Past in a future tense, Table 1, 2019
Hand-blown glass, whiskey glass, HVAC system, centrifugal fan, speed control, red oak, iron table base, paper receipt
327.7 × 426.7 × 238.8 cm
©Aki Sasamoto. Courtesy of the artist and Bortolami, New York and Take Ninagawa, Tokyo
Photo: John Berens

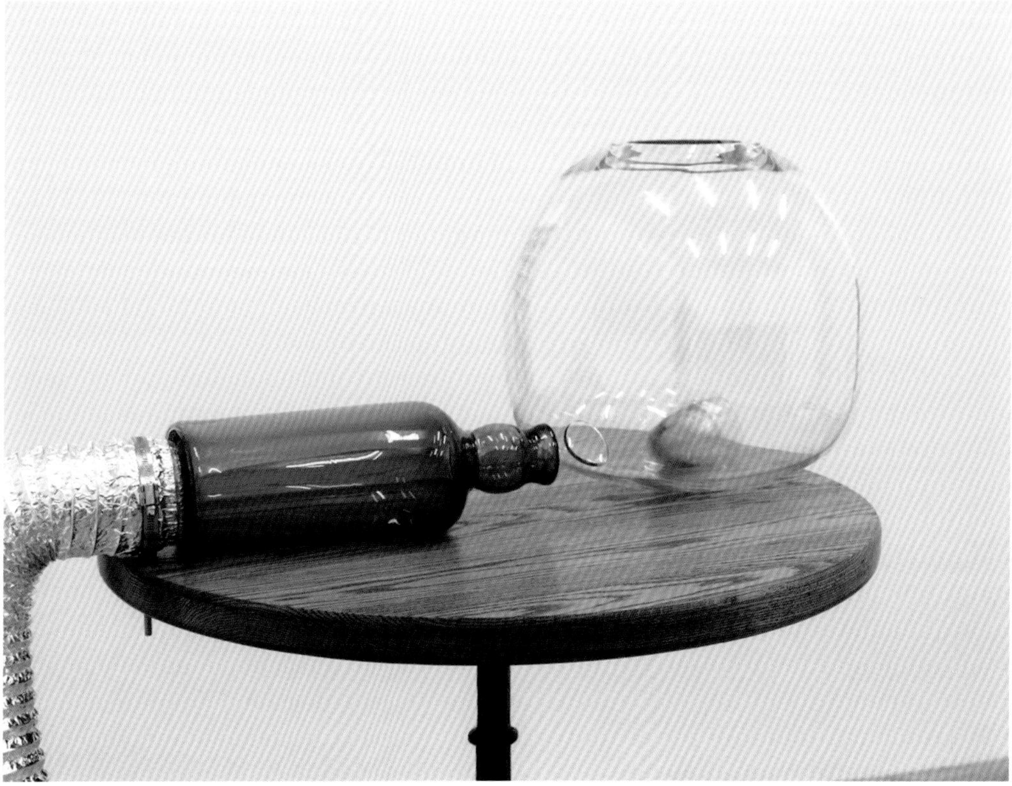

Transcription from Weather Bar Forecast #2

Hi, welcome back to the weather forecast.
We are getting a little worried over here. We have never seen the condition quite like this. This month is coming in with yet another climate surprise. If this is any indication of what's coming for the year ahead, this year is going to be a crazy year.
We worry about the tornados today in the blue and orange area, I know we think about tornado being a North American phenomenon, but they could also be seen in the southern hemisphere and parts of Asia as well.
Here is the storm.
Monday expect a tornado, Tuesday expect a tornado, Wednesday also a tornado, Thursday of course a tornado, Friday the tornado, the weekend more and most tornados...
This is unfortunately the simulation of where the tornados may be today. Be prepared.

校舎内に設置されたバーで、天気予報を見る（＝飲む）インスタレーション。空港のコンコースのような過渡的な場所からインスピレーションを受け、教室に設置された天気バーは、過渡の意味を人生へと拡張するかもしれない。レクチャーであり、スポーツバーでもあり、天気のもたらす恐怖と美しさのシュールな絡みを。

このバーは、ひとりまたは少人数の孤独な客にサービスを提供するものである。このバーでは、「ドリンク」としてウイスキーグラスが回転する現象を提供する。天気予報の映像ではほかにもいくつかの飲み物が紹介されており、デモンストレーションとしてつくられている。天気予報が進むにつれ、科学と神秘は融合し、近頃の異常な世界情勢や気候変動に対する風刺も多く含まれていく。

天気バー予報 #1より書き起こし

こんにちは、天気予報をご覧いただきありがとうございます。広範囲にわたって気候が変動します。この先数日間、同じような日はありません。ロンドンとパリの天気予報を見ればわかるように、雨もあれば、晴れ間もあります。相当激しい雨、この雨はバルカン半島を通過しイタリアを抜けていきます。そして別の嵐が地中海で発生し、コルシカ島とサルデーニャ島に影響を与えるまで長くはかからないでしょう。
さて、東寄りでは暖かくなってきました。イランからカザフスタンにかけて、この時期の例年よりかなり高い気温になっています。黒海沿岸に荒れ模様の天気が戻ると同時に中東では雨の勢いが弱まることがわかります。
ヒマラヤ山脈は冬型の気圧配置となり、冷気が中国、ビルマ、タイ、フィリピンまでおよび、気温が下がります。
月曜日までは地中海沿岸でかなり不安定な天気となります。しかしその後は前線が通過し、乾燥して晴れた天気になります。アテネでは暖かくなり、よく晴れそうです。

では、あなたの身体の中の各地の天気を見てみましょう。交通の乱れが予想されます、混乱が起きるでしょう。旅行の計画は柔軟に立ててください。胃腸の中は、東と西に挟まれた乾燥した場があります。液体は時速30マイルの突風に逆らって乾燥した前線に沿って移動し、食道を通過する過程が長引きそうです。ウイスキーの酒気はすぐに蒸発して、重い胃酸の雨をたくさん含んだ雲を形成します。胃の中では、時速45マイル。脾臓が激しい風を吹かせると、散発的な突風を経験するかもしれません。時速60マイル。さて、この熱い空気が腎臓の冷気と混ざると、空気は時速70マイルで急速に収縮します。これによって、小腸全体にわたり雹を降らせる雲が発生します。大腸では、想像のつかないほどの嵐になることでしょう。絶対に傘をもっていってください。

嵐の後は晴れ、時速5〜7マイルの微風が吹き、今後数日間は順風満帆でしょう。体を動かしたり、子どもが公園で転がったりするには良いお天気でしょう。次の雲が来る前に、洗濯物を済ませておくことをおすすめします。

Aki Sasamoto

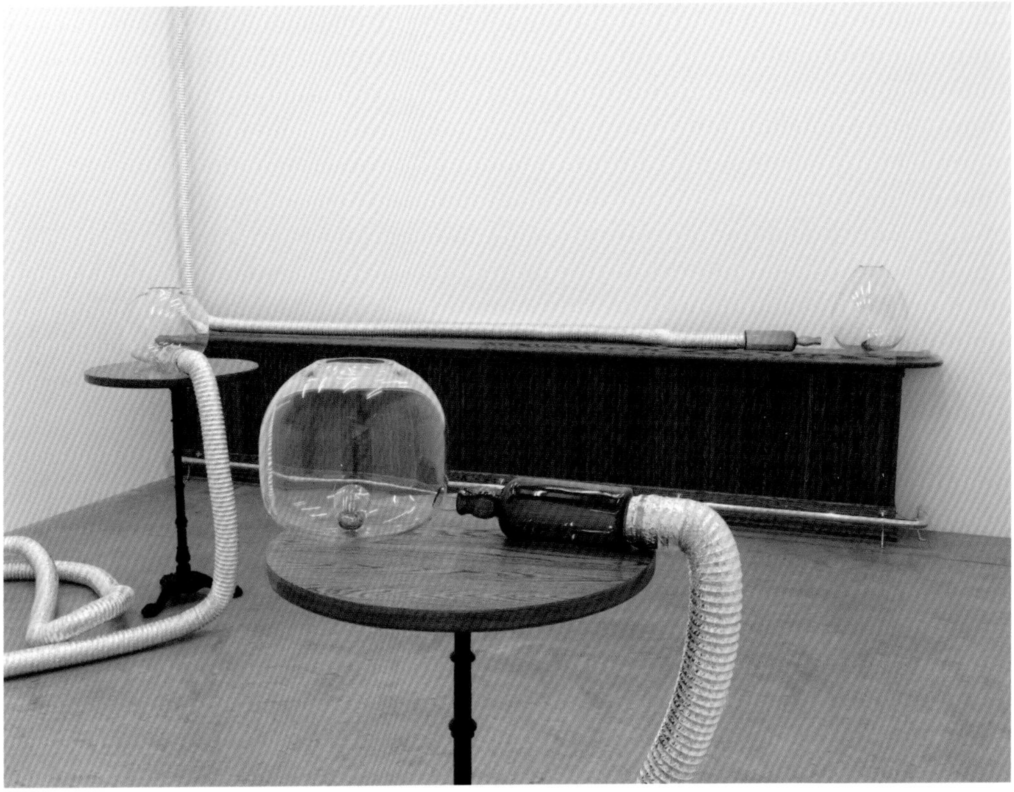

Past in a future tense, 2019, Bortolami, New York, installation view.
©Aki Sasamoto. Courtesy of the artist and Bortolami, New York and Take Ninagawa, Tokyo
Photo: John Berens
ニューヨーク、Bortolamiでの《Past in a future tense》展示風景

天気バー予報#2より書き起こし

こんにちは、天気予報へお帰りなさい。すこし心配になってきました。見たこともないような天気模様です。今月はまた新たに異常な気象がやってきます。これが今年の見通しの兆候だとしたら、今年はとんでもない一年になりそうです。
今日は青とオレンジの地域で竜巻の恐れがあります。竜巻は北アメリカの現象だと思われていますが、南半球やアジアの一部でも見られる可能性があります。
こちらがその嵐です。
月曜日は竜巻、火曜日は竜巻、水曜日も竜巻、木曜日はもちろん竜巻、金曜日も竜巻、週末はさらに多くの竜巻……。
これは残念ながら今日の竜巻が発生しそうな場所のシミュレーションです。覚悟してください。

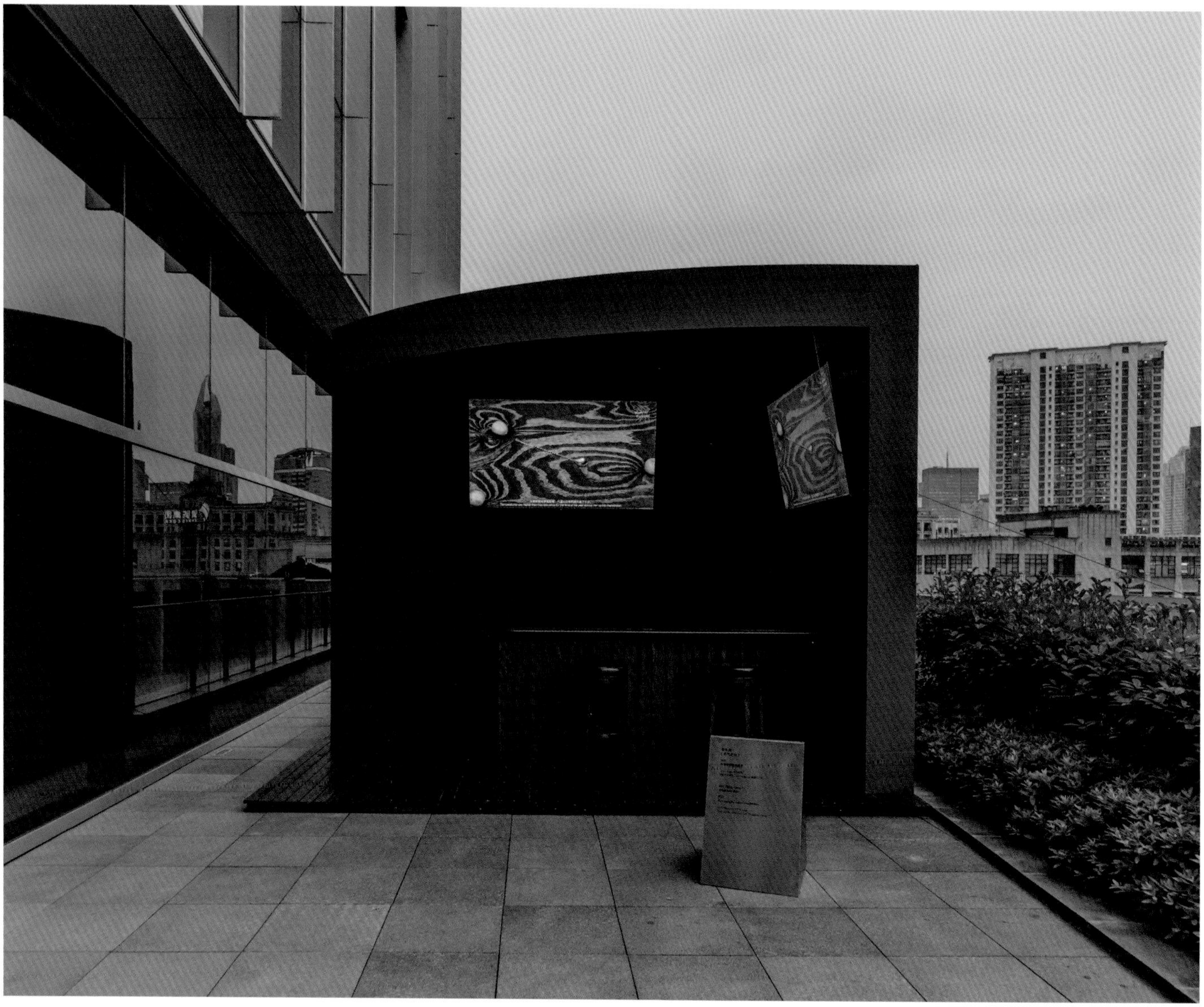

Weather Bar, 2021
Site-specific video installation
©Aki Sasamoto. Commission by UCCA Edge, courtesy of the artist and Take Ninagawa, Tokyo
Image courtesy of UCCA Center for Contemporary Art

ALL
YOU
NEED
IS
DYNAMITE

NO
FIRE
NO
ASHES

Jacolby Satterwhite

ジャコルビー・サッターホワイト

Jacolby Satterwhite is celebrated for a conceptual practice addressing crucial themes of labor, consumption, carnality and fantasy through immersive installation, virtual reality and digital media. He uses a range of software to produce intricately detailed animations and live action film of real and imagined worlds populated by the avatars of artists and friends. These animations serve as the stage on which the artist synthesizes the multiple disciplines that encompass his practice, namely illustration, performance, painting, sculpture, photography and writing. Satterwhite draws from an extensive set of references, guided by queer theory, modernism and video game language to challenge conventions of Western art through a personal and political lens. An equally significant influence is that of his late mother, Patricia Satterwhite, whose diagrams for visionary household products and ethereal vocals serve as the source material within a decidedly complex structure of memory and mythology.

Jacolby Satterwhite was born in 1986 in Columbia, South Carolina. He received his BFA from the Maryland Institute College of Arts, Baltimore and his MFA from the University of Pennsylvania, Philadelphia. Satterwhite's work has been presented in numerous exhibitions and festivals internationally, including most recently at the FRONT International: Cleveland Triennial for Contemporary Art (2022); Miller Institute for Contemporary Art, Pittsburgh (2021); Haus der Kunst, Munich (2021); Gwangju Biennale (2021); Fabric Workshop & Museum, Philadelphia (2019); Pioneer Works, New York (2019); Whitechapel Gallery, London (2019); MoMA, New York (2019); Museum of Contemporary Art, Chicago (2018); Fondation Louis Vuitton, Paris (2018); New Museum, New York (2017); San Francisco Museum of Art (2017); and Institute of Contemporary Art, Philadelphia (2017). His work is included in the collections of the Museum of Contemporary Art Kiasma, Helsinki; MoMA; Studio Museum in Harlem, New York; and the Whitney Museum of American Art, New York, among others. Satterwhite has collaborated with several musicians, including Solange Knowles in 2019 on her visual album, *When I Get Home*, and Perfume Genius in 2022 on his album, *Ugly Season*. He was awarded a public art commission in collaboration with the Studio Museum in Harlem and the Public Art Fund to inaugurate Lincoln Center's new David Geffen Hall, debuting in October 2022 in New York.

1986年、サウスカロライナ州コロンビア生まれ。

労働、消費、肉欲、想像などのテーマを、没入型インスタレーション、仮想現実、デジタルメディアを通して提起するコンセプチュアルな創作活動で知られる。様々なソフトウェアを駆使して複雑かつ緻密なアニメーション／実写映像を制作し、現実と空想が絡み合った世界観を表現。アーティストや彼の友人がアバターとして登場し、イラスト、パフォーマンス、絵画、彫刻、写真、テキストなど作家が手がける多様な表現を融合させている。クィア理論、モダニズム、ヴィデオゲーム言語などを幅広く参照し、個人的・政治的な観点から従来の西洋美術の概念に立ち向かう。また亡き母、パトリシアからも強い影響を受けており、彼女が想像した日用品のスケッチ、そして軽妙な歌声をインスピレーションに、記憶と伝承という複雑な構造を編んでいる。

The Maryland Institute College of Artsで美術学士号を、ペンシルベニア大学で美術修士号を取得。多数の国際的な展示や芸術祭で発表しており、近年の主な展示に2022年FRONT International 2022：クリーヴランド現代美術トリエンナーレ 、2021年Miller Institute for Contemporary Art（ピッツバーグ）、2021年ハウス・デア・クンスト（ミュンヘン）、2021年光州ビエンナーレ、2019年Fabric Workshop & Museum（フィラデルフィア）、2019年パイオニア・ワークス（ニューヨーク）、2019年ホワイトチャペル・ギャラリー（ロンドン）、2019年ニューヨーク近代美術館、2018年シカゴ現代美術館、2018年フォンダシオン ルイ・ヴィトン（パリ）、2017年ニュー・ミュージアム（ニューヨーク）、2017年サンフランシスコ近代美術館、2017年インスティテュート・オブ・コンテンポラリーアート（フィラデルフィア）など。作品はヘルシンキ現代美術館キアズマ、ニューヨーク近代美術館、ハーレム・スタジオ美術館、ホイットニー美術館（ともにニューヨーク）などに所蔵されている。2019年にソランジュ・ノウルズのヴィジュアルアルバム『When I Get Home』、2022年にパフューム・ジーニアスのアルバム『Ugly Season』など、音楽家とのコラボレーション作品も手がけている。現在、2022年10月にリニューアルオープンを予定しているニューヨークのデイヴィッド・ゲフィン・ホールの事業委託を受け、パブリック・アート・ファンドとハーレム・スタジオ美術館との共同事業として、パブリックアート制作を行う。

Reifying Desire 7 – Dawn

2022
Two channel HD color video and 3D animation with sound
27 min. 25 sec.

Courtesy of the artist and Mitchell-Innes & Nash, New York

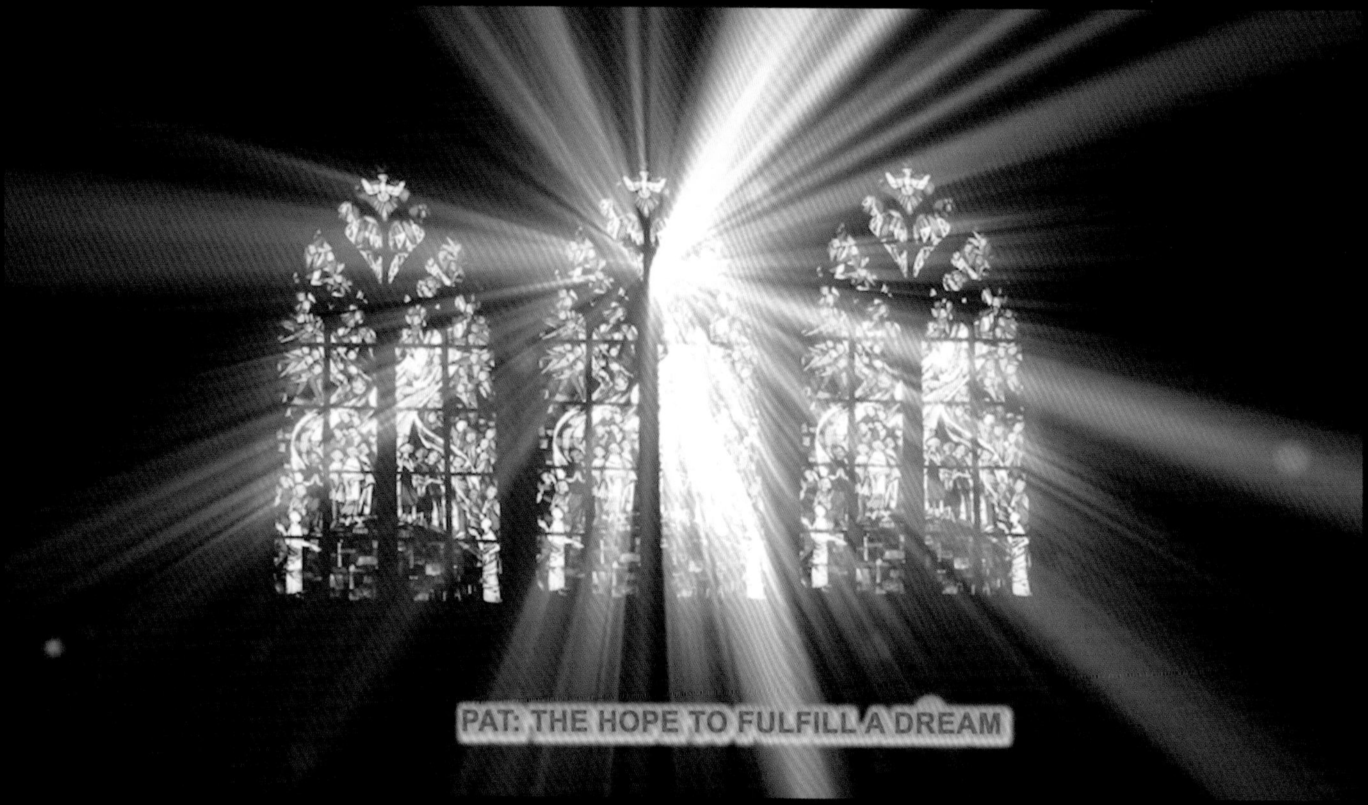

Reifying Desire 7—Dawn is an ambitious multimedia project by Jacolby Satterwhite that includes drawings gathered from residents of Cleveland's Fairfax neighborhood; an immersive video-game environment translating these drawings into a 3D world; a two-channel film installation with sound; and a layered graphic wallpaper, maypole painting, and more. Taken together, the project offers a 360-degree view of Satterwhite's unique creative process as well as a milestone in a long-term dialogue between the artist and the residents.

The installation is in dialogue with a previous work commissioned in 2021 by The Cleveland Clinic for which Satterwhite was asked to conceive of a public artwork for its new BioRepository facility in the neighborhood. He solicited texts and drawings from Fairfax residents responding to the prompt, "What does Utopia look like to you?" Their creations—nearly one hundred unique drawings—formed the inspiration for the successive stages of Satterwhite's work. Satterwhite transforms this material into the media on view by painstakingly digitizing and animating the drawings by hand.

In bringing his wide-ranging artistic process to both the Clinic and the Cleveland Institute of Art, Satterwhite's work offers a vision for how emergent forms of art-making can be boundary-crossing and multi-disciplinary yet socially-rooted.

《Reifying Desire 7—Dawn》は、ジャコルビー・サッターホワイトによる意欲的なマルチメディア・プロジェクトである。ここに盛り込まれているのは、アメリカの都市クリーヴランドのフェアファックス地区の住民たちから集められたスケッチの数々、そのスケッチを3Dの世界に変換した没入型のヴィデオゲーム・システム環境、サウンド付きの2チャンネル映像インスタレーション、自作のグラフィックが層をなす壁面、「メイポール・ペインティング（五月祭を描いた絵画）」などだ。総括すると、このプロジェクトは、サッターホワイトのユニークな創作過程を360度、全方向から見渡すことができると同時に、アーティストと地域住民たちとの長期的な対話のマイルストーンともなるものだ。

このインスタレーションは、2021年にクリーヴランド・クリニックから依頼を受けた前作に取り組むなかで生まれたものだ。その依頼は、地域に新しく建設されたバイオリポジトリ施設のために、パブリックアート作品を構想するというものだった。企画ではまず、フェアファックス地区の住人たちに、「あなたにとって、ユートピアはどんなふうに見えますか？」と問いかけ、これに答える短いテキストやスケッチを募った。約100点におよぶユニークなスケッチが集まり、サッターホワイトの制作プロセスに次々とインスピレーションをもたらしてくれた。この素材を手作業で丹念にデジタル化した彼は、それをアニメーションにすることで、今回展示されるメディアアート作品へと展開したのである。

広範におよぶ芸術的なプロセスの成果をクリニックとクリーヴランド美術大学の両方にもたらすことによって、サッターホワイトの作品は、芸術制作における新たな方式がいかに境界を越え、学際的でありながら、なおかつ社会にも根づいた営みになりうるかという展望を示している。

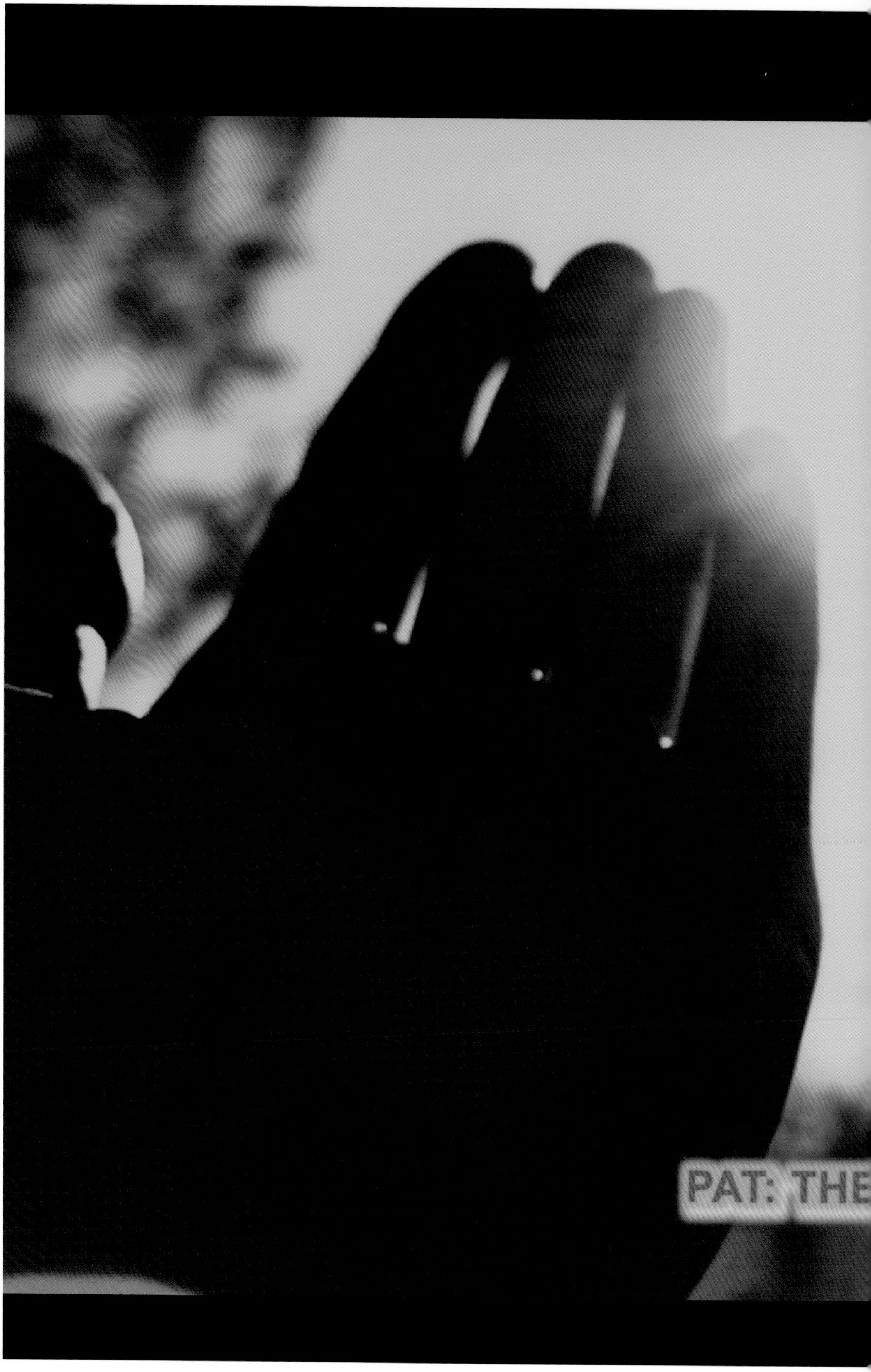
PAT: THE

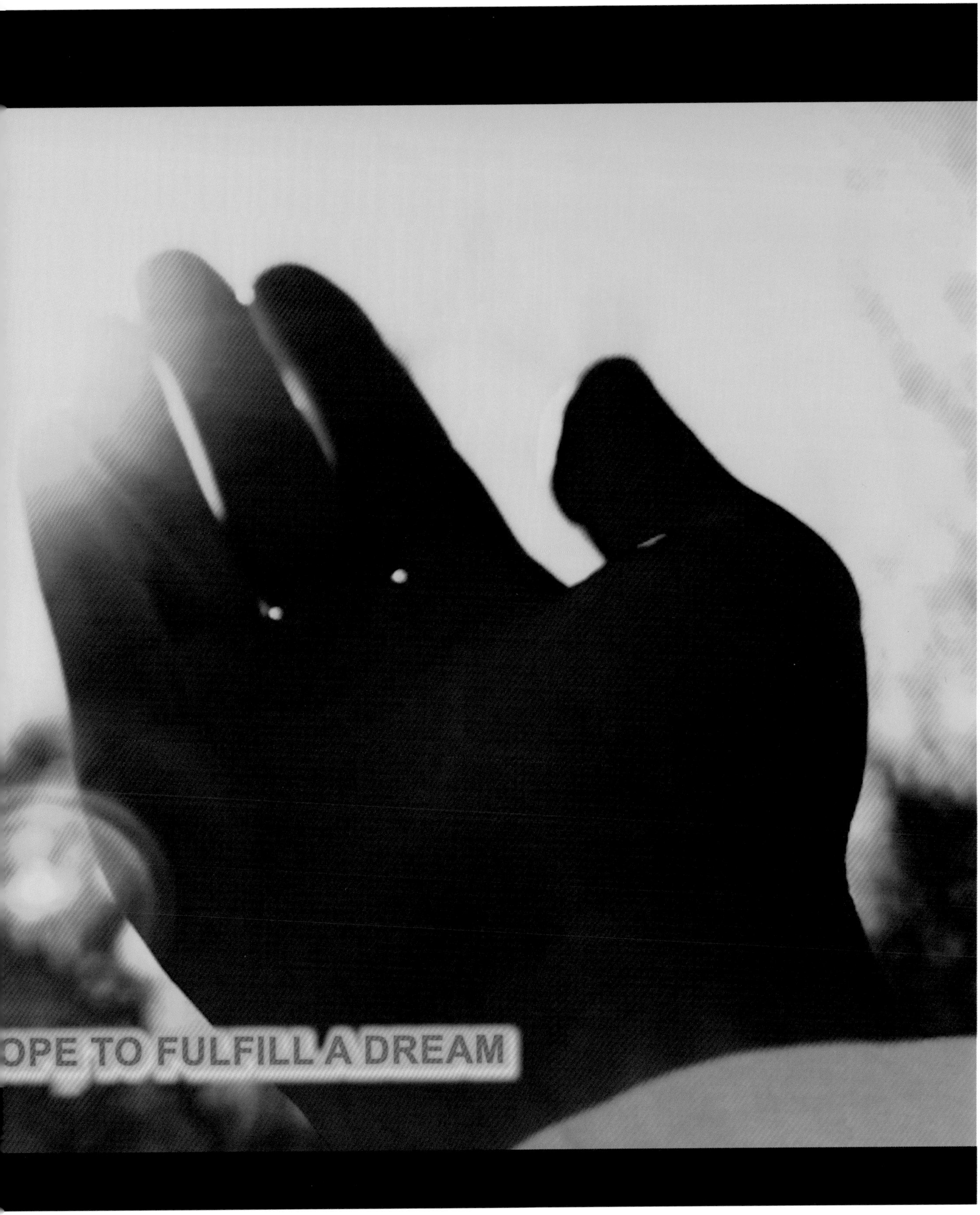
OPE TO FULFILL A DREAM

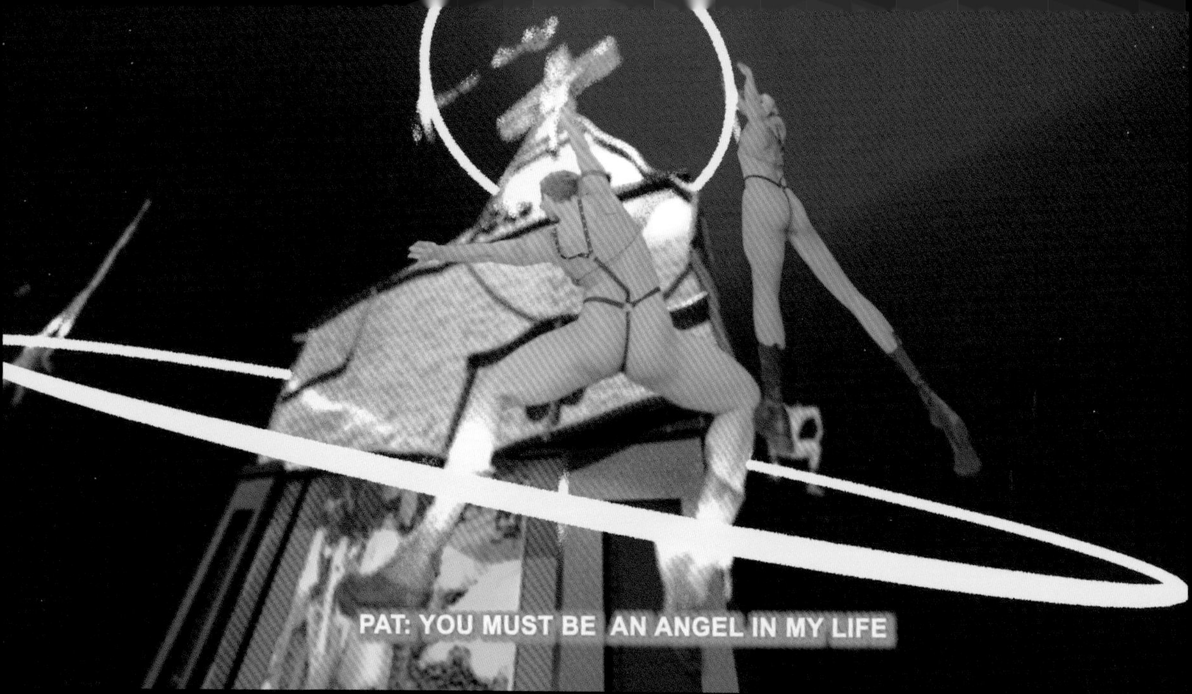
PAT: YOU MUST BE AN ANGEL IN MY LIFE

Shimabuku

島袋道浩

Born in 1969 in Kobe, Japan. Currently lives in Naha and works around the world.

Since the early 1990s, Shimabuku has traveled to many places, both in Japan and abroad. He produces videos, sculptures, performances, and installation works revolving around new ways of communication and the lives and cultures of people living in the places he visits, with his works often referring to the relationship between creatures and humans. His style, which is filled with poetic features and humor, provokes us in a metaphorical way, and has been acquiring international acclaim.

Shimabuku has participated in many major international exhibitions, including the 57th Venice Biennale (2017), the 14th Lyon Contemporary Art Biennale (2017), the 12th Havana Biennial (2015), the 9th Taipei Biennial (2014), the Sharjah Biennial 11 (2013), the 27th São Paulo Biennial (2006), the Liverpool Biennial (2006), and the 11th Biennale of Sydney (1998).

Recent major solo exhibitions include WIELS in Brussels (2022), Nouveau Musée National de Monaco (2021), and Le Crédac in Ivry-sur-Seine, France (2018), as well as Kunsthalle Bern in Switzerland (2014), and Ikon Gallery in Birmingham (2013).

1969年、神戸市出身。現在は那覇市を拠点に世界各地で活動。

1990年代初頭より国内外の多くの場所を旅し、その場所やそこに生きる人々の生活や文化、新しいコミュニケーションのあり方に関する映像、彫刻、パフォーマンス、インスタレーションなどを制作。その作品はときに生き物と人間との関係にもおよぶ。詩情とユーモアに溢れながらもメタフォリカルに人々を触発するような作風は世界的な評価を得ている。

主要な国際展にも数多く参加しており、そのなかには2017年第57回ヴェネツィア・ビエンナーレ、2017年第14回リヨン・ビエンナーレ、2015年第12回ハバナ・ビエンナーレ、2014年第9回台北ビエンナーレ、2013年第11回シャルジャ・ビエンナーレ、2006年第27回サンパウロ・ビエンナーレ、2006年リヴァプール・ビエンナーレ、1998年第11回シドニー・ビエンナーレなどがある。

主な近年の個展として、2022年ウィールス現代アートセンター（ブリュッセル）、2021年モナコ国立新美術館、2018年クレダック現代アートセンター（フランス・イブリー）、2014年クンストハーレ・ベルン、2013年アイコン・ギャラリー（バーミンガム）などがある。

Swan Goes to the Sea

2012, 2014
Video installation
HD video, framed poster (inkjet print: 1544 × 1118 mm)
2012: 4 min. 48 sec.
2014: 6 min. 30 sec.

One day, I visited the Asahikawa river bank in Okayama, which was my mother's hometown.
I used to play with the swan boat there when I was child. The same swan boat was still there. And nothing changed in 40 years!
While the swan boat had stayed on the same small stretch of river, I was traveling all over the world.
I decided to take the swan boat to the sea.

ある日、ひさしぶりに母の故郷の岡山を流れる旭川を訪れた。
子どもの頃、そこで白鳥のボートに乗って遊んだ。その白鳥のボートがまだそこにあった。40年経って何も変わらないまま！
白鳥のボートが旭川のほとりにとどまっている間、僕は世界中を旅してきた。
白鳥のボートに乗って、海へゆくことにした。

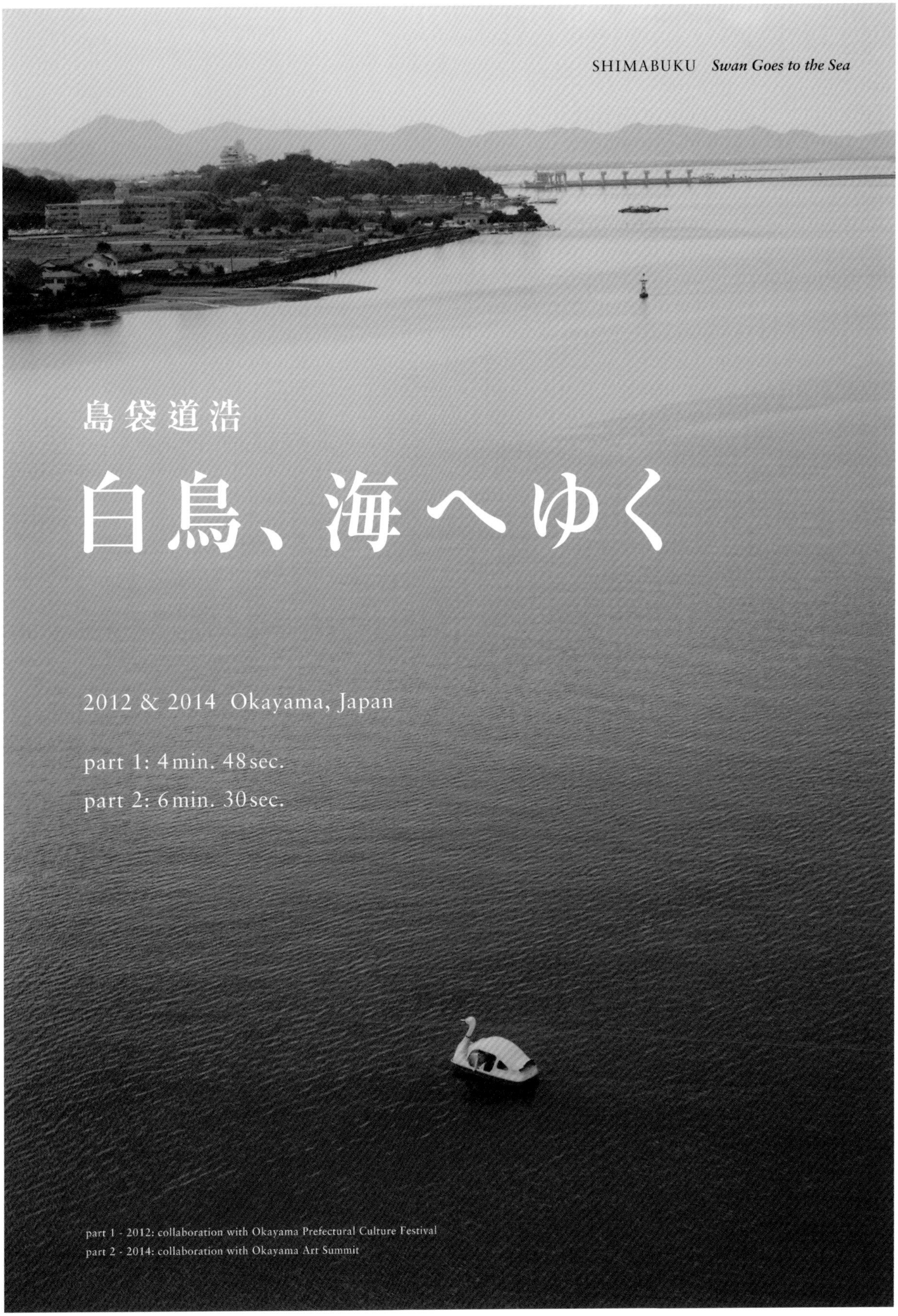

島袋道造

白鳥、海へゆく

2012 & 2014 Okayama, Japan

part 1: 4 min. 48 sec.
part 2: 6 min. 30 sec.

part 1 - 2012: collaboration with Okayama Prefectural Culture Festival
part 2 - 2014: collaboration with Okayama Art Summit

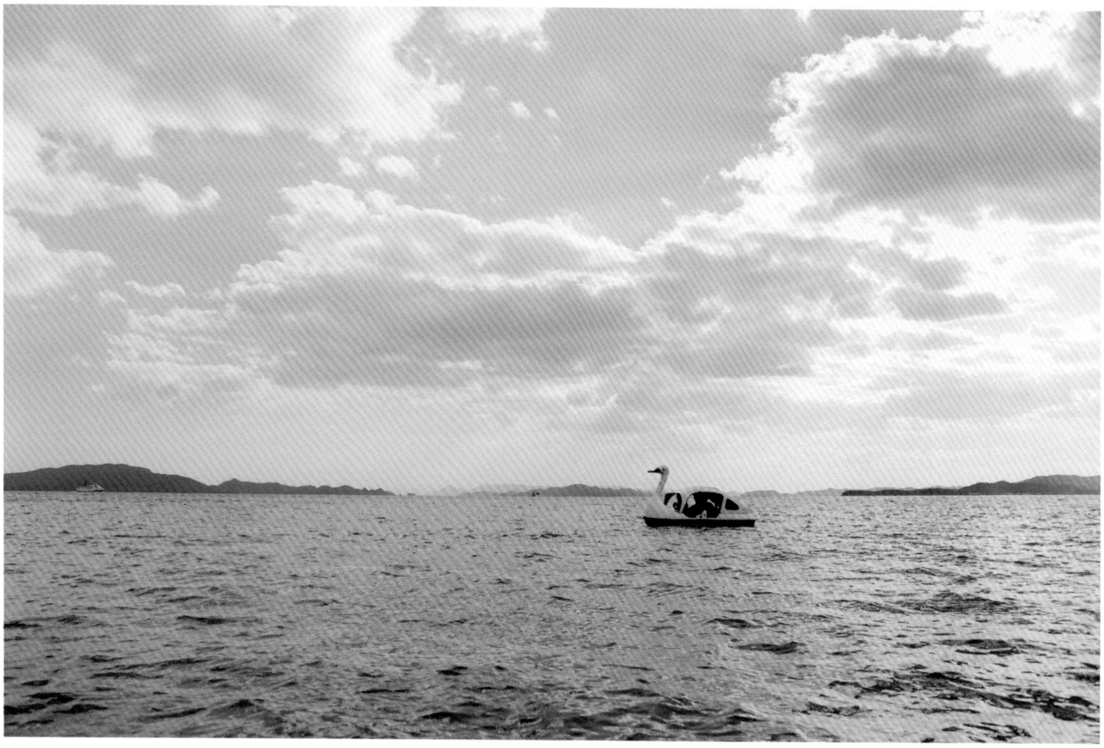

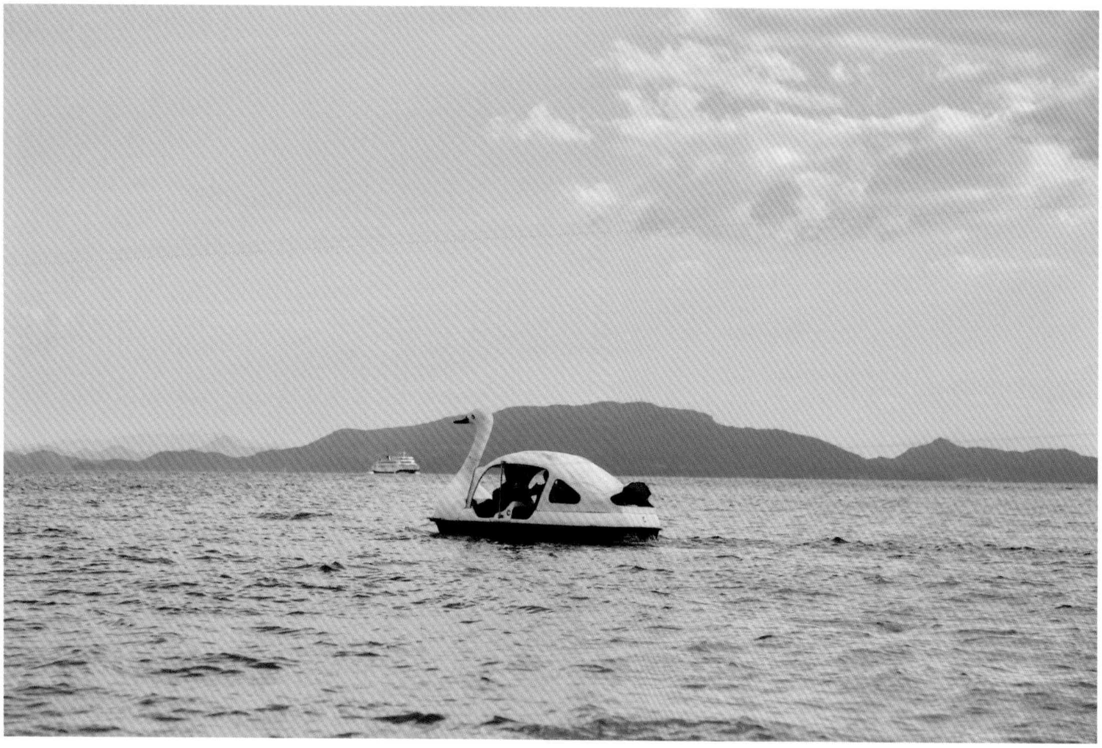

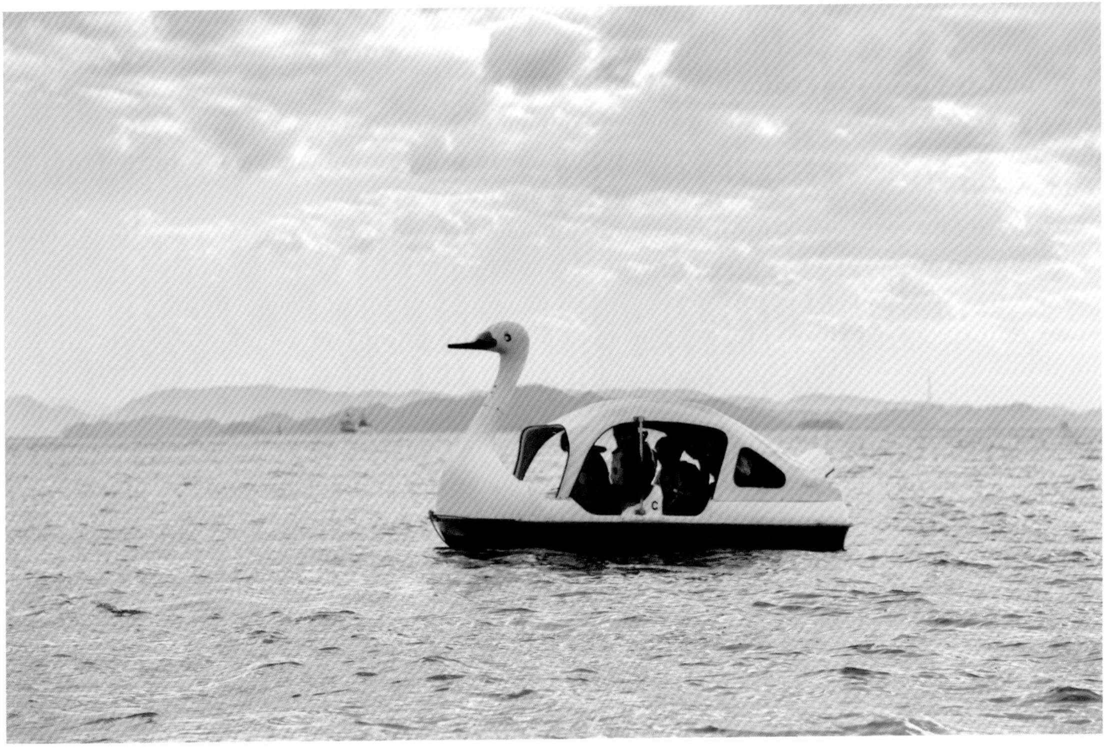

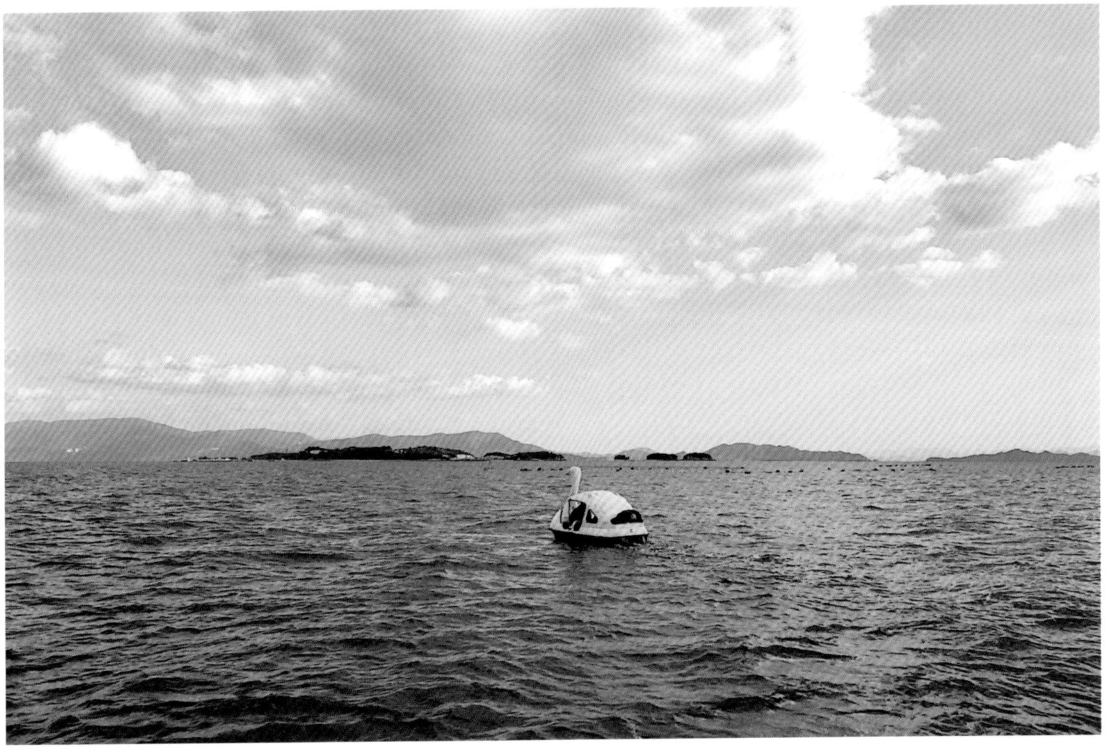

148–149

All works on pp. 147–150: courtesy of the artist, collection of Ishikawa Collection

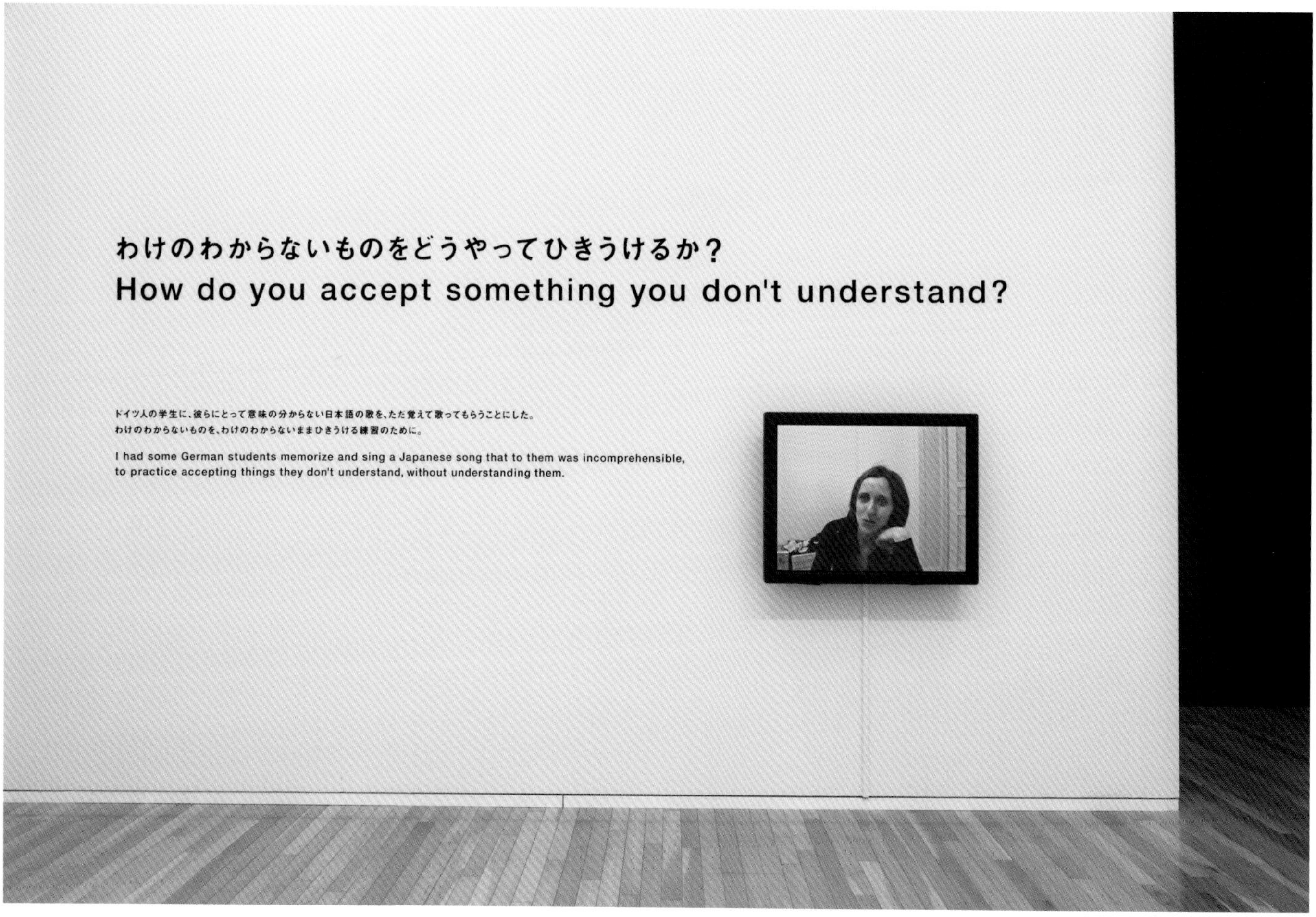

I had some German students memorize and sing a Japanese song that to them was incomprehensible, to practice accepting things they don’t understand, without understanding them.

ドイツ人の学生に、彼らにとって意味の分からない日本語の歌を、ただ覚えて歌ってもらうことにした。
わけのわからないものを、わけのわからないままひきうける練習のために。

How do you accept something you don’t understand?
2006, 2008
Video installation
HD video, wall text
Video: 5 min. 08 sec.
Installation view at Tokyo Opera City Art Gallery, 2014
Photo: Keizo Kioku
《わけのわからないものをどうやってひきうけるか？》2014年、東京オペラシティアートギャラリーでの展示風景

Yutaka Sone

曽根裕

Born 1965 in Japan. Lives and works in China, Mexico, Belgium, and Japan. His major solo exhibitions include *Obsidian*, Sifang Art Museum, Nanjing, (2017), *Day and Night*, David Zwirner, New York (2016), *Perfect Moment*, Tokyo Opera City Art Gallery (2011), *Like Looking for Snow Leopard*, Kunsthalle Bern (2006), *Travel to Double River Island*, Toyota Municipal Museum of Art, Aichi (2002). Major group exhibitions include *Tokyo Independent*, Tokyo University of the Arts (2019), *Sanguine: Luc Tuymans on Baroque*, Prada Foundation, Milan (2018), Whitney Biennial, New York (2004), *Heterotopias,* Japan Pavilion, 50th Venice Biennale (2003), *Egofugal: Fugue from Ego for the Next Emergence*, 7th Istanbul Biennial (2001), *Cities on the Move* (Vienna, Bordeaux, New York, Humlebaek, London, Bangkok, Helsinki, 1997–1999), Sculpture Projects Münster (1997).

1965年生まれ。中国、メキシコ、ベルギー、日本にて活動を行う。主な個展に2017年「Obsidian」四方当代美術館（南京）、2016年「Day and Night」デイヴィッド・ツヴィルナー（ニューヨーク）、2011年「Perfect Moment」東京オペラシティアートギャラリー、2006年「Like Looking for Snow Leopard」クンストハーレ・ベルン、2002年「ダブル・リバー島への旅」豊田市美術館（愛知）など。主なグループ展に2019年「東京インディペンデント」東京藝術大学大学美術館陳列館（東京）、2018年「Sanguine: Luc Tuymans on Baroque」プラダ財団（ミラノ）、2004年ホイットニービエンナーレ（ニューヨーク）、2003年「ヘテロトピアス（他なる場所）— 曽根裕 小谷元彦」第50回ヴェネツィア・ビエンナーレ日本館、2001年「EGOFUGAL」第7回イスタンブール・ビエンナーレ、1997–1999年「移動する都市」（ウィーン、ボルドー、ニューヨーク、フムレバク、ロンドン、バンコク、ヘルシンキ）、1997年ミュンスター彫刻プロジェクトなど。

The Last Night of the Stone Age

Repeating ceaselessly, in the dark, dark night. Decisions were made only and solely to ensure our survival.

This was long, long ago in a time much, much before time, when I did not rely on landscapes to distinguish myself from the stones, birds, animals, and rivers.

I am amid a din of noise that my people make. I do not know how many there are, I do not know where they come from, I have never seen so many of us, and there may be enemies amongst us, but perhaps amid this noise, it is only the cowardly me that thinks such thoughts. I do not know how long this has been happening, it probably has been happening for a very, very long time.

We are knowledgeable about many things, and we do not yet know that there are things we do not know. Trees and grass, mountains, and creatures around us have names, and so words exist as names to be yelled out. Each name has an image attached, so there are very few words besides names that exist. Or, even the rarest, the most memorable impression is given a carefully selected word, thus a single name, or it is expressed through its repetition and through the number of times it is repeated. The poets weave together many words, and because it is pleasing to the ear, we all imitate them.

When we encounter those who are not one of us, we kill that enemy, or we are the ones killed. Even amongst our people, should that sense of comradeship be tested, we kill. Or we will be the ones to be killed.

Normally, two to three families live together in a cave. As long as I remember, we have been holding the festival, so I do not know what it is like to live a normal life. None of us really knew what we were all trying to achieve through the festival.

Throughout the years of the festival, our family has been working ceaselessly to make sure the fire will not die out by gathering things to burn. In the first few years, there was a forest nearby where we would gather wood. But it has been many years since we burned the last tree there, so now we walk two days to another forest to gather wood.

There are about twenty-two of us in our family and my brothers, father, and mother all have the same name. But there are beautiful landscapes that define each and every one of us, and so we have been able to call out to each other without confusion.

That said, even though we are a family, the spot to dig up the black rock that can easily be split vertically is still a secret to all of them. This is because the sharp rock can be peeled flat and be readily used as a tool and a weapon.

Usually, most killings are done very very easily, by picking up rocks that are lying around to hit each other with, or sometimes to throw them at each other. Most living humans have had the experience of killing. That is why we are still alive.

But with this festival, fights spurred by discontent and frustration never happen. Sounds could be heard from morning to afternoon to night, someone would sing and someone would dance. When the sun rises in the morning, the mountain's long shadow would tread across our land. It will be at that moment when we would be born again, so we would sing songs to be born again. When night falls, everything would die, so we would sing songs.

This was before we had connected death to fear.

There was fear, and there was joy. Sadness was a very, very precious emotion, so the poets had to be called upon to express it.

And so none of us know what the festival is for, but as a whole, we feel we know why this is taking place. And that is because there is steady and sure music that plays and plays.

October 1, 2015
Yutaka Sone

石器時代最後の夜

ただただ暗い夜の無限に続く繰り返し、ただただいきるためのほうほうだけがえらばれた。

石や鳥や動物や川、それを取り巻く風景と自分のくべつがなされる、そういったことがおこるずっとまえの話だ。

わたしは、仲間がならすおとのこうずいのなかにいる。なんにんまわりにいるのだろうか、どこからかあつまってきた、みたこともないようなかずの仲間たち、この中に敵が紛れ込んでいるのではとおもっているのは、このおとのなかで、小心もののわたしだけかもしれない。なんにちこのさわぎがつづいているのか、きっとづーっとだ。

わたしたちは、かなりおおくのことをしっていて、まだ知らないことがあるのを知らなかった。木や草、山や、周りの生き物に名前がついていたのだから、ことばは、その名前だけをさけぶことになる。

名前の中にすべてのそれに関係のあるイメージがあるのだから、それいがいのことばはとてもすくなかった。または、ほとんどなかった、心に残る感動さえも選ばれた単語つまりひとつの名詞、またはその連続と連続する回数でかんじょうをひょうげんしあった。詩人は複数の単語を織り交ぜて使い、それでとても音感がよかったので、みながそれをまねし、そしてたのしかった。

わたしたちは、私たちの仲間でないものたちに出会うとその敵を殺す、またはころされる。仲間内でもその感覚の違いでけんかになったときは、相手を殺す。でないと私たちはころすあいてにころされてしまうのだ。

普段は、わたしたちは、それぞれ2－3家族ごとに洞穴にわかれてすんでいる。しかしわたしが物心ついたときすでに、このながい祭りがはじまっていたので、わたしにはふだんの生活を送る経験をしたことわまだない。わたしたちが、このまつりで、いま何を達成しようとしているのかだれもしらなかった。

わたしたちのかぞくは、ただひたすら、この何年にもわたるまつりのなかで、火を消さないように燃えるものをちょうたつしてまわった。最初の何年かは、ちかくに森がありそこで木を調達できた。しかしもう何年もまえにその森はすべて、燃やしてしまったのでいまは2日かけて歩いて行った先のもりからもえるものをさがさなくてはならなかった。

わたしたちのかぞくは、22にんぐらいで、兄弟も父も母もおなじなまえだった、しかし常にそこに横たわる美しい背景がことなることから、わたしたちは、それぞれをうまく呼び合い、わかりあっていた。

ただ、家族といえども、あの黒くてたてに簡単に割れる石が採れる場所は秘密だった。たいらにはがれるするどいいしは、たいした苦労もかけづにそのまま道具として使えるし、武器としてもつかえるからだ。

たいていのころしあいは、もっともっとかんたんなやりかたで、そこらへんの石を拾い上げてそれで殴りあう、ときにはなげつけるといったほうほうがとられた。生きているほとんどすべての人間が殺しのけいけんがあった。だからいきていた。

しかし、いまこの祭りの中では、わたしたちは、そういった、不満やイライラから始まるけんかはまったくしなかった。あさもひるもよるもおとがなり、だれかが、歌いだれかがおどった。朝、太陽があがるとき、大きな山の影がわたしたちのばしょをよぎっていく。そのとき、わたしたちはうまれかわるのだから、生まれ変わるためのおんがくをうたった。夜がくるときは、すべてがしにゆくわけだから、そのためのうたをうたった。

まだ死と恐怖がむすびつくまえのわたしたちだった。恐怖はあったし、喜びもあった。悲しみはとてもたいへんたいへん高級なかんじょうだったので、それを表現するには詩人をよばなければならなかった。

さて、この祭りはなんのためのものなのか、だれもしらなかった、しかしわれわれという集団はそれがなんのためにおこなわれるのかしっていたようなきがする。なぜなら、それにしては、継続的で、確信にみちた音楽がつづいているわけだから。

2015年10月1日
曽根裕

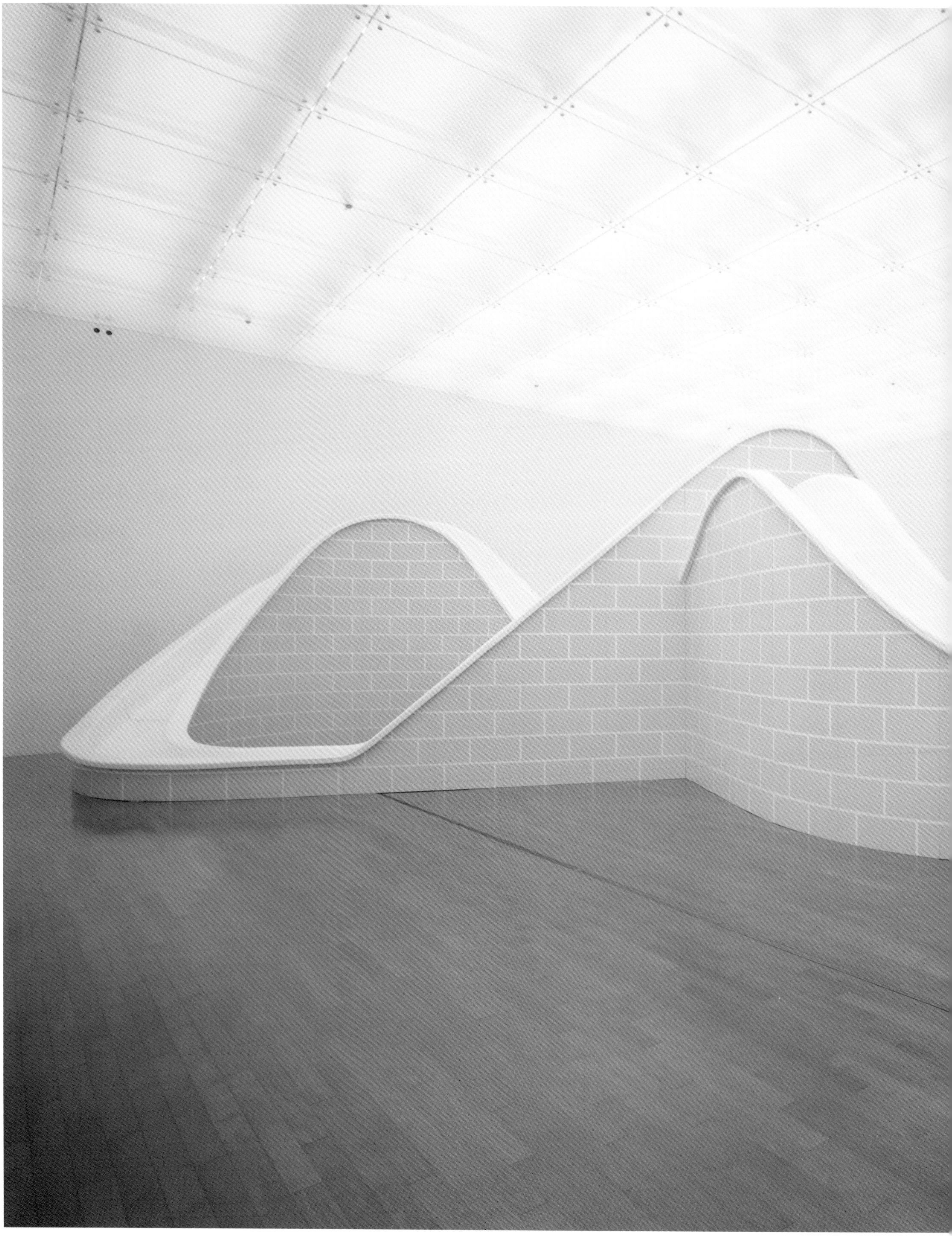

Yutaka Sone

HAPPINESS
IS
A
WARM
GUM

THE
TRUE EYE
OF
THE SOUL
IS
WATER

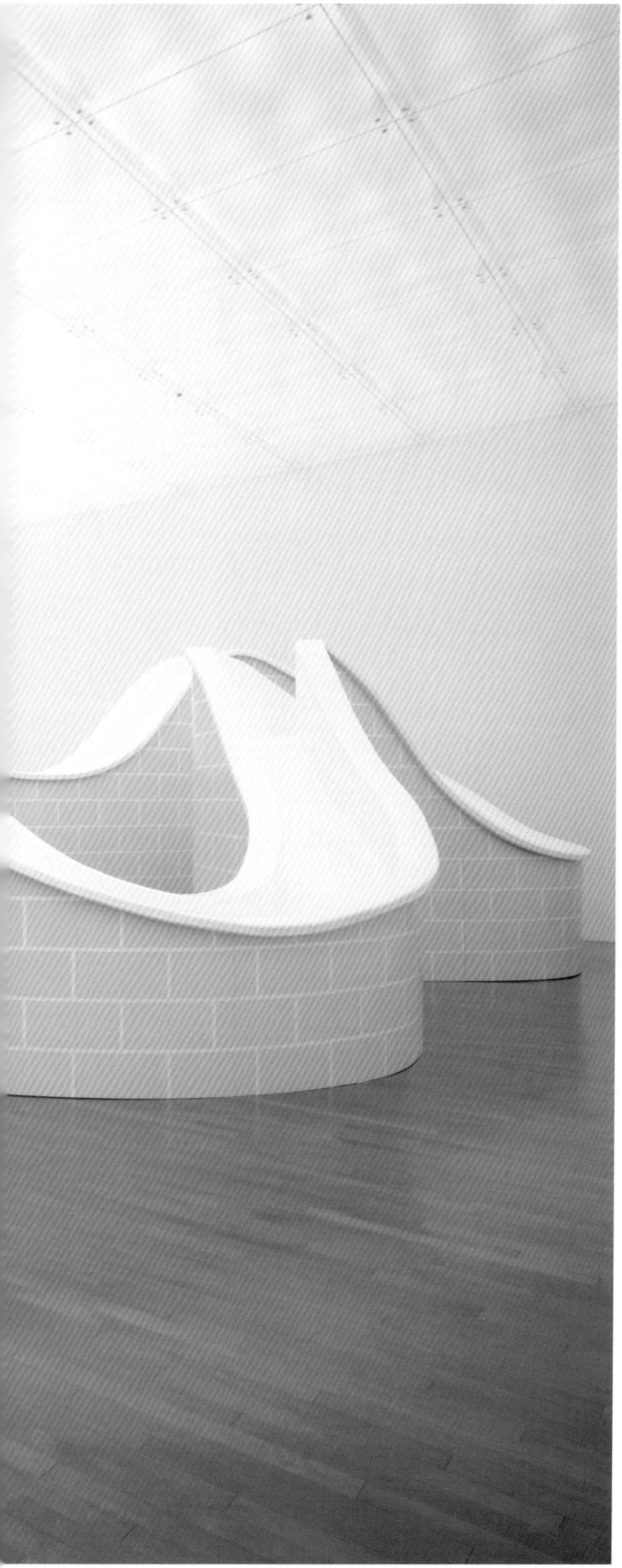

Amusement Romana, 2002
Wood, paint, FRP
400 × 1650 × 1025 cm
Collection of 21st Century Museum of Contemporary Art, Kanazawa
Photo: Keizo Kioku
Courtesy of 21st Century Museum of Contemporary Art, Kanazawa

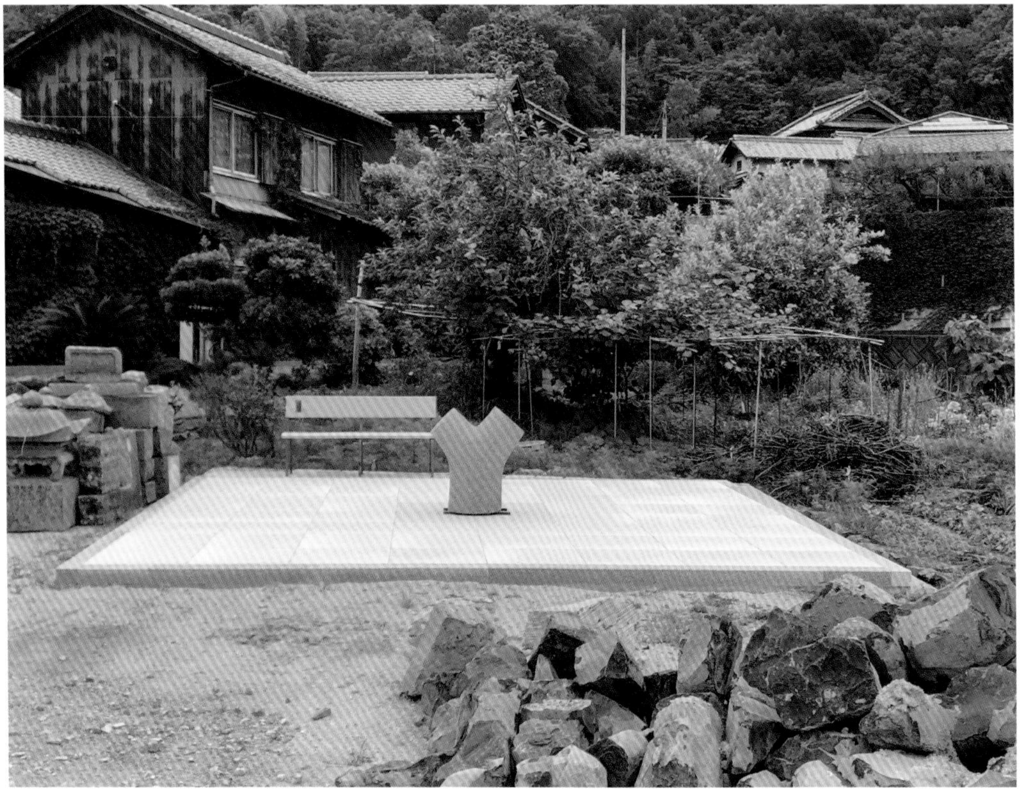

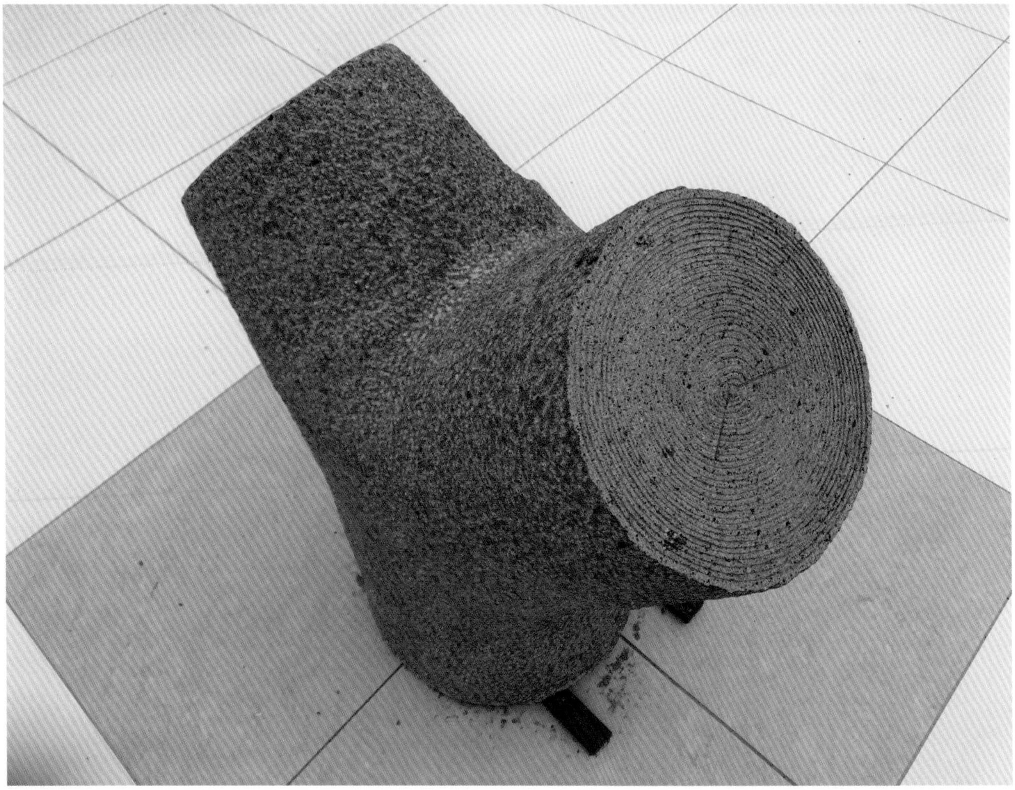

Double Log, 2020

Apichatpong Weerasethakul

アピチャッポン・ウィーラセタクン

Born in Bangkok in 1970 and spent his childhood and youth in Khon Kaen, Northeast Thailand, Apichatpong Weerasethakul is a filmmaker and artist working mainly in Chiang Mai. He won the Palme d'Or at the Cannes Film Festival in 2010 for *Uncle Boonmee Who Can Recall His Past Lives*, and received the same Jury prize for his most recent work *Memoria* released in 2021. He is highly recognized in the field of art as well and has participated in a number of large-scale international exhibitions, including the Venice Biennale in 2019, the Sharjah Biennale in 2013, documenta 13 in 2012 and the Yokohama Triennale in 2011. In 2015, he created his first theatre production of projection-performance *Fever Room* which was performed in various locations. He is now expanding his field of activities with a plan of presenting his first VR work at Aichi Triennale 2022 in 2022.

1970年バンコクに生まれ、タイの東北部コーンケンで育つ。現在チェンマイに主な拠点を置く映画監督、アーティスト。2010年にカンヌ映画祭の最高賞のパルム・ドールを『ブンミおじさんの森』にて受賞、2021年に公開された最新作の『MEMORIA メモリア』は同審査員賞を受賞している。アートの分野でも高い評価を得ており、2019年のヴェネツィア・ビエンナーレをはじめ、2013年シャルジャ・ビエンナーレ、2012年ドクメンタ13（カッセル）、2011年の横浜トリエンナーレなど多数の国際展に参加。2015年には映像を使った初の劇場作品『Fever Room』を発表し各地で上演。2022年の国際芸術祭「あいち2022」では初のVR作品を発表する予定で活動の幅をさらに広げている。

The Word Silence Is Not Silence

2022
Installation

A blackboard, the chairs, the sunlight. In a classroom, one learns about time. One also learns about the convenience of thoughts and memory. In another kind of classroom, one may ask: Is it possible not to learn?

A: Is it possible not to learn?
B: Do you mean not to repeat?
A: Is it possible not to record?
B: Do you mean not to remember or not to take a photograph?
A: To not record anything. Is it possible to understand a word without having to write it down or speak it?

A blackboard, seats, and sunlight all add to the memory of repetition. In March, I found myself in the stillness of an Okayama classroom. The room presented itself as a setting where one could acquire the skills necessary to shape an experience. I had a dialogue with it, much like A and B did above. It became clear that the room may also serve as a place to unlearn, a place of complete silence. Is it possible to comprehend silence?

A brain requires time to process a large amount of information in order to generate an image or an experience. No one can look up at the trees and take in the entire sky at the same time. You can't just read a word and become it. The thinker Krishnamurti stated that we are conditioned by time and words. Saying the word "silent" is not the same as being silent. The component of time must be removed.

I've spent the last few years walking along the trails near my house. I was looking for silence. I recognized a few of the birds and trees in the area. They exchanged words. The seasonal shifts had brought new shapes, hues, and sounds. In July, the rain delivered the intense greens. Plants sprouted in all directions. The cold air in December shriveled them and rendered them brittle yellow. The leeches went back underground where they had been. In April, the forest fire began. The flames raged through the mountains. The trails had been set ablaze, making them inaccessible. A haze of smoke blanketed the city and the bedrooms.

When you couldn't see the surroundings, there was a semblance of silence. As if memory had been wiped clean, a brain couldn't generate information beyond the grey clouds. The stillness of the carbon dioxide-rich air muffles your sensations and renders you formless. We did not dream under the same sky. Due to the lack of tangibles, we were unable to establish any sort of emotional or intellectual separation. In April, I briefly understood Krishnamurti.

Later, a trek through the woods was resumed. The sound of my footsteps, the koels, the crows, the pigeons, and the wind all came back. But I had observed that there were occasions when I simply vanished. At those moments, the surrounding environment began its loud monologue. The birds then vanished, leaving only their sounds behind. Later, without the birds, the sounds lost their meaning, and they, too, disappeared, as did time.

As one sat in an empty classroom, listening to childhood memories, one saw oneself learning. He or she was the blackboard. Words were being written and erased. In a different kind of world, no one had ever written on it and it had never asked any questions.

August 4, 2022
Apichatpong Weerasethakul

黒板、椅子、太陽光。教室では時間について学ぶ。また、思考や記憶の便利さについても学ぶ。別の教室では、「学ばないということはあり得るか」と問うかもしれない。

A：学ばないということはあり得るか？
B：繰り返さないということか？
A：記録しないことは可能か？
B：覚えないということか、それとも写真を撮らないということか？
A：何も記録しないことだ。言葉を書いたり、話したりしなくても理解することは可能か？

黒板、座席、太陽光が、繰り返しの記憶を高める。3月、私は岡山のある教室で静寂に包まれている自分に気がついた。その空間は、経験を形にするために必要なスキルを身につけるための場として存在していた。私はそこでAとBが上記で行ったように対話をした。その空間は、学ぶことを捨て去る場所、完全な沈黙の場所としても機能するであろうことが明らかになった。沈黙を理解することは可能だろうか？

脳は、イメージや体験を生み出すために、大量の情報を処理する時間を必要とする。木々を見上げながら、同時に空全体を見渡せる人はいない。言葉を読んだだけで、その言葉になれるわけでもない。思想家のクリシュナムルティは、我々は時間と言葉によって条件づけられていると述べている。「沈黙」という言葉を口にすることは、沈黙していることとは違う。時間の要素を取り除かなければならない。

私はここ数年を自宅近くの小道を歩くことに費やしてきた。沈黙を求めていた。ほんの一部だが、そのエリアの鳥や木々の見分けがついた。それらは言葉を交わしていた。季節の移り変わりは、新しい形、色合い、そして音をもたらしていた。7月、雨が強い青菜をもたらした。植物は四方八方から芽を出した。12月の寒気はそれら植物を縮みこませ、もろい黄色の状態にした。ヒルはもといた地中に戻っていった。4月、ふたたび森林火災が始まった。炎は山々を焼き尽くした。登山道も燃え上がり、立ち入ることができない。煙霧が街や寝室を覆った。

周囲が見えなくなると、そこには沈黙のようなものがあった。まるで記憶をきれいに拭き取られたように、脳は灰色の雲の向こうの情報を生成することができなかった。二酸化炭素を多く含む空気の静けさが、感覚を消し去り、形をなくす。同じ空のもとで夢を見ることはなかった。具体的なものに欠けていたことから、感情的、知的な区別を一切確立することができなかった。4月、私はクリシュナムルティのことを少し理解した。

その後、森のなかのトレッキングが再開された。自分の足音、オニカッコウ、カラス、ハト、そして風の音も、すべて戻ってきた。しかし、私は、自分が消えてしまうことがあることを観察していた。そういうとき、周囲の環境は大声で独白劇を始めた。鳥は、その音だけを残して消えた。その後、鳥なしでは、音がその意味を失い、そして、その音も消え、時間も消えた。

ひとり、誰もいない教室に座り、子どもの頃の思い出を聞きながら、自身が勉強している姿を見た。その人は黒板だ。言葉が書かれては消される。異なる世界では、誰もそこに書いたことがなく、何も質問したことがなかった。

2022年8月4日
アピチャッポン・ウィーラセタクン

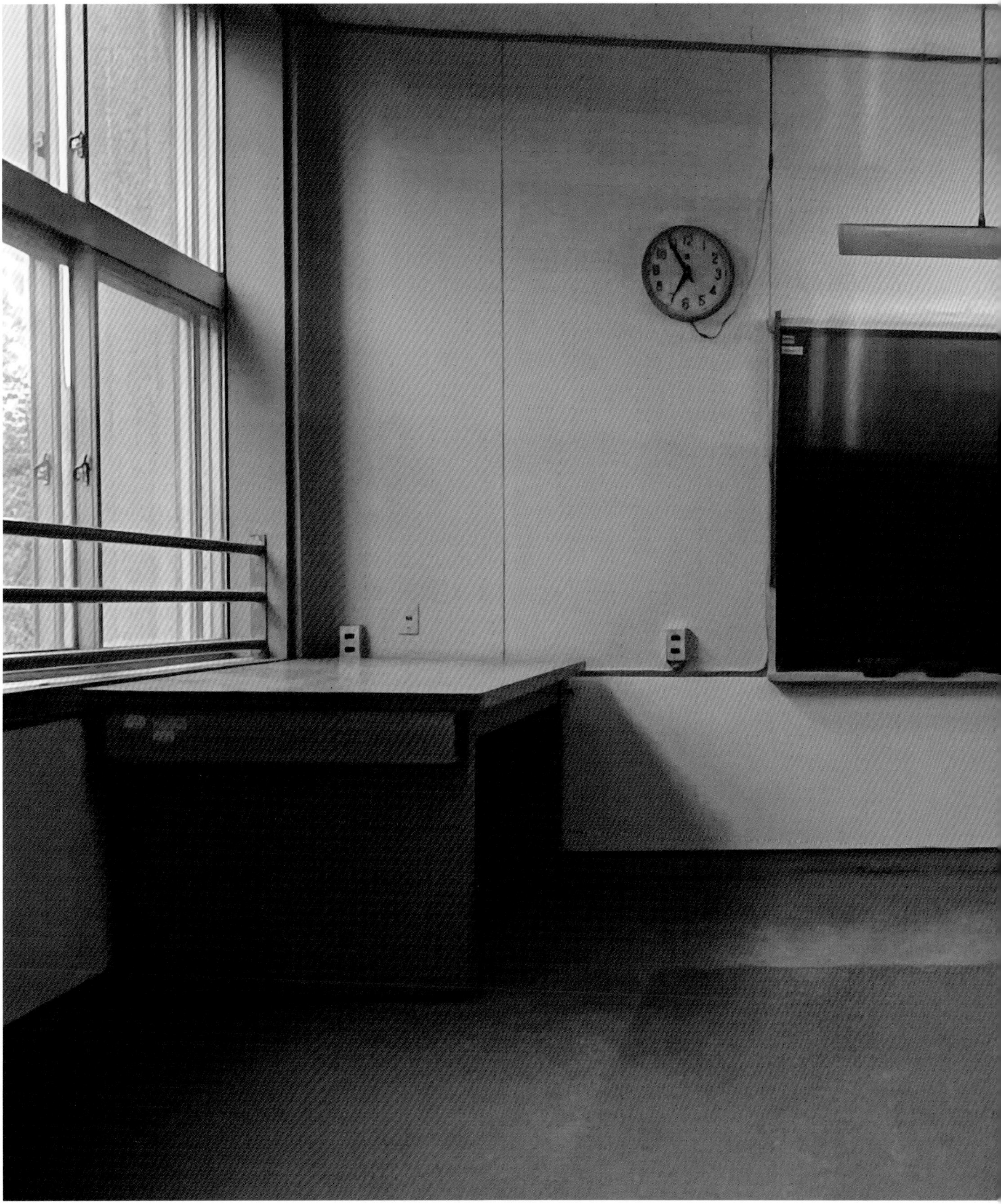

Apichatpong Weerasethakul

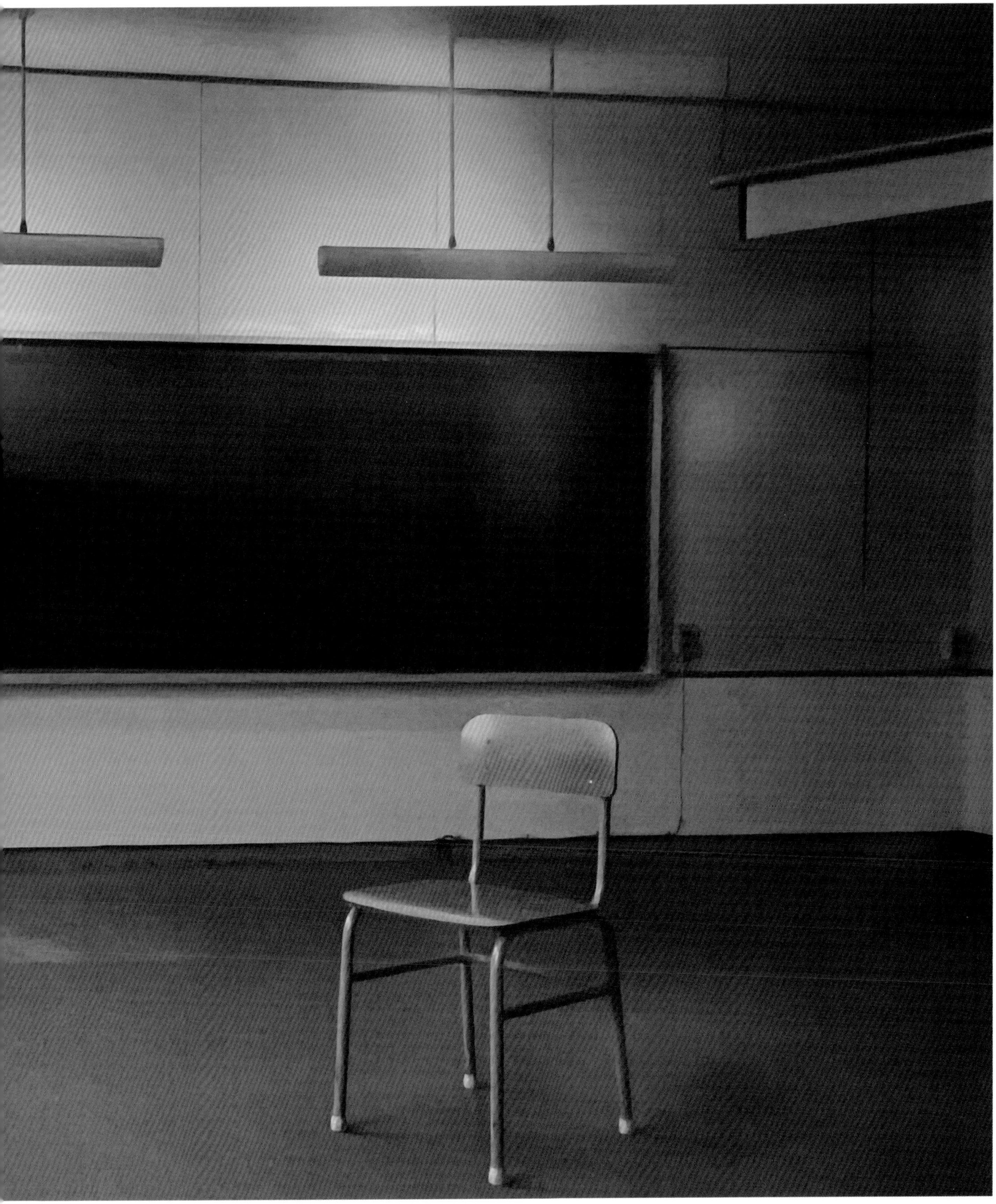

The Word Silence Is Not Silence

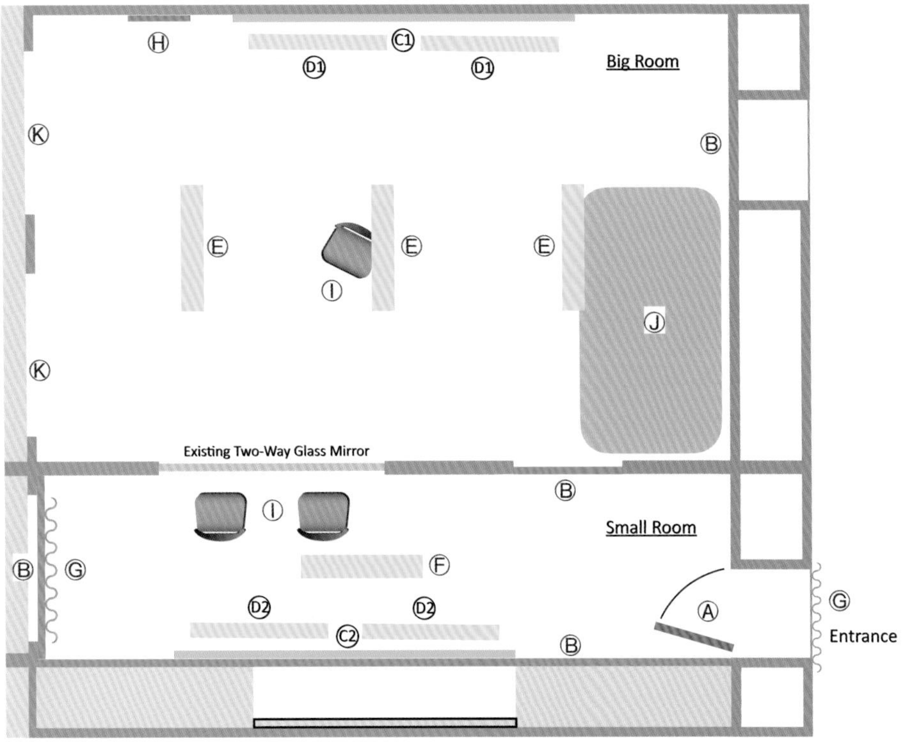

Ⓐ Door (Existing)

Ⓑ Temp wall, sealed section.

C1 Blackboard (Existing)

C2 Blackboard, same size and style as C1

D1 Lights in front of the blackboard (Existing)

D2 Lights in front of blackboard, same style as D1

Ⓔ Lights in big room (Existing)

Ⓕ Light in small room

Ⓖ Curtains that seal off lights, brown color

Ⓗ Rirkrit's poster "Do We Dream Under the Same Sky"

Ⓘ Classroom Chairs (3)

Ⓙ Swan

Ⓚ Windows, keep as they are (Existing)

Design plan for *The Word Silence Is Not Silence*, 2022

《The Word Silence Is Not Silence》の配置図

Haegue Yang

梁慧圭（ヤン・ヘギュ）

Born in 1971, Seoul. Lives in Berlin and Seoul.
Spanning a vast range of media—from collage to kinetic sculpture and room-scaled installations—Haegue Yang's work links disparate histories and traditions in a visual idiom all her own. The artist draws on a variety of craft techniques and materials, including venetian blinds, metal bells, *hanji* (Korean traditional paper made from mulberry bark), artificial straw, and bricks, as well as their cultural connotations. Her multisensory environments activate perception beyond the visual through immersive experiences that treat issues such as labor, migration, and displacement from the oblique vantage of the aesthetic. Ensuring that her references remain wayward and personalized, Yang prizes fluidity over unified narratives. A recipient of the Wolfgang Hahn Prize in 2018, Yang has presented solo exhibitions at institutions worldwide, including the Statens Museum for Kunst, Copenhagen (2022); the Art Gallery of Ontario, Toronto (2020); Tate St. Ives, United Kingdom (2020); National Museum of Modern and Contemporary Art, Korea, Seoul (2020); MoMA, New York (2019); Museum Ludwig, Cologne (2018); Centre Pompidou, Paris (2016); Leeum Museum of Art, Seoul (2015); Haus der Kunst, Munich (2012); and the Korean Pavilion of the 53rd Venice Biennale (2009).

1971年、ソウル生まれ。現在はベルリンとソウルを拠点に活動。
梁慧圭の表現はコラージュ、キネティック・スカルプチャー、空間インスタレーションなど幅広いメディアにおよび、作家独自の視覚表現を通して異なる歴史と伝統をつなぐ。ブラインドや鈴、韓紙《ハンジ》（楮《こうぞ》の樹皮からつくられた韓国の伝統手漉き紙）、人工藁や煉瓦など、様々な工法や素材とそれらが有する文化的な意味合いを扱っている。多感覚に訴える没入型インスタレーションは、視覚を越えた先の知覚を触発し、労働、移民、難民の問題に美学的見地から切り込んでいる。一貫して不定形かつ個人化されたモチーフからは、統一的なナラティブではなく流動性に立脚した彼女の視点が見て取れる。2018年ヴォルフガング・ハーン賞受賞。これまでに、2022年コペンハーゲン国立美術館、2020年オンタリオ美術館（トロント）、2020年テート・セント・アイヴス（イギリス）、2020年国立現代美術館（ソウル）、2019年ニューヨーク近代美術館、2018年ルートヴィヒ美術館（ケルン）、2016年ポンピドゥー・センター（パリ）、2015年サムスン美術館リウム（ソウル）、2012年ハウス・デア・クンスト（ミュンヘン）、2009年の第53回ヴェネツィア・ビエンナーレ韓国館など、世界で個展を開催している。

An Opaque Wind – Trifid Seating in Six Folds

2022
Clay bricks, concrete bricks, mortar, turbine vents, soil, various local plants
154 × 949 × 596 cm
Courtesy of the artist

Haegue Yang's work frequently explores the geometries and modular systems that persist across various regions and eras, as recurring forms of visual language that unify otherwise disparate cultures. Under the title of *An Opaque Wind*, Yang has realized several related, outdoor architectural structures that function like small landmarks since 2015.

Commissioned by Okayama Art Summit, Yang has conceived a new brick sculpture in public space. Yang is drawn to the materiality of the brick as both universally available and locally inflected, and the size and proportion of the bricks in use dictates the process of the structure's design. Comprising towers of varying sizes and winding, double-sided benches, *An Opaque Wind – Trifid Seating in Six Folds* is located in an open area at Ishiyama Park.

Extending outward from a concave, hexagonal center, these brick benches enable different contemplative views of the natural and man-made surroundings. Made of clay-fired bricks in tones of white, beige and grayish-brown (with accents of colorful concrete bricks throughout), the components of each bench are arranged in alternating patterns. Both the ornamental bricks and turbine vents were sourced domestically. The configuration of the benches and towers lies on a hexagonal matrix. The drawn shapes are extruded vertically, such that the work unfolds in a modular yet rhythmic manner. Used by Islamic designers and artisans since the seventh century, six-fold, symmetrical geometries symbolize perfection and a divine order made visible in the material world, manifested in the use of the hexagon to represent a universal being.

Unlike earlier iterations of *An Opaque Wind*, the recent structures integrate seating or beds for potted plants. The works emphasize holistic, environmental integrity and distinctive, modular geometries in equal measure. Meanwhile, the rotating turbine vent is evidence for the continuous movement of air around the piece, the forces that circulate within and beyond it.

Both images on pp. 166–167:
An Opaque Wind Habitat, 2022
Concrete bricks, mortar, turbine vents, soil, various plants
Dimensions variable
Courtesy of Kukje Gallery
Photo: Chunho An

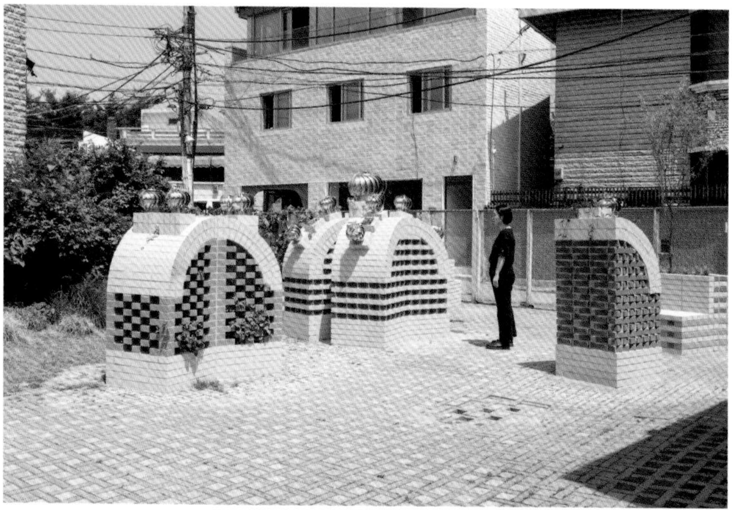

梁慧圭の作品は、ともすればバラバラになりがちな異質な文化を統合する反復的な形態をもつ視覚言語として、様々な地域や時代を超えて存在する幾何学的な形態やモジュラーシステムを探究したものが多い。《An Opaque Wind》というタイトルのもと、梁は2015年から、小さなランドマークのような役割を果たす一連の屋外建造物を制作してきた。

岡山芸術交流の委嘱を受けた梁は、公共空間に設置する新しい煉瓦彫刻を構想している。あらゆる場所で入手できると同時に地域性も感じさせる煉瓦のもつ物質性に惹かれている彼女は、使用する煉瓦の寸法や全体のバランスから、構造物をどのようにデザインするかを決めている。様々な大きさの塔と、両側から座ることのできる屈曲したベンチを配した今回の作品《An Opaque Wind – Trifid Seating in Six Folds》は、石山公園の開かれた空間に設置される。

この煉瓦のベンチは、凹六角形の中心から3方向に伸びており、腰掛けた人々が周囲の自然や人工物を異なる方向から静かに眺められるようになっている。用いられているのは、白、ベージュ、灰褐色の粘土を焼成した煉瓦で（全体的に、コンクリート製のカラフルな煉瓦もアクセント的に加えられている）、それぞれのベンチの構成要素は異なるパターンで配されている。装飾的な煉瓦と、塔につけられたタービン式の排気ファンは、いずれも国産のものを使用した。ベンチと塔は、六角形のマトリックス上に配されている。二次元に描かれた図形が垂直に立ち上がることで、作品はモジュール式でありながらリズミカルに展開されていく。7世紀以来、イスラム圏のデザイナーや職人たちによって使われてきた上下左右対称な六角形の幾何学模様は、物質界に可視化された完璧さと神の秩序を象徴する。その象徴性は、普遍的な概念を表す六角形を用いることで示されてきたのだ。

《An Opaque Wind》の初期作に繰り返し見られた様相とは異なり、最近の作品では、鉢植えのための台座が組み込まれている。こうした作品は、全体的な環境保全に対する意識と、一律の基準を用いた特徴的なモジュール方式の幾何学的形態を強調するものだ。一方、回転するタービン式の排気ファンは、作品の周りの空気の持続的な動き、作品の内部と外部を循環する空気の力を示唆している。

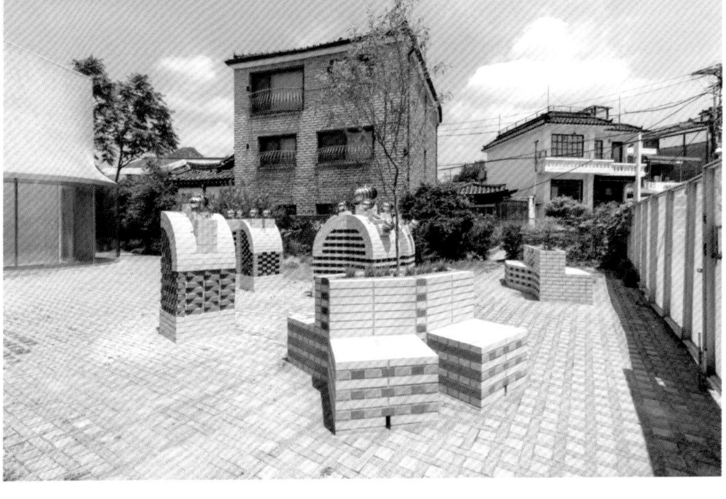

Wave-Powered Gilled Soul Streamers – Mesmerizing Mesh #115

2022
Hanji on alu-dibond, framed
92 × 62 cm

Wave-Powered Webfooted Soul Sheet – Mesmerizing Mesh #116

2022
Hanji on alu-dibond, framed
92 × 62 cm

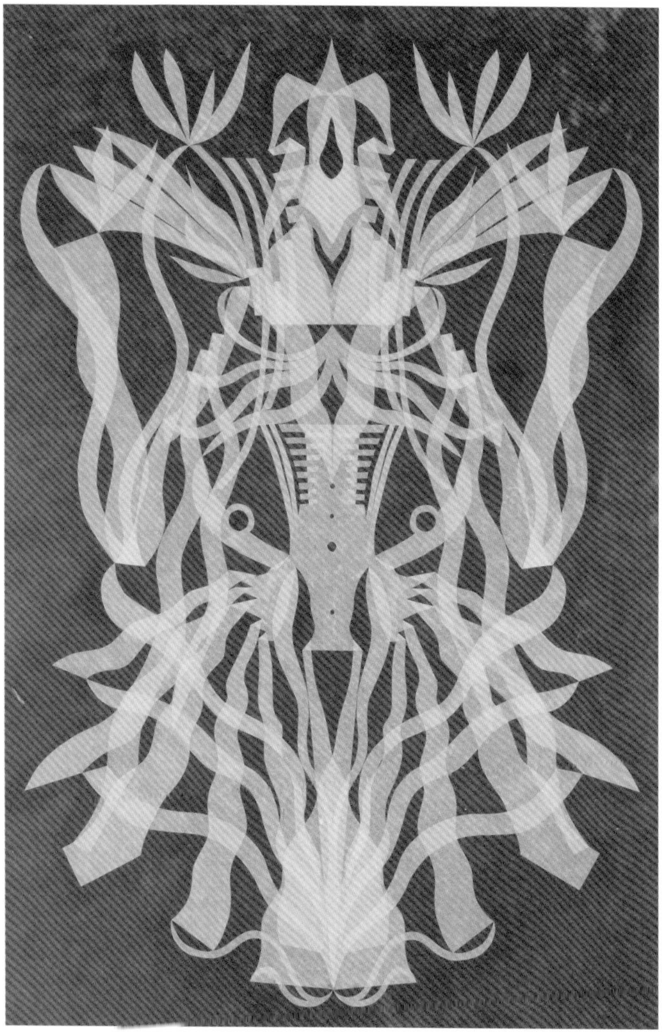

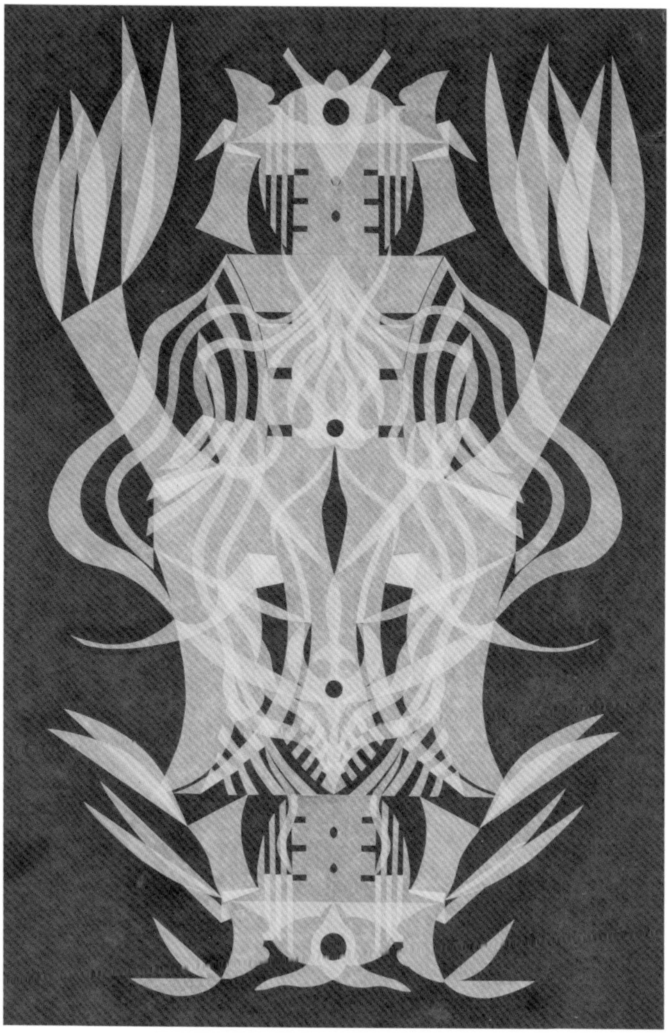

Both images on this page: courtesy of the artist
Photo: Studio Haegue Yang

Mesmerizing Mesh is based on Yang's longstanding inquiry into the relationship between spirit and matter, which in recent years has led her to deepen her artistic research into mystical practices ranging from European paganism to Asian shamanism. That pursuit has resulted in a new series of paper collages, loosely inspired by ritual props made of paper. Called *hanji* in Korea or *washi* in Japan, these highly specialized papers are made from the inner bark of the mulberry tree, and are used to create objects reserved for purifying, healing, exorcising, or cleansing rites. Usually folded before the cutting, the resulting paper motifs are characterized by strong symmetries in their compositions. For Yang, these paper objects speak to the human impulse to fashion objects for intercessory purposes, using matter to reach the dematerialized realm.

Two *Mesmerizing Mesh* pieces are presented in the Okayama shrine devoted to Inari, one of the principal deities associated with foxes, fertility, rice, agriculture, prosperity, and success in business. Against a monochromatic backdrop, white paper builds an intricately layered, creature-like motif at the center of each sheet. The works refer to traditional paper props found in religious context across Asia, from *gohei* (wooden wands decorated with symmetric paper streamers) in Shinto practices, to *nukjeon*, which symbolize the soul of the deceased in Korean shamanism and are installed at ritual sites to guard against evil spirits.

《Mesmerizing Mesh》は、精神と物質の関係についての梁の長年にわたる探究に基づいて制作された作品だ。この探究によって、近年の彼女は、ヨーロッパのペイガニズム（キリスト教到来以前の信仰の総称）からアジアのシャーマニズムに至るまで、神秘主義的な営みに関する美術面からの研究を深めてきた。その結果、祭祀用の紙製の祭具からゆるやかに着想を得た、切り紙の新しいコラージュ作品のシリーズが生まれた。韓国では韓紙《ハンジ》、日本では和紙と呼ばれるこのきわめて特殊な紙は、クワ科の楮《こうぞ》の樹の内皮からつくられ、浄化や治療、お祓いや清めの儀式に使われる祭具をつくる素材となる。通常、折りたたんだ紙を切って祭具とするため、結果として生まれるモチーフは、左右対称性の強い構成となるのが特徴だ。梁にとって、こうした紙のオブジェは、神へのとりなしを目的としたオブジェをつくり、その物質的なオブジェを使って非物質化された領域に到達したいと願う人間の衝動を物語っている。

今回、2点の《Mesmerizing Mesh》が、岡山の稲荷神社に展示される。日本の主要な神のひとつである稲荷は、狐、豊穣、稲、農業、繁栄、商売繁盛と結びついている。単色を背景に白い紙が複雑に重なり合うこの作品では、それぞれの中央に生き物のようなモチーフが表されている。ここで参照しているのは、日本の神道の祭祀で見られる御幣《ごへい》（木製の串に2本の紙垂《しで》を左右対称に折り下げたもの）や、韓国のシャーマニズムで死者の魂を象徴し、悪霊から身を守るために祭祀場に設置される切り紙の人形（ヌクジョン）など、アジア全域の宗教的な場面で見られる伝統的な紙製の祭具である。

Sonic Cosmic Rope – Gold Dodecagon Straight Weave

2022
PVD-coated stainless steel bells, stainless steel bells, stainless steel chains, split rings
Dimensions variable

Installed in the Okayama Orient Museum, Yang's *Sonic Cosmic Rope* consists of a nearly ten-meter length of metallic bells woven into a geometric constellation, with golden bells in the outer rows and silver in the inner ones. As the title suggested, the work resembles a rope, suspended from the ceiling to almost touch the first floor. Ropes are often featured in fairytales as modes of escape, and Yang drew inspiration from a Korean folk tale about two siblings who escaped danger on the ground by climbing up a rope that connected the Earth and sky. Upon reaching the safety of heaven, the siblings turn into the Sun and the Moon.

Like many of Yang's works, the sculpture has a kinetic element, activated by human touch. When manipulated by hand, the bells in *Sonic Cosmic Rope* produce resonant, rattling sounds, and the pliable structure moves in curving sweeps. Both effects cause our eyes to ascend, following the structure as it spans the building's full height. Yang's multisensory sculptural piece transforms the museum's soaring architecture into a mystical space, evoking prehistoric tales and cosmic orientations shared across civilizations.

**Sonic Cosmic Rope* will be activated by facilitators twice a day, at 11 am and 3 pm. For further inquiries on the activation, please consult the gallery attendants.

岡山市立オリエント美術館に設置された梁の《Sonic Cosmic Rope》は、金属製の小さな鈴を幾何学的なパターンで編んだ全長約10メートルの作品で、外側の列は金色の鈴、内側の列は銀色の鈴で構成されている。タイトルが示す通り、ロープ状の作品は吹き抜けの天井から吊り下げられ、1階の床に届かんばかりだ。童話に登場するロープは、脱出の手段として用いられることが多い。梁が着想を得たのも、韓国の昔話のひとつで、地上と空を結ぶ綱を登って危険を逃れた兄妹の物語だ。天上の安全な場所にたどり着いた兄妹は、太陽と月に姿を変える。

梁の作品の多くがそうであるように、この彫刻も人が触れることによって動くキネティックな要素を備えている。《Sonic Cosmic Rope》の鈴を手で操ると、共鳴してシャランシャランという音を発し、柔軟な構造をもつ作品が曲線を描きながら振動する。この2つの効果によって、観る者の視線は、建物の高さいっぱいにおよぶ作品の構造を目で追いながら上昇していく。いくつもの感覚を刺激する梁の立体作品は、美術館の高層建築を神秘的な空間に変え、文明を超えて共有される昔話や宇宙的な視座を思い起こさせる。

＊《Sonic Cosmic Rope》は1日に2回、午前11時と午後3時に稼働します。詳細は会場の係員にお問い合わせください。

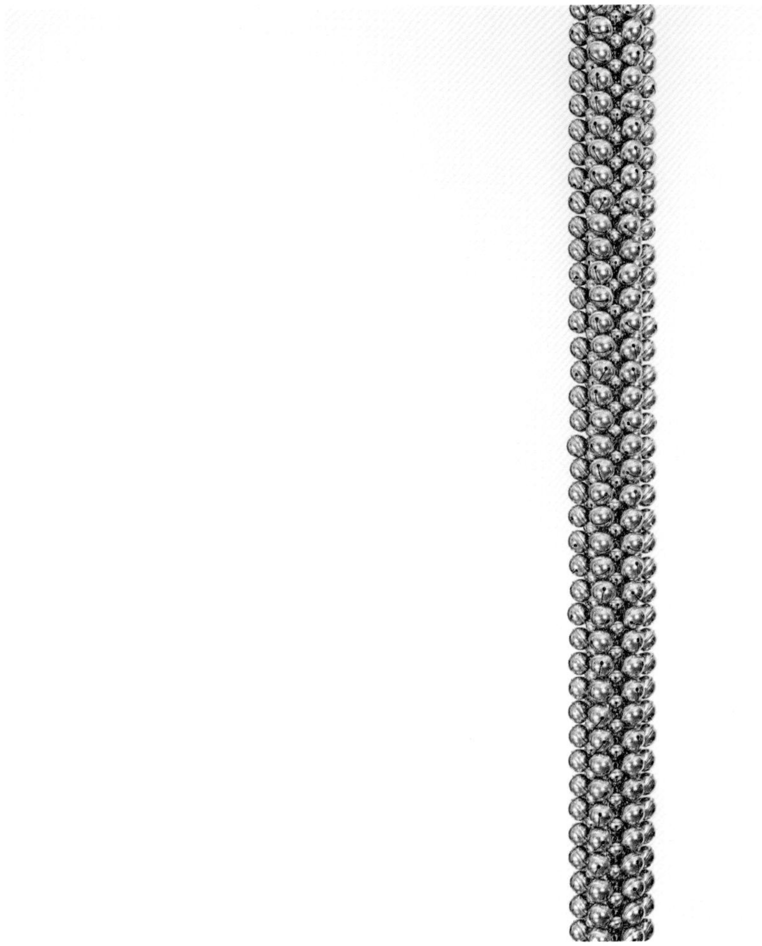

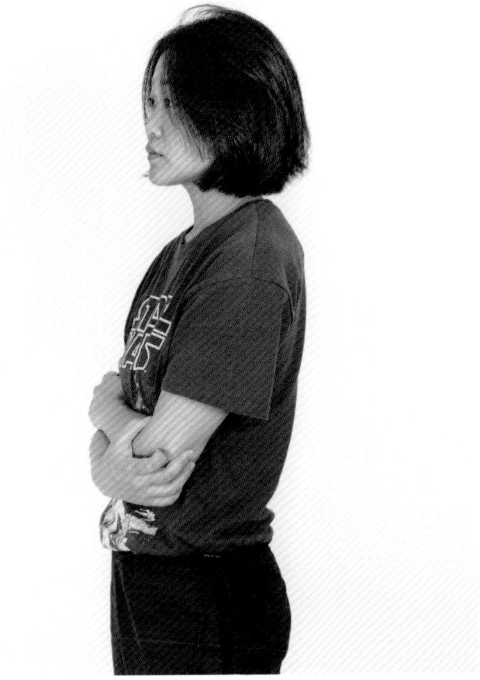

Both images on pp. 171–172:
Courtesy of Kukje Gallery
Photo: Studio Haegue Yang

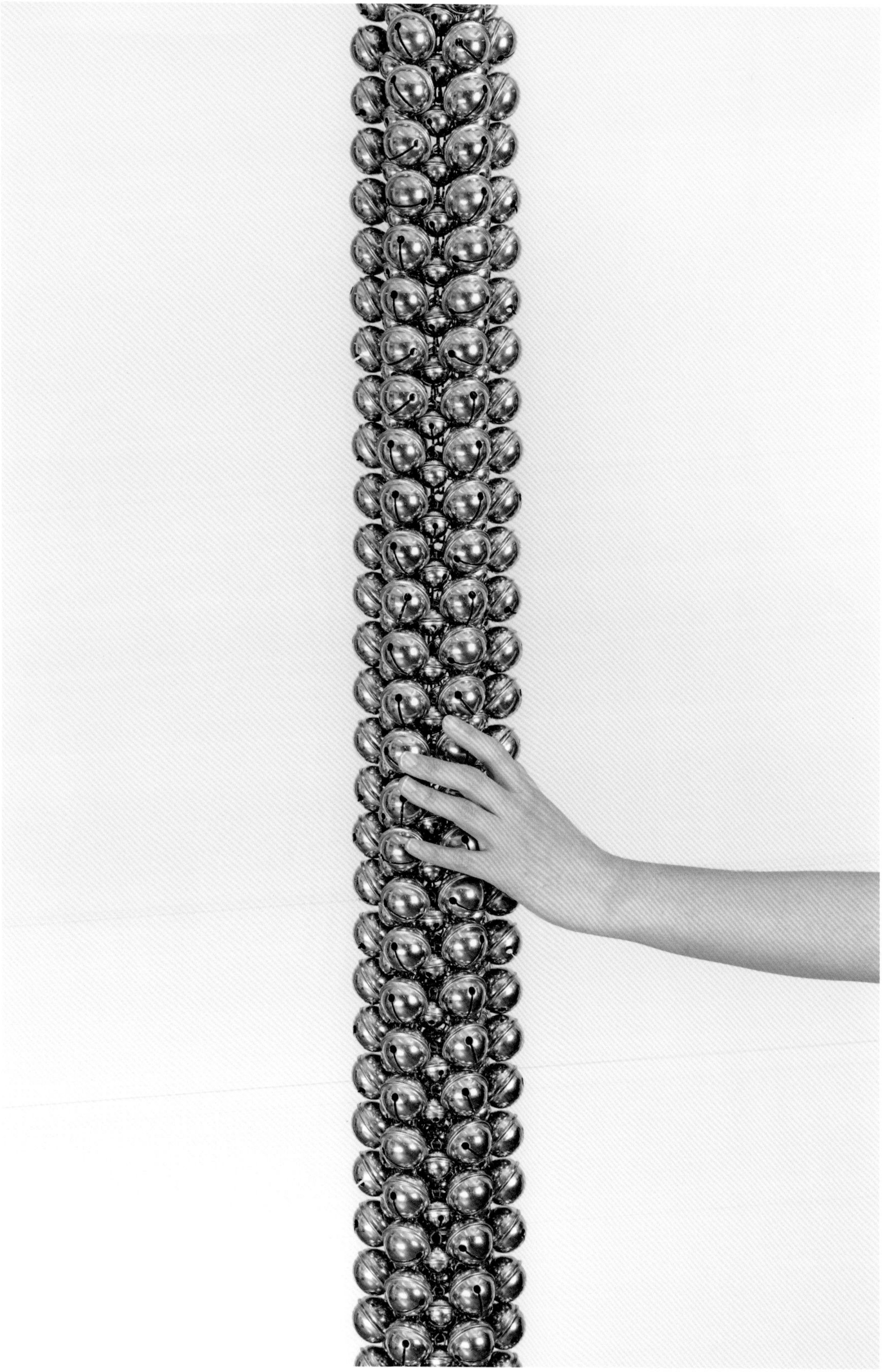

THE
DAYS
OF
THIS
SOCIETY
IS
NUMBERED

SUBMIT
TO
THE
BLACK
COMPOST

THE FUTURE IS NATURAL

EVENT

Gert Robijns

ゲルト・ロビンス

Born in 1972, Sint-Truiden. Lives and works in Borgloon, Belgium.
Over the course of his career, Gert Robijns has crafted extraordinary and unfamiliar compositions, ambitious and sometimes outlandish versions of things we know to be familiar. Dislodging everyday objects from their traditional frameworks, Robijns simultaneously deconstructs the quotidian from its contexts while foregrounding poetic dimensions that can be found just beneath the surface of his chosen subjects.
Robijns has spent the past decade working on his RESET concept, wherein the recreation and revaluation of the (social) landscape are key. In 2010, Robijns made a copy of the small town of Gotem, his birthplace, out of white wood and metal on a scale of 75:100, including the church and rectory. From then on, he became dedicated to following this idea of RESET in various projects, among them *Reset Charbon*, a reflection on Limburg's mining history, and *Reset Mobile*, a temporary structure that has been travelling as an unprogrammed freespace around the world.
Gert Robijns first attended the Hogeschool Sint Lukas Brussel from 1992–1996 and then did further research in the department of fine arts of the Jan van Eyck Academy, Maastricht. Later he participated in the artists residency programmes: MoMA PS1, New York and the Künstlerhaus Bethanien, Berlin. Since 2001 he has been visiting lecturer at KASK in Ghent.
Gert Robijns is represented by Tommy Simoens, Antwerp.

1972年、ベルギー、シント=トロイデン生まれ。現在は同国ボルフローンを拠点に活動。
見慣れた物を大掛かりなオブジェや異様なものに変化させるなどし、奇抜な構造物を制作。日常的な物体から既存の枠組みを取り除くことで物の文脈から日常性を解体し、同時にその表面下に潜む詩情的な特性の前景化を図る。
過去10年間にわたり、(社会的)景観の再生と再評価を主軸とする「RESET」シリーズプロジェクトを各地で展開している。2010年に白色木材と金属で生まれ故郷の小さな町、ゴーテムの複製を制作し、75:100の縮尺で教会や牧師館を再現。以来、リンブルフ地域の炭鉱の歴史を振り返る《Reset Charbon》や、世界各地で仮設の構造物を建てフリースペースとして活用する《Reset Mobile》など様々なプロジェクトを発表し、「RESET」のコンセプトを追求している。
1992–1996年までブリュッセルのLUCAスクール・オブ・アーツで学んだのち、マーストリヒトのヤン・ファン・エイク・アカデミーの芸術学科で研究活動を続ける。その後、ニューヨークのMoMA PS1やベルリンのクンストラーハウス・ベタニエンでアーティスト・イン・レジデンスプログラムに参加。2001年よりゲントの王立芸術アカデミーで客員講師を務める。
現在、トミー・シモンズ・ギャラリー(アントワープ)に所属。

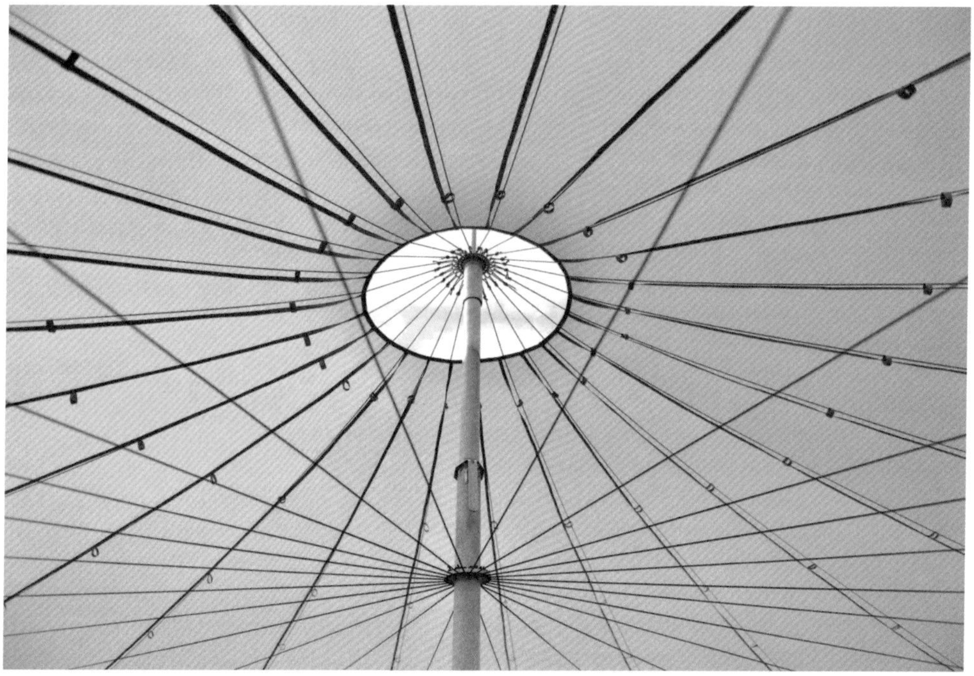

Reset Mobile (Yellow), 2020
Rib stop, ropes, metal beams
200 × 520 cm

Courtesy of the artist and Tommy Simoens, Antwerp

EVENT

Live House PEPPERLAND

ライヴハウス ペパーランド

Founded in 1974 at the dawn of the 'live house' (live music club) in Japan, PEPPERLAND was started with the intention to create a place like Andy Warhol's "Exploding Plastic Inevitable." The long-standing institution established the live music culture in Okayama and has continued to emphasize activities that transverse, connect, and intermix all cultural fields, from music to other forms including movies, plays, lectures, and poetry readings. Music is the fastest medium with which one can express the vision of the next generation, and PEPPERLAND has maintained an attitude of respecting, accepting, and nurturing the sensibilities of youth, regardless of genre. With a shirt and autographed photo of Joseph Beuys on display inside, the live house is unique in its respect for the Situationist approach to "social sculpture" through music.

ライヴハウスという存在が全国でも珍しかった黎明期の1974年に設立。アンディ・ウォーホルの映像作品に登場する「エクスプローディング・プラスティック・イネヴィタブル」のような場所をつくろうとスタートし、岡山にライヴ文化を定着させた老舗である。設立当時から音楽と共に映画、演劇、講演会、ポエトリー・リーディング…など、あらゆる文化領域を横断・接続・混淆する活動を重視してきた。次の時代のヴィジョンを連れてくる最も早いメディアが音楽であり、ジャンルにこだわらず若い感覚に宿る衝動を尊重し、受け止め、深め育てる姿勢を貫き通している。音楽を通じて「社会彫刻」するシチュアシオニスト的活動を尊重し、店内にはヨーゼフ・ボイスのシャツとサイン入り写真が展示されているライヴハウスは類例をみない。

Iseo Nose

能勢伊勢雄

Photographer, art exhibition organizer, and music critic.
Born in 1947, Iseo Nose has presided over Live House PEPPERLAND since 1974. While developing activities that transcend boundaries, he was involved in editing and writing for Yuzuru Agi's *Rock Magazine* from 1983 until the publication ceased. His major exhibitions include *Spectacle: Nose Iseo 1968-2004* (2004), a collaborative cultural project between Okayama and Kurashiki City; *X-COLOR Graffiti in Japan*, which he organized at Art Tower Mito in Ibaraki (2005); *The photograph as seen from Goethe morphology* at Nagi Museum of Contemporary Art in Okayama (2013); and *OPAM x Nose Iseo Theater in Museum* at Oita Prefectural Art Museum in Oita (2016). Among other places, Nose has lectured at Art Biotop in Nasu "Shule im Berg (The Mountain School)" (2009–), and Kyoto International Film and Art Festival (2015–). He also formed silver halide photography group, Phenomena (2008–), and opened Bigakko Okayama (2010–), an accredited school of Tokyo's Bigakko, which has a history of over 50 years. Nose authored many books and critiques, including, *Shin Ongaku no Kaisetsu* [New Music Decoding] (2013), published by disk union; and *ISEO NOSE MORPHOLOGY* (2014), a photography collection published by AKAAKA Art Publishing Inc. He received the Fukutake Cultural Award from the Fukutake Education and Culture Foundation in 2018, and his work has been featured in the collection of Keio University Art Center, Tokyo.

写真家・美術展企画・音楽評論家。
1947年生まれ。1974年よりLive House PEPPERLANDを主宰し、脱領域的活動を展開する一方で、阿木譲の『Rock Magazine』に1983年から廃刊まで編集・執筆として関わる。主な展覧会に、2004年岡山・倉敷市連携文化事業「スペクタル能勢伊勢雄1968–2004」展開催。水戸芸術館「X-COLORグラフィティ in Japan」展企画、2013年奈義町現代美術館「能勢伊勢雄写真展MORPHOLOGY・遊図・PORTOGRAPHの世界」展、2016年大分県立美術館「OPAM×能勢伊勢雄シアター・イン・ミュージアム」など。2009年よりアートビオトープ那須「山のシューレ」、2015年より京都国際映画祭などで講演会も多数行っている。2008年銀塩写真家集団Phenomenaを結成し、2010年に50年以上の歴史をもつ東京「美學校」の公認校「美學校岡山校」を開校する。書籍では2013年『新・音楽の解読』(disk union社)、2014年写真集『ISEO NOSE: MORPHOLOGY 能勢伊勢雄：形態学』(赤々舎)を刊行するなど、著作・評論等多数。2018年福武教育文化振興財団より「福武文化賞」を受賞。慶應義塾大学アート・センター収蔵作家。

Photo: Live House PEPPERLAND

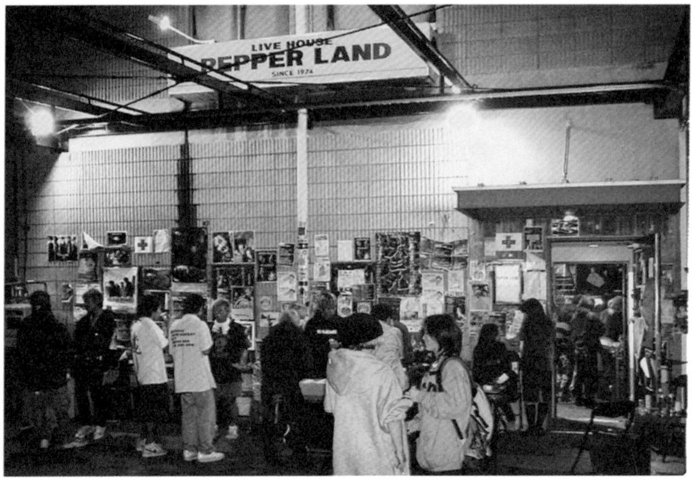

Performers on the Oil Drum Stage
produced by PEPPERLAND

PEPPERLANDプロデュース
オイルドラムステージ出演者

R58
赤田晃一
Asari Noriko
アストロノーツ
Atsushi
Adiantum Raddianum
Atoms Lost in Space
A Tribe Called NoiZ
untitled band (Shun Owada and friends)
アンバーアクアマリン
磯田護
板谷咲希
1Fuji
1.40秒
犬養佳子
ヴィヴィアン佐藤
VJ HIDE
上園桂祐
Wednesday
うろつき亭夜汰助
aaps
N-style
ELECTRIC BANANAMOON
大木裕之
大森悠平
大和田俊
小川陽子
奥市ばんど
オッス！オラ和人！
女8♡3
KHACT BOMB CHOSS
加治昇一郎
かちゃ
KANAD
カメラマンズ
刈馬カオス
河原龍峰
川元梨奈
カヲルSUN
金孝妍
木村匡孝
旧こいけ
KIYOSHI OKABE
きんたんめん
ぐうたらマジック
9ues
クラタカナデ
黒田秀徳
クロミツ
ケッチ
ケッチ茂毅
Koji Nakamura + duenn
小林俊幸
小林正秀
壊れたホテル
サイコロ
桜子
佐藤幸雄
THE NOUP
SEE EMILY PLAY
軸原ヨウスケ
刺激ex.
しばキチ
Schau-Essen
写真家集団Phenomena
Ja-3
Jean Pierre Tenshin
synchre
神闘歌
strike three!
スモール・ソルジャー
閃光玉
Senzadios presenta ABRAxASS
そ〜ざんす
曽根裕
武田充貴
竹本法人
田中恵一
谷本進
2me
DXNXB
DJ ISSON
DJ KAWANO
DJ KENPA
DJ FLASH PISTON
DJ MASAAKI
DJ RYO
Deixa Fofocar
DVJ-MY
TILL EWING
David Lee Ruest
Tem bo
トキコウジバンド
NAAGA
ナカタケ&カオナシ
中西明博
中村隆子
navire
ナマステクラブ
成瀬遠足
NOISECONCRETEx3CHI5
野澤収
能勢伊勢雄
能勢慶子
能勢聖紅
能勢遊神
☆NORi☆
Norimitsu Moriyama
86B210
Bad Blood
バナナ通信
ハナムラチカヒロ
林健太郎
VANCO -HENDERSONS
VENUS & CIRCUS
Bizarre Clown
ファネス佳乃
藤原重利
plugman
Brutal Springsteen & E.street garage band
ペック石井
HEP BURN
ホイスピナーユウヤ
possession
BOMB KETCH
murmur
舞原義人
前田留菜
Masayoshi Sakaguchi
まちだこうぞう
MACCOY
マッシュ星川
松村圭一郎
MANISDRON
マビキ団
丸山徹
My-Linh Le
MIU
水色赤
Minamiguchi Eri
村岡充
村西淳史
揉美山しおり
Momose Yasunaga
MOLMO PLUG
やっほー
薮下明弘
吉田省吾
良口病
RAMZAx田辺舞
Ryu & Blue Dragon
RUINS alone(吉田達也)
冷凍人間
朗読詩人・ホムラ
Rrose Selavy/Celine
ロバQ
和山太郎

GROUP

OVERCOAT

オーバーコート

OVERCOAT is a fashion brand founded in 2015 by New York resident, Ryuhei Oomaru (born in 1977 in Fukuoka). Under the concept "Wearing New York," the brand aims for sizeless, genderless, and ageless craftsmanship, with a special focus on the shoulder line. The collection has expanded into department stores and concept stores, mainly in Japan and the USA and has been acclaimed by the art industry and creative community.

OVERCOAT（オーバーコート）はNY在住の大丸隆平（1977年福岡生まれ）が2015年に創立したファッションブランド。「Wearing New York（ニューヨークを着る）」というコンセプトで、特にショルダーラインに工夫が凝らされており、サイズ、ジェンダーそしてエイジからも解放されたものづくりを目指している。コレクションは日米を中心とする主要百貨店やコンセプトストアで展開され、アート業界などクリエイティブ層からの支持も高い。

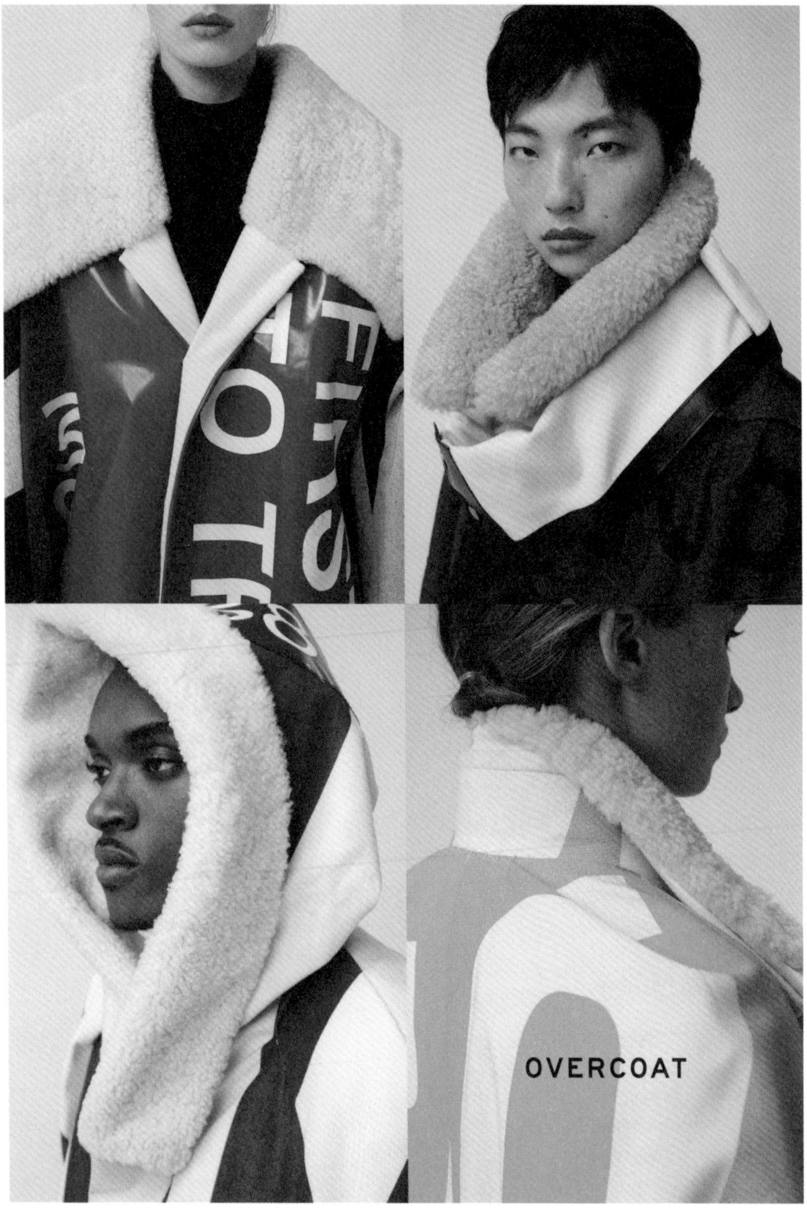

GROUP

Shu Isezaki (Bizen) Ethan Shogo Smith De’Andre Kiguchi (Ujobori)

伊勢﨑州（備前焼）
スミス一三省吾
木口ディアンドレ
（烏城彫）

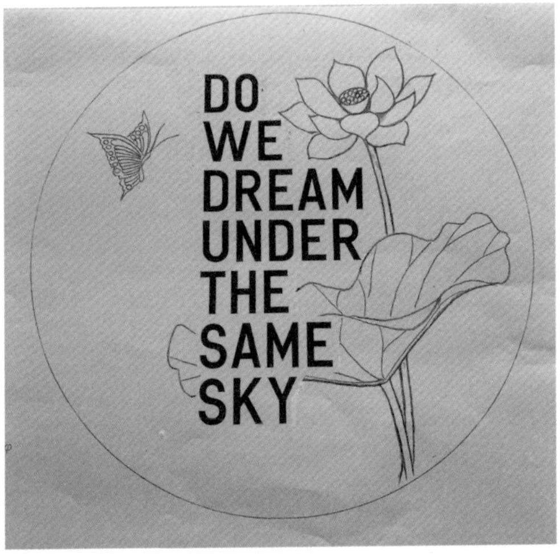

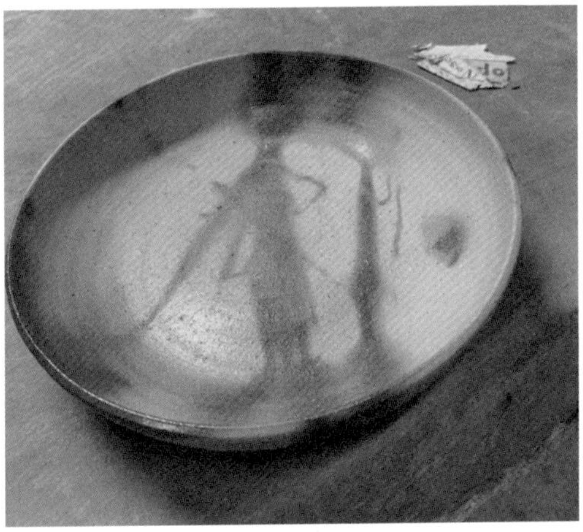

Bizen-yaki is prototypically produced in Bizen City, Okayama Prefecture. It is characterized by the technique of firing with a high-temperature flame without a glaze. Having the longest history among the six oldest kilns in Japan, we can trace the roots of Bizen-yaki back to the Kofun period. Shu Isezaki, Bizen-yaki artist and son of Kyo Isezaki, began training at his father’s kiln after studying abroad and gaining experience at a culinary school.

Shu Isezaki
Born in 1996
Lives and works in Okayama Prefecture

Ujobori is a style of wood carving and was first produced in 1925 by sculptor, Kyuhou Kiguchi. This lacquerware craft is characterized by delicate carvings and realistic representations. Kiguchi is said to have named “Ujobori” after Okayama Castle, also known as “Ujo.” The high level of skill and specialization that goes into producing Ujobori has made it a regional specialty of Okayama. De’Andre Kiguchi and Ethan Shogo Smith are young carvers working to fuse tradition and modernity.

Ethan Shogo Smith
Born in 1998
Lives and works in Okayama Prefecture

De’Andre Kiguchi
Born in 1998 in the US
Lives and works in Okayama Prefecture

備前焼は岡山県備前市を代表的な産地とする。釉薬を用いることなく高温にて焼き締める手法が特徴とされる。日本六古窯のなかで最も古い歴史を有する備前焼はルーツを古墳時代に遡るという。伊勢﨑州は備前焼の作家、伊勢﨑競を父とし、海外留学や調理師学校での経験を積んだ後、父の窯にて修業を始めたばかりである。

伊勢﨑州
1996年生まれ
岡山県にて活動

烏城彫とは1925年、彫刻家の木口九峰によって始められた木彫。繊細な彫りと写実的な表現を特徴とする漆器工芸品である。烏城彫の名称は、岡山城の別名を「烏城」ということに由来して木口自らと名づけたという。分業による高い技術力でつくり出される烏城彫は、岡山の誇る特産品となっている。木口ディアンドレとスミス一三省吾は若い烏城彫職人として伝統と現代の融合に取り組んでいる。

スミス一三省吾
1998年生まれ
岡山県にて活動

木口ディアンドレ
1998年生まれ
米国に生まれ岡山県にて活動

PERFORMANCE

Untitled Band (Shun Owada and friends)

The band, led by Shun Owada, consists of artists including Ju Muraoka, Masataka Kimura and Yutaka Sone. Initiated by Sone, the group formed in Okayama in the fall of 2021.

大和田俊を中心に、村岡充、木村匡孝、曽根裕らアーティストで構成されるバンド。曽根裕の声かけにより、2021年秋に岡山で結成。

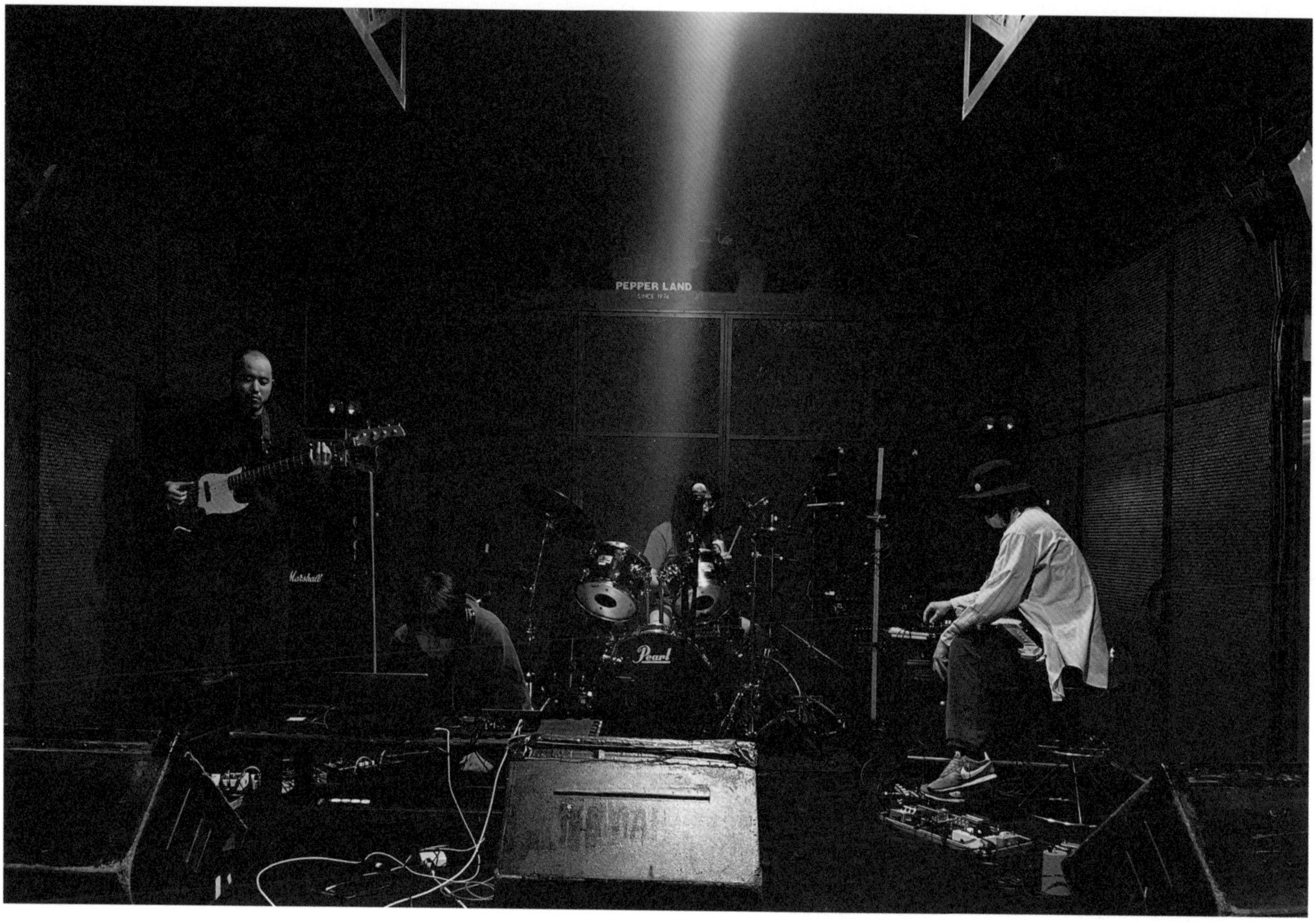

© Yutaka Sone Studio

About this book
本書について

This is an official concept book for the "Okayama Art Summit 2022: Do we dream under the same sky." Under the supervision of Rirkrit Tiravanija, the artistic director of the program, the contents of the book are organized as follows:

Tiravanija's slogans for the Okayama Art Summit 2022 can be found throughout the book (on pp. 9–16, 33–34, 51–52, 85–86, 103–104, 137–138, 155–156, 173–175). Japanese translations are summarized on p. 8.

For the 22 participating artists, biographies, statement texts newly-written for the Okayama Art Summit 2022, images of their exhibited works (and/or related past works), and their proposed images are included.

Biographies for each of the five artists presenting events and performances at the festival are also featured (pp. 177–182).

The contents included in the concept book are current as of August 31, 2022. However, they may differ from the actual exhibited works at the Okayama Art Summit 2022.

本書は、「岡山芸術交流2022　僕らは同じ空のもと夢をみているのだろうか」の公式コンセプトブックです。アーティスティックディレクターのリクリット・ティラヴァーニャ監修のもと、以下の構成をとっています。

・本全体に点在する形で、ティラヴァーニャが「岡山芸術交流2022」に寄せたスローガンを掲載しています（pp. 9–16、33–34、51–52、85–86、103–104、137–138、155–156、173–175）。和訳はp. 8にまとめています。

・岡山芸術交流2022に参加する22組のアーティストのバイオグラフィー、および今回の参加にあたって書き下ろしたテキスト、出品作（またはそれに関わる過去作）の画像や提案イメージを掲載しています。

・同芸術祭でイベントやパフォーマンスを行う5組のアーティストについては、バイオグラフィーを掲載しています（pp. 177–182）。

掲載内容は2022年8月31日時点のもので、「岡山芸術交流2022」での展示内容と異なる可能性があります。

Acknowledgements
謝辞

We would like to express our deepest gratitude to the following individuals, institutions, and others for their generous assistance and contributions to the realization of Okayama Art Summit 2022. (The listed names are in alphabetical order.)

岡山芸術交流2022開催に際しまして、右記の方々に多大なるご協力を賜りましたことをここに御礼申し上げます。
(敬称略・五十音順)

特定非営利活動法人アートファーム
artless Inc.
アール・アンド・ディー
RSK山陽放送株式会社
RSKホールディングス株式会社
社会福祉法人あいあい
アイサワ工業株式会社
atelier LA NOTE MUETTE
ELD INTERIOR PRODUCTS
イシカワホールディングス株式会社
株式会社イルカ
植島コレクション
株式会社烏城彫協会
内山下地区体育協会
内山下地区連合町内会
学校法人内山下保育会内山下幼稚園
株式会社NTTマーケティングアクトProCX
特定非営利活動法人ENNOVA OKAYAMA
学校法人KTC学園おおぞら高等学院岡山キャンパス
食事処おかべ
ナチュラルワイン食堂okuto
岡山エフエム放送株式会社
岡山上之町商業協同組合
一般社団法人岡山経済研究所
岡山県教育庁
岡山県高等学校文化連盟
岡山県小学校長会
岡山県中学校長会
岡山県天神山文化プラザ
岡山県内市町村教育委員会
公益社団法人岡山県文化連盟
岡山県立岡山東商業高等学校
岡山県立岡山芳泉高等学校
岡山県立図書館
岡山県立博物館
岡山県立美術館
岡山後楽園
協同組合連合会岡山市表町商店街連盟
岡山市教育委員会
岡山市小学校長会
岡山市中学校長会
岡山シティミュージアム
岡山市ほっとプラザ大供
岡山市民会館
岡山市立旭公民館
岡山市立岡山中央小学校
岡山市立オリエント美術館
岡山市立中央図書館
岡山市立馬屋下小学校
岡山神社
岡山大学教育学部附属小学校
国立大学法人岡山大学
岡山トヨペット
公益財団法人岡山文化芸術創造
岡山放送株式会社
株式会社岡山ランドリー
日本酒バル解放区
片山工業株式会社
季節料理かたやま
金沢21世紀美術館
CAFE & RESTAURANT & BOATING 碧水園
イタリア料理Carapan
キッチンかいぞく
木下商店
GALLERY SIDE 2
KAMP inc.
京都府文化スポーツ部文化芸術課
株式会社京橋クルーズ
九眼橋
学校法人加計学園倉敷芸術科学大学
GREENFIELDGRAFIK INC.
そば切り來輪
株式会社Coaマネジメント
株式会社コウデザインアンドビルド
社会福祉法人弘徳学園いち・にのさん
ごう原

国際芸術祭「あいち」組織委員会
古美術 今出川
株式会社サウンド・スケッチ
山陽学園大学
株式会社山陽新聞社
三和式ベンチレーター株式会社
株式会社ジーシーディ
株式会社シーマ
株式会社JTB
株式会社茂山組
シネマ・クレール丸の内
CIFAKA, Inc.
シンニチロ建工株式会社
新和シッピング株式会社
株式会社ジンプラ
SUPER-FACTORY
SCAI THE BATHHOUSE INC
Stand foundation Co.,ltd.
ワインショップ&スタンド スロウカーヴ
瀬戸内国際芸術祭実行委員会
株式会社瀬戸内海放送
続！おかやまケンコー大作戦
タグチアートコレクション
Take Ninagawa
税理士法人タッグ島原事務所
玉野市産業振興部商工観光課
TARO NASU
株式会社The Chain Museum
株式会社チクバ装飾社
中国学園大学
学校法人第一平田学園 中国デザイン専門学校
株式会社チュウブ
株式会社ティー・シー・シー
テレビせとうち株式会社
株式会社デンショク
株式会社電通西日本
株式会社天満屋
株式会社東京スタデオ
トモ・スズキ・ジャパン有限会社
有限会社ドラムカン
協同組合中之町商店会
奈義町現代美術館
西川アイプラザ
西日本放送株式会社
日本たばこ産業株式会社（JT）
日本通運株式会社
日本通運株式会社 岡山支店
株式会社日本旅行
ワイン食堂Bacco
株式会社ハブネット
一般財団法人林原美術館
株式会社ヒト・コミュニケーションズ
株式会社びより
藤本壮介建築設計事務所
株式会社双葉店飾社
PEPPERLAND
Penguin Translation
Porte Baseball Scool
White Sound with Studio
株式会社マクアケ
THE MAGRITTE
一般社団法人みるを楽しむ！アートナビ岡山
LOVE SONG
LABOCCA
リバーフューズ合同会社
株式会社リョービツアーズ
臨済宗蔭涼寺
鷲之山石材商会

相田翔吾
青山昌史
赤星賢太郎
秋田周治
浅田彰
足羽憲治
有元仁彦
安東信哉
飯田志保子
池田理寛
石井謙次
石川昌子
石川祐子
伊勢崎競
伊勢崎晴代
磯田敏子
市川暁子
市川靖史
井出はるか
稲本貴男
猪野ほのか
井上治郎
今川喜博
今出川朋樹
今吉考弘
岩田淳
岩淵泰
上岡弘明
宇治田達
内田章文
内田清吉
内海慶一
宇野孝伸
梅野和幸
漆中誠
江見肇
大杉宏明
大隅勝利

大林剛郎
大森誠一
岡坂正典
岡崎伸二
岡崎有紀
小笠原ヒロ子
岡田智美
岡武裕二
奥山隆史
尾崎敦志
小崎哲哉
越智早良
小野修司
加瀬部敏志
片岡真実
片山聡
片山進平
片山眞理
加藤淳子
加藤秀章
金光一孝
唐川美音
川角礼子
川上俊
川口真義
河西延彰
岸本和明
岸本留奈
喜多里律
木下阿佐美
木村稔将
金城泰成
久山信太郎
桑田奈美枝
河野広幸
越宗孝昌
小林弘昌
小山幸三

近藤弦之介
近藤龍
近藤季樹
金万純子
作元大輔
佐々木貴朗
佐藤兼郎
佐藤竜吾
里見俊樹
澤原一志
四角隆二
軸原ヨウスケ
篠原真祐
渋谷竜司
島原実
塩飽哲文
神辺英明
杉原匠
鈴木義治
須藤寛史
洲脇孝俊
十川智基
高橋英理子
高橋良典
高畑誠
滝沢忠孝
竹内愛二朗
竹重悠登
竹重優真
武田一夫
武久顕也
武本賢治
田附滋大
田中林太郎
谷一尚
種艸智和
田野口希
趙宇森

簗澤和記
土井雅人
遠山正道
徳山知永
鳥越亜矢
鳥越達夫
中一恵
中尾美月
中川弘之
中沢優喜
中静敬一郎
中島基善
中藤祝夫
中藤歳浩
長原正明
中村美南子
名木田いづみ
名合貴洋
西高辻信宏
西川達樹
沼本具德
能勢伊勢雄
野田尚子
土師浩子
浜田高夫
林克朗
林田堅太郎
原憲一
原見修司
坂東美都子
小童谷靖則
平井智之
平井優子
平松隆
廣瀬誠
藤井和子
藤本幸三
藤原達

藤原健史
藤原直樹
舟越俊司
船曳麗
ホリグチイツ
益田昌昭
松浦満
松川えり
松田一晟
松田正己
藺山俊
三上真理子
南雄大
三宅範尚
三宅幹夫
虫明純
室山賢司
物部一宏
森弥生
森佳子
森田潔
森本涼子
安井祥二
矢延里織
八巻真哉
山口陽子
山下晴海
山瀬徹夫
山田真理子
矢本奈央
横田さなえ
横山定
横山拓二
吉野誠一
若林昭吾
渡邉渓
渡辺俊文
渡邉友太

Alison JacquesAlison Jacques
rossogranada + Valeria Diaz Granada
Galerie Chantal Crousel
QUINN HARRELSON GALLERY
Ryoji Ikeda Studio
Krimanzutto
KUKJEGALLERY
Lygia Clark Association
GALERIE NORDENHAKE
Tommy Simoens
White Light Studio
"The World of Lygia Clark" Cultural Association

Hamid Amini
Belle Elizabeth Anne Charter
Haru Heshiki
Isabelle Hogenkamp
Iihong Kong
Thitiphorn Kotham
Junseok Lee
Paloma Hidalgo Monroy
Emmanuelle de Montgazon
Jan Pfeiffer
Jardy Santiago
Truong Minh Tuan
Heejung Ye

Okayama Art Summit 2022

Do we dream under the same sky

[Period]

September 30 to November 27, 2022

10:00–17:00 Closed on Monday

[Locations]

Former Uchisange Elementary School

Tenjinyama Cultural Plaza of Okayama Prefecture

Okayama Orient Museum

Cinema Clair Marunouchi

Hayashibara Museum of Art

Okayama Korakuen Garden

Okayama Shrine

Ishiyama Park

Okayama Castle

Okayama Tenmaya

[Organizer]

Okayama Art Summit Executive Committee

[Chairman]

Masao Omori, Mayor of Okayama City

[Vice Chairmen]

Yuuji Yokota, Vice-Governor, Okayama Prefecture

Hisashi Matsuda, President, Okayama Chamber of Commerce and Industry

[Auditor]

Shinji Inoue, Inoue Certified Public Accountant's Office

[Producer]

Yasuharu Ishikawa, President, Ishikawa Foundation

[Director]

Taro Nasu, Owner, TARO NASU

[Artistic Director]

Rirkrit Tiravanija

[Public Program Director]

Chieko Kinoshita, Associate Professor, Osaka University

[Design Director]

Shun Kawakami, Founder, artless Inc.

[Advisors]

Takeshi Wake, Chairman, Okayama City Council

Hirofumi Makino, President, Okayama University

Masato Miyanaga, Chairman, Chugoku Bank

[Affiliated Entities]

Okayama City

Okayama City Board of Education

Okayama Prefecture

Okayama Chamber of Commerce and Industry

Okayama Visitors & Convention Association

Okayama Culture Zone Liaison Council

The Consortium of Universities in Okayama

Sanyo Shimbun

RSK Sanyo Broadcasting Co., Ltd.

Okayama Broadcasting Co., Ltd.

Setouchi Broadcasting Co., Ltd.

Okayama Bus Association

Okayama Taxi Association

West Japan Railway Company

Okayama cultural arts Creation Foundation

Ishikawa Foundation

Inoue Certified Public Accountant's Office

岡山芸術交流2022
僕らは同じ空のもと夢をみているのだろうか

[会期]
2022年9月30日–11月27日
10:00–17:00　休館日・月曜日

[会場]
旧内山下小学校
岡山県天神山文化プラザ
岡山市立オリエント美術館
シネマ・クレール丸の内
林原美術館
岡山後楽園
岡山神社
石山公園
岡山城
岡山天満屋

[組織運営]
岡山芸術交流実行委員会

[会長]
岡山市 市長 大森雅夫

[副会長]
岡山県 副知事 横田有次
岡山商工会議所 会頭 松田久

[監事]
井上公認会計士事務所 井上信二

[総合プロデューサー]
公益財団法人石川文化振興財団 理事長 石川康晴

[総合ディレクター]
TARO NASU 代表 那須太郎

[アーティスティックディレクター]
リクリット・ティラヴァーニャ

[パブリックプログラムディレクター]
大阪大学21世紀懐徳堂 准教授 木ノ下智恵子

[デザインディレクター]
artless Inc. 代表 川上 シュン

[顧問]
岡山市議会 議長 和氣健
国立大学法人岡山大学 学長 槇野博史
株式会社中国銀行 取締役会長 宮長雅人

[構成団体]
岡山市
岡山市教育委員会
岡山県
岡山商工会議所
公益社団法人おかやま観光コンベンション協会
岡山カルチャーゾーン連絡協議会
大学コンソーシアム岡山
株式会社山陽新聞社
RSK山陽放送株式会社
岡山放送株式会社
テレビせとうち株式会社
公益社団法人岡山県バス協会
一般社団法人岡山県タクシー協会
西日本旅客鉄道株式会社
公益財団法人岡山文化芸術創造
公益財団法人石川文化振興財団
井上公認会計士事務所

Okayama Art Summit Executive Committee Office
岡山芸術交流 実行委員会事務局

[Chief Officer]

Osamu Iwata

[Assistant Chief Officer]

Miyuki Eda

[Operation Staff]

Katsunori Niida

Nobuyuki Satou

Reiko Kiyohiro

Daisuke Yabuki

Aya Kodama

Yoshitaka Ando

Yousuke Yamashita

Shogo Mikada

Misato Nakai

Izumi Fujiwara

Shinji Kishimoto

Kayo Sakamoto

Riho Shishido

Yoko Abe

[Operation PR]

Akihiro Mochizuki

Ai Yoshida

Ken Horinishi

Nobuko Mori

[Director Support]

Masako Hosoi

Daisuke Harada

[Curatorial Staff]

Mao Hashinokuchi

Yasuhisa Kawada

Sayaka Kawamura

Kazuki Akimori

[Operation Support]

Yuji Arai

Tetsuo Tachibana

Takamichi Kataoka

Yoso Mouri

Ataru Yoshida

Kazumi Hattan

Fumihiro Kobayashi

Masato Okada

Naomi Kimura

Nanako Hosoda

Ayumi Uemoto

Naoki Masaki

Reina Kawasaki

［事務局長］

岩田修

［事務局長次長］

江田美幸

［事務局スタッフ］

新居田克則

佐藤宣之

清廣玲子

矢吹大輔

児玉文

安東義貴

山下陽介

三ヶ田匠吾

中井美里

藤原いずみ

岸本真治

坂本賀代

宍戸里帆

阿部葉子

［事務局 広報］

望月章宏

吉田愛

堀西賢

森信子

［総合ディレクター補佐］

細井眞子

原田大輔

［キュレトリアルスタッフ］

橋之口真央

川田泰久

河村清加

秋守一希

［事務局支援］

新井祐二

橘哲生

片岡孝通

毛利洋壮

吉田中

八丹和美

小林史博

岡田真人

木村尚美

細田菜納子

上本鮎美

柾木直紀

川崎玲奈

助成 | Granting Agencies

文化庁

一般財団法人 地域創造
Japan Foundation for Regional Art-Activities

日本博
JAPAN CULTURAL EXPO

公益財団法人
吉野石膏美術振興財団

特別協賛 | Special Sponsors

Ishikawa holdings ltd.

山陰新聞社

ちゅうぎんグループ

JR西日本

JT

registART

協賛 | Sponsors

TOYOTA
岡山県トヨタ販売店グループ

総合環境クリエイト
サピックス

山陽ヤナセ

TOMIYA

NAKASHIMA
We Go Beyond

RSK

OHK

TSC

岡山純心会グループ

デンショク

rossogranada
art angels

Ryobi シンク

後援 | Supporting Agencies

AUSTRALIAN EMBASSY TOKYO
在日オーストラリア大使館

Embassy of Belgium in Tokyo

EMBAIXADA DO BRASIL
駐日ブラジル大使館

中華人民共和国駐大阪総領事館
Consulate-General of the People's Republic of China in Osaka

MÉXICO
EMBAJADA EN JAPÓN

Norwegian Embassy
Tokyo

駐日フィリピン共和国大使館
Embassy of the Republic of the Philippinc, Tokyo, Japan

駐日韓国文化院
Korean Cultural Center in Japan

在東京タイ王国大使館
Royal Thai Embassy

ブリティッシュ・カウンシル
British Council

United States Consulate General Osaka-Kobe

Okayama Art Summit 2022

Do we dream under the same sky

Published on | September 30, 2022

Produced by | Okayama Art Summit Executive Committee

Catalogue Director and Text | Rirkrit Tiravanija

Artists | Rasel Ahmed, Art Labor in collaboration with Jrai artists, Wang Bing, Daniel Boyd, Lygia Clark, Abraham Cruzvillegas, Enku, Ryoji Ikeda, Mari Katayama, My-Linh Le, David Medalla, Asif Mian, Precious Okoyomon, Frida Orupabo, Vandy Rattana, Bárbara Sánchez-Kane, Aki Sasamoto, Jacolby Satterwhite, Shimabuku, Yutaka Sone, Apichatpong Weerasethakul, Haegue Yang, Gert Robijns, PEPPERLAND, OVERCOAT, Shu Isezaki, Ethan Shogo Smith, De'Andre Kiguchi, Untitled Band (Shun Owada and friends)

Catalogue Editors | Satoko Shibahara, Taylor Stewart, Mai Hashiba

Translators | Takafumi Akimoto (p. 8),
Yukari Nakayama (pp. 35–42, 73, 84, 115, 122, 126, 141, 167–170),
Penguin Translation (all the biographies of the artists [except for p. 151, 180, 182], p. 61, 92, 102),
Kae Shigeno (pp. 20–23, 27–30, 46–47, 78, 89, 108, 161)

Art Direction and Design | Yuri Suyama

Design | Nanako Toriya

Catalogue Coordinator | Nao Asuma (Culture Convenience Club Co., Ltd.)

Printing and Binding | LIVE Art Books Inc. (Daishinsha Group)

Publisher | Kazuki Yamashita

Published by | Culture Convenience Club Co., Ltd.

Sale by | Bijutsu Shuppan-sha Co., Ltd.
5F, Meguro Central Square, 3-1-1
Kamiosaki, Shinagawa-ku, Tokyo
141-8203 JAPAN
Tel: +81-3-6809-0318
https://www.bijutsu.press

Printed in Japan

ISBN 978-4-568-50650-1 C3070

岡山芸術交流2022

僕らは同じ空のもと夢をみているのだろうか

2022年9月30日　初版第一刷

[企画]
岡山芸術交流実行委員会

[監修・執筆]
リクリット・ティラヴァーニャ

[参加アーティスト]
ラゼル・アハメド、アート・レーバーとジャライ族のアーティストたち、王兵、ダニエル・ボイド、リジア・クラーク、アブラハム・クルズヴィエイガス、円空、池田亮司、片山真理、ミー・リン・ル、デヴィッド・メダラ、アジフ・ミアン、プレシャス・オコヨモン、フリーダ・オルパボ、ヴァンディー・ラッタナ、バルバラ・サンチェス・カネ、笹本晃、ジャコルビー・サッターホワイト、島袋道浩、曽根裕、アピチャッポン・ウィーラセタクン、梁慧圭、ゲルト・ロビンス、ペパーランド、伊勢﨑州、スミス一三省吾、木口ディアンドレ、オーバーコート、Untitled Band (Shun Owada and friends)

[編集]
柴原聡子、テイラー・スチュワート、橋場麻衣

[翻訳]
秋元孝文（p. 8)、中山ゆかり（pp. 35–42、73、84、115、122、126、141、167–170）、
Penguin Translation（全アーティストのバイオグラフィー [p. 151、180、182を除く]、p. 61、92、102)、
重野佳園（pp. 20–23、27–30、46–47、78、89、108、161)

[アートディレクション&デザイン]
須山悠里

[デザイン]
鳥屋菜々子

[制作]
遊馬奈歩（カルチュア・コンビニエンス・クラブ株式会社）

[印刷・製本]
株式会社ライブアートブックス（大伸社グループ）

[発行人]
山下和樹

[発行]
カルチュア・コンビニエンス・クラブ株式会社
美術出版社

[発売]
株式会社美術出版社
〒141-8203　東京都品川区上大崎 3-1-1 目黒セントラルスクエア 5F
電話：03-6809-0318（代表）　03-6809-0349（編集）
https://www.bijutsu.press